SLIGHTLY BEYOND SKEPTICISM

SLIGHTLY

BEYOND

SKEPTICISM

Social Science and the
Search for Morality

LEONARD W. DOOB

Yale University Press
New Haven and London

Designed by Sally Harris
and set in Meridien type by
David E. Seham Associates Inc.
Printed in the United States of America by
Halliday Lithograph, West Hanover, Mass.

Library of Congress Cataloging-in-Publication Data

Doob, Leonard William, 1909–
  Slightly beyond skepticism.

  Bibliography: p.
  Includes index.
  1. Ethics. 2. Skepticism. I. Title.
BJ1031.D66 1987   171'.7   86–22400
ISBN 0–300–03823–2

10   9   8   7   6   5   4   3   2   1

To
Aristotle and Eveline

Contents

PART 1: INTRODUCTION   1

1. The Probing Questions   3
    1.1 Skepticism   8
    1.2 Principals as Observers, Observers as Principals   11
    1.3 Salient Values   12
2. Principals, Observers, and Groups   24
    2.1 Genesis   24
    2.2 Identification   25
    2.3 Events   27
    2.4 Perception   29

PART 2: PRINCIPALS   35

3. Personality   37
    3.1 Predispositions   40
    3.2 Motives and Goals   41
    3.3 Beliefs and Knowledge   43
    3.4 Attitudes   46
    3.5 Skill   47
    3.6 Interrelation of Predispositions   49
4. Rules and Duties   58
    4.1 Inevitability   59
    4.2 Habitual Morality   63
    4.3 Changes   64
    4.4 Comprehensibility   65
    4.5 Variability   66
    4.6 Obligation and Responsibility   67
5. Anticipations   79
    5.1 Options   80
    5.2 Accuracy   82

5.3 Immediate versus Future Consequences 86
5.4 Other Persons 87
5.5 Predictability and Hope 91
5.6 Means and Ends 93
6. The Imperative 100
    6.1 Conscience 100
    6.2 Self and Others 101
    6.3 Happiness 105
    6.4 Freedom 107
    6.5 Justifiability 109
7. Intention 115
    7.1 Multivariance and Weighting 117
    7.2 Situation at Hand 119
    7.3 Exceptions 120
    7.4 Reasoned Judgment 126
    7.5 Feasibility and Procrastination 130
8. Behavior 143
    8.1 Inaction 144
    8.2 Risk 145
    8.3 Rewards and Punishments 146
    8.4 Future Effects 148

PART 3: OBSERVERS 155

9. Roles and Inferences 157
    9.1 Observers' Motives 158
    9.2 Sources 159
    9.3 Responsibility 160
10. Fallibility 169
    10.1 Lay Observers 171
    10.2 Social Scientists and Historians 177
    10.3 Scientists 182
    10.4 Experts concerning Ethics 183

PART 4: MORAL PERSONS 195

11. Dreams and Reality 197
    11.1 Natural Naturalistic Fallacy 199
    11.2 Social Utility 201
    11.3 Love 202
    11.4 Justice 204
    11.5 Truth and Predictability 207

11.6 Beauty   208
11.7 Perfection   209
11.8 Utopia   212
12. Constraints   222
    12.1 Disagreement and Unreality   222
    12.2 Human Frailties   224
    12.3 Limited Judgments   228
    12.4 Complexity   233
    12.5 Inelasticity   238
13. Struggles   241
    13.1 Awareness   242
    13.2 Interpersonal Sensitivity   245
    13.3 Cautious Indoctrination   247
    13.4 Ethical Codes   250
    13.5 Searching for Means   255
    13.6 Eternal Tussle   256
14. The Future?   275
References   281
Index   307

PART 1

INTRODUCTION

CHAPTER 1

The Probing Questions

Every human being forever asks questions about himself, about other persons, about events, and about judgments and actions. The answers to the questions, whether he or others provide them, are the bases of *morality*. The first, the last, the eternal, and the most crucial question, the one pointing directly to morality is: *why* should I (or we, he, she, you, thou, they) do or not do whatever is contemplated or *why* should I have or have not done what occurred?

The why-question is, however, much too general to embrace the myriad problems and details considered by theologians, humanists, philosophers, scientists, and ordinary men and women before offering themselves or others at least a partial answer to the *why*. What they do is to provide answers to one or more probing questions, the scope of which includes basic or behavioral problems. The questions may first be stated in a form applicable to the single, isolated, and hence hypothetical person with reference to himself in the present or future (rather than the past) and in the affirmative (rather than the negative) mode:

I. Basic
   1. Personality: what *will* I do?
   2. Potentiality: what *can* I do?
   3. Rule: what *may* I do?
   4. Duty: what *must* I do?
   5. Anticipation: what *would (might)* the consequences be?
   6. Imperative: what *ought (should)* I do?
II. Behavioral
   7. Intention: what *shall* I do?
   8. Behavior (action): what *do (did)* I do?

These eight questions, when handled cautiously, are the parameters of morality;* they shall serve that modeling function in the analysis that follows. The questions are modifiable to fit the person or persons and the situation at hand. The individual may judge himself in retrospect: what did I wish to do, what were the consequences of what I did, what should I have done, what judgment did I intend to carry out, and what did I actually do? The same questions can be phrased in the negative. Similarly they may be directed at another person or persons simply by substituting another pronoun for *I:* what will we do, what can she do, what may he do, what must we do, what did they anticipate?

A reply to a probing question is potentially *a moral judgment* when it affects or is affected by a reply to question 6, that of *ought* or *should,* which is derived from a superordinate or imperative value. Let the concept of value be abruptly defined:

> A value is the actual or inferred expression of a belief that a goal or form of behavior is approved or disapproved in a variety of comparable relevant situations.

The cumbersome, belabored definition is explained and justified in the third proposition of this chapter. For the moment its role in defining morality can be merely illustrated. Thus a person who says:

> I like spinach,
> I am going to order spinach,
> I have eaten a dish of spinach,

is not passing a moral judgment. That he likes spinach is one of his predispositions (#1), that he plans to eat some is an objectively stated

---

*In this first and only footnote I hastily explain why the concept of morality has been selected to designate the contents and scope of the book. For over a year I avoided the word because it has acquired political connotations in the United States (Moral Rearmament, Moral Majority) and because it slips too easily into everyday speech. Instead I substituted *virtue,* but it soon seemed awkward in too many sentences; besides, if I may make a personal and perhaps meaningless statement, it sounds a bit too virtuous. Obviously *ethics* is a possibility. Here my ear agrees with a distinction in *A Dictionary of Modern English Usage* which appeared more than half a century ago: *"ethics* is the science of morals, & *morals* are the practice of ethics" (Fowler, 1926). I think that sparkling writer has employed *science* a bit too loosely to apply to the discipline of philosophy; instead I am assigning the study of morality to the social sciences as well as to philosophy. I am not happy about the choice of *morality,* but one word is needed and it will have to do. Generously, however, I allow the words *virtue* and *ethics* and their variants to be left undisturbed in quotations from other writers toiling in the same vineyard.

intention (#7), and that he has consumed some is a behavioral fact (#8). He comes close to making a moral judgment if he says he believes that spinach is "good" for him, but even then he may only be indicating an anticipated consequence of spinach (#5). Eating spinach enters morality when the spinach eater justifies his preference in terms of a superordinate value such as health or some other claim of vegetarianism (#6).

A *morally complete judgment* is a judgment affected by as many of the five basic probing questions as are relevant in the situation; a *morally incomplete or deficient judgment* fails to consider all the relevant ones. *Morally complete behavior* results from an intention (#7) to behave in accordance with a morally complete judgment; *morally incomplete or defective behavior* results not from such an intention or from an intention to carry out a morally incomplete judgment. "Moral judgment" or "moral action" without a qualifying adjective means that no decision is or can be reached as to whether the judgment or action is complete or incomplete.

Again and again morally deficient judgments are passed as if they were complete:

> He meant well.
> She did not know what she was doing.
> They were deprived as children.
> We were only obeying what we were told to do.

Statements like these are used to justify behavior, but each deals with only one of the probing questions and fails to mention other relevant questions as well as an underlying value, if any. His intention may have been to mean well (#7), but what he in fact did may have had disastrous consequences (#5 or #8); besides we are not told what his motive was (#1), whether his action resulted from a sense of duty (#4), and so on; also we do not know what value he followed (#6).

The same action may evoke a morally incomplete judgment or action in one person and a complete one in another. A policeman arrests a citizen for buying a drug on the black market. He observes the man (#8) and knows he has broken a law (#3); his judgment and action are morally incomplete because presumably he need only have considered the value of upholding the law (#6). A conscientious bystander approves of the policeman's action and his judgment is morally complete if he weighs the consequences of taking the drug and of the arrest upon the man (#5) and if he believes the arrest should occur because he also believes that drugs (#6) and black markets (#3) should be banned, and because he assumes that the policeman is capable of taking the man to the police station (#2) and wishes only to enforce the law (#7).

Equivalent problems arise—or should arise (#6)?—in areas concerned with morality. In strategic planning by the military, the chiefs of staff consider the goals (#1), the capabilities (#2), and the intentions (#7) of their own side and those of the enemy. They know they have a duty to their own government (#4). Perhaps they wonder whether storing nuclear armaments or devising ways to combat them will infuriate or deter potential enemies (#5). The replies to such probing questions are either factual or hypothetical; no moral judgment is made unless the military officers justify their judgments or actions by invoking some superordinate value such as that of doing one's duty already mentioned, or the need to defend one's country or to defeat an enemy. When they settle on the value, they then may have to consider its effect upon the replies to the other probing questions, and they may or may not try to make their moral judgment as complete as possible; for example, should or can they try to avoid war?

America's most influential philosopher referred in the opening pages of perhaps his best known treatise to "the evils which have resulted from severing morals from the actualities of human physiology and psychology" (Dewey, 1922, p. 4). John Dewey was saying in effect that moral judgments are deficient unless at a minimum they are linked to other questions, the ones concerned with human needs (#1) and capabilities (#2) and societal rules (#3). The statements of many philosophers about morality are often accompanied by a loophole such as "other things being equal" or the more elegant "ceteris paribus," by which they mean that they are assuming answers to one or more of the probing questions they do not mention. Nor is it sufficient to discuss a central problem like obligation (#4 or perhaps #6) without raising other probing questions. If they say you are obligated to do such-and-such, then you must be capable of doing so (#2).

In my opinion, the probing questions are adequately mentioned, and not simply in passing, by Aristotle whose philosophy, as a modern philosopher has suggested, unlike Plato's, was "mainly directed to and modelled on biology and the social sciences" (Körner, 1979, p. 256). We, therefore, can only echo Aristotle's insights; I shall refer to him frequently and unabashedly. Perforce my own references are expressed in a language and form better suited to our age and supported, it must be hoped, by the additional knowledge if not the wisdom that has been accumulated in the meantime. Who would now dare say, as Aristotle did, that "the male is by nature superior, and the female inferior?" (Aristotle, 1944 ed., p. 21). I take courage, consequently, from the conviction that anyone approaching the overall problem of morality is attempting to function as "a cultural broker, mediating between ages and nations, and bringing about the gradual re-unification of divided humanity" (Bauman, 1978, p. 28). All writers on morality must feel humble when they dip into the vast literature of philosophy or politics: can anything be said that some sage has not already said or, according to one or more of his friendly or unfriendly critics, that he intended to avow or not to avow? In addition I take courage from the observation that "no one can keep up with all that is written in philosophy today" (Bahm, 1979, p. 80); and, I add, no one should be expected to do so since the same or similar perplexities keep being expressed with slightly new twists as each publication appears.

A few necessary words concerning the structure of this book:

1. Frequent reference is made to the eight probing questions in parentheses by repeating the first-person phrasing as suggested above when the questions were unveiled.

2. To knit together the principal arguments, the central themes are also numbered as propositions with distinctive titles. Admittedly the propositions are a mixed bag: generalizations that seek to summarize current knowledge; commonsense banalities that must be brought within the stream of thinking concerning morality; and challenges for the future. If there is to be "an organized convergence of science, philosophy, and religion," which a theologian once believed had been occurring in the United States (Muelder, 1983, p. 164), the basic problems and assertions must be exposed in the manner these propositions nervously seek to express. Each proposition is explained, justified, and illustrated, and ends with a "Skeptical Note" for reasons to be immediately explained below; but chapters are concluded with optimistic thrusts called "Envois," all of which contain the crucial word "nevertheless."

3. Since the bulk of available treatises on morality by the various disciplines is staggering, I obviously cannot claim to have plowed through all that has appeared since the time of the ancients, including the publishing flood of our era. Often, therefore, I have tried to offer a sample of additional data or insights at the end of the chapter which I do not call notes but "Meanderings" because they are just that. A reference to each meandering is made in the text. Immediately, therefore, see, if you wish, *Meandering 1.1: A Confession.*

1.1 SKEPTICISM

Proposition: Perfect knowledge and perfect guides to morally complete judgments and actions are unattainable but approachable.

Throughout the history of philosophy, beginning with Heraclitus ("you cannot step into the same river twice") and Protagoras ("man is the measure of all things") and including such modern writers as Santayana (our "animal faith" in knowledge) and Camus (only "human solidarity" remains), skepticism has appeared as a significant way to view the validity of both knowledge and morality and to argue against the claims of "dogmatic" philosophers (Dewey, 1928) and other opinionated thinkers. I shall not assume the task of outlining that history since "skepticism comes in many varieties" and forms (M. G. Singer, 1973, p. 78). Excellent accounts exist, and any dictionary of philosophy overflows with references. With such a history, the concept has been so variously explicated (Naess, 1968, pp. 2–4) that its meaning has become as obscure and ambiguous as most other philosophical terms, such as idealism, realism, and indeed morality. For the task at hand it is not helpful to belabor an epistemological or ontological skepticism concerning the reality or the perception of the external world. These are intriguing metaphysical problems that will forever tease or excite some of us, but they have little practical importance, if I may crudely suggest, when we have an overwhelming impulse to scratch an itch, drink cold water, or prevent a nuclear war *(What will I do?)*. On the other hand, theological skepticism cannot be excluded from some consideration because an individual's beliefs concerning gods and his attitudes toward them, unlike the private worries of philosophers with which he is unacquainted, influence his thinking and his behavior. My skepticism consists of suggesting that vital questions remain unanswered, new problems protrude (Weischedel, 1976, p. 38), and "our claims to objective knowledge involve an absolutism that cannot in fact be realized" (Held, 1984, pp. 3, 51, 271). In addition, like others who have been affected by the uncertainty and chaos of our era (Rescher, 1980, p. 28), I am convinced that we cannot find a single value or theory that is useful or applicable to all the different "domains" in which moral judgments are passed *(What should I do?);* we must be eclectic. All knowledge perforce, in short, is tentative; deviations or exceptions to almost all propositions is almost always to be anticipated.

Self-evident in the last sentence is the repetition of the qualifying "almost," which is the counterpart of the "slightly beyond" in the title of this book. There are, I insist, glimmerings of universality in every sphere of human activity. The sun will rise tomorrow, I have no wings and for better or worse cannot fly like a bird, you and I are mortal *(What can I do?)*. While it is unrealistic, impractical, or whatever to expect the moral judgments of the ancients, the medievalists, or even the romantics to be specifically helpful with reference to the perplexing problems associated with computers, contraceptives, and civil liberties in a nuclear age, it does not follow that their abstractions or modes of reasoning may not be useful or inspiring. The tenets and hence the values of religious organizations like the Catholic church have survived for centuries; does their durability rescue us from skepticism? No, I think not, when I note, for example, the courageous opposition to the Vatican during the eighties by some Catholics in the Netherlands, Latin America, and elsewhere.

Many philosophers and many human beings throughout historical time have espoused the doctrine of skepticism or—like Descartes and Kant—have had to cope with what they considered to be its fallacies or shortcomings. A historian who traced the rise of skepticism in religion from the seventeenth century to the present has noted that "in many cases" that doctrine has been "accompanied by some form of believing" (Baumer, 1960, p. 31). My own skepticism is likewise accompanied by a belief that there is something slightly beyond skepticism enabling us to cope with existence. A cogent critic of philosophical skepticism begins his analysis by saying that skepticism is "in one sense irrefutable" because "one cannot dislodge the skeptic himself from his position by rational counterargumentation," but then concludes that "the skeptic is right on virtually the entire gamut of the subsidiary issues regarding the inadequacy of our knowledge. . . . One need not know everything to know anything; our getting *something* wrong does not entail our getting *everything* wrong pervasively" (Rescher, 1980, pp. 1, 250, 251; Klein, 1981). I do not claim to be dislodging myself; rather social science has dislodged me—slightly. Another personal word: it matters not how this approach is labeled; I have no objection to terms like neoskepticism or pseudoskepticism.

If social science has made me slightly skeptical concerning skepticism, I must immediately add that, for reasons that will become abundantly clear, I am also skeptical concerning social science. Relatively recently some social scientists—and among them psychologists floating a banner they call cognitive psychology—have been reporting in journals and in books a superabundance of studies devoted to moral issues, especially those concerned with values, altruism, justice, and attribution. The generalizations have been phrased in confusing, idiosyncratic jargon, yet glimmerings of uniformity are evident. The data, because they are precise, are limited in scope, limited to the situation and persons giving rise to them. More frequently than not, each writer would contradict another investigator's findings (and thus hope for academic immortality); of necessity he discloses, even within the narrow scope of the study, central tendencies with fairly large deviations. These studies from the social sciences will be either described in the text or relegated to a meandering at the end of a chapter. Sometimes they as well as ideas gleaned elsewhere have served merely to suggest the thought being expressed; to relieve them of responsibility for what I have written, references to them are preceded by the symbol "cf."

Whether or not a study mentioned in this book is typical—however typicality might be defined—it is cited, nevertheless, because it appears to advance the analysis and perhaps also to diminish my own skepticism a trifle. Any good investigation, no matter how limited its scope, suggests one of the parameters that conceivably might or must be considered in the future. My own favorite analogy: the approach of the consultant whose expertise is called upon to increase productivity in a factory. Past research has demonstrated that in other plants sometimes wages, illumination of the factory floor, union recognition, and so on, on, and on, have affected productivity. For the factory at hand one or more of these same factors, after investigation, may turn out to be significant and the others may be irrelevant; having a list tells the consultant what to look for. In an analysis of morality, consequently, studies are culled from the published literature in order to illuminate factors that appear relevant to the problem being discussed; each situation or each person, however, must be examined de novo with the aid of compelling clues from the past study. The examples, in a word, are hints, whereas those employed by philosophers are usually simpler and more dramatic. Suppose you are in a crowded lifeboat which will sink if a person you see struggling in the water and about to drown is rescued. Suppose a person in extreme pain demands to be killed. Hypothetical illustrations may cause the reader to think and may reveal something about him to himself or to others, but the data thus gathered are personal and unsystematic. But do they "prove" more than those of social scientists gathered systematically under controlled but usually artificial conditions?

Skeptical Note: Can one be skeptical about skepticism?

1.2 PRINCIPALS AS OBSERVERS, OBSERVERS AS PRINCIPALS

Proposition: To pass moral judgments and to act morally, principals function as observers; to observe principals, observers may also function as principals.

By definition principals are concerned with themselves, observers with others. Observers include persons who evaluate principals, whether professionally or informally. This distinction between the two, though obvious, must be stated explicitly since popular and philosophical writers on morality do not always indicate whether their judgments stem from themselves as principals who are introspecting or as observers who are appraising other persons or groups. The distinction, however, is not sharp and hence the proposition is double-barreled.

In the first place, a principal almost always observes other persons as well as himself as he passes a moral judgment, whether consciously or unconsciously, in a clearly verbalized or even in a completely unverbalized form *(Propositions 5.4 and 6.2)*. He pays some if not complete attention to those other persons as he is socialized: they are his models, he sees them behaving, he listens to them, he obeys them, and thus he becomes acquainted with the rules he must follow and the duties he must discharge in specific situations *(What may, what must I do?)*. We do not and cannot live alone, we interact with our fellows, we judge them, we observe them. Parents, police, priests, and philosophers do not have a monopoly on observation, although their motives for passing judgment may be more transparent than those of the rest of us. That person out there: should he be accepted as a friend or an enemy, is he or she a worthy spouse or trustworthy associate in some joint affair, should he be recommended for a particular position, should he or should he not be helped?

Then the reverse of the proposition is also true under many circumstances. Observers become principals when they try to imagine the judgment they would make or the action they would take if they were the principal they are observing. Observers are likely to become principals after they have observed and passed judgment; they perceive situations and then they themselves evaluate what is occurring and do or do not take appropriate action. He is a good citizen, or a thief, or a child, and therefore I must . . . At this point the observer has turned principal; his action, if any, depends upon his relation to the principal or principals being observed as well as his own values and predispositions. The momentary situation may also be influential; thus persons with knowledge of the Holocaust, or even directly involved, but "at a distance from the actual gassings, burnings, and shootings" may have failed to pass judgment on the atrocities, or even while disapproving of them, they took no action (Sabini and Silver, 1982, p. 60, cf. pp. 40–49).

Every man or woman is a principal during many phases of his or her existence when he or she passes judgment in order to choose between alternative courses of moral or nonmoral action. Philosophers in particular observe other persons in order to reply to one or more of the probing questions such as duty *(What must I do?);* whether they are better qualified to do so than other professionals or laymen is an issue that plagues us and should plague us forever. They are, let us remind ourselves, human even when they believe that one or two of their number, preferably deceased (for example, Aristotle, Kant, or a more obscure favorite), have had superhuman insights; consequently, the principals they observe in large part may be themselves, with the result that their philosophies of ethics inevitably reflect those selves and their own experiences. These comments concerning philosophers are not intended to be gratuitous insults; rather they would alert us to the fallibility of all human beings and the tenuousness of their judgments, and they therefore would strengthen our skepticism *(Proposition 10.4).*

Skeptical Note: The morality of which principals and observers merit attention?

1.3 SALIENT VALUES

Proposition: Salient values affect judgments and actions.

Let the definition of value at the outset be repeated with numbers inserted to indicate the sections that must now be clarified below.

A value is (1) the actual or inferred expression (2) of a belief that (3) a goal or form of behavior (4) is approved or disapproved (5) in a variety of comparable, relevant situations.

In the first place, principals are able to express their values: they are conscious of them and can put them into words. They praise what they call "honesty," they condemn "dishonesty." Observers may infer that principals have the values and could or do express them; in fact, they must also infer the remaining components of the definition from the standpoint of those principals.

Then, second, it is presumed that principals must possess their beliefs in order to express them. The "goal" suggests that they are appropriately motivated or are appraising their own or others' behavior. The fourth phrasing concerning approval or disapproval is necessary to emphasize that individuals are seldom neutral; in any situation they like or dislike aspects of what they perceive, whether human or not. Evaluation falls along a continuum, ranging figuratively or literally from approach to avoidance, and with an infinite number of degrees in between. The fifth and final component would limit the definition by insisting that the expression of the value be confined not alone to the situation at hand but to many situations. A principal who is honest on an occasion and clearly praises honesty is expressing a value only if he approves of honesty either because he knows he has been honest in the past or because he plans to be honest in the future.

Even without the significant word *salient*, Proposition 1.3 follows from this definition of value. For the concepts of expression, belief, goal, form of behavior, and approval or disapproval by themselves suggest the potentiality of values affecting judgments and actions. The very term, therefore, vibrates with judgmental and behavioral potential. Unless they become "salient," however, a principal's values may remain dormant. At a given moment, although honesty is one of his values, it does not occur to him that cheating at a game or deceiving an opponent in a business or a disarmament conference is an instance of dishonesty. His value of honesty is not salient, until for some reason or in some way he reminds himself or is reminded that he is in effect cheating. When the values of a religious creed are called "Sunday values," the presumption must be that they are not salient on weekdays.

Noteworthy is a tendency of scholars and laymen to locate values within human beings, and not within the objects or conditions that make them salient (Veatch, 1971, pp. 108, 110). Yes, money or diamonds have value, but only to persons who value them. A vocabulary exists everywhere that includes the equivalent of good or right at one end, and bad or wrong at the other. "Nothing," for example, "is evil—not even an earthquake, an atomic bomb, or a mass murder—until someone calls it that" (Doob, 1978, p. 6), until a salient value is attached to it.

The present concept of value, although oriented toward the probing questions, does not violate appreciably the way in which the word is customarily employed. It has been said, for example, that values are "personally held, internalized guides in the production of behavior"; they "are found in the large and diverse universe of selective

behavior" and hence are not to be identified with beliefs, needs, motives, or even social norms (R. M. Williams, 1968); they are "properties or attributes" that are "present in greater or lesser amount"
(Margenau, 1964, pp. 107, 261). The labels affixed to values, however, are most varied, which may be a tribute to human versatility
but which hinders analytical precision. Imagine calling the element
oxygen a score of different names and then evoking more than one
symbol to designate it; or, still worse, using the word *oxygen* as a label
for different compounds *(Meandering 1.2: Value Nomenclature).* Having
said that, nevertheless, I must make two major distinctions that refer
to the scope of values. The first refers to the number or importance
of the situations to which the value applies, the second to its present
status:

Values	*Scope*
Situations	
Particular (principal or	
society)	limited, relatively specific
General	
Imperative (principal)	superordinate: broad range, fre-
	quently evoked
Universal (society)	existing in many or all societies
Status	
Descriptive	current, actually utilized
Prescriptive	recommended, pursued

The values of principals and their societies may thus be particular or
general. A particular value might be the approval of a specific form
of dress; for a principal this might mean clothing to his liking, for the
society, a distinctive type of clothing (like a toga or jewelry) not
prevalent in any other society. A general value for a principal would
be an imperative high or highest on his scheme of values such as being
extremely religious or ambitious; for the society, values allegedly
modal within a particular society or allegedly common to most or
even all societies. Why allegedly in both cases? For two different,
skeptical reasons. It is difficult to determine the modal values of a
principal and especially those of a society that is changing, and then
even when they are thought to be known, to decide whether the values of a principal or a number of principals conform to the norm.
For societies, the search for universal values is an ancient one and
has not produced agreement among either philosophers or social scientists. A few social scientists believe that "basic similarities or analogies between the lower and higher cultures" are discoverable and

include a dedication to one's community, the importance of sanctions, and a system of powerful metaphysical beliefs (Dawson, 1959). Such an abstract cataloguing may strengthen a belief in the essential unity of mankind, but the details produce the disunities and conflicts that forever plague us. For present purposes it would be futile to inquire into the problem of how the particular values have originated; sufficient is the flabby statement that their origin cannot be traced to "a single factor" (Ossowska, 1970, p. 99). It is not in the least surprising to discover that the social scientists who would investigate and measure values show no indication whatsoever of coming to an agreement concerning the names of the values lying within their purview *(Meanderings 1.3: The Pursuit of Universal Values)*.

At first glance the distinction between descriptive and prescriptive (or normative) values is clear-cut. What does he do? He is not conscientious, he almost never does a thorough job, he seldom keeps his word (descriptive value). Too bad that he was never taught by his parents to be conscientious, for all persons should be conscientious, good citizens (prescriptive value). The difference between the two types of value may be self-evident, but the relation between them raises the most profound problem of what is usually called the *naturalistic fallacy:* many philosophers believe that significant prescriptive values should not or cannot be derived from descriptive ones (cf. Moore, 1903, pp. 10–58; Douglas, 1983); what we are doing is not necessarily what we should be doing. And yet we cannot be told what we should do unless we are capable, in some sense, of doing it (helping the malnourished): *What can I do?* Likewise we cannot avoid doing what we are compelled to do for some biological reason (sleeping: *What will I do?*) or as a result of a social custom we know to be unavoidable (respecting aged parents: *What must I do?*) To claim a sharp distinction between descriptive and prescriptive values under all circumstances is patently absurd; nevertheless, we must return again and again to the fray *(Proposition 11.1)*.

Descriptive values appear in connection with all human existence. A principal favors certain foods, music, political systems, bodily appearances. Historians and social scientists prefer to remain on a descriptive level, for they presume the descriptive values they isolate can be verified by others as competent, presumably, as they themselves are. Prescriptive values, on the other hand, are elusive in part because, resulting from an act of faith, they are not independent of the tastes and prejudices of the principals and observers who advocate them. Admittedly, although we must repeat "de gustibus non disputandum est," we must also skeptically inquire whether there may be a universal preference for symmetry in the human form and in works of art wherever one looks. Obviously faith is unquenchable.

Skeptical Note: Is not the concept of value too slippery to be useful?

Envoi: Although we must be skeptical, especially because many judgments and actions are morally deficient and because various values pervade all phases of existence, *nevertheless* we are perhaps ever happily doomed to struggle on and somehow to try to lead a good life—whatever that means.

MEANDERINGS

1.1 A Confession

This paragraph should really be not only a meandering but a confession in very fine print so that it can be easily skipped: as modestly as possible I would offer personal testimonial concerning the utility to me of the probing questions. As this book has undergone too many drafts for me to remember with any degree of comfort, I often would have new ideas or stumble upon new ideas I wished to incorporate into the text. Truly I have experienced almost no difficulty in fitting them into the analysis without, from my admittedly biased standpoint, forcing them upon what was already there. The schema works for me; it enables me to utilize tidbits or profundities in a systematic manner. I can only hope the reader will have a similar experience.

After formulating the probing questions, for example, I have also searched for sympathetic writers in the literature of philosophy and social science because I believe that no schema can be original, certainly not my own. "The process hypothesis" of one psychologist comes close to this formulation; he believes that every "adaptive decision" goes through four stages:

(a) establishing the purpose or goal whose achievement is to be advanced by the decision.
(b) analyzing the information relevant to the decision.
(c) synthesizing a solution by selecting the alternative action or actions most likely to lead to the purpose or goal.
(d) implementing the decision by issuing a command signal to carry out the action or actions (Miller, 1978, p. 100).

Although the author rates his own "personal confidence" in the formulation as "low," it should be evident that the four stages cover the same ground as the eight probing questions, but that the "relevant"

information and the "synthesizing" are too elliptical: they lump together and do not differentiate the questions of potentiality, rule, duty,
anticipation, and values.

1.2 Value Nomenclature

Admittedly other concepts besides value could serve a similar analytic
function. One candidate might be "moral rules" which are "abstract
and general principles of conduct that have to be applied to all kinds
of concrete situations" (Wright, 1971, p. 14). Another is "sin," provided it is less glibly defined than "something you do that is wrong
. . . much more likely to be not doing something that may be right"
(Emerson, 1974, p. 67). "Value," however, seems sufficiently flexible
to be applicable to all probing questions. While any unabridged
dictionary reveals that in English the term is employed in countless
ways, it has been called, nevertheless, "the core concept across all
the social sciences" (Rokeach, 1973, p. ix). Often the word itself may
appear in another guise. Thus Kant's "one categorical imperative" is
the well-known statement, "Act only according to that maxim by
which you can at the same time will that it should become a universal
law" (Kant, 1969 ed., p. 44). Kant is functioning here as an observer
who is prescribing a superordinate value to justify the use of a maxim
or principle *(What ought I do?)*. When an anthropologist writes that
in a traditional African society men have plural wives, implicitly he
is reporting one of the values to which the inhabitants subscribe: as
an observer he is stating that polygyny is a marital rule securing their
approval *(What may I do?);* he is not philosophizing about that rule.

The concept of value creeps into diverse disciplines whenever the
allegedly distinctive attributes of human beings are discussed. A distinguished neurobiologist, for example, when he reflects upon the
state of the world and what is known concerning the nervous sytem,
is convinced that values are at the apex of the numerous factors affecting behavior, yes, affecting behavior. Human beings are not created
completely by environmental pressures, he asserts; they can control
their own destinies when their values at a conscious level direct what
they do (Sperry, 1983, pp. 12–13, 33). In my opinion, such a view
suggests that sometimes values are crucial, sometimes they are not,
which is the approach of the present analysis. The approach, however,
is pragmatic in the sense that in some instances the value can be called
the immediate cause without inquiring into the environmental pressures responsible for its arousal. One of the same writer's critics who
is enthusiastic about sociobiology places greater emphasis upon the
sources of behavior and views the brain as a "value-driven decision

system"; thus he also believes that "human values provide the guiding criteria for all personal decisions" (Pugh, 1977, pp. 6, 9, 49–54). Only in an ultimate sense does it become necessary to consider the genetic or biological versus the learned components of values; for present purposes it is sufficient to note that proponents of both extremes agree in allocating a central role to values as a determinant of ongoing judgments.

Unlike some philosophers, one of whom has frankly stated that "the absolute . . . indicates that there is a farther realm beyond thinking which thinking itself cannot reach" (Roubiczek, 1969, p. 70), psychologists and other social scientists seldom hesitate to name values and to treat them as measurable variables and hence the object of thought. But unlike chemists who agree on a table of chemical elements, these investigators do not possess a body of common knowledge concerning the values that is supposed to be helpful within their discipline. Virtually every investigator emerges with his own list of values, each of which seems reasonable, even compelling until the next one is published. Here are the "fifteen major themes of value-belief orientations that have long been salient in American society," according to one sociologist: activity and work; achievement and success; moral orientation; humanitarianism; efficiency and practicality; science and secular rationality; material comfort; progress; equality; freedom; democracy; external conformity; nationalism and patriotism; individual personality; racism and related group superiority. Who would dare quarrel with such a list, the items of which are said to have been derived from "a large and diverse body of data from historical, economic, political, and sociological studies" (R. M. Williams, 1979, pp. 30–31)?

A psychologist, on the other hand, has made a distinction between terminal values ("beliefs or conceptions about ultimate goals or desirable end-states of existence that are worth striving for") and instrumental values ("beliefs or conceptions about desirable modes of behavior that are instrumental to the attainment of desirable end-states"), under each of which he postulates the following values, which turn out to be—mirabile dictu—for each list exactly eighteen in number, no more, no less:

Terminal	Instrumental
1. Wisdom	Intellectual
2. Freedom	Capable
3. Self-respect	Honest

4. A sense of accomplishment	Responsible
5. A world at peace	Imaginative
6. Equality	Independent
7. A world of beauty	Broad-minded
8. Inner harmony	Logical
9. Family security	Ambitious
10. Social recognition	Helpful
11. Happiness	Courageous
12. An exciting life	Self-controlled
13. A comfortable life	Loving
14. True friendship	Forgiving
15. Mature love	Cheerful
16. National security	Polite
17. Pleasure	Clean
18. Salvation	Obedient

The above schema has proven to be extremely useful in aiding the author's own research as well as that of others especially because he has embodied the two sets in an easily administered paper-and-pencil questionnaire which, without further specification, asks the respondent only to arrange the values in order of their importance to him, "as guiding principles in YOUR life" (Rokeach, 1979).

Finally, an empirically inclined philosopher once detected "thirteen ways to live" in the world's religions and in the responses of American college students to a questionnaire expressing those ways. He then sought to extract—by means of the statistical technique of factor analysis—the various values they embodied. Five emerged, which are, in his words, social restraint and self-control, enjoyment and progress in action, withdrawal and self-sufficiency, receptivity and sympathetic concern, and self-indulgence (or sensuous enjoyment) (Morris, 1956, pp. 32–34).

It is noteworthy that all three of the above schemas are in one sense in agreement: although their words differ significantly, the values they describe refer to the self, to others, and to society in general. In addition, their progenitors have been able to express them in a form that is acceptable on a commonsense, intuitive basis and that can also be embodied in paper-and-pencil questionnaires intelligible to principals who, in spite of different experiences in the past and varying languages, are able or at least are willing to respond. Values thus ascertained, as will be suggested later *(Proposition 3.6)*, always have a statistical relation with various demographic and personality factors, a tribute both to the possible validity of the so-called instruments and to the principals' plasticity. A tour de force could construct one schedule embodying all the values of these and other schemas, a thankless task I shall not undertake. Here it is sufficient to note both the diversity and the possible unity of the schemas; therefore our skepticism stemming from the former is modified by the latter, perhaps.

Enough: the present treatise is not a textbook either on values or on ethics; by themselves the cited sources demonstrate the tremendous variability in nomenclature and the referents of values. The demonstration of that variability does not claim to be exhaustive. Any social scientist or especially any philosopher who mentions the subject of values, because he is dealing with culture, personality, economics, ethics, or axiology perforce must have his own nomenclature—and an exhaustive review would be exhausting and fruitless. Undoubtedly the explanation for the variability must be, as one writer has said, the fact that "almost any aspect of culture can become the basis for values" (Miller, 1978, p. 804), and therefore attention is focused on different phenomena. In addition, as one browses through the elaborate and changing vocabulary employed by scholars and writers in the Western world to refer to values, it is impossible to repress a deep skeptical note: maybe they have been seeking only a unified vocabulary by ignoring the distinctive connotations and denotations attached to the words. Yes, we seek justice, truth, and all the rest, but just what do the words mean in everyday life?

1.3 The Pursuit of Universal Values

Why is the pursuit of universal values seemingly futile? The changing complexity of mankind has contributed significantly to the futility, as have differences among individuals. The challenge was once clearly stated by Hobbes:

> *Good,* and *evil,* are names that signify our appetites, and aversions; which in different tempers, customs, and doctrines of men, are different: and divers men differ not only in their judgment, on the senses of what is pleasant, and unpleasant to the taste, smell, hearing, touch, and sight; but also of what is comfortable, or disagreeable to reason, in the actions of common life. Nay, the same man, in divers times, differs from himself; and one time praiseth, that is, calleth good, what another he dispraiseth, and calleth evil: from whence arise disputes, controversie, and at last war. (Hobbes, 1946 ed., p. 104, italics his)

And a modern philosopher, somewhat but not completely out of context: "Whatever is decidable or can be determined by deliberation is right or wrong . . . anything under the sun may be good or bad" (Łewis, 1955, pp. 20, 59). But is this really so? I repeat: nowhere presumably is starvation a positive, normal value that men ordinarily seek to realize, unless they would achieve a political goal through a hunger strike or unless they torture an enemy. In one breath a philosopher realizes that "different cultures may have different concepts of truth-telling, different codes of honesty," but in the next he quite rightly points out "there *must* be a norm of truth-telling in any conceivable society," for how else can we "teach a child to speak a language without reproving him when he makes false statements" (Norman, 1971, p. 136, italics his)? Yet another philosopher asks, "is there a single property by virtue of which all intrinsic or inherent goods are good?" and then replies: "this question has often been answered affirmatively, but none of the affirmative answers has met with general favor" (Olson, 1967).

Although anthropologists are not reluctant to suggest that the "same basic physiological needs" are satisfied everywhere and that every society provides for its "organization, operation, and perpetuation" (Linton, 1952), they offer copious and convincing evidence that particular values fluctuate from society to society. Cultures differ with respect to the patterning of their values, the emphasis they place upon those values, the referent to which the values apply, and the consistency with which the values are organized (R. M. Williams, 1979, pp. 17–18). There is thus a vast difference between persons living in the upper-class section of an American city and those Somali nomads who inhabit the desert of their country, but it is equally evident that both groups also share significant values concerning the sanctity of human life, the importance of tradition, the need for security, and so on—on and on. Even when an observer believes that two peoples are similar in some respect, however, closer examination may reveal differences with respect to apparently similar behavior; or dissimilar behavior may be judged similarly by them. Hunting animals is a food-gathering necessity in one society, sport in another. In seeking a basis for moral judgments, no observer is able to say, without suggesting the modifying role of culture, that "human nature" requires very specific values. What Luther called "sinful" callings—"robbery, usury, public women," and the officials within the church from which he had rebelled (cited by Passmore, 1970, p. 14)—may or may not be universally so labeled; certainly Catholics would object to the reference to officials of their church. Of late, however, some anthropologists have expressed doubts concerning the validity of anthropological analyses of the particular values in other societies: in reporting data from their own fieldwork, they may not have been able to grasp the subtleties and the interconnections of the prevailing values, their interpretations may not be valid, and perforce what they write in their monographs must be filtered through their own language and adapted to their prospective readers (Geertz, 1983; Marcus and Cushman, 1982). Projective techniques—having informants respond to drawings of traditional and modern activities—have been tried with moderate success (Goldschmidt and Edgerton, 1961).

That social science is not an infallible guide to establishing the basis for universal values is also suggested again by one of its prime findings as well as by historical investigations: changes in values over time. These changes occur for various reasons ranging from the influence of outside forces to rearrangements within the society itself, which, as one writer has phrased it, are needed to prevent "the harmony of the group" from being threatened (Schneiderman, 1979). Values move like a slow or a rushing stream; the warning comes from social science that we can only glimpse them as they pass by. All of us, including the best of our philosophers, are victims of the ambience in a specific milieu.

Universal values are also pursued slightly indirectly by considering the "rights" to which all human beings presumably are entitled. One social scientist, after surveying the history of the doctrines of human rights since World War II, concludes that "votes in the United Nations and other international organizations indicate a substantial degree of consensus on the question, what are human rights"—but then he ends the sentence with the clause, "when the answer is confined to general principles." In connection with a "right to life," "to regulate family size" or "conception by artificial methods," "to enter a country other than one's own," to "conscientious objection in war," and so on, "no very serious effort has yet been made to achieve agreement" among nations (Van Dyke, 1970, pp. 242–43). Again, the path to universality is strewn with controversy, inconsistency, and exceptions.

I have the impression that usually the search for universal values among both philosophers and social scientists is directed toward the positive rather than the negative. Torture, poverty, and alienation, it could be said (Doob, 1978, pp. 53–56), are universally to be avoided. Avoided for whom: only one's own group or also one's enemy? In addition, the concepts can be worded positively: persuasion, plenty, satisfaction are somewhat equivalent. More important, negative values or practices require a more superordinate value such as an interest in humanity before they can be condemned.

Perhaps this dissection of prescriptive values can be forced to end on a less skeptical note by going off on an apparent tangent. When large organizations, such as corporations, are surveyed, it has been said that in a highly competitive market and with the need to adopt innovations, the changes in routines occur slowly and can be considered—at least metaphorically—in an evolutionary context: the new must be built upon the old (Nelson and Winter, 1982, chap. 6). More generally it is clear that in spite of complexity—and confusion and constraints—some values in society endure. In fact, their very endurance offers some reason for believing them to be prescriptive rather than descriptive values: they must be reflecting basic needs within human beings. They transcend the person or persons originally formulating or epitomizing them and also the periods in which they appeared. This attribution of duration is applicable in fields other than morality. The writings of great men such as Shakespeare, Goethe, Cervantes evoke profound responses in modern audiences, maybe equally as profound, whether different or not, as once occurred among their contemporaries. Even the achievements of outstanding scientists, such as Galileo, Newton, Lavoisier, Darwin, and Einstein, though superceded and revised by succeeding generations, continue to be venerated. And so it is also with the exponents of values: Aristotle, Confucius, Jesus, Mohammed, Marx, and maybe even Kant. The fact that their values are appreciated must mean that they are satisfactory either as guides to current practices or as models to be achieved. A synthesis of enduring values is not easy, nay, impossible to come by, but clearly on slightly different abstract levels they are all concerned with the relations among human beings and with an emphasis on reciprocity in those relations. This criterion, however, must be cautiously employed. Wars, for example, have existed perpetually, if periodically, which cannot mean that they therefore merit moral approval.

Skepticism concerning universality is thus gently justified and challenged: principals play very diverse parts during their exits and entrances, but perhaps those parts have not undergone appreciable alteration even when the stage sets change.

CHAPTER 2

Principals, Observers, and Groups

The relation between persons and their society is a well-worn, hackneyed topic. But it cannot be avoided since reference, for example, is often made to the values and morality of the individual as well as to the groups to which he belongs. The state is supposed to make decisions even as principals pass judgments. A straight path through this essentially verbal jungle must be hastily hacked, however skeptical we may feel concerning the chances that it will ever be hailed by those necessarily addicted to convenient group metaphors.

2.1 GENESIS

Proposition: Replies to the probing questions, however buried, stem originally and ultimately from human beings either individually or collectively.

It is misleading and can be dangerous to lose sight of possibly identifiable persons and to refer to the values of a society, a social class, a church, an army, or a neighborhood. Aristotle states somewhat glibly that "the happiness of a state is to be pronounced the same as that of each individual" and that "everyone would agree" with that proposition (Aristotle, 1944 ed., p. 538). After discovering "the virtues found in the State"—wisdom, courage, temperance, and justice—Plato beclouds the procedure with a semantic twist: "Let the discovery which we made be now applied to the individual" (Plato, 1928 ed., pp. 152–62). In general, close inspection of the assertions by these ancients and their successors invariably reveals that the allusion to groups in reality is a reference to the modal values or "happiness" of members of the group, to those of an influential minority, or to those of the group's actual or potential leaders. At best, in short,

24

praising or condemning the values of the group may be a necessary metaphor; yet often it is a sloppy form of shorthand. Conventionally, it may be said that groups, whether temporary or more or less permanent, influence their members. Such rephrasing masks the fact that some persons in the group affect other members, principals, or observers who refer their behavior to it.

Similarly when entire societies are characterized in sweeping terms—their "morale" is high or they are permeated by "moral decay"—a moment's reflection suggests that some or more of the citizens in those societies are eager and optimistic or are making the kind of moral judgments the speaker or writer chooses to call bad.

Often philosophers maintain that they should not trouble themselves with examining or explaining principals and groups. For example: psychology is said to be "concerned with processes, with the question of how individual actions are motivated and performed," whereas ethics "tries to evaluate the motives and actions themselves, to apply values which are independent of the individual, and to discover the principles on which these values rest" (Roubiczek, 1969, p. 44). A persuasive reply is simple: any system of moral principles has little or no impact unless it is related to what is known about persons and groups; the separation is artificial and dysfunctional. Or in different words: the nature of human nature or ideas about human nature inevitably affect both evaluations and policies; specifiable principals and observers dare not be avoided if morality is to be comprehended *(Meandering 2.1: The Values of Institutions).*

Skeptical Note: Why quibble? Is it not perhaps easier and more fruitful to refer to groups of all kinds rather than persons?

2.2 IDENTIFICATION

Proposition: Locating principals or observers concerned with moral judgments or actions is essential; when this proves difficult or impossible, the substituted basis should be clearly indicated.

The proposition recognizes that the locus of moral judgments and actions is within human beings but simultaneously admits the possibility of slips twixt practice and the ideal. A child who is told by his parents to behave in a particular way knows with complete certainty who has made the judgment to which he is supposed to respond. But does he? No, the parent's injunction springs from personal and cultural values concerning all the details of which both he or she and the child are unaware. Only an observer like a political scientist or a journalist, if he is persistent and perhaps lucky, may be able to name the political leaders responsible for the legislation that affects the individual citizen who has neither the incentive nor the information to identify them.

The principals or observers of groups that, according to the metaphor, pass judgments are frequently especially difficult to identify. Even when the discussion leading to a decision is brief, the interaction of principals and their influence upon one another may have been quite different from the ways in which they could have behaved in isolation. Some principals may have had more prestige and power than others, so that their views prevailed; others may have disagreed but conformed. The consequences of an interaction rather than the precise mode of arriving at a decision, whether that decision must be rapid (as in a nuclear power plant) or prolonged (planning the strategy of a political campaign), may be known, unknown, or kept secret. Additional difficulties arise when the effort is made to locate the persons responsible for the networks or connections groups have with one another (cf. Marsden, 1983), especially in complex systems whose human and mechanical constituents are so tightly "coupled" that the role of any particular person cannot easily be ascertained (Perrow, 1984, pp. 89–94). The extremely useful sociological concept of reference group raises a similar problem when a principal states—and quite correctly, too—that his values or his moral judgments originate in some institution like a church, a political party, or a community without being able to locate the specific members of those groups who have been influential; rest assured, however, that the influence has not come out of the air but from persons now forgotten or never clearly observed.

Indeed, let us admit that the principals ultimately responsible for some actions, good or bad, may never be located. He is a genius or an arsonist—who is responsible? If a genius, the genes of his parents and the parents themselves must have played a role; should they be praised? But their genes in turn came from their own parents, and so on back to Cain or perhaps Abel. If he is an arsonist, again his parents and maybe not his genes but someone in the community may have inspired him to commit the crime. In either case, the groups of persons to be identified in order to affix total responsibility are elusive. Even when a principal admits responsibility for an action—he believes he is telling the truth; he is an egoist or a masochist—his admission may not necessarily be true in some sense an observer may either know or posit.

According to a somewhat unconventional psychiatrist, "the assertion that a person is mentally ill involves rendering a moral judgment about him" (Szasz, 1966). The assertion itself stems from an observer, perhaps a psychiatrist, perhaps a relative, who knows the person and who therefore can be located. But that observer has obtained his conception of mental illness from a variety of sources that ultimately may not be located. If he is a psychiatrist, he has been influenced by the official definitions provided by his profession or by his mentors when he was a medical student: their identity is unknown or unknowable in detail like most phenomena with long histories. If he is an ordinary citizen, he has been affected by a prevailing view in the society transmitted to him by his parents or other role models.

A key concept in the present analysis is that of judgment, which inevitably and unequivocally refers to human beings. When a principal calls himself, another person, or an entire group, for example, "good" or "evil," he is applying the epithet to an individual or individuals. He may be unable to find the specific persons in the group and he may not care to do so, but he judges the actions of those unknowns. Ignorance, deliberate or otherwise, is no excuse for abandoning the search which, even when fruitless, at least makes the searcher aware of the human problem.

It should now be evident, even to the skeptical, that there is nothing mysterious about the ancient questions concerning whether the group is more than its members, whether the whole is more than the sum of its parts. The mystery arises because observers are ignorant concerning the details of the interactions among the members. When such information is not available, it is convenient or necessary to use the metaphor of the group. But the metaphor drags us only a trifle beyond skepticism; we may still remain dissatisfied or puzzled. All we can do is qualify our statements when we are ignorant or confess our leap. "The government has decided . . ." Who? Which persons? Who informed you about a decision? Can he be trusted? *(Meandering 2.2: Who Told Them to Be Good?)*.

Skeptical Note: What happens when all relevant persons are not located and comprehended?

2.3 EVENTS

Proposition: Judgments and actions, moral or nonmoral, are elicited by events or changes in the environment.

From the standpoint of the ordinary citizen it may be convenient to say or believe that "government" demands that taxes be paid, that the "church" requires and observes rituals under specified circumstances *(What must I do?)*. Government, I repeat, means officials, tax collectors, or police; and church means clergymen, parents, and peers. The elicited judgments—shall I pay all I am supposed to? shall I follow a golden rule?—depend on the events as well as on the principals' groups. Potentially all events are controllable by human beings. The control may be negative, as when wild animals are curbed or reforestation is allowed to occur after trees have been cut down. At this technological moment weather may still be beyond direct control, but adaptation is possible—for example, by heating, air-conditioning, and taking shelter during a storm. Otherwise, most events originate within the society, especially those affecting interpersonal relations, although some come from outside, as when a country is invaded by a hostile army or by carriers of an infectious disease. According to the assumptions of some or many persons in every society, supernatural events are especially compelling when metaphysical beings such as gods or a god intervenes in human affairs; nevertheless, the assumptions are transmitted by leaders and members of groups. How events are actually perceived, consequently, also depends on what the principals bring to them: their own predispositions. Any event, moreover, may have moral implications; thus an impartial arbitrator of a dispute may refrain from expressing his own values, but the very role he plays reflects his own judgment that the conflict between the parties can or should be resolved (cf. Stevenson, 1963, pp. 3–15).

The actions of some persons are events for others, as a result of which new issues requiring judgments become salient. Until recently, for example, moral judgments were not made by most Americans concerning the rights of blacks and women or concerning pollution and the gradual destruction of the natural environment. Now organizations of interested citizens have formed pressure groups whose publicity and activities have made these issues salient, and therefore new or modified judgments and actions have been required.

It is or should be self-evident that much of behavior occurs in groups. Hunters in pairs or parties may more effectively find and slay game than a single person, and the kill may be shared. Obviously the sexual drive normally demands the existence and presence of another individual whose feelings and proclivities are somehow taken into account. One or more persons are needed to play most games. The values corresponding to such cooperative activity, therefore, include a reference to people who influence events.

Locating all the details of an event produced by or affecting principals *(Proposition 2.2)* is another difficult, if not impossible task upon
occasion. Skepticism concerning the "complete" explanation or even
description is inescapable. Shortly before the end of World War II,
for example, the open city of Dresden was firebombed by American
and British planes. At least 135,000 lives were lost and the city itself,
with its rich cultural monuments, was virtually destroyed. Those
making the decision to conduct the raid must have been swayed by
immediate considerations that would provide the Russians with a
demonstration of American and British air power or that would bring
the war in Europe to a quicker end so that attention could be concentrated upon the Japanese. The question of who authorized the raid
and for what reasons is perhaps insignificant when one considers the
far-flung repercussions for the Germans and others who had been
living or who had fled there, or for the postwar relations of Germany
with Great Britain and the United States. The probing is complicated
by the fact that thousands of persons were involved in the bombing—
those making the decisions and those suffering the consequences. Less
important than locating the persons responsible for the bombing is
the question of its moral significance. We shall never know what the
consequences would have been if Dresden had not been bombed,
consequences relating to the ongoing war, to the relation between
the Soviets and Anglo-Americans, and to the warlike peace that followed the formal ending of hostilities. Desirable skepticism in this
instance is insufficient: a crime was committed and should not be repeated. Never?

Skeptical Note: Can any event ever be completely described, no
less adequately judged and assessed?

2.4 PERCEPTION

Proposition: Events must be perceived if they are to affect moral
judgments and actions.

Perception may be direct or may occur as a result of communications from intermediaries. Values are transmitted directly in face-
to-face situations, as when a psychiatrist or counselor offers advice.
Or they may reach principals through models or symbols. Models include parents, peers, clergymen, educators, political leaders, the values
behind whose words or behavior must be inferred on many occasions.
Symbols refer to the contents of any medium that would induce the
audience to react to the implications of what is perceived. Commu-

nicators may communicate informally, as when they praise or condemn an action with or without an additional reward or punishment. Perhaps an expletive or curse slips off their tongues: any language has innumerable, concise ways to appraise the behavior of another person or of the communicator himself. Networks exist through which values are assumed to be transmitted to persons and groups, such as those between parents and children, or between managers and workers.

The problem of whether a communication is effective is too vast to be considered here *(Meandering 13.2)*. One illustration must suffice to suggest that guidelines are uncertain because the variables and the variations are numerous. In some instances the difficulty arises because oranges and apples are compared. An orange: after listening to stories, young children tended to recall more readily the intentions of the characters whose behavior they were asked to judge when those intentions were reported toward the end (recency) rather than at the beginning of the tale (primacy) (Austin et al., 1977). An apple: experiments with American college students suggest that the nature of information may be more influential than the presentation order, and that a silent film tended to be more effective than a written communication, again regardless of presentation order (Luchins and Luchins, 1984). Thus skepticism is warranted concerning research that mixes children and young adults or that uses different kinds of material to be perceived without a thorough analysis of the intervening variables, even though each study seems intriguing or potentially useful in its own limited right.

Except when a group is very small or when a large group can be viewed from afar (by observing a crowd from a tall building or a helicopter, for example), the principal or the observer cannot directly perceive all the actions. Even then only the externalities of the behavior are communicated. Also, as previously indicated, the decision of a group communicated by a leader, spokesman, or a written document does not reveal how the decision was reached and who played various roles *(Proposition 2.2)*. Sometimes, moreover, inferences concerning members of a group are made from a knowledge of the reported or stated predispositions of one of its members or from his behavior. Perhaps such a generalization from the individual to his fellow members may be more likely to occur and be valid when it is believed that he is representative of them, when what he says or does can be attributed to situational rather than idiosyncratic or predispositional factors, or when his behavior is truly salient (Zuckerman et al., 1982).

Skeptical Note: Does one ever know adequately what another person perceives?

Envoi: Although we are dealing directly or indirectly with human beings and can never make a complete or enduring analysis of all the individuals affecting and being affected by events, *nevertheless* we can pass judgments that are momentarily, tentatively, but pragmatically useful.

MEANDERINGS

2.1 The Values of Institutions

A psychologist sounds like a sociologist when he boldly states that "it is just as meaningful to speak of cultural, societal, organizational, and group values as it is to speak of individual values." But what in fact does he himself do when he seeks to determine the values of an institution? He lists and skillfully employs five methods to investigate such values, all of which are related to one another in varying degrees: the content analysis of documents or publications transmitted from the institution; the "personal values" of the elite who control or lead the institution; the "personal values" of persons belonging to the institution; the "perceived values" of the institution by its elite; and the "perceived values" of the institution by members of the society who have some knowledge of that institution (Rokeach, 1979). The last four measures are not the least bit mysterious: they are assemblages of values possessed or transmitted by principals or ascribed to members—individual human beings—of the institution. The first, the documents or publications, likewise reflect the values of their creators or of what those creators assume or wish to be the audience for which they are intended. We learn about institutions not by looking into the clouds but by seeking to locate and then query their members or surrogates.

Over decades the values of a society and other guides to action become embodied in proverbs, which thus contain some of the wisdom of the society. These functions are clearly evident in traditional lands. In many African societies the ability on occasion to quote appropriate proverbs increases the speaker's prestige and may have meaningful, concrete advantages in contests and trials. In the West, however, proverbs may be part of tradition, but their role in affecting moral judgments and actions is less clear; thus we know that "a penny saved is a penny got" but also that we should not postpone until tomorrow what we can do today. Traditional societies, moreover, are changing and therefore proverbs may sometimes be effective, sometimes not. One way to test their effectiveness is to see whether they are known to principals. In one study I found, as might be anticipated, that a sample of nomadic Somalis tended to be better acquainted with Somali proverbs (as well as with Somali poetry) than another sample of Somali cultivators living in the neighborhoods of the capital city; thus the more traditional Somalis must have employed the proverbs more frequently than the semiurbanized group. But a third group of Somali students who were having meaningful contacts with Western culture were as well acquainted with the proverbs as the nomads, not because they necessarily followed the values expressed therein, but because they maintained contact with their nomadic parents and deliberately sought to preserve the traditional heritage (Doob and Hurreh, 1970–71). In another study, this time among Twi-speaking students between the estimated ages of thirteen and sixteen, I learned that knowledge of allegedly traditional Akan proverbs was spotty, that some were better known than others, that a slight but perceptible increase in knowledge was evident with increasing age, and that of course knowledge tended to vary from student to student (Doob, 1972).

2.2 Who Told Them to Be Good?

Research concerning moral behavior may produce statistical norms without indicating precisely the persons originally or ultimately responsible for that behavior. Children in more than a dozen countries, for example, were confronted with hypothetical dilemmas and were asked whether or not a person in effect would yield to temptation. Should a child continue to view an exciting TV show after the hour at which his absent parents had told him he must go to bed? Some of the children were told that their verbal judgments about these situations would be shown to adults, others that peers would see them, and still others that their replies would be kept confidential. In Israel the age of the children affected their replies: the younger the individual, the less the tendency to believe the hypothetical child should yield, regardless of who allegedly was to see their responses (Guttmann, 1982). In other countries the tendency to state that temptation should be avoided was more pronounced when the children had been told that adults rather than peers would see their replies. In the Soviet Union, Hungary, and Brazil, more children tended to claim that they would obey authority and not succumb to temptation than did those in Canada, Scotland, and Switzerland, regardless of who allegedly would be shown their responses (Scheibe and Spaccaquerche, 1976). Clearly the cultural norms regarding authority and temptation, as here artificially measured, functioned differently in the countries where the children were being socialized. But why, oh why had they been indoctrinated differently, or why had their parents, their peers, or the school authorities indoctrinated them differently? When age was a factor, did this mean that the indoctrinators adapted their communication to the children's age or that the children themselves could learn and practice the values only as they matured? The questions are unanswerable directly, but the established differences point the way, if one wishes, to investigate the methods of the socializers, the parents or peers, in each of the societies.

In another study, secondary school boys in northern Nigeria tended to be "more advanced in moral judgment" when they were enrolled in a residential school containing boys from a variety of cultural subgroups than did those in a school having virtually only boys from the same cultural group (Maqsud, 1977). Presumably the values of the boys in the mixed school had been challenged more frequently than had been those in the homogeneous school; hence they must have been more salient. We are thus left with an intuitive guess, and concerning guesses it is always wise to be grateful but somewhat skeptical.

PART 2

PRINCIPALS

CHAPTER 3

Personality

The distinction between principals and observers *(Proposition 1.2)* will now be scrupulously honored, at least for the time being. In this second part, attention is concentrated, almost exclusively, upon principals and the problems arising as they seek to answer the eight probing questions. Observers receive their due in part 3. Let there be no illusion: understanding is only the first step in any quest for prescriptive values. Whether a leap can be attempted from descriptive to prescriptive values is the momentous, ever recurring problem meriting a skeptical sigh.

The accompanying figure, hereafter referred to as the Morality Figure, skeletonizes the complicated processes to be reviewed. The principal's personality (circle A) is at the top: it embodies his predispositions, no matter what the event. When he introspects, he may well ask himself at least two of the probing questions: *What will I do?* and *What can I do?* These two and perhaps other predispositions are activated by an event (B), an event not in the abstract but one perceived by the principal. He responds to that event in one of two ways:

1. The principal passes judgments or acts (or both) as a result of a previously established habit, which may or may not be cognitively judged.
   a. If the habit is not cognitively judged, a habitual judgment (C′) occurs and then perhaps action (D). When confronted with temptation, the principal does not hesitate, he does not succumb, he acts accordingly. In the figure, arrows go directly from the perceived event to habitual judgment and then to action.
   b. If the habitual judgment itself is cognitively judged, that

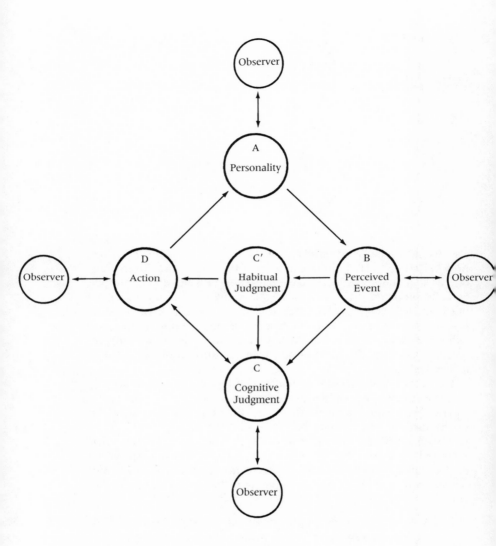

Morality Figure

cognitive judgment (C) follows after the habitual judgment or the action. In this case the honesty-prone principal wonders whether he should be honest either before or after acting; he may raise one or more probing questions. In the figure, arrows go from the habitual judgment and action to the cognitive judgment.

2. The principal may raise one or more of the probing questions; he does not pass a habitual judgment but passes a cognitive judgment, which may or may not be moral (C) and which may or may not lead to action (D). He is puzzled; a cognitive judgment may not occur immediately but only after reflection concerning the probing questions that he raises and perhaps weighs, possibly in accordance with a particular or imperative value. This cognitive judgment may or may not be expressed in action. In the figure, arrows go from perceived event to cognitive judgment (avoiding habitual judgment) and from there to action.

With a cognitive judgment one or more of the probing questions are raised and answered and thus produce a morally complete or incomplete judgment or no moral judgment; the arrow from it to action is double-pointed since the last of the questions, *What do I do?*, occurs only after action. Finally, when and if there is action, it may have an effect upon the principal's personality later on as he perceives future events—hence the arrow connecting action and personality.

The possible presence and reactions of observers is noted in the small circles on the edges of the figure; the arrows are all double-pointed since an observer not only observes but may also affect the principal.

The figure and hence the mode of analysis seek to embrace the concepts and theories of those scholars who confront themselves with the same related problems. It would include the numerous factors or parameters of interest to students of ethics (J. E. Smith, 1963); it would reflect concepts previously employed by others (Brandt, 1959) and by me in other contexts (Doob, 1961, 1971, 1975, 1981, 1983); and it would refer to the subjective or internal factors of interest to cognitive psychologists and phenomenologists as well as to the objectively observable ones preferred by behavioral psychologists and other social scientists. Originality is not being sought; rather emphasis is placed upon concepts common to all of us *(Meandering 3.1: Metaphysical Implications)*.

3.1 PREDISPOSITIONS

Proposition: The principal's predispositions always affect his judgments.

This proposition would be an unnecessary banality were it not for the fact that often human beings are overlooked when reference is made not only to groups but also to their alleged judgments in a society *(Proposition 2.2)*. A simple proverb such as "honesty is the best policy" is a formula that can be said, without quibbling, to make innumerable assumptions: the best for whom, under what circumstances, and who defines honesty? No matter where one dips into available research or commonsense observations, a relation, strong or weak, between personality and moral and nonmoral judgments can be noted. As Plato constructed his Republic, he referred explicitly to what he called mankind's three predispositions: "the rational principal of the soul," "the irrational or appetitive, the ally of sundry pleasures and satisfactions," and "passion or spirit" (Plato, 1928 ed., book 4). Most, many, some—a useless survey would be necessary to select the appropriate adjective—philosophers also conceptualize human nature before or while they embark upon the prescriptive values they prefer. Indeed, descriptive values are likely to be attached to, and to become salient in connection with, the replies to all the probing questions *(Proposition 11.1)*.

There is, therefore, no escape from the fact that personality affects judgments of all kinds as well as behavior. Some persons, for example, are prone to be submissive and to comply with legal or social regulations *(What may I do?)*; and some are likely to be idealistic, others pragmatic, no matter how those terms are defined *(What ought I do?)*. Obedience may be a habitual trait or a value employed to elicit a cognitive judgment; idealism and pragmatism embody other values. Almost everywhere mothers take care of their children and *wish* to do so *(What will I do?)*; but the ways in which they express this universal goal—whether they tend to be permissive or strict—result from experiences in their society *(What must I do?)*.

Out-of-bounds in this discussion must be, with one exception, the attempt to account for a principal's predispositions. Here is a psychological and psychiatric problem requiring detailed examination in its own right. Even a question concerning the predispositions likely to be salient during the life span of American males leads to complexities relating not only to their own background as children and adolescents but also to the roles they are expected to play and the difficulties they must face as they grow older (Levinson, 1978). The exception, however, is noteworthy: discussions of responsibility, unquestionably a key challenge both for principals and for observers, almost inevitably lead to a consideration of the genesis of a particular set of predispositions *(Proposition 9.3)*.

Skeptical Note: Can the real—whatever that means—predispositions of a principal ever be grasped?

3.2 MOTIVES AND GOALS

Proposition: Moral judgments and behavior occur after motives have been evoked and consequently incline a principal to seek one or more general or specific goals.

This proposition encompasses a good deal of what is usually meant by human nature, for it suggests why persons wish to behave as they do; hence it embodies the first probing question, *What will I do?* When an individual blinks reflexively in response to a bright light striking his retina, however, only in retrospect and then metaphorically can it be said that he was motivated to protect the retina by blinking. When an appeal is made to contribute money to a charity, a principal's response obviously is more complex. What he then does depends to some extent upon his goals and the motives sustaining them. By any definition, including mine *(Proposition 1.3)*, values refer to approved or disapproved behavior, whether in particular situations or more generally; they become salient only when a motive has been aroused by a source (a stimulus, an event) external to or within the principal. Ethical codes are violated when the motivation to achieve a goal is more powerful than that which ordinarily produces obedience to the code *(What must I do?)*. At the same time individual freedom and the right to conduct one's own affairs as one wishes refer to achieving the goals associated with motives. Whether we like it or not, however, men cannot live by motives alone. Motives and values, therefore, are inextricably intertwined: values guide the expression of motives, which in turn may be evoked by values. You wish to do something; the value of altruism affects your judgments and your behavior; you are altruistic and therefore decide to do something.

Motives vary in strength. The stronger are basic to existence and usually have a genetic, though modifiable foundation. Such motives are almost always inescapable. I must thus reiterate the obvious—and shall continue to do so—because the obvious may be overlooked in lofty, philosophical discussions: human beings seek food, drink, various forms of activity, and sleep, as well as air to breathe and the avoidance of pain. Although they cannot be permanently diverted, frustrated, or repressed unless death through suicide is sought, goals under some circumstances may not be realized or they may be momentarily ignored.

Nobody including clergymen would dare deny what is variously called "human nature"; according even to one bishop, "Facts in the real world around us, not authoritative laws imposed from the outside, are these: persons count more than things; the well-being of persons requires certain things" (Pike, 1968). Usually but not always the basic motives bring immediate satisfaction when the goals are achieved. You eat the meal and are gratified. Food or physicians may be esteemed in the abstract, but ordinarily you do not eat unless you are hungry in some sense or visit a medical doctor unless you are ill (cf. Köhler, 1938, especially chap. 3). The value of the objects or persons of concern, like all values, resides not in them but in the principals whose motives are the basis for their significance.

Secondary, acquired, learned motives—terminology is not standardized—are usually weaker and can be extinguished, unlearned, or ignored. A principal strives to be successful in a new profession after abandoning his old. But on occasion a secondary motive may be stronger than one that is basic: a martyr chooses to perish rather than abandon his beliefs. Some meaningful goals may never be completely achieved. You are a Christian or a Buddhist and therefore your "ideal life is unrealizable in this world," although you may and can "strive after this ideal" (Körner, 1976, p. 201).

When a principal's genetic and physiological structure determines or affects the motive, precious values may have to be violated. Persons reared in the Western and almost universal tradition, when driven desperately by hunger, have been known to overlook the taboo on cannibalism in order to remain alive (cf. McGlashen, 1940, pp. 84–87). Secondary or derived motives that become self-sustaining may be judged good or bad by principals or observers: they may range from being obedient or benevolent to being negativistic or dishonest. One cannot expect a principal to be a hero or a villain unless he or she is motivated to behave appropriately. Whenever a principal asks himself or is asked not only *What will I do?* but also *What ought I do?*—whether the action is the pursuit of scientific truth or murdering a father-in-law—the values of what is contemplated become an issue.

For an observer and also sometimes for a principal, the goal of an action may be easier to ascertain than its motive. Objectively when one person helps another, does he do so only to help him or to ingratiate himself with that other person? Is his motive conscious or unconscious? When a large hydroelectric dam is constructed in a developing country, can one immediately state that its function and the goal of its sponsors are to generate electricity? As leaders of the country their motive may have been to introduce modern technology and thus to raise the country's standard of living. Or perhaps they commissioned a single large dam rather than a number of smaller ones because they believe its very size will be more impressive and hence will enhance their own prestige at home and abroad *(Meandering 3.2: Naming Motives)*.

Motives and goals always have accompanying values. Primary moves are likely to be assessed positively but not necessarily their methods of attainment. Yes, hunger must be satisfied but not by stealing food. Secondary motives are variously assessed. Perhaps a will to power is approved by some persons and in some societies but not by or in others.

Skeptical Note: Can one ever know, in an ultimate or even a nonultimate sense, what a principal seeks?

3.3 BELIEFS AND KNOWLEDGE

Proposition: Judgments and behavior are accompanied and affected by, and also affect, beliefs and the knowledge related to them.

Beliefs serve many functions. For morality, by definition they play a central role in values: I believe I ought to do that. More often than not, when principals "explain" their judgment to themselves and others they are more likely to provide reasons (their immediate goals, intentions, or even values) than causes (antecedent-consequent analysis) (A. R. Buss, 1978; Grice, 1967, chap. 1). On occasion, however, truthfully or not, they have no explanation: I don't know why I did that. Beliefs affect judgments: I believe it is important to go to the trouble to vote in elections. They may affect behavior: I believe he is powerful and therefore I shall be cautious in his presence. They suggest how knowledge may be increased: I believe computers are faster and more accurate than human beings in solving certain problems.

A long continuum of beliefs is thus available. At one end is a reference to a precedent and the status quo: I do this because that is the way it has been done in the past *(What did I do?)*. At the other end is sheer rationalization: I do this because I wish to do it and I really think that I shall be helpful to others *(What will I do? What would the consequences be?)*. Rationalizations, especially when accompanied by excuses, give rise to skepticism among observers concerning the validity of many beliefs, which therefore are thought to be self-serving and to enhance self-esteem (Snyder et al., 1983). A Freudian therapist and a Marxian theoretician may brand a principal's belief false because it is said to belie, respectively, his unconscious impulses or the "true" state of affairs in society. Somewhere in between seemingly rational and rationalizing beliefs are other possibilities: I do this because I believe I ought to do it *(What should I do?)*. Compulsion may be admitted: I do this because otherwise I shall be punished *(What must I do?)*. Finally, some beliefs stem from knowledge having few behavioral consequences. Many Christians, for example, are able to repeat some of the Ten Commandments and even a portion of the Sermon on the Mount without following those principles in their daily existence.

Beliefs are held with varying degrees of certainty, and hence principals have beliefs concerning beliefs in the manner of an infinite regress. A scientist, for example, has greater confidence in a belief he believes to have a scientific basis than one based upon the testimony of a friend or even upon his own conviction: he believes that scientific beliefs are more likely to be valid than nonscientific ones. Beliefs, like motives and goals, can be classified in as many ways as the experiences from which they are derived.

Beliefs do not function in isolation. If a principal holds a belief concerning another person, he simultaneously is likely to ascribe other beliefs to him. That man is immoral and therefore—and additional beliefs are probably associated with the very ascription. Stereotypes concerning ethnic groups or nationalities are clusters of beliefs; for this reason reference is frequently made to belief systems. Then, too, beliefs are affected and accompanied by attitudes. An action by a person who is liked may strengthen a principal's belief that he is a good person, but the same action will contribute to a belief concerning his badness when he is disliked. Part of the debate in the West concerning the morality of abortion hinges on a belief as to when the fetus may be considered to be a human being: those with a value opposed to abortion believe it lives after it has been conceived since it has the potentiality of developing into a person; those with a value favoring abortion believe that its life becomes significant, for example, only at the end of the trimester. The dividing line between potential and actual living is hazy.

Additional evidence may be needed before a judgment can be passed. In the Western tradition a person accused of a crime is seldom tried until the state and his own attorney gather the "facts" relating to his alleged action. The accused, however, may lack adequate knowledge as a result of which he "not only fails to take what externally appear as his formal decisions, but he also does not take advantage of his formal rights because the costs of doing so are structured so that they usually exceed the benefits"; as a result, as is reported in a Canadian study, frequently he "typically complies with police searches whether or not they have the authority of a warrant, usually does not remain silent in the face of police questioning, infrequently seeks or obtains access to a third party while in police custody, often does not obtain a lawyer, rarely demands a trial, often does not speak out in court when he has the urge to do so, and very rarely entertains an appeal of the outcome, let alone actually seeks one" (Ericson and Baranek, 1982). Ignorance obviously has serious consequences.

In contrast, the plea of "let me think it over" may mean that the principal believes he has inadequate knowledge to arrive at a moral or nonmoral cognitive judgment. Or he knows he must weight the opinions and values confronting him through the application of his own imperative value. In other situations additional facts are not needed: a principal may not hesitate to help someone in distress *(Proposition 13.1)*.

Relevant knowledge may exist but remain untapped. The principal lacks adequate motivation *(What will I do?)* or he is unable to utilize that knowledge *(What can I do?)*. Or one person may be knowledgeable, but only another may be in a position to use that knowledge, which happens so often when government officials ignore the expertise of individual citizens or the "expert" reports or recommendations even of those they themselves have appointed.

Beliefs are not like sacred objects to be worshiped without critical appraisal. They spring from experience which may have been motivated not only by apparent facts (the sun rises in the East and sets in the West; I have seen it do that) but also by the principal's own motives and values (you will live longer if you get out of bed before the sun rises). Indeed, if we recall some of the sacred beliefs from the past (the sun revolves around the earth), it is impossible not to agree with the sad if stimulating observation that "nothing we say about reality is definitive, authoritative, and fully settled" (Rein, 1983). Beliefs, nevertheless, play a crucial role in judgments concerning actions; does a principal believe that the assumed benefits from an activity are likely to be greater than the risks accompanying it (cf. *Proposition 8.2*)?

Skeptical Note: When are beliefs and knowledge well founded?

3.4 ATTITUDES

Proposition: The feelings and emotions associated with beliefs and hence with the principal's judgments concerning his milieu and himself affect the arousal and expression of motives as well as his behavior.

The concept of attitude is sufficiently elastic to be applicable to a variety of contexts. A principal may have a favorable or unfavorable attitude toward a particular goal, rule, duty, or person, whether or not—again by definition—the feelings of approval or disapproval on occasion may differ from the related attitudes. Many duties, for example, are considered unpleasant (unfavorable attitude) but are believed to be essential (favorable belief and value). Just as a person may have a belief concerning his own belief, so he may have an attitude toward his own attitude; for example, he has a strong, favorable attitude toward smoking cigarettes—he just likes to smoke—but he is also unfavorably disposed toward this inclination as a result of a belief—smoking he knows can damage his lungs (Körner, 1976, pp. 92–93). Some attitudes result from the more or less unique experiences of each principal; others are the subjective counterparts of the sanctions and taboos within his society.

An attitude can function either as a precipitating cause or as a precipitated effect. As a cause, common sense and a speck of empirical evidence suggest, principals may make more complex and detailed judgments concerning persons they dislike than those they like or toward whom they feel neutral (Irwin et al., 1967). Conceivably they are more vigilant when they are unfavorably disposed than under the other two attitudinal conditions. They may wish to avoid future disagreeable experiences similar to those they must have had in the past. One consequence may be a tendency for moral judgments to be more likely or frequent under unfavorable than under favorable circumstances. Crises test principles. The principal may also come to have an unfavorable attitude toward persons he has harmed. He thus avoids dissonance within himself by rationalizing what he at first believed to have been an unjust action on his part by convincing himself that they merited the harm. Avoiding dissonance in this manner, however, is not automatic. Perhaps a principal's attitude will not be unfavorable unless he convinces himself that he could not have avoided hurting the other persons or that he will have no future contact with them (Davis and Jones, 1960).

Attitudes are so subjective that they constitute one of the reasons for skepticism concerning the predictability of behavior and hence for seeking to ignore descriptive values in the formulation of prescriptive ones. Slightly beyond such skepticism is the fact, yes, the fact that those very attitudes may affect some of the lofty values posited by well-intentioned thinkers everywhere. For example: a temporary mood—another way of describing salient attitudes—may influence a principal's readiness to aid others (cf. Berkowitz, 1972). Generosity or miserliness may be traced to a good or bad night's sleep *(Meandering 3.3: Attitudes and Attitudes)*.

Skeptical Note: Are not many, maybe most attitudes prejudices?

3.5 SKILL

Proposition: Under most but not all circumstances action occurs only when principals possess or believe they possess the necessary skill.

Unless the principal's reply concerning his capability *(What can I do?)* is affirmative, he may ignore all the other questions when contemplating possible action: his strongest motive or his best intention cannot overcome an assumed inability to carry out a judgment; in fact he may even be less likely to pass an affirmative judgment. A principal's beliefs concerning his skill in a particular situation may or may not be accurate from the standpoint of a detached observer. Those beliefs may be derived from personal experience or they may be communicated to him by someone else. Is he sufficiently self-confident to believe he has the ability to take the initiative in a variety of situations? In a more general sense, as investigations of what is called locus of control have demonstrated, persons believing their destiny by and large to be affected by external events and hence not appreciably or frequently under their own, internal control are perhaps less likely to pass moral judgments in Western society, such as resisting authority or temptation (Lefcourt, 1976, pp. 48–49).

Observers of skill employ the concept to refer to intelligence, adaptability, or any kind of aptitude or talent. Designating the components that are genetically determined and those that are more or less completely affected by forces in the milieu is a fascinating problem in its own right which need not detain us here, especially since the topic is once again under intensive review on both the animal and the human level (Gardner and Dudai, 1985). One competent summary of relevant research in the United States indicates that at the moment the much maligned intelligence quotient (IQ), even though or perhaps because it is affected by the socioeconomic status of parents, turns out to be "the childhood test best predicting adult adjustment"; however, the measures of "adjustment" are poor, IQ must be considered "a necessary, not sufficient condition" for maturity, and its precise relation to adjustment varies throughout the life cycle (Kohlberg et al., 1984). In the analysis of morality, then, the concept of skill may be employed in a very general sense without seeking to establish its biological and experiential bases.

With rare exceptions (Roubiczek, 1969, p. 5), philosophers avoid the variable of skill as they construct their moral systems, perhaps because it seems too obvious to them. Whether or not it is true that prescriptive values cannot be derived from "facts" (Frankena, 1963, pp. 96–102), facts certainly may be utilized when judgments are made. The principal, for example, salvages his experiences from the past *(What do I do?)*; he must know what he is capable of doing *(What can I do?)*; he must utilize facts in order to be able to anticipate the consequences of his judgment or behavior *(What would the consequences be?)*; and so on for all the probing questions. He needs facts, relevant ones; and he uses them, correctly or incorrectly. Gathering such facts demands skill, however skeptical philosophers may be. Ordinarily an individual does not risk his life trying to save a drowning man unless he himself can swim. Conceivably some principals develop skill in passing moral judgments on the basis of their experience in doing so: jurists, philosophers, clergymen, anyone required to pass frequent judgment upon others and hence upon themselves.

Judgments about one's own skill are interwoven with other variables. In a simple laboratory experiment utilizing the usual American college students, for example, indeed the subjects tended to aid a contemporary when they believed not only that they were competent to do so but also that he was dependent upon them; furthermore, they were inclined to be helpful more readily when they knew they were being observed by others (Midlarsky, 1971). Skill is also related to other predispositions of the personality. Although the conventional values of a family or a society are learned by virtually everyone, the rate of acquisition varies from person to person, perhaps because the ability to role-play is associated with moral development (Selman, 1971): the child must learn to take another person's point of view before he can raise some of the probing questions (cf. Staub, 1979, v. 2, p. 7).

Skeptical Note: Can persons with different skills make similar or comparable moral judgments?

3.6 INTERRELATION OF PREDISPOSITIONS

Proposition: The predispositions of personality are closely interrelated, continually affect one another, and give rise to values, but their effect upon behavior is not invariant.

Social scientists offer tons of evidence suggesting that a particular predisposition of interest to them is related (but usually only in a statistical sense) to other predispositions. The relationship, however, is seldom straightforward because many different variables may be salient and because any one of the variables may be related to several others. Thus the values of freedom and equality, or their opposites, are embedded in the writings of communists and socialists as well as of ultraconservatives and fascists (Rokeach, 1973, pp. 117–21, 158–59, 171–80). Beliefs and attitudes can bolster one another; hence in modern society it sometimes makes sense to speak of liberal and conservative syndromes concerning such issues as conservation of natural resources, abortion, disarmament, and the role of government in everyday affairs. Or the components of personality may be at odds; thus many principals with favorable attitudes toward the knowledge acquired through science believe that such knowledge is more impressive than beliefs originating in religion, tradition, or common sense, as a result of which their attitudes toward the latter sources are less favorable or worshipful (Childs and Hickman, 1983) *(Meandering 3.4: Beliefs and Attitudes)*. The culmination of the interaction of the predispositions affects the emerging judgments and actions.

The relation of predispositions to actual behavior is usually so complicated that good observers like behaviorists, prison wardens, and sport coaches are prone to think that by their deeds rather than their beliefs, attitudes, or values shall ye know people. Of late several models have been proposed to relate subjective variables and objective actions, particularly because surface measures of attitudes through interviews and questionnaires are so easy to come by. Such models refer not only to the strength of attitudes (on the assumption that stronger attitudes are more likely to lead to appropriate action than weaker ones) but also to other variables that, their progenitors rightly contend, must also be measured if predictions are to stand a chance of being valid. For example: behavior depends upon the principal's "intention" *(What shall I do?)* which is affected by the attitudes in question; that intention depends upon his "belief" concerning the "outcomes" of so behaving and his "evaluation" of those outcomes *(What would the consequences be?)*; in addition, he is influenced by his own "norms" concerning the behavior as well as by the norms of "persons important to him" *(What ought I do?)*; that norm may be affected by society's norms and the individual's motivation to conform to them *(What may I do? What must I do?)*; finally, the social "context," the "time" at which the behavior is "performed," "personality traits," and "attitudes toward people and institutions" may play a role *(What will I do?)* (Ajzen and Fishbein, 1980). Clearly the suggestion is that the replies to all the probing questions, and sometimes also information concerning the principal's predispositions and his situation, must be available before predictions from attitudes can be made.

Even the multifaceted approach just mentioned, however, requires modification when applied to a specific situation (Kantola et al., 1982; cf. Darden, 1983); thus apparent surprises arise sufficiently often to justify a reserved skepticism concerning the validity of survey research. It might be supposed, for example, that strong motives and attitudes would affect relevant judgments. In one study based on survey data it was found that opposition to the busing of American schoolchildren in the interests of desegregation was unrelated to the principals' actual involvement in the issue, with involvement being signified by whether they had children or were the parents whose children were or were not in fact being bused to desegregating schools (Sears et al., 1979). In this instance, therefore, the moral judgment was not affected by the experience.

When and if predispositions are highly interrelated, the principal may be said to have a consistent set of values and to behave consistently. To some degree all of us are somewhat consistent; otherwise our associates would never be able to anticipate what we shall say or do. But if a principal is generous or aggressive in one situation, will he behave similarly in other situations? If not, in which situations will he be consistent and which not? When the situations are virtually identical, obviously consistency can be anticipated; he may never fail to contribute to the offering plate of his church, but does he pay taxes on absolutely all of his taxable unrecorded income? Psychologists have cracked their heads over this issue and have unloosed an avalanche of undecisive research. Two investigators have actually admitted, "It is tempting to tire of the consistency debate" (Mischel and Peake, 1982). Perhaps their fatigue arises from the fact that the issue cannot be settled: it all depends, it all depends. Complete skepticism, however, is unwarranted; without some consistency the relations of persons would be even more chaotic than they always appear (Royce and Buss, 1976).

This problem of consistency can be phrased in terms of salience: are similar predispositions so frequently evoked that they usually affect a principal's judgment and behavior? The fairly common expression, "felt needs," refers to motives of which principals are conscious. Often action occurs when relevant predispositions or values have not been salient: I didn't think of it, nobody reminded me. Salience may result from "sensuous experience," such as a church building or the sermon of a clergyman, or from an enduring heavily reinforced predisposition or formula stemming from experience, such as efficacious prayers (cf. Paton, 1947, p. 22).

At one extreme, consequently, is the disorganized schizophrenic whose behavior largely depends upon his fluctuating moods: he tends to respond habitually and allegedly with little or no reference to values unless his delusions are somewhat integrated into a paranoid outlook. At the other extreme is a saint like Gandhi whose behavior, at least after his adolescence, resulted more or less completely from his philosophy of life, his values, which were imperatives and almost always salient. Principals, according to one psychologist, can be more or less categorized in terms of the salience of their values; in his phrasing:

1. Situationist: rejects moral rules; advocates individualistic analysis of each act in each situation; relativistic.
2. Subjectivist: appraisals based on personal values and perspective rather than universal moral values; relativistic.
3. Exceptionist: moral absolutes guide judgments but pragmatically open to exceptions to these standards; utilitarian.
4. Absolutist: assumes that the best possible outcome can always be achieved by following universal moral values. (Forsyth, 1980; cf. Hardin, 1972, p. 134)

This classification or any one like it that suggests adherence or nonadherence to a set of values is highly significant for two reasons. First, associated with adherence or nonadherence are other predispositions within principals. And second, as will be emphasized later *(Proposition*

7.3), the trait, if it be a trait, plays an overwhelmingly significant role in passing moral judgments *(Meandering 3.5: Situationists versus Absolutists)*.

Principals, in short, are human beings, and therefore they must achieve certain goals, they possess imperfect knowledge, they are swayed by their feelings or attitudes, their skills may be inadequate, and they are not always consistent. Morally complete judgments and actions, when they are achieved, must be achieved with principals who are not angels. Let no one think otherwise.

Skeptical Note: Can nonangels be completely moral?

Envoi: Although the components of predispositions and hence the predispositions themselves are unique, *nevertheless* principals are convinced they understand one another and are able to exist more or less satisfactorily.

MEANDERINGS

3.1 Metaphysical Implications

The problem of monism and dualism which has plagued and intrigued both philosophy and psychology is avoided in the analysis here by including the predispositions of the personality as well as behavior or action. Assumed, of course, is a physiological basis for both which may sound like dualism but which is required by our inability to deal with the subtler aspects of human existence in physiological terms. The causal sequence within the chosen universe of discourse can begin at any point, whether outside the principal (events as they are perceived) or inside (the predispositions)—and this sounds like monism. From the outset in chapter 1, however, I have shoved aside the skeptical problem concerning the validity of the perception of events.

The Morality Figure is also eclectic with reference to the data to be surveyed. As the critics of orthodox behaviorism gleefully point out, merely dealing with objectively observable behavior prevents or obscures a crucial determinant of behavior, namely, the principal's own internal responses to events. The investigator does not become metaphysical when he seeks to determine whether a slip of the tongue was intentional, whether the accused deliberately destroyed another person, whether in brief any action is purposive or accidental *(What shall I do?)*. Certainly it is necessary also to know why specific predispositions exist and what makes them salient or dormant at a given moment, but simultaneously their nature must also be ascertained if the analysis is to be reasonably complete.

3.2 Naming Motives

The motives of principals can be labeled most variously or—not for-
tuitously—as variously as their accompanying values. Usually every
scholar or man-in-the-street quickly produces his own list if or
whenver he is asked to do so. In the first sentence of his treatise on
ethics, Aristotle states that "every art and every investigation, and
likewise every practical pursuit or undertaking, seems to aim at some
good. . . . the end of the science of medicine is health, that of the art
of shipbuilding a vessel, that of strategy victory, that of domestic economic wealth." He also postulates a very general motive, "one which
we wish for its own sake": "this one ultimate End must be the Good,
and indeed the Supreme Good" (Aristotle, 1934 ed., pp. 3, 4).

It seems sensible to be skeptical concerning all attempts to draw
up an inventory of human motives, so versatile and varied are human
beings, unless an abstract and almost meaningless term like *libido* turns
out to be helpful for some purpose. The naming of motives is of little
significance; perhaps it is more useful to attempt, as have two sociologists, to locate "a limited number of common human problems"
universally presented everywhere, although they are always "differ-
entially preferred." In fact, they list the following five which can be
expressed as orientations: toward human nature; toward nature in
the sense of the environment; toward time, whether focusing upon
the past, present, or future; toward human activity; and toward the
relation of human beings to one another (Kluckhohn and Strodtbeck,
1961, pp. 10–24, italics omitted).

The older generation of biologists and psychologists around the turn
of the century and during the first few decades of this century did
not hesitate to name human "instincts." One influential list included
thirteen of them called, in the writer's own words, paternal or pro-
tective, combat, curiosity, food-seeking, repulsion, escape, gregarious,
sympathy, self-assertion and submission, mating, acquisitive, and
constructive (McDougall, 1923, chap. 5). A difficulty even then was
that each writer had his own list, and though there was considerable
overlapping, the agreement was never complete. From our present
standpoint, every name on any list calls attention to a motive likely
to characterize some if not many persons everywhere; it is to be
doubted that the bases for all these motives are innate: some such as
"food-seeking" and "mating" may be primary, but "gregarious" and
"constructive" are undoubtedly secondary.

Usually but not always when motives are too strong, they are likely
to be given a negative evaluation. In the Western world the frequently

cited seven deadly sins have human or praiseworthy goals that are condemned because they are excessively pursued: (in alphabetical order) anger, covetousness, envy, gluttony, lust, pride, and sloth. Any one of them in moderation is either necessary or desirable; for example, the moderate form of gluttony is the pursuit of means to satisfy natural hunger. In their pristine form they are convenient labels for negative values, but be it noted that synonyms are employed for some of them (wrath for anger, envy for covetousness), and probably all the words have at least slightly different meanings when they appear in different languages.

3.3 Attitudes and Attitudes

Frequently the term *evaluate* is another way to refer to attitude. Contrast how persons in modern society react to garbagemen and gardeners, dentists and surgeons. They have different attitudes toward these occupations or professions; they evaluate them differently in terms of prestige or skill; but they also consider them essential. Behind the attitudes and the beliefs may also be a value that refers to education or specialization; and each evaluation has arisen within particular groups over historical time (Mannheim, 1937, pp. 178–79). A philosopher immediately denies that "attitudes or feelings are the sum and substance of moral judgments" (M. G. Singer, 1973, p. 103). I agree: even on a descriptive level, it is evident that more than attitudes enter into moral judgments, for which reason all the probing questions must be asked and the Morality Figure cannot be simple. Research on the relations of attitudes to one another and to other predispositions tends to be confusing and inconsistent because investigators feel free to select whichever variables and modes of measurements they choose in order to investigate their selected problem; in fact, so many factors can be explored and so many different techniques can be employed that unsurprisingly results from different studies by different investigators may not be comparable.

For purposes of understanding morality, a significant attitude may well be the one toward authority. Up to some point difficult to specify, the immature child inevitably accepts his parents as authorities, and then probably his peers. As he matures, he may or may not be convinced that their power is avoidable, the way, for example, probably most criminals believe at least in passing that they can evade law-enforcement officials. Perhaps the most compelling authority for the principal as an individual or as a member of a society comes from a supernatural source with whom or with which there can be no dispute and whose power rests largely on faith. That faith is strengthened whenever natural proof of the source can be said to be or to have been demonstrated. The power of a church derives in large part from the favorable attitude of its adherents toward an authoritative religious credo.

3.4 Beliefs and Attitudes

Attitudes are usually accompanied by beliefs that principals can spontaneously express or quickly generate. Some of the beliefs may be genuine in the sense that they are supported by what allegedly competent observers might call reality; others may be sheer rationalizations. In the modern Western world some principals rarely mistreat members of another race or ethnic group or have unfavorable attitudes toward them without being able to supply allegedly supporting evidence that they are, for example, genetically inferior; others "censure slavery because it involves the treatment of men as if they were not persons" (Harris, 1966). The reverse is also easy to illustrate: beliefs influence attitudes. American college students, for example, tended to associate the beauty of models in photographs with social status and also to believe that persons appearing attractive were more intelligent and competent than those considered ugly; their belief affected their views of other persons and perhaps also the ways in which they behaved in their presence (cf. Webster and Driskell, 1983).

Values variously ascertained among American children, students, and adults have been shown to be related statistically to phenomena as diverse as the speed with which words are recognized, cheating on examinations, the choice of friends—the list is impressively long (R. M. Williams, 1979, p. 23). Concretely: a sample of graduate students tended to a greater degree than undergraduates to be impressed with the claim that returning questionnaires to an investigator would increase human knowledge (McKillip and Lockhart, 1984). Supposedly the subculture of graduate students placed greater emphasis on extending knowledge than did that of undergraduates, but as ever exceptions to the trend are noticeable since some of the latter cooperated with the investigator and some of the former did not.

No matter how beliefs are phrased, they are associated with other aspects of the personality. One investigator distinguishes at a lofty level two kinds of beliefs: one stressing the "ethics of personal conscience," the other the "ethics of responsibility." A belief in conscience as the source of beliefs is said to rely upon intuition, a belief in responsibility upon legality and the welfare and happiness of society. American students replied to a paper-and-pencil questionnaire which presumably indicated whether they subscribed to conscience or responsibility. Those believing in conscience tended to be progressive, rebellious, and unconventional; they tended also to be activists. Those stressing responsibility, on the other hand, tended to be conservative, good-natured, and conventional (Hogan, 1970).

3.5 Situationists versus Absolutists

The fourfold classification offered in the text is provocatively descriptive, but it is also essential to inquire why some principals are consistent and others are not. The author of the schema has devised a paper-and-pencil scale to classify respondents in terms of the four types. For a sample of American college students, being in one category rather than another was somewhat related to their stage of moral development as determined by another questionnaire but not by a less formal open-ended interview. Among males, the absolutists, in contrast with the other three groups, tended to be opposed to creating human beings in a test-tube, to mercy killing, to abortion, to homosexuals, and to the use of marijuana; both males and females were inclined to render harsher judgments concerning a fictitious character displaying behavior with good and bad consequences for others (Forsyth, 1980). In two experiments, however, although the categorization was related to attitudes regarding cheating, it was unrelated to actual cheating in contrived situations (Forsyth and Berger, 1982).

A political scientist has provided a detailed and sophisticated "metaethical" schema outlining the "claims" principals supposedly make in behalf of their values. These claims can be considered to be special forms of beliefs—beliefs concerning the values on the basis of which judgments are and should be made *(What shall I do?)*. In the author's own words, judgments may be claimed to be:

1. Absolute: their inviolable character is rationally unquestionable.
2. Inviolable: objectively wrong ever to violate.
3. Objectively valid: considerations that anyone should accept, were he to view the problem from what is contended to be the appropriate moral perspective.
4. Universalizability: apply consistently to everyone.
5. Interpersonal: [apply] to others as well as oneself, [but not] consistently.

6. Self [directed]: [apply only] to oneself. (Fishkin, 1984, pp. 11–14)

It is further assumed that, if the principal believes one of these claims and if he is consistent, he rejects all the preceding ones and accepts all the succeeding ones in the series. If he believes that judgments should be "absolute," consequently, he also believes they should satisfy the remaining five; if he believes they must be "objectively valid," then he rejects the beliefs that they can be "absolute" or "inviolable" but accepts the remaining three. To illustrate the formulas, anecdotal evidence is offered that has been derived, with the exception of an unemployed English schoolmaster, from interviews with Cambridge and Yale students. The fact that the sample is casual and atypical is of little significance since the author did not purport to be conducting systematic research but was determined to show (a) that a somewhat rigid schema concerning "moral development" was not applicable to individual principals *(Proposition 7.4)* and (b) that a subjectivist approach could be supplanted by an objective one *(Proposition 7.3)*. For present purposes, the schema suggests that, with the exception of the first two beliefs, the remaining four presume that they come from situationists who allow exceptions as they pass judgments.

CHAPTER 4

Rules and Duties

For the first but not for the last time reference is made to freedom, here to the principal's freedom to seek whatever goal he would attain *(Propositions 6.4 and 13.6)*. Clearly no matter what position he occupies in society, he is seldom if ever completely free to achieve the goal of his immediate motive. He is engulfed in restrictive rules *(What may I do?)*, and he has duties to perform *(What must I do?)*, many of which are embedded in his own personality. When rules, especially external ones, are strictly enforced, he may have no choice other than to obey: he need not, cannot, or will not pass moral judgment. His behavior, nevertheless, may be considered by an observer to be moral even when he himself has reacted habitually and has made no moral judgment. Many, maybe most philosophers assert that human beings should or actually do respond to forces over which they have little or no control; they should think of themselves as masters of their fate. Perhaps, but first the unavoidable rules and duties must be examined.

Anthropological monographs provide details concerning the rules of the society in which their authors have carried on research; those rules are described under such headings as tradition, mores, stratification, and institutions. The rules indicate what is permitted and what is prohibited, with corresponding rewards and punishments in the offing which vary from verbal praise and reproof to material benefits and hanging. In any society every principal has certain rights: these refer to rules specifying the kind of behavior that he is allowed to perform and that is not supposed to be hindered or declared taboo by others. Philosophers refer to the obligations created by rules, laws, and customs (with the consequences being of secondary importance) as deontology, an esoteric pursuit that need not detain us here.

Rules may be formal or informal. In modern society, for example, factory owners until recently have been permitted to allow smoke from their furnaces to spew acid rain upon the environment near and far. Now knowledge of that damage has first aroused informal protests producing pressure upon them to mitigate the pollution, and gradually if slowly formal laws prohibiting the practice are being enacted even in the United States in spite of the pride many leaders take in what they believe to be a doctrine of laissez-faire. Perhaps a reference to rules provides the easiest way for a principal to avoid considering other probing questions and values: we have always done it that way. Among the informal rules that become formalized are abstractions pertaining to the goals of justice, freedom of speech, and privacy.

By definition and by practice rules prohibit certain kinds of behavior, but they also may impose an obligation, a duty to perform specified actions. The rule states that you may not avoid paying taxes and it also indicates that you must pay them, it is your duty to do so. The child knows he will be spanked if he is untidy from his parent's viewpoint, and he tries to put his toys or clothes where they "belong." The adult realizes he will incur disapproval or, in some societies, persecution if he marries his niece, and hence he allows his fancy to wander toward women not related to him. Positive overtones may also appear when the principal comes to value what he has learned to do or not to do. When such a positive value is self-imposed, he may be said to have a sense of obligation: he must do it. Usually rules and duties are complementary: you know you may or may not and then, rationalizing or not, you say you would or would not. A young man who is conscripted as a soldier in modern society is dealt with harshly if he refuses to serve; he is supposed to do his duty by being trained to become a member of the armed forces. But must he really become a soldier? What are his options? Doing one's duty to one or more other persons is a universal value and is likely to be at least partially selfless. Without a feeling of obligation, a principal may pass no moral judgment or at least he may avoid one; with the feeling, and especially when he perceives that the other person is dependent upon him and when the belief is salient, he is more likely to render assistance or to perform a service for him (cf. Schwartz, 1977).

4.1 INEVITABILITY

Proposition: Inevitably normal principals tend to obey or conform to the rules of the groups and of the society in which they find themselves, and they perform the roles and duties associated therewith.

Although principals are somewhat consistent from situation to situation as a result of enduring predispositions of their personalities, their reactions also depend upon the group in which they find themselves and the roles they are expected to perform therein. The behavior of a parent conversing with his or her child is different from the parent's responses to a stranger. Associated with every role, therefore, are implicit or explicit rules the players are expected to obey.

No principal is completely an island: he cannot live in isolation and hence rules are required to mitigate conflicts and to encourage and promote cooperation as well as a sense of duty. Even those who disobey rules and shirk duties usually remain aware of their atypical behavior. In a frontier society men quickly have sought "to establish the binding rules to govern the use of force" (Handlin and Handlin, 1961, p. 73). Any group, whether temporary or concerned with enduring occupations, social class, caste, and formal and informal associations and cliques, has its own standards, conformity with which is considered moral, nonconformity immoral or at least wrong. The codes of the principal's own group may not be applied to other groups; thus so-called honor among thieves is presumably not extended to those who do not steal. Inevitably, therefore, every normal principal must assume duties that may be at variance with his own motives: *What must I do?* Whether you like it or not, you have duties to perform toward your parents, your children, your community, your country.

The values behind the rules in a society possess a kind of undeniable sanctity. Many, but not all of them have been acquired through the experience of generations. Each principal cannot be expected to invent rules for himself or his society, just as he does not have to reinvent the wheel or modern medicine in order to benefit from using them. The case for conservatism in many forms is made to appear strong and convincing, although obviously improvement may be both necessary and recognized. The authorities of the society, moreover, often have a vested interest in status-quo rules and duties.

Everywhere rules regulate three human activities: age, sexual relations, and life-and-death. Status associated with age is necessary obviously because infants are dependent upon parents; also the elderly require care as they grow less active and deteriorate somewhat both physically and mentally. From a Western standpoint rules regarding sex may appear to vary from promiscuity to straitlaced puritanism embodied in an eternal marriage vow. Closer examination, however, reveals that some taboos exist in societies where sexual contacts are freer and more numerous than in the West, if only regarding those relations considered incestuous.

Rules concerning life-and-death are less universal, as a glance at any modern society easily suggests. Conflicting views exist concerning the very onset of life: May pregnant women have abortions? Should agencies of government permit or pay for the operation? At the other extreme of the life cycle are disagreements in the West pertaining to whether terminally ill patients should be permitted to die. If they are conscious and assert that they prefer to end their misery, it is by no means certain that their request is or should be granted. And if they are unconscious and remain technically alive only with the help of an expensive life-supporting apparatus, someone must make the decision to continue or discontinue that support: Should it be the next-of-kin? Should it be physicians and nurses? Should it be clergymen or officials of the state? Deliberately killing another human being who is not terminally ill is outlawed except under special circumstances, and those circumstances are by no means clear. Physicians in a New York hospital who perforce have been wholly or partially responsible for these decisions and who have been uncertain how to make the decision have sought advice from philosophers and other nonmedical persons ("Hospitals . . .," 1982), who in turn have no magical or satisfactory solutions.

Even in time of war, according to international treaties, limitations are placed upon those who may be killed: civilians are not supposed to be considered combatants, although the code does not evidently prevent the bombing of factories or residences. Methods of killing the enemy, such as the use of poison gas, may also be outlawed, again at least in theory. Here and there are instances in which modern soldiers hesitate to carry out orders to kill or to take advantage of situations in which they may do so; or their consciences pain them as their bombs strike the intended targets (Doob, 1981, pp. 35–37). In general, permitting the killing of identifiable persons raises doubts even when the person has been fairly and perhaps unequivocally convicted of a heinous crime; the issue of capital punishment has been debated throughout the centuries. In modern but not in all societies every principal is even discouraged from taking his own life; suicide may be considered a sin or a crime. There is thus variability; yet the challenge of life-and-death is never ignored.

The principal who transgresses the cultural or legal regulations of a group or society is likely to be punished if apprehended and then, according to existing procedures, found guilty. The victims, those who suffer as a result of the transgressions, may or may not be awarded damages. Compensation and restitution, though existing here and there throughout Western society, have not been universal, in fact have perhaps declined in importance (Schafer, 1970, pp. x, 8–12). The possibility of punishment for crime and then of the additional punishment embodied in mandatory restitution is supposed to be anticipated by principals tempted to transgress; it is assumed, however, that these threats are not efficacious unless the principal, as the proposition under discussion states, is "normal": he must be of sound mind, not seriously disturbed, and not under the influence of a passion or a drug—and he must be beyond the age of childhood. Punishments, it is obvious, vary over time and may not be administered uniformly.

Frequently duties and rights are associated with one another: duties are performed for the sake of the beneficiaries, which may include those discharging the duties. It is the duty of parents to feed and otherwise care for their infant children who in a sense have the right to that care (Melden, 1977, p. 72). Then in most traditional and to a certain extent in modern societies those children later have a duty to provide for their aged parents who have earned the right to that care. Usually some flexibility in the discharge of duties and in the accession of rights occurs. In Western society a mother must feed her infant, but she may decide whether to nurse the child or use a bottle. Flight attendants on planes are supposed to be courteous and cheerful, a commercially imposed duty they perform with varying degrees of effectiveness; but in an emergency they are not supposed to hesitate to discharge the duty of assisting passengers to safety.

Many of the rules and obligations are learned by children so thoroughly that they are forever considered sacrosanct and unchallengeable. An extreme but telling illustration is the so-called sexist bias of the English language, which has been only recently pounced upon by feminists and others advocating sexual equality: the use of the third person singular *he* and words like *mankind* and *chairman* to refer in context to both sexes and not only males. In spoken German the word *man* when followed by the third person singular is used like *one* in English, but it does not differ in pronunciation from *Mann*, which means, again in English, *man* and sometimes *husband*. Children learn correct grammar, therefore, without realizing that they are reinforcing a rule giving higher priority to males than females.

Skeptical Note: How is it decided whether rules and duties are necessary and unavoidable?

4.2 HABITUAL MORALITY

Proposition: Rules may be obeyed and duties performed without moral judgments or replies to probing questions.

Events may occur and principals then respond with little or no hesitation. Even as an individual without profound reflection avoids stepping into a puddle of water, so a parent almost unhesitatingly makes a general or specific sacrifice that benefits his child. A glance again at the Morality Figure in chapter 3 reveals arrows moving directly from the "Perceived Event" to "Habitual Judgment" and "Action." The sequence suggests that the principal does not pass a new judgment either because there is no need to do so or because he guides himself, however dimly, by a judgment previously made in the past. Principals who confine their morally incomplete judgments to answering the call of duty—*What must I do?*—have simplified their existence; meekly they avoid other probing questions or they avoid answering them. From many standpoints it may be efficient or it may be thought desirable to be, as it were, habitually moral.

Why doesn't a person steal as he walks through a large shop and sees a desirable object he can easily conceal in his pocket without being detected? It may not even occur to him to grab it—he is habitually honest. If for some reason he is tempted to steal, he may hesitate on two scores: someone may be watching and he will be arrested; or he considers it necessary to be honest under all circumstances. That latter judgment, whether arising from a knowledge of the rules or an obligation, takes time. Ignorance may prevent a moral judgment from being exercised: in the past the principal may have reached for another cigarette since almost through no fault of his own he was unaware of the possible health hazards from smoking. By and large, however, members of a society subscribe to what may be called a covenant in every sphere of activity, "the limits which we impose upon ourselves" (J. F. A. Taylor, 1966, p. 6). Codes of conduct decrease hesitation required to make minor and major decisions, especially those prescribed by the major religions embracing a philosophy or style of life. The principal follows the dictates of his creed: he adheres literally to the commandments, and he rightly receives the sacraments as well as the plaudits of his peers.

It may be convenient and simple to obey rules and respond to the call of duty, but habitual behavior of this sort often is disadvantageous in terms of the goals of other values. Not having to make a decision "alleviates man's search for meaning" (Frankl, 1970, pp. 56–57) and, more prosaically, may foster an undesirable ethnocentrism. A principal, convinced of his own righteousness that is reinforced by his peers, almost without reflection applies his own values to other groups or societies. Americans often condemn foreigners for being "different," but they themselves when abroad perhaps as often behave as they would at home; little wonder that they may be branded "ugly."

Aristotle distinguished between habitual and judgmental reactions. He maintained that a "moral virtue" is "the product of habit"; in contrast, an "intellectual virtue" is a function of reason through "instruction and requires experience and time" (Aristotle, 1934 ed., p. 71). A modern non-Aristotelian has maintained that without habits there would be chaos; yet principals cannot depend upon habits for all morally related judgments and behavior if they would satisfy "a hankering for certainty" (Dewey, 1922, p. 238). Exceptional circumstances arise *(Proposition 7.3)*, and inelasticity becomes unsuitable *(Proposition 12.5)*.

Skeptical Note: Can morality ever be habitual?

4.3 CHANGES

Proposition: Changes in rules and duties affect and are affected by changes in principals.

A prototype of this proposition is the modern political party in Western countries, which both responds to changes in the electorate and also influences voters' beliefs and attitudes regarding legislation, government, and the social system. It is necessary only to refer to sexual mores in modern society to dramatize the reciprocal relation between rules and principals. The reasons for changes in rules and duties cannot be easily supplied. A simple Darwinian explanation does not suffice. Rules may have some connection with the survival of the society and its citizens, but it is difficult to discern the relation between many changes and that value. A judicial system alters rules presumably to rectify injustices; yet then again the judges may render decisions that favor one group rather than another. It seems clear, therefore, that deliberate changes often reflect the morally deficient judgments of those effecting the change and that other judgments may spring from habitual responses to changes within the principals perceiving or requiring those changes. Whether the changes are for the better in any sense are decided in each instance either in the short or in the long run; overall generalizations must be skeptically greeted.

Skeptical Note: Can those changing chart the changes?

4.4 COMPREHENSIBILITY

Proposition: To be salient and effective, rules and duties must be understood and remembered.

In simple language, principals can obey rules only if they know what they are and what they demand. You cannot play chess until you have been taught the importance of each piece, how it can be moved, and the nature and goal of checkmate. A converted Catholic has stated that it is easier to pray not to an "inexplicable and mysterious force but to his intermediary, Christ" (Greene, 1983). If he is correct, he may be providing a simplistic psychological—not a theological—explanation for the power of his church throughout the ages. Effective rules may be stated as injunctions in simple language like the speed limits posted on highways or the Ten Commandments, but some laws may be so complicated that they require specialists such as lawyers, civil servants, or priests to be interpreted. Principals must know what they are supposed to do as well as the consequences resulting from disobedience.

One of the consequences of comprehending, yet disobeying a rule or failing to discharge a duty may be the arousal not only of anxiety but also of guilt. Either consequence constitutes a highly significant goad to change the content of moral judgments and actions. The very act of disobedience, whether or not accompanied by these affective states, may be an initial step in the direction of changing the rules. Revolutionaries as well as the young activists of the last quarter of the twentieth century are well aware of this relationship.

Principals may believe they comprehend a rule, a duty, or indeed most of the components of replies to the probing questions because events reaching them are interpreted in phrases and sentences. The very nature of language and the way in which words are used in everyday communication induce confidence in the belief that the message has been comprehended, even though the reverse may be true or at least there may be ambiguity. Perforce every principal has his own private meanings attached to words, whether those meanings originate with him or are received from others. The cry of "honor," "democracy," "communism," "equality," "happiness," "justice"— and the list can be infinitely extended—evokes different responses in each person but, more important for present purposes, halts doubt and any kind of judgment or a complete one. There is not even a clear-cut way of determining precisely what such glittering words mean to each individual. One unrealistic technique, that of the so-called semantic differential, comes as close as any to capturing the subtle meanings attached to words: on a fairly large number of scales the subject is asked to specify in degrees how he reacts to a word. Using a scale of 1 to 10, for example, he places a value such as "trust" close to or far away from end points labeled "desirable" and "undesirable," or "feasible" and "not feasible" (Osgood et al., 1957, pp. 18–30). This device, by artificially requiring the respondent to be self-conscious concerning the connotations of words, breaks down solipsism up to a point without indicating the relation of the verbal value to other values or to behavior. In other instances no measuring device is needed to indicate the more or less unequivocal meaning of a morally deficient injunction or statement: "you must not do this," "it would be impolite to act that way," "thou shalt not take the name of the Lord thy God in vain."

Skeptical Note: Does not each principal arbitrarily comprehend rules and duties according to his predispositions and experiences?

4.5 VARIABILITY

Proposition: Adherence to rules and obligations varies from person to person, from group to group, and from society to society.

Very young children are not expected to conform to adult standards; yet the age at which they are considered to have reached adulthood and hence to be responsible for conforming to socially approved standards is not universally identical. In addition, every person has more or less unique experiences as a result of unanticipated events and of influential role models, with the result, as emphasized throughout this book, that there is no sure-fire way to predict later judgments and behavior in detail on the basis of early socialization. We must rest content with macroscopic, not microscopic forecasts *(Meandering 4.1: The Learning of Rules and Duties)*.

On a social level, it is evident that the incidence of criminal behavior, which by definition is contrary to normal rules, differs from country to country and within a country over time, even when modes of detection, apprehension, and conviction are taken into account. Groups with distinctive cultures, such as minorities, have their own rules and respond differently to the rules of others. Membership in one of the three major religions in the United States may affect the guilt experienced by college students with reference to mundane actions such as smoking and social drinking as well as more significant ones such as cheating on examinations and not fighting back (cf. London et al., 1964).

Skeptical Note: Is not variability especially elusive?

4.6 OBLIGATION AND RESPONSIBILITY

Proposition: When rules and duties are constantly reinforced and are associated with a principal's significant predispositions, they facilitate a self-sustaining sense of obligation and responsibility.

A philosopher contrasts the obligations of two persons, both of whom observe that a hypothetical child is drowning: one is a passerby who happens to see the child; the other is a lifeguard at a beach who notices the child in distress (Arthur, 1977). Clearly the lifeguard has assumed the obligation to rescue people; if he fails to do so, he will probably be roundly condemned and lose his job; his obligation springs from the duty of his occupation. The passerby has no contract to rescue the child; whether or not he responds will depend upon some deeper predisposition within him; he probably does not consider whether responding or not responding will be rewarded or punished. In a crude sense the response of the passerby is voluntary and moral, that of the lifeguard involuntary, habitual, and nonmoral. Such a distinction cannot always be maintained with precision: a citizen does not voluntarily pay legally imposed taxes unless it can be said that he voluntarily—either because he is afraid he might be punished if he fails to do so or because he believes that citizens ought to pay tax-es—avoids taking advantage of a loophole.

Obligation and responsibility are the chief components of what is sometimes called character, usually defined in effect as the ability and tendency to act contrary to one's immediate or overwhelming motives. A principal with a "bad" character gives way to his impulses; he ig-nores those of other persons except in his own interest; he lacks a sense of responsibility. Accompanying irresponsibility may be some form of personal disorganization: the principal has a bundle of pre-dispositions attached to separate, uncoordinated, even contradictory values. In contrast, someone with a "good" character may rejoice in his responsibilities; he receives more gratification from discharging his duties than if he were not to do so.

The senses of obligations and responsibilities are weighted along a continuum ranging from the extremely significant to the trivial. In many instances the difference between two responsibilities is clear: if a choice is necessary, should a beloved pet or a child be rescued from a burning building? But very often the judgment is difficult to determine: in time of war, which obligation is more compelling to a good Christian, that associated with his country or his religion? Then each responsibility has its own weight. Adultery, for example, may be disapproved; the principal has the responsibility to remain faithful to his or her spouse. A philosopher reports that, when the Hopi Indians "discussed adultery, they expressed disapproval but definitely did not show signs of revulsion" (Brandt, 1954, pp. 67–68). If so, then perhaps they disapprove of adultery but do so more mildly than puritanical Americans.

The greatest challenge for everyone, including principals and observers of all kinds, is to determine the conditions under which obligations and responsibilities are or are not to be discharged. Clearly, since they usually require a sacrifice—in time, money, or the casting aside of some personal goal—a crude, somewhat behavioristic reply can refer to the rewards or punishments from the anticipated performance or nonperformance of the action. One experimental investigation illustrates the complications that ensue and that therefore induce skepticism concerning the possibility of meeting the challenge in a clear-cut manner. In that experiment it was contrived to have a student, a confederate, appear to be receiving a painful electric shock. His peers were less likely to permit him to be "shocked" when they believed that they themselves were responsible for "hurting" him than when they did not have this belief, provided also that they were aware of the alleged damage that would occur (Tilker, 1970). Responsibility, therefore, was not automatically evoked; it depended on the circumstances.

More compelling is the actual dilemma faced by a principal who may wish to assume the responsibility of donating a kidney to a relative who will in fact perish unless a donor is found. Noteworthy is a procedure followed in various American hospitals. When the need arises, prospective donors are carefully selected and briefed so that their informed consent may be obtained. After one of them is considered suitable on medical grounds, his decision to undergo the operation is usually made quickly. His obligation to donate a vital organ may have been painful, but afterward he is rewarded: he notes how rapidly the recipient improves and he himself is likely to experience an "important increase in self-esteem and a stronger feeling of self" (Fellner and Marshall, 1981).

A simple but also a complicated hypothesis might be that principals do not discharge their responsibility if they are uncertain what that responsibility should be. When he observes an unethical or dishonest practice by a superior, does a principal have a responsibility to remain loyal to him and others in the group, or should he be a whistle-blower and expose him to some higher authority (cf. Glazer, 1983)? Sometimes principals can discharge obligations without feeling completely responsible for their actions. Instead of a single marksman shooting a condemned prisoner, a small number of men composing a firing squad carries out the sentence. Generally the identity of executioners is concealed, sometimes literally with a mask or hood. Similarly, not one individual but a committee may make a report on almost any subject, so that accountability is thus spread. In many courts of law, not the judge but a panel of judges or members of a jury render the verdict. In general, I think, the claim of a Victorian philosopher that "duty is usually not a difficult thing for an ordinary man to *know*" (Sidgwick, 1962, italics his) must be treated skeptically. When, for example, is a contemplated action "beyond the call of duty"? When the principal is unable to perform the act, when no one notices his failure to do so, when he brings irreparable harm to himself, when he is not acquainted with the other person who will benefit from having the duty discharged?

If an obligation or a sense of responsibility is not salient, the principal may not realize that he has an obligation or a responsibility. In modern America, for example, although a good liberal may have been opposed to apartheid in South Africa, he may have allowed some of his excess income to be deposited in a savings bank, some of whose assets were invested in enterprises that bolstered the South African regime. He knew nothing about the investment policies of his bank, nor did he have the time, talent, or inclination to investigate them. His own money, therefore, was perhaps aiding a value inimical to himself. Was he obligated to investigate the bank's portfolio in order to discharge his sense of responsibility? Or a principal may never have perceived an event either at all or meaningfully; thus he does not know that persons not far from him are starving or he cannot visualize what real hunger means since he himself has never experienced it.

Principals may deny that they have a responsibility to take appropriate action. People in developing countries, it is asserted, are starving because they or their governments do not control the growth of population through the use of contraceptives. Often it is believed that other persons besides the principal have the responsibility, not he. Other things being equal, as they almost never are, a principal's own sense of responsibility tends to diminish with an increase in the number of face-to-face persons simultaneously having the opportunity to assume the same responsibility (Jones and Foshay, 1984). Frequently cited in the recent literature of social science and in popular references to practical morality is a real-life tragedy—the Kitty Genovese murder in 1964—in which nobody came to the rescue of a twenty-eight-year-old woman who was being attacked and beaten to death. Her screams were clearly audible to many of her neighbors who did not even call the police; they wished to avoid becoming embroiled. The most ghastly instance in which the leaders of an entire nation were able to remove a sense of responsibility from principals who committed deliberate murder is that of Nazi Germany (cf. Arendt, 1964; Dicks, 1972, p. 37). The cry of Eichmann and many SS officers—"What could I do, I was only a little man?"—must ever haunt us, even though apparently they were not disturbed.

This discussion of obligations and responsibilities could be endless since the relations of principals to one another are at stake. A principal may claim—rightly or wrongly is beside the point—that he has not been socialized to consider that he has a particular obligation. A young child is scolded by his parents, promises not to repeat the misdemeanor, and then does so because "I forgot." Has the child assumed a responsibility he has subsequently failed to execute? A relative promises a dying person to do something in the future, such as taking care of his child or carrying on a worthy crusade (cf. Melden, 1977). Has he an obligation to do just that forever? Enough: let three self-styled specialists in responsibility give their views.

First, it is useful, I think, to listen to a political scientist since government formulates rules, prescribes duties, and hence is a source of responsibilities *(Meandering 4.2: The Obligations of Citizens)*. Then I turn to psychologists who have investigated the consequences of believing in determinism and therefore perhaps irresponsibility *(Meandering 4.3: Locus of Control)*. Finally, the name of Kant inevitably is associated with the issue at hand. His influence, at least among members of his profession, has been so great; nevertheless, only a quick summary can be given here since his own writings and those about him are so extensive and seemingly opaque. For him responsibility was virtually synonymous with duty: the moral value of an action depends not on whether it is performed because the principal is so generally inclined or because he wishes to achieve a particular personal goal but on whether the action stems from an encompassing sense of duty. Kant had a broad definition of duty, so broad that it included these inclinations and goals: "To secure one's own happiness is at least indirectly a duty, for discontent with one's condition under pressure from many cares and amid unsatisfied wants could easily become a great temptation to transgress duties." After thus satisfying his needs *(What will I do?)*, the principal may have a respect for law and conform to a universal law, a slightly rephrased categorical imperative *(Meandering 1.3)*: "Always act according to that maxim whose universality as a law you can at the same time will. This is the only condition under which a will can never come into conflict with itself, and such an imperative is categorical" (Kant, 1969, pp. 18, 63). In less dignified but perhaps more effective language: ask yourself, what if everybody did that? It would be quite presumptuous for me or anyone to evaluate Kant's contribution. The fact that he is so frequently cited possibly suggests a significant impact not upon principals but upon observers; yet his influence upon society may well have been negligible in comparison with Hegel's influence upon Marx and Marx's influence upon the world. Kant's metaphysical challenges remain, but their practical importance can be greeted with skepticism.

The conclusion must be that a morally relevant question cannot be avoided: are principals everywhere responsible for all the suffering and evils in and outside their immediate milieu when deliberately or through neglect they are in fact indifferent to the plight of others? If they ignore the evil and the suffering, should they be accused of complicity in their perpetuation? Here is perhaps the supreme challenge to the range of responsibility. Again, nevertheless, we must remind ourselves that human beings are not angels, or at least few of them are. They may be told by authorities what they may or may not do, and the best of goodwill may motivate the regulations, but not all of them will obey or all of them will not obey some of the time. Perfection in these respects is beyond our reach; yet this does not mean that the regulations cannot be improved so that less disobedience ensues.

Skeptical Note: How sacred or complete is any obligation or responsibility?

Envoi: Although rules are never completely obeyed, although duties may not be completely carried out, although changes in persons add to complexity, and although a sense of responsibilities varies, *nevertheless* the rules, obediences, and responsibilities are of supreme importance to principals and their society.

MEANDERINGS

4.1 The Learning of Rules and Duties

The rules and duties are learned or are supposed to be learned as the child is socialized by parents, other adults, and peers; they stem, therefore, from persons in the culture and society under consideration. Both culture and society metaphorically, consequently, contribute to or determine perceived events. It has been said that human beings are "rule-formulating and rule-following" beings; hence they acquire the rules not only to be law-abiding but also to make moral judgments in a social context (Hogan, 1973). This learning is usually a slow process, but even during the first and second years children react to the vagaries of their milieu both realistically and symbolically (Gardner, 1982, pp. 92ff.). According to one survey of largely American research, the learning occurs in three ways. First, parental discipline may consist of the assertion of power, the withdrawal of love, and deliberate tutoring. Here behavior "designated as moral often amounts to nothing more than compliance with an adult's arbitrary prohibition." Then children and adults may identify with or imitate other persons who serve as role models for rule-adhering behavior considered good or bad. Or the maturing child himself, with whatever resources he has at his disposal, seeks to make sense of his own behavior and that of others in terms of experience he has had and is having, a process frequently proclaimed by Piaget and his followers (M. L. Hoffman, 1977).

A sample of "essentially middle-class" American parents was observed as they interacted with their children during the first three years of life. The kinds of obedience they demanded could be classified into three different "domains": those they believed to be dangerous, those they claimed required consideration of other persons, and those they admitted were trivial. The children's measured intelligence and their self-concept tended to be positively related to their tendency to obey sensible demands concerning danger and social consideration, but the same attributes were negatively related to the trivial commands (Zern and Stern, 1983).

Considerable experience and skill, therefore, are required before rules and duties can be learned and then affect behavior in relevant situations. Presupposed is a memory for what has occurred in the past: the circumstances under which a rule has been required as well as the ensuing behavior and its consequences. Such learning may be deliberate or voluntary; it may be motivated as a means to an end or be an end in itself. Undoubtedly the learning is not specific in the sense of being autobiographical and situation-specific ("episodic memory"); rather it tends to be abstract, verbally formulated, and hence generalizable to numerous situations ("semantic memory") (cf. A. L. Brown, 1975). Possession of semantic memory is crucial for the application of rules and other aspects of moral behavior because, as suggested in the definition of value *(Proposition 1.3)*, the tendencies become salient not only whenever they are relevant but also when details change as a result of afterthoughts and the changes wrought by time. With semantic memory, utilization of previous knowledge can thus expand or contract. It is possible for a person to "know" something he has not learned, such as the applicability or nonapplicability of a rule in a novel situation, even as semantic memory (what letter in the English alphabet comes before *p?*) is less spontaneous than episodic memory (what letter comes after *p?*) (cf. Tulving, 1972).

It is all very well to emphasize the importance of early socialization, but the precise connection between early training or learning and later behavior is unclear both to researchers and to parents. In fact, there are reasonably good grounds for accepting the following conclusion by three writers who have evaluated the systematic research among Americans: with the exception of schizophrenic and sociopathic behavior, the "common belief that the experiences of the first few years of life determine the development of a person for the rest of his or her life" is "generally a myth." Why? The myth springs from what quite rightly is called "follow-back" rather than "follow-forward" studies; that is, the ex post facto recollections of childhood by adults can be linked to their present behavior, but the tendencies measured in advance at an early age may in fact be altered by experiences later on. The twig is not inevitably bent as it matures. In the voluminous writings of Freud, who may be partially responsible for the so-called myth, we read, for example, "if we start from the premises inferred from the analysis and try to follow these up to the final result, then we no longer get the impression of an inevitable sequence of events which could not have been otherwise determined" (Kohlberg et al., 1984). Similarly, an unresolved problem, according to the conclusion reached by a conference of experts (Social Science Research Council, 1984), is the determination of the factors leading to a crusading sense of responsibility by some outstanding principals such as Gandhi and Einstein. Certainly experiences in their childhood must lead them to develop a strong interest in the welfare of mankind. Possibly they are so intelligent that they recognize the plight of human beings every-

where and therefore devote their lives or segments of their lives to
their fellows, but clearly a highly intelligent principal may employ
his skills toward selfish ends. Knowledge of and attitudes toward rules
and duties, therefore, like other judgments and behavior, may have
their origin but not their final destiny in the early years.

4.2 The Obligations of Citizens

A political scientist has made a valiant attempt to determine the conditions under which participants feel obligated to discharge their responsibilities (Fishkin, 1982). His views merit a summary at some
length; his original phrasing is not being followed but, I believe, has
not been violated. According to him, a feeling of responsibility or obligation does *not* arise when a principal experiences no or virtually
no conflict between or among alternative options *(What will I do?)*;
when a contemplated action appears trivial or unrelated to a value
(What ought I do?); when for realistic reasons (physical, psychological,
geographical) he believes he is unable to carry out the contemplated
action *(What can I do?)*; or when he cannot directly perceive other
persons who require assistance or who will benefit from his action
(What would the consequences be?). On the other hand, that sense of
obligation arises when the principal is confronted with options in-
clining him either to accept or to reject the obligation. Factors affecting
acceptance or rejection by a principal include inclinations to behave
heroically or beyond the call of duty; to expend effort, to incur costs,
or to make sacrifices that in his own terms are minimal; to abandon
a moral ideal; to apply a moral principle to a specific situation or
person or to any person having a specified status or possessing a
specified authority; to add to possibly burdensome obligations he already has in various situations or with reference to various other
persons; to contemplate the action because other persons are or are
not contemplating it or because they can or cannot be expected to
do so; to favor the action because he has a strong, meaningful bond
with a particular person, a community, or perhaps with the world;
to secure additional information, if possible, for reaching a decision.
The reader can immediately note that these negative conditions refer
not only to what are called here habitual judgments but also obviously
to many of the probing questions.

No one, including myself, would contend that a principal reaches
a decision only after considering all the alternatives just reeled off.
Usually he does not need to do so; the decision to rescue a person
from drowning or from a burning house is not likely to include, at

least at the moment of decision, the consequences of heroic behavior now or for future generations, and so on down the list. The analytic challenge is to determine the circumstances under which one or more of the propositions has a critical effect on the decision to discharge an obligation. Is it always true that principals feel a greater sense of obligation to persons whom they know or can perceive than to those they have never met or who appear only as strange abstractions to them?

The same political scientist, moreover, has provided commonsense illustrations of the specific, time-bound conditions, largely in Western society, that actually evoke or might be expected to evoke a sense of responsibility:

Should a participant contribute to famine relief?
Should he go to the trouble to vote at election time?
Should he pay taxes when failure to do so will not be detected?
Should he attempt to rescue a person in peril when the risk is negligible or when it is high?
Should he walk on the grass?
Should he sacrifice himself in behalf of his peers?
Should he take an apple from another person's orchard when the petty theft will go unnoticed?
Should he be a vegetarian in a world rife with starvation since one pound derived from meat requires the prior expenditure of twenty-one pounds of grain?

From the standpoint of the present analysis, skepticism must be expressed concerning the assumption that the principal's sense of responsibility plays the exclusive role in making decisions concerning such situations; rather more of the probing questions must be raised and answered. Famine relief, for example, poses questions concerning the effects of that disaster upon the principal's own country *(What might the consequences be?)*, his ability to make e a financial contribution *(What can I do?)*, the opinions of other persons who believe that he should contribute *(What must I do?)*, and so on down the list.

4.3 Locus of Control

Psychologists have also valiantly approached the problem of determining principals' beliefs concerning responsibility for their own behavior. The research has been conducted in part under the appropriate banner of "locus of control." On the basis of their responses to standardized questionnaires, individuals are divided into two groups:

internals who believe that in effect they control their own destinies, and externals who believe that by and large they are buffeted about by forces over which they have little or no control (Rotter, 1966). The technique of appraising locus of control suggests a systematic way of obtaining data concerning the replies to two of the probing questions: potentiality *(What can I do?)* and duty *(What must I do?)*. The fact that the proportion of principals falling into the two categories varies from society to society is also of interest because it demonstrates that the concept at least is not ethnocentric and that the beliefs have a strong cultural component. A skeptical warning in passing: it is dangerous to anticipate that the proportion of externals and internals will conform to some ad hoc hypothesis. One investigation of black, Indian, and English-speaking white students in South Africa, for example, revealed no significant differences with respect to the proportion of internals and externals when the three samples were compared; only within the white group was there a significant difference (women tended to be more externally oriented than men) (Moodley-Rajab and Ramkissoon, 1979). Since the three ethnic groups occupy clearly different positions in the society, such similarities were not to be expected.

An examination of the original locus-of-control questionnaire, which has fruitfully inspired so much research, indicates that the respondent reveals his belief in a sense of responsibility by agreeing or disagreeing with some of the items; for example:

> Many of the unhappy things in people's lives are partly due to bad luck.
> Unfortunately, an individual's worth often passes unrecognized no matter how hard he tries.
> Getting a good job depends mainly on being in the right place at the right time (Rotter, 1966).

Presumably the externally oriented participant tends to disclaim responsibility for his actions and hence feels less obligated toward others; and the reverse may be true of those with an internal orientation. Just as the scores on the questionnaire range between two extremes, so it is to be anticipated that most principals are convinced they control some matters and not others; hence in some situations and not in others they experience a sense of responsibility. A humanist believes we are more likely to find two souls within a single breast: man "asserts himself as a pure internality against which no external power can take hold, and he also experiences himself as a thing crushed by the dark weight of other things" (Beauvoir, 1948, p. 7).

When a principal places responsibility upon forces external to himself, in effect—with the exception of natural events beyond human control—he is shifting his sense of duty to other persons. If he lives in an environment he considers cruel, ultimately he must be convinced that cruelty has been inflicted upon him by persons now living or dead. From his standpoint, however, such an analysis is either meaningless or metaphysical: he believes he lacks the ability to control what happens to himself here and now. Undoubtedly, even the most externally oriented principal recognizes a distinction between a reflex action, such as occurs when the knee is tapped in the right place, and premeditated murder; or does he?

The most extreme form of the external orientation is a belief in the doctrine of determinism. If it is true that "determinism is the epistemological basis of the human search for knowledge" and that "we cannot even conceive the image of an undetermined universe" (Von Mises, 1957, p. 74), then most of the probing questions are answered or are meaningless: the freedom to judge options and to pursue alternate courses of action comes not from the principal but from forces beyond his knowledge and control (Gergen, 1982). In a society that encourages a belief in fatalism or predestination, a principal may more readily discharge some duties, especially those endangering him, since whatever happens he knows will happen and will not be affected by his own decisions (cf. Guitton, 1970, pp. 137, 143). What he does is determined by forces over which he has no control; if human beings are included among those forces, they also cannot be blamed because their behavior is likewise determined; and so on through an infinite regress that ends—well, where does or can it end? It usually ends in some kind of metaphysical assumption, attributing ultimate responsibility to God (and then one has a duty to Him) or to reckless nihilism. In fact, probably most principals have a strong tendency to blame authorities or outside forces for their misdeeds or shortcomings (Milgram, 1974, pp. 7–12), but they may also hold themselves responsible in situations over which they have no direct control. Such self-blame may be confined to the situation at hand or, if phrased more generally, may affect future judgments (Abramson et al., 1978).

The discussion of responsibility and locus of control concludes on a somewhat prosaic note. Again and again studies have shown that this variable is related, at least statistically, to demographic and personal factors within principals. One investigation based upon interviews with over one thousand American male workers has shown a stronger tendency among blacks than among whites and among those dissatisfied than among those satisfied with their work to attribute success in their jobs to luck rather than to hard work (Vecchio, 1981). The effects of these differences on the moral judgments of the principals in the specified groups are not indicated; let them be skeptically imagined.

CHAPTER 5

Anticipations

Anticipating consequences is an essential ingredient of moral judgments (Schwartz, 1977). In fact, many writers pay almost exclusive attention to this particular probing question under the heading of teleology, whether the consequences involve the principal himself or other persons (Boyce and Jensen, 1978, pp. 21–34). Thus a philosopher suggests that an activity itself should not be judged in isolation; rather reference must be made to its "relationship to the development of my own life in the community of men" (Melsen, 1967, p. 94)—the consequence, in short, for the principal and his society. On the other hand, "consequentialism" is attacked as a one-sided system of evaluating moral judgments; "ideals" (that is, values) are said to be neglected (Held, 1984, pp. 18, 32). The present analysis, it should be obvious, avoids this charge of one-sidedness by considering anticipations to be only one of the eight questions relatable to morality.

Existentially and otherwise, anticipatory judgments mean that the principal is consciously evaluating various options for the immediate present and for the future. The phenomenological attribute of consciousness must be considered distinctly human; whether animals are or are not conscious in this sense is only a tantalizing question. Children, however, gradually acquire the values of their society as their experiences enable them to anticipate the rewards and punishments they obtain in and beyond the immediate present. Instantaneous and habitual actions, whether or not they are judged subsequently by principals and observers, may lack this moral component at the moment when the action occurs.

Some kind of leap is usually necessary before the principal selects the value to guide him, before he passes judgment, and before he acts. The leap is required because knowledge is never completely accurate or available or because the present and the future are never—or seldom ever—like the past. A philosopher thinks the leap into the unknown occurs as an act of faith into "the better known" when the principal has confidence in his moral principles (cf. Roubiczek, 1969, p. 310). Perhaps—but more than confidence is needed, or at least we try to fathom the conditions generally bolstering confidence.

5.1 OPTIONS

Proposition: The possible consequences of alternative courses of action are anticipated and weighted.

Unless they respond habitually, principals may be said to have options available to them. Often, however, one alternative in effect may be only hypothetical when external compulsion is present. A principal may ignore a bandit who demands that he surrender his money, a traffic policeman whose siren demands that he halt, or a dear relative who requires assistance so as not to perish; but he is much more likely to respond in the manner required by the situation; from his viewpoint he has no option other than to do nothing, and that will bring only disaster or grief.

Real options arise as a result of events in the milieu or of the principal's own experiences in the past. In a restaurant the diner immediately orders a cup of coffee, although he knows he has the options of ordering tea, beer, or nothing. Habit determines his choice, not a moral judgment. Similarly a devout Muslim or Jew, confronted with the options of pork or another meat, immediately rejects pork: he knows the dietary rules of his religion, and, if challenged, he could say that the devout are expected to follow them; he may also anticipate disapproval from his peers. If the option of pork were not available, he would not make a moral judgment resulting from the imperative value of his faith. An understanding of options requires insight into the circumstances of their appearance and into the principal's anticipation as to whether they are realistically available to him *(What can I do?)*.

Humanists are likely to insist that additional options are available if only the principal would reflect and find them: "the possibility of opposing choices" exists (Beauvoir, 1948, p. 118). Revolutionaries, on both the Left and the Right, also assume alternatives as they urge their followers to take actions against the regime in power. But often there is no effective alternative; we are prisoners, either literally or metaphorically, and we must either submit or flee into fantasy. Revolutionary activities are suppressed by the authorities of police states, if not forever, then at least for short or long periods.

Whenever there is a breakdown within a society, problems such as unemployment, poverty, crime, and terror arise, as a result of which leaders and ordinary citizens are confronted with the challenge of selecting options whose consequences they try, however vainly, to anticipate. Traditional societies having contact with one another and particularly with the West are faced with the alternatives of retaining their way of life or of changing. Heretofore principals in those societies have not been confronted with apparent choices; they have followed customs and have adhered to the values of their group with a minimum of change. Their contacts with outsiders may begin on a material level: bicycles are viewed as efficient modes of transportation, and tin roofs are clearly more durable and fire-resistant than thatched roofs. But with these material innovations comes the realization that they and other changes are achievable only in a cash economy accompanied by the values of the marketplace. Whether or not missionaries seek to alter the religious superstructure, those who acquire or who would acquire the bicycles and the roofs begin, perhaps dimly at first, to question some of the old values and to try to comprehend the morality of the system under which they have previously been functioning. It is not as if a tribal, colonial, or independent council is assembled to revise the old code and substitute a new one: the principals permit the old and the new to continue side by side until they or their descendants find it rewarding gradually to absorb the new but also to retain some if not all aspects of the old. Then perhaps for the first time principals make note of the fact that they have been selecting alternative ways of living, and hence they begin consciously to anticipate the consequences of their options—and possibly too late to halt what they then begin to call the evil of modernization.

Somewhat similarly principals come to appreciate the options ahead of them when they reach crucial points in their development. They anticipate the consequences of remaining with their parents, of pursuing one career rather than another, of continuing to lead an active life or retiring (cf. Erikson, 1959). Do they really anticipate which opinions will be more or most satisfactory from their standpoint? The pain ensuing from having to make a choice may be avoided by failing to admit the existence of options, so that principals manage to judge and act as they have in the past. For a confrontation of options to be compelling, they must be able to anticipate that they possess the relevant skill (What can I do?) to pursue the alternatives and to achieve the gains anticipated from them. Infants behave impulsively and only gradually reach the "stage" at which they can recognize options. A principal with an "uncontrollable" impulse resulting, as one says, in a strong passion is not likely to be either able or in the mood to contemplate alternatives for any length of time: one value from the past is salient, the consequences of the alternatives cannot be quickly anticipated, and impulsive behavior or withdrawal may be the outcome. When options are recognized and a choice is made, the principal may note that he has cut himself off from what he has rejected. He may then suffer from pangs of conscience and be plagued with the desire to have done what he did not do. The pain and the reactance may be even greater when he believes he must select one of two apparently incompatible actions (Brehm and Brehm, 1981); for example, in replying to a good friend, should he be frank and honest and criticize him justly, or should he be silent or evasive?

Skeptical Note: Are most persons able to have options concerning actions of real significance and also be aware of them?

5.2 ACCURACY

Proposition: The consequences of options and judgments are anticipated with varying degrees of accuracy.

Obviously some future consequences can be correctly anticipated: if you shoot a person point-blank in the head, he will almost certainly die; if a young child is vigorously spanked by his parent, he will cry. But, wait, there are flaws even in such hypothetical illustrations. The victim may die, but the assailant may not be able to predict his own fate. The child will cry, but what effect will the spanking have on his willingness to obey in the future or upon his immortal character? Telling a harmless white lie may achieve an important goal; yet may not the reward therefrom facilitate a tendency to avoid the truth in many other situations?

It is also clear that principals can anticipate numerous aspects of the future, if not perfectly, then with some degree of accuracy. They know their own skills on the basis of past experience *(What can I do?)* and so they believe correctly that they will or will not succeed at a given task. There is convincing evidence that an individual can perhaps improve his skill beforehand by practicing mentally the physical movement (even landing an airplane) required in a future situation (Prather, 1973). Any principal, moreover, must remember the obligations to which he has committed himself or has been committed; otherwise all promises and contracts would be forgotten and become worthless.

In modern times, however, principals find it difficult to anticipate the future correctly. Parents may not know how best to socialize their children in order to make them good citizens or to achieve whatever goals they postulate for them, yet they must continually, whether consciously or not and whether for pedagogical or selfish reasons, administer punishments and rewards. Such a simple matter as reading may have consequences not anticipated by teachers; learning to read by rote methods, it has been affirmed, postpones the enjoyment of literature when it is assumed that the pleasure will come later, an assumption that may well be false (Bettelheim and Zelan, 1982). In the United States competent persons with diseases considered incurable may be "legally entitled" to refuse medical treatment, but the peaceful death they anticipate as a consequence may be elusive as painful symptoms intensify (Battin, 1983).

Accurate anticipations usually become increasingly difficult if not almost impossible as the number of persons potentially affected by a judgment increases. How can there be, the question is asked, "intelligent citizen participation in a society increasingly directed by scientific and technical processes often beyond the comprehension of any save the experts?" (Prewitt, 1983). These processes range from religion to economics, from recreation to politics. Decisions of groups, like those of the persons composing them, are especially prone to error. Rather than considering the evidence that could be gathered or, if at hand, that could be utilized to serve as the basis for anticipating consequences, principals may rationalize their own predetermined goals, they may make decisions that please their own egos, or they may succumb to pressure of their peers as they interact (Janis and Mann, 1977, especially chap. 3). One writer suggests that, even when these human tendencies can be overcome, the decisions have only "limited rationality": principals for reasons beyond their control cannot accurately anticipate either the future consequences of their decisions or their own attitudes toward those consequences (March, 1978). Even preliminary discussions among associates of an organization, if there be any, may not produce sure-fire procedures to facilitate new proposals: often the experts themselves disagree concerning the optimum actions to be taken (Brewer, 1978–79) (Proposition 5.6).

The most extreme challenge for mankind at the moment clearly pertains to nuclear weapons. No one except an idiot doubts the desirable value: to prevent a nuclear war. The problem, as one writer suggests, is how to make a "rational choice" when confronted with "conditions of uncertainty" (Kavka, 1980). Options include decisions concerning not only the stockpiling of such weapons to deter the leaders of the potential enemy country but also their actual use during a war and especially in retaliation. Knowledge is imperfect: the wisest statesmen cannot anticipate precisely how their opponents will react to what they themselves do. Under these circumstances, each leader believes or at least avows that he is performing his duty, a moral judgment that in fact is truly deficient.

Similarly the decisions by principals in any high position, such as in industry or religion, are likely to have far-reaching and to some extent unanticipated consequences. The owners declare their corporation bankrupt; leaders of a church maintain abortion is or is not a sin. Such decisions by a few affect scores, hundreds, even millions of persons; often the experts themselves are able to anticipate only a small number of the consequences either because their expertise is limited or because unanticipated events intervene. Revolutionaries may topple a regime in power but the consequences for their society and for other societies that hear about the event cannot be etched in detail. Would Lenin be surprised by what has occurred in the Soviet Union since his death? And even during his lifetime did he not have to alter his blueprint when he installed the New Economic policy?

Sometimes, therefore, decisions backfire and produce consequences different from those that have been anticipated. Banning pornographic materials for seemingly virtuous reasons, for example, may stimulate interest in them: tritely but factually we know how attractive forbidden fruit can be. New housing projects, whether privately or publicly financed, may be motivated by profit or by the welfare of the underprivileged, but eventually the occupants are affected in ways relating to their family life, friends, buying and recreational habits— the list is almost endless and its contents depend upon the situation being changed.

Actuarial reasoning is often employed to increase the accuracy of anticipations. On an informal level a principal anticipates that a given action will please or hurt another person because that has been the consequence in the past. His reasoning, however, may be flawed by the fact that the future may be quite unlike either the past or the present for reasons he himself does not anticipate. His knowledge may be imperfect or events in the society may alter the situation in which he expects to implement his moral judgment. His reasoning from the past may also be faulty: he recalls the last or most recent event but not the sequence of events as his basis for predicting the future. He may misinterpret his own experiences and weight them more or less heavily than they merit as a result of his successes or his failures. He may rely on knowledge from others that may or may not be accurate.

In modern societies many persons believe they can anticipate the benefits and risks from nuclear power plants on the basis of the information or misinformation they have acquired from the mass media or from hearsay. Whether the estimates of others are well founded offers a moot challenge. For lawmakers and others in power the utilization of the past is particularly challenging. In the United States from 1919 to 1933 both the Congress and forty-six of the forty-eight states prohibited "the manufacture, sale, or transport of intoxicating liquors" as well as importing and exporting them. That Noble Experiment, as it was sometimes called, failed: so many Americans continued to buy and sell liquor that the amendment and the laws were repealed. What is the significance of this experience for the future either in the United States or elsewhere? Does it mean that on some or all occasions judgments of behavior cannot be changed by fiat or that Americans will always be fickle?

In spite of its defects, principals must use actuarial reasoning if they are to profit from past experience. The principle of stare decisis, precedent, guides the decisions of judges in Anglo-Saxon countries; thus many, maybe most laws in any society in part salvage from past experience precepts believed to be necessary or useful in the future. The "facts" from the past that are at hand—all of them, a selection of them, perhaps almost none e of them—are recalled and taken into account. Then principals, including judges, look forward: what effect will a present judgment have upon future precedents and hence on actuarial reasoning? A principal and his associates would find living too chaotic if there were not a degree of consistency between past and contemplated judgments and action; yet the past cannot, should not be the only guide if there is to be change for the better, however better may be skeptically defined.

Some areas of human existence are quite predictable after they have been subjected to actuarial analysis in the best scientific sense. The profitability of private insurance companies in the West offers convincing evidence on this point. Their estimates of the future, however, are based upon probabilities for masses of persons, which are applicable to the individual only with extreme caution. In contrast, a principal must often base his own anticipations concerning future consequences upon hunches that range from the sagacious to the reckless. For him no hedonistic calculus is available that can function like a computer programmed with the best available data. Perfect reasoning, alas, is elusive; but slightly beyond such skepticism, some lawfulness must be noted.

Skeptical Note: Are not critical consequences frequently over-looked, ignored, or miscalculated?

5.3 IMMEDIATE VERSUS FUTURE CONSEQUENCES

Proposition: When they must anticipate rewards and punishments likely to be associated with immediate and future consequences, principals usually feel more confident concerning the immediate than the future.

Any kind of preparation or planning requires a momentary sacrifice for the sake of gratification at some future time. Thus a principal may be confronted with an attractive goal attainable almost immediately, but simultaneously he may anticipate that its attainment may produce far-flung, undesirable consequences (cf. Heider, 1958, pp. 221–22). Emergencies may be anticipated and their effects mitigated by precautionary efforts in the present. Again, however, the unforeseen consequence intrudes. Einstein may have been gratified by his own significant scientific achievements, one unintended consequence of which—the creation of atomic weapons—eventually horrified him. According to one writer, mankind throughout the ages has freed itself from dependence upon many of the vagaries of nature, yet unanticipated consequences have included less freedom from the state and other powerful groups resulting from the development of science and technology (cf. Rosinski, 1965, pp. 22–23, 79–88) *(Meandering 5.1: Renunciation)*.

Principals may worry about immediate consequences and fail to foresee future consequences. Parents in a modern community, having deep concern for children generally, may lobby in behalf of smaller classes in schools on the assumption that thereby education can be more effective and hence students will acquire additional knowledge and the values of the society. Having achieved that objective, they may lose interest and not investigate whether in fact diminishing the number of students in a room has achieved the original objectives. What is needed for a project that seeks to induce change is an explicit criterion for success. And the criteria for success in social affairs burst out of a cornucopia of possibilities ranging from creativity to survivability.

Skeptical Note: When two birds in the bush rather than one in the hand are necessary, then what?

5.4 OTHER PERSONS

Proposition: A principal almost always anticipates the consequences of his judgment or action upon other persons actually present in the situation or likely to be affected in the future.

The effects from the anticipation of others vary with the nature of those others and their relation to the principal. Another person close at hand—one belonging to the principal's own ingroup such as his neighborhood or his country, one who appears friendly, one who is identifiable, or one who is in need, for example—influences the principal's anticipation differently from, respectively, another at a distance belonging to an outgroup such as an enemy country, appearing hostile, not identifiable, or seemingly content. A modern philosopher in fact believes that a "question or judgment" relating to morality is "at least *relevant* whenever the conduct or life of a person or rational being, insofar as it is voluntary, impinges, or may impinge directly or indirectly, on the feelings, beliefs, happiness, well-being, etc., of other persons or rational beings" (Frankena, 1977). If the influence of the others is to be salient, the principal must first perceive them or in advance possess beliefs and attitudes regarding them.

Immediately or ultimately, directly or indirectly, the principal judges other human beings. Whether present or absent, they may be identifiable or not. When an epithet is hurled at a place—Sodom, red-light district, ghetto, slum—the persons, or their behavior therein are being condemned or at least viewed negatively regardless of who presumably is thought to be responsible. Attitudes are evoked that then may or may not affect the judgment and the action. Thus a philosopher once wrote in a book containing "so much in praise of the Jews" that he would add a "deplorable fact" about himself, namely, that he had met "few Jews" he liked and that his first reaction when meeting a Jew was "one of defensive distrust" (Joad, 1939, p. 228). Natural phenomena like droughts or hurricanes are condemned even by principals not experiencing them because of their adverse effects upon potential or actual victims.

The kind of relationship associated with other persons can be variously expressed. In large part the principal must be able to anticipate the behavior of those persons. That anticipation may be derived from experience with them: he knows how they will react because they have reacted that way in the past. Or else he has been given the equivalent of a contract and he trusts them to execute its terms. Part of his trust may spring from the conviction that they trust him. It is not sentimental to conclude that much of social and moral behavior is based upon mutual trust (Easterbrook, 1978, pp. 174–75) while alluding to the possibility that blind or naive trust in other persons can lead to disappointment or disaster.

The principal may be compelled to consider the sheer number of the others who will be affected by his action. Melodramatically a philosopher discusses a situation in which a driver is "forced to hit and kill you with [his] car in order to avoid hitting a dozen children" (Aiken, 1977). The dilemma, though hypothetical, is a cruel one that at the time would have to be instantly resolved. More often deliberation is possible, and the outcome is determined not only by a calculation of costs and benefits but also by the principal's own enduring predispositions. Shall I buy a new suit of clothes or pay the university fees of my child rather than give the money to a charity that will aid—infinitesimally, so far as my contribution is concerned—homeless persons in my own community or starving persons in Africa? The identical action may affect different persons differently as any official knows who attempts beforehand to anticipate the effects of a piece of legislation upon the different groups, classes, or interests in a society.

The anticipated effects upon others need not be conscious or verbalized. No learned documentation is necessary to indicate that the mere presence of other persons almost certainly has an effect upon judgments and behavior *(Proposition 4.6)*. The principal conforms or does not conform to what he assumes to be their expectancies and therefore unwittingly he judges them and anticipates their reactions. We need not seek at this point to identify the attributes of those others who influence the principal; it is sufficient to note their effect upon him.

The anticipated or actual consequences for other persons are explicitly stated or implied in virtually all the desirable values postulated by philosophers and especially by social scientists *(Proposition 6.2)*. However hackneyed the proverb "man cannot live by bread alone" may be, its compelling truth must be recognized: the diversified goals of human beings—ranging from murmurings of immortality to appreciation by family and contemporaries—include other persons. Even the most alienated principal shows some concern for others, no matter how withdrawn he is or how badly he treats them; and he has memories of those who once socialized him. Other persons, it is anticipated, will benefit from or be hurt by an intended action *(What will I do?)*, or else it is known or believed that it will or can be they who would administer the positive or negative sanctions provided by existing rules *(What may I do?)*. While thus anticipating the reactions of other persons, the principal is functioning in the role of an observer; hence some of his problems will be more appropriately analyzed in part 3, which is devoted to him in that role.

The person or persons of interest to the principal may be present, and so his or their immediate reaction is anticipated. He is approached, directly or over a telephone, by someone collecting money for a charity; he anticipates that the solicitor will be pleased or disappointed by his response. If a general appeal is made by mail, he may anticipate that his virtual anonymity will have little or no effect upon that solicitor. National leaders try to anticipate the effect of their decisions upon the protagonists and antagonists they may never see when their constituency is large and scattered *(Meandering 5.2: Tragic Consequences)*.

The anticipated effects of actions upon others who are absent appears in most dramatic, poignant form when contact with those others can never occur, as is true when the referent is great-grandchildren or the vaguely stated "future generations." What values require that their reactions or welfare be taken into account? The principal who considers them usually must pass a series of prior morally incomplete judgments. He may feel, when others now alive know of his concern for persons in the future, that he himself will be praised. In almost a metaphysical sense he may be convinced that he has been the heir of persons now dead, a debt he can discharge by considering his own future descendants. He may feel that by considering those at a temporal distance he strengthens values in the here and now. His own welfare may be directly involved; avoiding a nuclear holocaust, for example, benefits both present and future generations. In any case, no direct reciprocation from the recipients is anticipated.

In addition to anticipating the responses of other persons, the principal may anticipate his own responses to them. He ignores a stranger who passes by. But if he observes that the stranger is in distress, or particularly if he seems to be experiencing pain, he will probably express concern and may respond helpfully. With nonstrangers he may be more concerned with his own and their judgments. A principal's response to one person may have anticipated repercussions upon other persons; thus the "rights" of a dying patient in a coma concern not only him but also his relatives and friends, which in turn evokes a more general challenge concerning the sacredness of human life under all conditions (cf. Melden, 1977, pp. 215–20).

Ordinary taboos concerning strongly held values can more easily be violated when those affected are not present or are at least invisible as human beings, so that their reactions can be ignored. "Napalm is dropped on civilians from ten thousand feet overhead; not men but tiny blips on an infrared oscilloscope are the targets of Gatling guns" (Milgram, 1974, p. 118). Modern warfare may require this kind of psychological distance, but sometimes anger or frustration may also remove a taboo, as when one frustrated spouse kills his or her frustrating mate.

Whether present or absent, therefore, the other person or persons evoke beliefs and attitudes within the principal. People can so easily be thrown into categories, and, if they are viewed as threats, they can be stereotyped as "devils or monsters, germs or vermin, pigs or apes, as robots, or as abstract menaces" and hence "they are thus removed from the company of men" (Sanford and Comstock, 1971, p. 7). Corresponding values are then evoked and the principal is able to justify his anticipations, his judgments, and eventually his actions. When a sociologist states that "there is nothing in the least anomalous about the fact that an Aristotle or a Jefferson owned slaves," he could be saying in effect that those principals employed different values when judging distinctive groups within their society (Patterson, p. ix). Another person in clerical garb or bearing a symbol such as a cross, a crescent, or a star may remind the principal that religious values are supposed to guide him. But then, according to Ovid, possibly the reaction can be "video meliora, proboque, deteriora sequor" (cited by Szanlawski, 1980).

Anticipated rewards also inevitably include a reference to other persons. Sometimes, as has been indicated, those persons are "an intrinsic part of social contact" (their presence, their attentiveness, their responsiveness, their initiation of action); at other times what they do can be rewarding (they demonstrate deference, sympathy, or affection, or they offer praise). These social rewards are subtle since they must be distributed, as it were, in the right amounts; for example, a principal may wish others to be attentive, which means he does not seek to be shunned but also that he would not become thereby too conspicuous (A. H. Buss, 1983). For these many reasons, principals are likely to anticipate the consequences upon others as they pass judgment *(Meandering 5.3: Judging Other Persons)*. The problem of determining the conditions under which principals become altruistic is also relevant and is considered later *(Proposition 6.2)*.

Among the persons whose reactions are anticipated, more often than not, is the principal himself. If I do this, what will be its effect upon me in the future? Shall I be proud or ashamed of myself?

Skeptical Note: Exactly which persons concern principals both generally and in specific situations?

5.5 PREDICTABILITY AND HOPE

Proposition: When principals pass moral judgments, they believe and hope they can make sufficiently accurate predictions concerning other persons and events.

Whether or not he resorts to actuarial reasoning, a principal must make some kind of leap into the future. He knows he has experienced surprises and therefore concludes, quite sensibly, that surprises will be inevitable. By and large, however, even though some surprises may be gratifying, he wishes to anticipate the future correctly, which means that he will be able to predict more or less accurately how other persons will respond to his contemplated behavior. To "do unto others as you would have them do unto you" also expresses the hope that others will behave like you, and hence enable you to predict their behavior. Principals, to be sure, may fail to reach a decision or to run a risk when they are unable to anticipate future events or consequences. Predictability implies trust: anticipating that others will react as they have previously agreed or will agree to react. Clearly a high degree of trust among members of the same family, group, or society is both desirable and inevitable if principals are to achieve their own goals with a minimum of friction or conflict. Informally and legally it is anticipated that promises will be kept. Reciprocal trust probably reaches its peak in friendship, which therefore, according to Aristotle, is "one of the most indispensable requirements of life" (Aristotle, 1934 ed., p. 451).

An exceptionally thorough analysis of promises from a legal and moral standpoint suggests that a whole array of psychological components within the promisor and the promisee must be considered before, for example, a promise can or should be considered binding. Is a promise "a moral commitment"? What does the promisor intend? What does the promisee expect? Under what conditions may a promise be broken? When may a promise be relied upon? When are promises explicit, when implicit? The raising of these questions suggests the intricacy of the interpersonal factors that go beyond the simple commonsense injunction, "you must always keep your promise." The relation between the principals affects the binding character of the promise. Promises, in general, raise two "moral questions": What is the right course of action to be followed by either party with reference to a promise made or received? Why is it socially necessary for promises to be kept (Atiyah, 1981, pp. 123–24)?

Not surprisingly, trust is related to other predispositions. In national surveys Americans have been willing to indicate whether they believe people can be trusted. A positive belief in this respect has been found to be related to another belief, namely, the conviction that their "financial situation," rather than worsening, has either improved or remained the same in the "last few years." This relation tended to hold for all ages of respondents; for whites but not for blacks; for those above but not below a certain income level; and for those with an education up to but not beyond a high school level (Ostheimer and Ritt, 1982).

Most, maybe all principals have hopes and beliefs concerning what they call good and evil. Whether optimistic or pessimistic, they anticipate some kind of success or failure for themselves or for others. The mixture of good and evil appears frequently in theological systems. "God is good," a philosophical theologian has stated, "and means only good, but His purpose is to realize His ends with our cooperation; and in some sense evil is necessary that they may be revealed to us, and striven after by us" (Niven, 1922). More generally: "It is hard to believe in Christ the Redeemer without at the same time believing in his antagonist, the devil" (Valensin, 1972). Beliefs in the existence of gods and eternal life cannot be verified in the normal sense, although efforts are made to find relevant facts by pointing, for example, to divine interventions and perceived miracles. Human beings also struggle to achieve or at least to conceive of a more perfect society on earth. Lost paradises project fantasies concerning the past into the future. Utopias, whether potentially realizable or merely imagined, suggest the possibility of future bliss: the inhabitants are expected to live in harmony with one another, conflicts are supposed to disappear, basic and secondary needs will be fulfilled. The bliss, however, may not be equally distributed as in the various Marxian ideals; or even in imagination, it may be restricted to a privileged group, so that servants or even slaves are portrayed as exploited.

Skeptical Note: Are not hopes and anticipations too often blasted?

5.6 MEANS AND ENDS

Proposition: The consequences of employing particular means to achieve a designated end cannot always be accurately anticipated.

Few problems in the life of a principal or his society are as banal and important as the relation of means and ends. It is important because the noblest of goals must somehow be achieved, yet it is banal because so often there are no clear-cut answers. In advance of a later discussion *(Proposition 7.4)* I would borrow from a psychologist a hypothetical, somewhat abused dilemma: a husband cannot afford to buy a drug essential to save his wife's life and wonders whether he should steal it. Saving her life is the end; stealing could be the means. What will happen if he does steal the drug and is caught and punished? Obviously the husband and we are enmeshed in the ancient problem of deciding whether the end justifies the means; part of his and our decision rests on estimating the probable consequences of the means adopted to achieve the end. On a realistic and not a hypothetical level, consensus among American policymakers concerning national goals may be greater than the means or indicators, especially the quantitative ones, that can be employed to determine whether the goals have been achieved (Biderman, 1966).

Utilizing the wrong means may not lead to the desired end: a principal seeks to win approval from another person by means of ingratiation and thereby antagonizes him. There may be no apparent means to achieve a desirable end, such as abolishing all violent crime or obvious evils, and sometimes any means can be justified by the end. A philosopher has remarked that "the principal that the end cannot justify the means is easily breached," as every child and social theorist knows. We must never kill or murder, but may we not assassinate "a tyrant who is systematically murdering his opponents and anyone else he dislikes?" (P. Singer, 1979, pp. 183–96).

Conflicts occur between means serving different ends. Political leaders of major and not so major countries in the modern world may wish to achieve greater self-sufficiency in order to decrease dependence upon imports, hence making their country less likely to become embroiled in a war for economic reasons. To achieve this end, however, they may have to destroy parts of their own natural environment to increase, for example, the production of oil, coal, or even wood. Which value should triumph, avoiding war or preserving the environment?

Similarly principals often find it difficult to draw a line between conflicting means to achieve desirable values. Surely, in democratic countries, the value of free speech and of free communication in general is deeply appreciated; but so is the value of protecting persons from physical and psychic injury. In the justly famous words of Justice Holmes, "The most stringent protection of free speech would not protect a man in falsely shouting fire in a theater and causing a panic" (cited by Boyce and Jensen, 1978, p. 250): one value is sacrificed in behalf of another; the means employed to achieve one value is attained by neglecting another. Additional perplexities are evident in our perplexed, skeptical age *(Meandering 5.4: Baffling Means)*. It is not surprising, therefore, that modern philosophers often avoid searching for the means to achieve the noble values they espouse, except when philosophizing concerning a contemporary problem such as prostitution (cf. Pateman, 1983); then quite rightly they may become empirical and utilize social sciences to try to uncover efficacious means.

Skeptical Note: Means and ends, ends and means, must they keep going round and round?

Envoi: Although one never knows exactly what will happen until it happens, especially in the most distant future, *nevertheless* aspects of close and distant future are and can be anticipated.

MEANDERINGS

5.1 Renunciation

Parents, even though they cannot anticipate the ultimate effects of their own regimens, perforce usually make sacrifices in behalf of their children who, they believe, eventually will become self-supporting adults. Some of these sacrifices, however, bring immediate joy: being in the presence of children almost always does. For their part children endure many travails during later socialization and hence may anticipate that eventually they will be able to control more of their own existence. Experiments among French children suggest that such delays are easier to tolerate with increasing age (Fraisse, 1982).

Adults also labor, too frequently with little immediate joy, in order to obtain some of the luxuries of living. A pay envelope at the end of a day or month can be more gratifying than the hours spent earning it. Yearly medical examinations serve to detect unnoticed symptoms of diseases: the costs and the often slight unpleasantness in the present prevent more serious problems later.

A summary of contemporary experimental literature suggests that the ability to be patient and "to act in the light of anticipated future consequences," although it may be "fundamental for planning" and other complex activities directed toward the future, is not a unitary skill; rather it depends upon many factors such as the principal's age, his goals, other persons affecting him, and indeed his own actions during the delay (Mischel, 1974). When choices are available—and for principals in some societies and for others in certain social classes or at particular economic levels they are not readily or at all available—the future effects of alternative careers must be carefully anticipated in terms of current ability *(What can I do?)* and interests *(What will I do?)*. Some religious persons behave morally and sustain certain beliefs because they anticipate that these may be the keys to everlasting life after death which they know to be inevitable.

5.2 Tragic Consequences

Chains of events permeate societies, so that the actions of important principals in the present may have such profound effects upon others in the future that it becomes difficult to assign responsibility to the original principals *(Proposition 9.3)* and impossible for them to have assumed responsibility *(Proposition 4.6)*. Consider the Holocaust perpetrated by the Nazis upon Jews, Gypsies, and Christian opponents. It is difficult to know where to begin or to describe the chain of events that led to that ghastly tragedy. Surely Lloyd George, Woodrow Wilson, Georges Clemenceau and others did not foresee that consequence: they believed they were making reasoned judgments when they forced the Treaty of Versailles upon Germany after World War I. The treaty played a role in producing the economic and social conditions facilitating the rise to power of Hitler and the Nazis. Those Germans and Austrians arrived at a morally deficient judgment when they decided that the final solution for Jews and others would be extermination. In turn the survivors of the Holocaust, it is now known, have had to make various judgments concerning their own roles in the concentration camps; and even now they must cope with whatever horrors still pervade them, some must also deal with the question of guilt (whether they could or could not have behaved differently while inmates), and all of them somehow must continue to live in terms of a new value system (Danieli, 1981). The survivors necessarily affect their children who then affect their children, on and on and on (cf. the bombing of Dresden, *Proposition 2.3*).

Sometimes a single principal is the originator of a tragic consequence of which he could not conceivably have been aware when he acted as he did. An extreme but telling example is that of the creator of Agent Orange, the defoliant employed by Americans against North Vietnam. Its origin can be traced to a botanist's Ph.D. thesis, which reported that a particular chemical improved soybean yields. He had noted that the chemical, when applied to the plant in higher concentrations, caused the leaves to fall off. Army chemists then seized upon the incidental, accidental finding, and with "a less-than-zealous attempt to understand the possible biological consequences of using this chemical," they employed it against the enemy in Vietnam. The botanist, a broad-gauged person opposed to war in general and certainly to chemical warfare, is appalled because "unwittingly, in my attempt to solve a basic problem, I had spawned a destructive weapon" (Sides, 1984).

5.3 Judging Other Persons

The anticipated reactions of others depend in large part on the principal's appraisal of them; hence the problem of what has been called person perception is relevant to the analysis of morality (Doob, 1975). Sometimes the consequences of their actions, at other times their demographic characteristics, and at still other times their inferred intention may function as the basis. When American children between the ages of five and twelve, for example, judged the behavior of other children in hypothetical situations, they tended to be more lenient toward those of the same age than toward those known to be older or younger. Obviously these young principals anticipated that the behavior of others would or should fluctuate with age, but it was not absolute age but age compared with their own (Buldain et al., 1982). Or Canadian workers, managers, and students, when asked to judge occupational groups with respect to the "justice of their position compared to other occupations in society," tended to be influenced not only by conventional indices but also to some degree by their feelings about their own occupation and their conceptions of its "standing" from the standpoint of comparative justice (Taylor et al., 1985). In face-to-face situations "the manner" in which another person speaks conveys considerable information about him generally (for example, his background, his social class) and specifically (his current mood, his conception of his formal or informal relation to the other person) (cf. Giles and Powesland, 1975).

The very resiliency of persons under many circumstances creates problems in anticipating consequences. Suppose, for example, the principal does or says something that injures another person's conception of himself. Ordinarily, as therapists can testify, it is difficult to change the way in which such a victim views himself; yet sometimes a swift insult or a painful rejection can produce a change not anticipated by the principal. Even then, however, the person insulted or rejected may make every effort to "refute and undermine feedback that threatens" the existing self-conception: we would think well of ourselves in the face of adversity (cf. Swann and Hill, 1982).

Principals may also seek to explain the past or the anticipated behavior of others. Evidence has been accumulated indicating that a sample of American students tended to attribute their own behavior to situations or external factors and that of others to personality traits or other internal factors (Jones and Nisbett, 1971). As ever, these are only tendencies; exceptions are all too easy to find. Patients were asked why they sought therapy; their therapists were also asked why they thought the patients sought the therapy; contrary to the tendencies just mentioned, the two groups tended to agree concerning the stated and ascribed motives (Gibb et al., 1983). Subtler aspects of the other's behavior can sometimes be anticipated, however, as when Scottish students fairly accurately indicated how persons of an opposite political viewpoint would respond to o a schedule seeking to measure moral reasoning (Emler et al., 1983).

5.4 Baffling Means

The search for adequate means to achieve desirable ends leads principals and observers into bypaths of infinite complexity that usually require replies to other probing questions and hence additional values. A compelling value, for example, is that of beauty *(Proposition 11.6)*, which is achievable in various ways, often in the West by seeing and appreciating works of art. Should those works be privately owned or exhibited in galleries? If they belong to the wealthy, their owners have an opportunity to live with them and enjoy their subtleties, but other persons are prevented from seeing them. The socioeconomic system, however, rewards those who succeed; hence they are the rightful owners. But suppose the owners are persons who acquire art objects through inherited wealth? The value of inheritance in the society then must be assessed. If the art works are exhibited publicly, all persons have the privilege of enjoying them, whether or not admission is charged. But the aesthetic reaction in a gallery to piles of paintings or sculptures is likely to be different from what ensues when the viewer is able to see one or more of the objects constantly in his home or in a public place such as in a post office.

To achieve victory over Germany, Japan, and Italy in World War II, the leaders of the United States and the United Kingdom used various savage means, such as firebombing German cities and dropping two atomic bombs on Japan. The end was achieved at the cost of millions of lives, of broken families, and of destroyed cities and cultural artifacts. Those means had other consequences that probably were not anticipated, such as the cold and hot wars that have followed World War II, the ghastly expenditures allegedly to secure military security, and the violence and terror almost everywhere. We dare not neglect, however, the perceived benefits from the war: the wiping out of the Nazis, the closer and friendly relations between France and Germany, the feeble yet frequent achievements of the United Nations, and numerous instances of postwar international cooperation.

Noble-sounding values can be easily formulated by someone steeped in the traditions of his society and capable of translating them into appealing language. Consider the following "beliefs," all of which are quoted verbatim from one document:

a rule of law which respects and protects without fear or favor the rights and liberties of every citizen

a system of democracy which insures genuine choice in elections freely held, free expression of opinion, and the capacity to respond and adapt to change in all its aspects

the political and economic systems of our democracies

close partnership among our countries in the conviction that this will reinforce political stability and economic growth in the world as a whole

the need for peace with freedom and justice

Also "genuine nonalignment" is to be respected and there must be a "determination to fight hunger and poverty throughout the world" ("Text . . .," 1984). The statement containing these phrases was released toward the end of the tenth annual economic summit meeting of seven powerful nations, including Great Britain, Japan, and the United States. But the means to achieve this "Declaration on Democratic Values" were not specified and perhaps never can be. Possibly also the declaration itself was not supposed to have implementing means; the series of clichés may have been meant simply to convince citizens everywhere that their leaders were on the side of conventional morality.

CHAPTER 6

The Imperative

It would be impossible and hence foolhardy to attempt to specify the imperative values that can become salient and produce a principal's moral judgments and behavior. Every philosopher or human being who dips into ethics or morality points to some of these values. Many social scientists who would "measure" values, I have indicated at the outset, do likewise if a bit more explicitly. For the moment the aim is more modest. I would suggest only the most general referents of the imperative values that are the responses to the probing question, *What ought I do?* The resolving of conflicts between values, or between values and the replies to other basic questions, I leave to the next chapter *(What shall I do?)*; and dreaming concerning prescriptive values is postponed until chapter 11. But first, if I may employ a metaphorical expression, I would invade the seat of values, conscience.

6.1 CONSCIENCE

Proposition: When habitual judgments do not guide judgments and behavior, when values are in conflict, and when a resolution is not immediately salient, principals may nevertheless pass judgment and behave in a manner they themselves consider both moral and appropriate; their conscience is activated.

Usually a principal can express verbally to himself if not to others the requirements of conscience, so defined. He may be aware of other motives and goals, of other rules and duties, of other consequences, but for him a prescriptive value becomes salient. Otherwise "what really prevents men who have authority from abusing their authority?" *(What can I do?)* and "what is it, if it is not force, that leads men to give obedience to authority?" *(What must I do?)* (Radcliffe, 1952,

p. 3). For both questions the reply can be some kind of internalized inhibition or conscience which, if violated, leads to remorse or regret. Presumably saints deliberately follow a set of inperative values to which they consistently adhere and which they may intuitively formulate; for them conscience is no problem, their response has become habitual. Nonsaints are less strict or consistent with reference to their own values, and they may regret lapses from their formulas.

Conscience or superego may be a flabby term, but there is no other way existentially to highlight a distinctly human attribute. An animal or a very young child who avoids desirable, attainable food as a result of punishment in the past is not obeying a conscience: in simple conditioning terms, perceiving the food evokes the anticipation of punishment associated with eating it and the judgment is nonmoral. But an older child who succumbs to temptation may suffer from pangs of conscience, whereas presumably the animal does not suffer. The pangs eventually may cause him not to eat the forbidden food; he makes a conscious choice; he follows, as it were, the dictates of a salient value; his judgment and behavior are morally related. Conscience is, or functions like, an imperative value concerned with more than a specific bit of behavior such as eating; its scope is more general; guilt results whenever a principal believes he himself has violated an important or imperative value or when he feels that someone else believes he has transgressed. The guilt may be as compelling as the threat of the lash from authority.

Skeptical Note: When does one follow the dictates of conscience?

6.2 SELF AND OTHERS

Proposition: Whether goals may be oriented toward the self, others, or self and others depends upon the principal's replies to the basic probing questions.

Incompatibility of goals or values is not inevitable since self does not necessarily mean selfishness: pride in one's own achievements may include concern for the welfare of others *(What will I do?)*. Time and resources are always limited, however, so that often a choice must be made, for example, between self-satisfaction and altruism or sacrifice for others *(What can I do?)*.

During social crises, the principal may well feel compelled to ask himself whether he should be guided by his own goals or those of his society. He may have no alternative, as when a draft-eligible male cannot or will not prevent himself from being inducted into the armed services *(What may I do?)*. Parents postpone or abandon their own plans for the benefit of their children. In an individualistic society the principal may believe that he himself has "inherent worth," and hence the "recognition and respect" he believes he merits from others enables him to ignore or slight them (Winch, 1972, p. 185).

Integrating or reconciling an interest in oneself and in others may not be easy. Inequality in some form exists or is tempting in all societies *(What shall I do?)*. In classical Marxist terms, exploitation occurs whenever the goods purchased by a worker embody "less labor time than he has worked" and hence the temporal exchange is inequitable; in socialist societies such "differential remuneration" is supposed to be given on the basis of skills or as a privilege associated with status (Roemer, 1982, pp. 121, 237, 240). Reconciliation of conflicting goals may be attempted and may even succeed without damaging the other interests within an industrialized society, such as productivity and efficiency.

Various measures can be adopted to avoid damaging others *(What do I do?)*. A principal obtains informed consent from the person with whom he will have contact so that the other person knows his intention and hence can agree or disagree to participate, for example, in an experiment, a bargaining session, or an informal social occasion *(Meandering 13.3)*. A surgeon almost never operates until the patient, if conscious, is willing; he outlines or should outline beforehand some of the problems and risks that may occur. But can the patient really grasp what he is being told? Is his consent therefore truly "informed"? Indeed the value of consent must constantly be violated. An infant is unable to give his consent except perhaps by smiling or howling as he is forced to carry out an action. Too often the principal's target has no alternative other than to obey. A dictator issues decrees without the consent of the governed, although ultimately he must accede to some of their needs if he or his successors are not to be overthrown. An unemployed worker may have to accept whatever work he can find.

The most consistent and poignant cry throughout the ages and especially perhaps in our time has been in behalf of justice. According to Aristotle, most institutions of a society are concerned with two types of justice: distributive ("the distribution of honor, wealth, and other divisible assets of the community, which may be allotted among its members in equal or unequal shares") and corrective (remedying a faulty exchange either in "voluntary" or in "involuntary"—"furtive" or "violent"—transactions) (Aristotle, 1934 ed., p. 267). In this context, too, reference is frequently made to some significant doctrine of human rights: the recognized positive and negative privileges that are supposed to be accorded principals (cf. Grice, 1967, pp. 39–40), almost regardless of their status within society and no matter under what political regime they chance to be living. One tenet of justice in the West and sometimes elsewhere, for example, is the right of anyone accused of a crime to fair treatment and a fair trial, which means, according to the laws and customs of the country in which he has been apprehended, that he is not held incommunicado, that he knows the charges being leveled against him, that his trial is not long delayed, and that the judge or jury is unbiased.

A principal concerned with administering distributive justice to another person is often torn between the values of equality and equity. Should the pie literally or figuratively be divided into equal slices or on the basis of each person's contribution or need? The question is unanswerable for all time and all situations, but it must be discussed as we dream about justice *(Proposition 11.4)*. In contrast, a principal who believes he has experienced injustice is likely to be counteraggressive, to engage in hostile behavior, or to seek restitution: his judgments are focused upon the other person or persons believed to be the cause of his misery. He may be, however, masochistic: I deserve to be punished or to be treated unjustly.

On occasion a principal bestows benefits upon others or seeks benefits from them. Although an impulse to be altruistic is directed toward others, the possibility is not excluded that the altruistic principal thereby benefits himself and increases his own satisfaction *(What might the consequences be?)*. Being altruistic rather than selfish is one of the central problems of morality: to transcend the self even for self-seeking reasons requires principals to reflect upon many of the probing questions and to possess a relevant value. It is not surprising, therefore, that both the literature on altruism and research concerned with helping others or being generous toward them are abundant.

Although most of this abundance looks toward the altruist, let us first consider the recipient. The reaction of a principal who is the potential or actual recipient depends, as might be anticipated, upon his own predispositions and the situation in which he finds himself. Receiving help, he may judge, can be embarrassing: it can threaten his own self-esteem; it may leave him indebted to the donor; it may result in a loss of power. Help may be rejected when the number of other persons witnessing his plight increases or when those witnesses are of higher rather than of lower status than himself (cf. Williams and Kipling, 1983). When the principal is desperate, he is likely to cast convention and pride aside and to seek or accept assistance. Anecdotally, however, most of us know persons who prefer to suffer rather than to be dependent upon others or otherwise to humiliate themselves. As might be expected, in various studies employing recipients who almost always were American undergraduates, these principals were often but not always grateful for receiving aid that turned out to be "a mixed blessing" and that could even seem threatening. Sometimes the donor was liked less after giving aid and was even derogated (Fisher et al., 1981).

Whether or not the principal himself is altruistic in general depends upon his own predispositions, which stem in large part from the way in which he has been socialized according to the mores of his society and from the teachings and practices of his parents. Conceivably even in Western society altruism can be a personality trait or a frequently salient value; at least some persons tend to be helpful fairly consistently in a variety of situations (cf. Zelden et al., 1984). Sociologically and anthropologically inclined theorists have stressed socialization per se as well as the demands of the principals' reference groups; the psychoanalytically oriented, the developments of conscience and "ego ideal," which means in part the structure of the ego; the devotees of social-learning theory, the habits that are reinforced, with particular emphasis upon modeling; and those enthusiastic about cognition, the manipulation of children's role-playing and efforts to change their perspectives. It is not wishy-washy to declare, as one psychologist has written, that each of these theories "complements the others by drawing attention to aspects of the nature and development of moral behavior that they neglect, and at the same time provides a language for studying these aspects" (Wright, 1971, p. 49).

Forward, then: in adults a variety of factors affects altruism (cf. Macaulay and Berkowitz, 1970; Staub, 1978, v. 1, pp. 44–45, 122). An ongoing motive may be decisive when the principal anticipates a material reward or some kind of social recognition or gratitude *(What might the consequences be?)*. He may or may not have the resources or skill enabling him to help *(What can I do?)*. He judges the type of assistance to be rendered *(What shall I do?)*. He is affected by the presence or absence of others in a position to assist the needy *(Proposition 5.4)*. If he lives under favorable circumstances, he may remove or prevent a sense of guilt by rendering assistance to others. Occasionally and for some persons the motive to help others rather than himself is overpoweringly salient *(What will I do?)*: the hypothetical or real mother who throws herself in the path of an oncoming car to save her child; parents who forgo their own pleasures so that their children may be properly educated; the soldier who truly regrets that he has but one life to give for his country; Jesus who allowed Himself to be crucified to atone for mankind's sins; and Gandhi whose prolonged and devastating bouts with voluntary starvation must have pained him physically but enabled him to attain many of his political objectives. Martyrs who perish rather than recant undoubtedly are thinking of others both now and in the future.

Often but not always critical is the principal's attitude toward the person or persons who need help. Sometimes he may believe all human beings contain a divine spark and should be both respected and assisted, but simultaneously he must note that some of them are rogues and dictators whose evil deeds do not encourage generosity. While believing strongly in justice or equity, he perceives that the other person violates these values. The reaction of others to the altruistic action may be anticipated: Will they be grateful? Will they reciprocate? Are demographic factors related to altruism? All the statements and questions in this and the preceding paragraph have been illustrated in experiments *(Meandering 6.1: The Diversity of Altruism)*. The emerging generalizations, when there are any, must be skeptically greeted: at the most what we have are sagacious hints.

Skeptical Note: But generally why is altruism so rare?

6.3 HAPPINESS

Proposition: Principals seek happiness for themselves.

Merely stating the proposition most certainly elicits groans from those philosophers who have convinced themselves that any doctrine of hedonism has been thoroughly punctured by their own keen analyses. If the concept of happiness makes the critics unhappy, let them use some other concept; but some word is essential to refer to a subjective state considered both desirable and attainable by everyone (Dewey, 1922, p. 179) *(Meandering 6.2: Happy Philosophers)*. Every human being wishes to be happy, however he defines this subjective state. He may deliberately make himself unhappy for the moment in order, he anticipates, to achieve greater happiness in the future. Almost any theory of learning contains an affective component relating to happiness, though the words are varied: gratification, drive re-

duction, positive reinforcement, and so on. One does not deliberately
lacerate one's own skin unless the hurt brings some kind of satisfaction, which may then appear perverse from an observer's standpoint. Imperative values are significant because they are associated
with a desirable, desired subjective state in which the positive out-
weighs the negative.

But, but—there are many buts philosophers and others are eager
to indicate. Only three need be mentioned here. First, the value and
the goal may be that of happiness, but achieving that state is admittedly ever a challenge *(Proposition 5.6)*. Then the happiness of the
selfish or unselfish principal may interfere with that of others in his
group or society. For this reason the value of happiness must be re-
considered as an essential dream under the heading of utilitarians
(Proposition 11.2); and for this reason, too, other values are instru-
mentally or pragmatically important. Finally, critics of this imperative
value take delight in pointing out that "happiness too long becomes
a bore," to which an astute engineer-philosopher has commented:

> Happiness is the one thing that people never get tired of; but they
> confound it with its causes—eating or drinking, or kissing or playing
> a harp—and so they mistake the thing they are tired of. They are
> tired of the cause for the very reason that it has ceased to be a cause
> of happiness. Hence they say exactly the opposite of what they
> mean. They *say* they don't like happiness when they *mean* they
> don't like unhappiness. (MacKaye, 1924, p. 284)

To avoid other misunderstandings, perhaps empirical research is
desirable. But that research has been both scarce and unproductive.
In the 1970s, for example, thousands of Americans responded to a
long questionnaire on happiness containing such questions as "In
general how happy have you been?" and "Was your first sexual experience a good one?" ' The analysis appears disappointing, essentially
banal, until it is remembered that these respondents were pointing
in the same affective direction. For example, in the words of the investigator: "people generally agree about what they mean by happiness . . . a positive, enduring state that consists of positive feelings
about the self and the world and . . . includes both peace of mind
and active pleasures and joy"; "happiness . . . depends on comparing
yourself to other people" since, if "you are doing better than they
are, you are happy; if you are doing worse, you are unhappy"
(Freedman, 1978, pp. 34–35, 220). The least that can be said is that
these Americans were able to respond to the questions, so that it is

clear that on a verbal level, as the author says in the first sentence of his book, "For most people happiness is what life is all about": the word triggers responses.

Any exposition concerning happiness, including this one, makes us think skeptically that we are not going to agree upon the name of the optimal state. No consensus can be forced upon us. And yet you surely wish to be healthy even when you are not conscious of your good health; and do you not prefer to laugh and smile rather than groan and cry?

Skeptical Note: And what is happiness?

6.4 FREEDOM

Proposition: At some point in each day and throughout his existence a principal is motivated to act as he wishes: his response to being blocked ranges from being superficially annoyed to being deeply frustrated.

One principal's freedom may be another's restraint or may require his consent. The dependence of infants upon their mothers and others is as compelling as is the requirement that two persons cooperate before and during normal sexual relations. Within limited spheres, freedom means the opportunity to choose between options and hence to engage in different kinds of behavior. Regardless of the motives of self and others *(Proposition 6.2)* and of the lure of happiness *(Proposition 6.3)*, the principal usually prefers to pass his own judgment and select his own action. Legal systems perforce are established to regulate some freedoms and to curb others; in democratic countries, it is assumed (or hoped) that authorities will not invade or disturb the privacy of the individual. But privacy cannot be easily defined or protected.

The nature and value of freedom are variously operationalized by principals and observers, but are likely to include a subjective feeling, first, that one may express oneself and select one's own goals and the means of achieving them—one is master of one's own destiny *(What will I do?)*, and, second, that one possesses the ability in fact to carry out one's judgments and intentions *(What can I do? What do I intend to do? What do I do?)* (cf. I. D. Steiner, 1970; Bidney, 1963). As a result, "a threat to or loss of freedom motivates the individual to restore that freedom," and hence, other things being equal, he is likely to value highly something he cannot have or an action he cannot perform. In different words, the desirability of an object or an action may increase when the freedom to acquire the object or perform the action is blocked. Such a tendency within recent years has been labeled "reactance" by a small, vocal group of American psychologists who suggest, on the basis of common sense and evidence ingeniously assembled largely in laboratory settings, that principals—and they mean their own subjects who are Americans—seek to restore or preserve a course of action when it is threatened or abandoned. The occurrence of reactance depends upon the importance of that action to the principal, the strength of the threat, and the simultaneous penalty for other actions (Brehm and Brehm, 1981, pp. 1–6). Thus any right protected by a constitution or custom will not seem important until an obstacle appears to prevent its exercise; curbing a desirable action limits the individual's freedom and results in reactance.

Although in Western society the word *freedom* tends to be used, especially by politicians, as an attractive cliché, its concrete reality in many contexts cannot be gainsaid. Unquestionably the child must metaphorically seek to stretch himself beyond the confines of his clothing or the embraces of his parents. The degree of freedom granted principals at different ages fluctuates from society to society.

The imperative value of freedom requires at least a small dose of skepticism: its desirability can be challenged on various grounds. Some principals and observers demand routines: making a decision for them may be difficult. When the options are too numerous or complex, according to a lay psychoanalyst whose way of life had been grievously hurt by the Nazis, principals may seek to "escape from freedom" (Erich Fromm, 1941, pp. 3–23). In addition, one person's freedom may curb another person's freedom of choice, so that in any society complete license is impossible. The variability that is ever present reflects an adaptation to diverse needs, which within each society are arranged along some hierarchy. Freedom of speech or assembly is abridged or abolished in time of war, presumably because it interferes with the war effort. Again the decision is a pragmatic one, which is not to say that safeguards for personal expression are superfluous.

To feel free to choose, therefore, the principal with or without power must be able to distance himself from options and weigh them carefully and reach a judgment favoring one value rather than another. As he compares the relative merits of options, eventually he must be skeptical concerning one or more of them; or he may be skeptical concerning the choice offered or dictated by someone else (cf. Weischedel, 1976, pp. 155–56). An occupation or profession, even one's mate, may be predetermined in some societies at birth, so that the principal's freedom is limited in such respects, even though within the restrictions and in other spheres he may exercise some discretion. Whether one principal can exercise his own freedom without interfering with "the right of another person to do and say as he pleases" also seems utopian (cf. Garcia, 1971, p. 25), but the skepticism dare not be pushed too far: however limited the options, they offer more freedom than masters and dictators ordinarily grant their serfs and followers.

Skeptical Note: Can the freedom of different persons or groups ever be compatible?

6.5 JUSTIFIABILITY

Proposition: Principals may select imperative values to guide their judgments and actions which they believe they can justify or, having selected the values, they then supply beliefs to justify them.

The prior or ex post facto beliefs accompanying imperative values may be true or false from the standpoint of an observer *(Propositions 3.3 and 9.1)*. To tell a lie deliberately the principal must be able to discern the truth (cf. Buber, 1953, p. 7): in any case, he specifies the reasons for acting or not acting as he does; these reasons are not necessarily the causes of his behavior (cf. Veatch, 1971, pp. 11–13). Justifications are legion, yet arbitrarily they may be divided into two pairs: those referring to the past and present or to the future, and those pointing to the principal himself or to others. The past may stress the will of a deity or the tradition of the society: we are commanded by the gods or by our ancestors or contemporaries to do this, and hence we do it. Or new conditions in our midst require a change in values, and hence we must adjust to them. The other type of justification suggests that the principal has good reason for his value or his action, or that the value is needed for the good of society.

Philosophers and others, as might be imagined, feel impelled to deal with justifications in a manner that leaves the rest of us skeptical concerning the possibility of finding solid bases for values other than by descending to a metaphysical, arbitrary level. Sometimes reference is made to a specific kind of justification, "metaethical," as the meaning of values is analyzed (cf. Frankena, 1963, p. 11). A modern philosopher suggests that principals justify values in five different ways, which can be briefly summarized, with apologies to the author, by ignoring his labels and substituting very approximate verbal translations: (1) almost everybody believes this; (2) I believe it, I'm not quite sure why; (3) it's important, otherwise there would be confusion or chaos; (4) I do my best under the circumstances; and (5) that's what I'm supposed to do (Becker, 1973, pp. 26–37). A typology of this sort is a tribute to the versatility of human reasoning, although it leaves us with no solid basis for distinguishing between rationalizations and truth.

Skeptical Note: When are justifications credible?

Envoi: Although principals grope to be at ease with their conscience and with other persons, although they possess varied imperative values, and although they seek elusive goals, *nevertheless* they catch glimpses of their heaven on earth.

MEANDERINGS

6.1 The Diversity of Altruism

Considerable research on altruism has been conducted in a nonaltruistic era. Many theorists have devoted their efforts to validating their own theories. Perhaps, as one writer notes, the research may remain after the theories "have been modified out of recognition" (Wright, 1971, p. 49). Let it be noted that typical of the best of the research is a volume containing numerous ingenious experiments performed in laboratories or in real life and employing questionnaires, simulations, and realistic demands; the witting or unwitting subjects have been American children, college students, and normal adults (Macaulay and Berkowitz, 1970). Illustrations follow.

Socialization. When samples of American children between the ages of four and six were given the opportunity to help another child, the percentage actually helping did not fluctuate as a function of the kind of preschool they were attending, but did with the type of help they rendered (Mussen and Eisenberg-Berg, 1977; Simmons and Sands-Dudelczyk, 1983). So far other studies on the topic have been inconclusive for two reasons. Again, the investigators have been wedded to their own theories, which have made them narrow the scope of the investigation. Then operational definitions of altruism and helping have almost always been employed (does the child help a peer? will he give some of his candy to someone else?), so that, as one competent review of this literature suggests, there have almost never been direct investigations of "what the intention was behind the child's actions" (Rushton, 1976). Thus the viewpoint not of the principal but of the observer has been reported, and necessarily so, since very young children cannot supply answers concerning their intentions.

Rewards and Recognition. Scattered evidence suggests that principals who were paid to help others tended to find what they did to be less interesting and less morally compelling than when they received no material rewards. In a carefully rigged experiment, however, Hebrew students who were rewarded for helping in a meaningful situation tended also to claim they were satisfied with what they had agreed to do, but only when they knew their statements would be seen by others and not when they were duped into believing they would have to tell the truth (Kunda and Schwartz, 1983). The presence of others may inhibit altruistic behavior as well as a sense of responsibility *(Proposition 4.6):* why should I do it, why not they? Both in the laboratory and in experimentally manipulated real situations it has been impressively and almost consistently demonstrated that the reward recognized by Americans is the presence of others: both students and adults have tended to assist persons in distress or otherwise to be generous in responding to the call or the need for help to a greater degree when they were alone and hence would be exclusively praised or thanked by the beneficiary than when they were in the company of others and hence would share the reward *(Proposition 5.4).* In fact, there was almost a negative linear relation between rendering assistance and the size of the group. Thus Canadian students were inclined to contribute more to charity when the appeal reached them alone rather than in a group. Of course other variables such as the sex of the person asking for help or the size of the donation could also have an effect (Wiesenthal et al., 1983).

Recipients. American undergraduates were asked to volunteer to supervise allegedly handicapped children. Those generally empathic toward others tended to volunteer when they believed the children would be responsive rather than unresponsive; the reverse tended to be true for those generally not empathic and hence preferring impersonal encounters (Barnett et al., 1983). Interacting with empathy may be the principal's view as to whether he can escape from the person needing assistance (Toi and Batson, 1982). The context may also be important: perhaps a principal is more likely to honor a request, especially in a worthy cause, when he has previously refused another request he has judged to be quite unreasonable (cf. Goldman et al., 1984) or if he has suffered from guilt because he did not comply. An exhaustive review of the research reveals that the reactions of the recipient likewise may depend upon various factors, such as the condition of the donor (for example, the resources at his disposal), the kind of assistance being rendered (solving a puzzle, receiving money for performing a task), the attributes of the recipient (his or her sex or needs), and the nature of the context (opportunity to reciprocate, appropriateness of the aid). Each new study turns up additional factors (such as the physical attractiveness of the recipient, the legitimacy of his request, the similarity of his political views) (M. Wilson, 1985), but the factors always interact with one another.

Predispositions. Although no compelling systematic model has emerged from the varied studies of altruism (cf. Staub, 1978, v. 1, pp. 17–22), one trend can be discerned: whether or not a principal helps is highly likely to be dependent upon his own predispositions. When he would have freedom for himself and be altruistic toward others, he may be able to resolve the conflict in favor of altruism by invoking another value such as a sense of justice referring to equity or equality. Thus again various values interact.

Under conditions of stress, it has been shown both in the laboratory and in a real situation that American undergraduates and adults who believed or actually possessed the necessary skill or competence *(What can I do?)* were more likely to be helpful than those who believed themselves deficient or who had not had relevant previous experience (Form and Nosow, 1958, pp. 22–29; Midlarsky, 1971). Without the necessary skill, therefore, altruistic judgments were less likely to be made or, if made, to be translated into behavior. And sociopaths—persons who reported tendencies considered antisocial—may have been less likely to render assistance than those not so classified, regardless perhaps of the anxiety experienced when viewing another person in distress (cf. Marks et al., 1982).

Demographic Factors. This line of research, though followed in most studies, is strewn with surprises. In one study, for example, children between the ages of four and five were told that donating gifts of candy to poor recipients either would make them happy or would give them "a tummy ache"; the control group was told nothing. Which communication, in comparison with the controls, affected the donation rate? No, the positive communication did not increase the donation, but the negative one did (Rosser, 1982). Perhaps size of community is relevant: principals in large cities are too overburdened to render assistance to their fellowmen and those in villages are more likely to be friendly toward their fellows. The experimental evidence in real-life situations, however, has produced contradictory results, at least among Americans. One Australian study perhaps throws the clearest light on the problem. It was conducted in fifty-five communities of varying sizes, and for five of the "informal" measures (for example, helping a confederate who apparently had a hurt leg, correcting inaccurate instructions given by one confederate to another), the percentage of those offering help decreased as the community size increased; but for a "formal," archival measure (filling out a census form), the reverse association appeared (Amato, 1983).

6.2 Happy Philosophers

I turn once again to Aristotle who apparently was not unhappy about happiness, for he stated the problem clearly:

> Inasmuch as all studies and undertakings are directed to the attainment of some good, let us discuss what it is that we pronounce to be the aim of Politics, that is, what is the highest of all the goods that action can achieve. As far as the name goes, we may almost say that the great majority of mankind are agreed about this; for both the multitude and persons of refinement speak of it as Happiness, and conceive "the good life" or "doing well" to be the same thing as "being happy." But what constitutes happiness is a matter of dispute. . . . Men have good reason therefore to pursue pleasure, since it perfects for each his life, which is a desirable thing (Aristotle, 1934 ed., pp. 11, 599).

Elsewhere Aristotle even suggests in effect the means to attain happiness: "good birth, the possession of many friends, the possession of good children, the possession of many children, a happy old age; further, such physical excellences as health, beauty, strength, stature, athletic ability; also fame, honor, good luck, virtue, . . . various kinds of power" (Aristotle, 1932 ed., pp. 24–25).

When a philosopher defines what he calls "teleological perfection" as "attaining that end in which it is one's nature to find final satisfaction" (Passmore, 1970, pp. 16–19), presumably he is referring to achieving goals in accordance with the principal's predispositions *(What will I do?)* and capabilities *(What can I do?)*, the net effect of which is some kind of hedonistic state. However compelling hedonism appears as a doctrine in view of the undeniable role of motives in determining or at least affecting behavior, either doctrine, as another philosopher has suggested, is only "a minimal one, a first base which we reach by universalizing self-interested decision making" (P. Singer, 1979, p. 13); thereafter the principal is challenged to find ways to achieve that state, and hence he must be guided by other values such as justice and by temporal considerations regarding attainment in the present or in the immediate or far-flung future.

Another philosopher at the turn of the century seems to have abandoned the quest: "Good," he wrote, "is incapable of any definition, in the most important sense of the word. . . . It is one of those innumerable objects of thought which are themselves incapable of definition, because they are the ultimate terms of reference to which whatever *is* capable of definition must be defined" (Moore, 1903, p. 9). One can sympathize with that position since, as the same author also points out, in a sense the color yellow cannot be defined connotatively except in terms of its denotative properties as perceived by persons or physicists. Perhaps, however, "happiness" faces the same problems, although its subjective meaning may be a little more precise than "good."

Semantic twists concerning "happiness" are as easy to collect as well-intentioned platitudes from contemporary statesmen. It has been pointed out that "there have been men who preferred to *suffer* for a noble cause" and that asceticism has often been the value of important religious leaders (Margenau, 1964, p. 202). But then it is so easy to say that not to suffer for such a cause or not to be ascetic in behalf of one's faith would have produced in these particular principals a state of unhappiness. Or a quibbling distinction has been made between the affective state and its causes: "Men do not work to maximize pleasure and minimize pain. . . . they work to produce pleasant things and to avoid painful things" (Skinner, 1971, p. 107). Of course. Similarly it appears that means and ends can be confused in such noble sentiments as the following: "man is neither dominated by the will-to-pleasure nor by the will-to-power, but by what I should like to call man's will-to-meaning" (Frankl, 1959, p. 97). For a few persons in Western society, probably among the educated elite, that quest for meaning is one that brings them deep satisfaction, pleasure, or happiness.

CHAPTER 7

Intention

When the principal has made all necessary preparation by replying, as it were, to the half dozen basic questions, then like a sprinter at the start of a race he hears or should hear himself say, "Ready, on your mark, get set, and . . ." But he may not go; overt behavior requires more complete readiness. Readiness means collating the replies to the basic questions concerned with his goal, his capability, the rules, his duty, his anticipations, the relevant salient values, and even an imperative value. In fact, "morals has to do with all activity into which alternative possibilities enter" (Dewey, 1920, p. 278), for otherwise, from the standpoint of the principal, habits become the guide. It has been argued that the "possession of values alleviates man's search for meaning, because at least in typical situations he is spared making decisions." Immediately, however, the same writer—a philosophical psychiatrist and Holocaust survivor—also notes that all hesitation is not eliminated: two or more values may "collide." He then defines the possibility of collision inasmuch, he reminds himself, as values are arranged in a hierarchy; yet then again he eventually contemplates "decision-making": the principal is "always free to accept or to reject a value he is offered by a situation" (Frankl, 1970, pp. 56–57). The very fluctuations of this gentle man indicate his own hesitation. Few principals, moreover, have their values neatly ranked or rated so that they can immediately or even ultimately decide which is more pressing, which is imperative; they must contemplate what they intend to do.

Somehow the principal under these circumstances tries to reach a behavioral decision, unless he would avoid making one or unless he would rather procrastinate. On a conscious level he may seek advice from others or he may rehearse within himself his various options. Prayer may serve many functions, such as expressing gratitude to a

115

deity or seeking favors, and it may also enable the individual to reach an understanding with himself. A distinguished biologist, largely on the basis of data obtained in Great Britain from principals who report that they have had a profound religious experience, may be correct when he universalizes his findings: "The effect of general prayer is the sense of receiving help, strength, and encouragement, power, and a great zest to do much that one feels is worth doing for the good of the world and one's fellows" (Hardy, 1979, pp. 137–38). A principal with such a "sense" presumably has passed a moral judgment with increased conviction and he knows what he intends to do; under the circumstances the judgment seems to be demanding or required, although some judgments must be immediately or eventually rejected (Köhler, 1938, pp. 336–39).

The problem of intention, therefore, is at the core of the search for moral judgments and actions (cf. Franklin, 1968, p. 308). When an intention has been formulated, the principal has "one foot in the present and the other foot in the future" (Meiland, 1970, p. 192). If the other foot is thought to be guided by an imperative value, then the judgment is moral, whether complete or deficient. A neurobiologist has argued philosophically that by including intention within a purview it becomes feasible to distinguish between the apparent kindness and helpfulness displayed by animals toward one another (which he calls "instinctive" and considers to be "pseudoaltruism") and the altruism sometimes occurring among human beings (Eccles, 1980, pp. 202–07), especially, I add, when the generosity results from an imperative value. Principals who are consciously aware of alternative courses of action are forced or force themselves to pass judgment and to make a selection, even though philosophers and social scientists may maintain that, unknown to them, their choice has been predetermined. We are concerned now—in a nonpejorative sense—with casuistry, the principal's own effort to resolve conflicting tendencies within himself. Shall I tell a lie to avoid hurting my sensitive friend or shall I follow a value that orders me always to tell the truth? In the words of another philosopher, am I not entering "the sphere of meta-ethics" by reflecting upon what I am doing when I pass judgment (McCloskey, 1969, p. 1)? Aristotle observed, "If a man has struck a blow . . ., it does not follow that he has committed wanton outrage; the blow must be struck with a certain motive such as insult to the victim or the gratification of the striker" (Aristotle, 1934 ed., pp. 75–76).

It is at this point, as a principal contemplates action, that he does or does not guide himself by whatever values have affected his replies to the other probing questions. "To avoid stealing for fear of imprisonment is not a morally good reason in [presumably American or Western] culture" (Edel and Edel, 1968, p. 171). Why not? Such a person presumably estimates his own capability *(What can I do?)*, he is acquainted with rules concerning stealing *(What may I do?)*, and he anticipates punishment as the penalty *(What would the consequences be?)*, but he does not invoke the imperative value that stealing under any circumstance is immoral. The replies to the three questions may have evoked generally various values, but it is the presence or absence of another expressible value that must decisively affect intention before the judgment becomes morally complete.

7.1 MULTIVARIANCE AND WEIGHTING

Proposition: When moral or nonmoral judgments do not clearly and compellingly emerge, the salient variables are weighted.

In so many situations options are available and a choice must be made: there is hesitation; established habits do not point unequivocally to action. In conventional arithmetic, one psychologist suggests (Wertheimer, 1961), a gap can be filled in only one way unless one wishes for some reason to be perverse: there is but a single answer to the problem of $3 + 9 = X$. In contrast, there may be many ways to fill a judgmental gap, to find the value or to select the action when the principal is confronted with options; for example, should he take a vacation trip or donate the same money to help combat starvation in Africa? Which alternative is more important? Which receives more weight? A philosopher has called the solution to this dilemma "the priority problem" when two values or contradictory anticipations concerning justice are in conflict (Rawls, 1971, pp. 40–45). What then does the principal decide to do? It is all very well to maintain idealistically that "every man must decide for himself according to his own estimate of conditions and consequences" (Fletcher, 1966, p. 37); yet this cannot mean that a principal always permits himself, or is permitted by external circumstances, to take all the relevant probing questions into account or, for that matter, to achieve the individual optimization usually postulated by classical economists. The balancing is not perfect, but it is seldom fortuitous or completely irrational.

When or if a principal weights relevant variables, he might phrase the probing questions as follows:

Motive: Do I truly value what I wish to do?
Capability: Am I convinced I can accomplish what I wish to do?
Rule: What value do I place upon the relevant rule? Should or must I obey it or may I disobey it?
Duty: How important is my obligation to do that?
Anticipation: Can I be sure the consequences I expect will really come to pass?
Imperative: Is the value guiding me particular or imperative? Does it permit me to make an exception?

Merely raising the questions suggests that one or more of the replies are more compelling than the others and can influence the principal's intention. An individual or people generally in a particular society may believe that obedience *(What must I do?)* or concern for other persons *(What would the consequences be?)* should always or almost always be paramount, come hell or high water; other factors are then weighted much less or ignored. A modern philosopher notes that his colleagues, in the manner of skeptics, sometimes resort to intuition or a "gut feeling" when they are convinced that there is no "rational procedure" to establish priority among competing values (Melden, 1977, pp. 123–24). The problem of weighting is especially acute for leaders of large organizations; what is the best course owners or managers should follow to foster the welfare of their workers and safeguard their own profits?

The weighting is influenced by the event or the situation at hand as well as by the principal's predisposition. Possibly adults lay more stress upon consequences when the effects appear to be serious (other persons may be hurt or treated unjustly) than when conventional behavior is to be transgressed (wearing the wrong clothes or using an impolite form of address); but conventional rules are not easily ignored by most persons. Children may not begin to acquire "respect for [an] authority figure's power" until they have reached the age of nine or more (Damon, 1983, p. 167). It all depends, yes, it all depends; principals are frequently driven by many predispositions. It is for this reason, as will and must be trumpeted in part 3, that for the observer no easy solution to the problem of morality is ever or even conceivably possible; some skepticism is essential.

Any pressing problem demands that numerous factors be weighted. The assessment of risks in the modern world is a case in point *(Proposition 8.2)*. On a social or political level, leaders must estimate the capabilities of their constituencies and the possible consequences of decisions as they contemplate the risks created by measures related, for example, to social welfare or disarmament. The weighting of intent and consequences is especially challenging for jurists *(Meandering 9.2: Responsibility and the Law)*.

Another problem: can we believe a principal who after the fact states quite bluntly what his intention has been? The answer must be affirmative only if he or she is like George Washington who allegedly never told a lie. Perhaps also the consequence of the expressed intention may be taken into account. Someone confessing a crime in order to shield someone else is not telling the truth. The assassin of a public figure or the powers behind the suicidal bombing of an embassy may admit their responsibility and refer to a value that in their view justifies their intention.

Skeptical Note: Can one ever be certain that the "correct" weights are assigned to interacting processes?

7.2 SITUATION AT HAND

Proposition: Intentions are affected significantly but not exclusively by the situation at hand.

Social scientists, especially sociologists, mention again and again the obvious but significant fact that behavior tends to fluctuate with the role demanded by other persons in different situations and by the situations themselves. An individual acts differently in his various roles as parent, employee or employer, tennis partner, or hospital patient (Ossowska, 1970, pp. 64–66). Similarly, different values become salient as the situation demands. Americans are said to use one standard of values in their face-to-face contacts but another in political life; this could be phrased as a contradiction between private and public morality. When principals are dealing directly with other persons, values like kindness and fairness may predominate; but in politics ruthlessness and carelessness are more likely to be salient among many American political leaders, though not necessarily so. Sometimes such situation-determined judgments or behaviors are called opportunistic, sometimes adaptive. Studies of political preferences among Americans, for example, suggest that many or most voting decisions especially during presidential elections depend not upon a more or less constant political philosophy but upon the personality of the candidates, their performance in office and on television programs, the party platforms, party affiliation, the condition of the economy, and various demographic factors. One study, utilizing national samples prior to the 1980 campaign, indicates that prospective voters' emotional reactions to the candidates were then both positive and negative and tended to account statistically for their voting intentions to a greater degree than the traits they ascribed to the candidates (Abelson et al., 1982): their momentary attitudes spoke louder than their beliefs.

Although principals are situationists to some extent, all behavior is not situation-determined: varying degrees of consistency are evident, personality traits may prevail to some extent, and a touch of absolutism is inevitable *(Proposition 3.6)*. A supreme egotist, though perforce limited somewhat by the rules prevailing in each situation *(What may I do?)* and perhaps affected from time to time by the duty he knows he is expected to perform *(What must I do?)*, is likely to make moral or nonmoral decisions as a result of the personal goals he seeks *(What will I do?)*. Principals themselves, moreover, may recognize that exceptions occur as they contemplate their future behavior. They are able to distinguish between what they intend to do and what they expect to happen *(What might the consequences be?)*. Perhaps their expectations turn out to be more accurate or realistic than their intentions, especially when the behavior in question involves elements over which they do not have direct control. In addition, some principals may have been socialized or instructed in such a manner tthat they may never see the far-flung implications of the values they acquire. Religious values are sometimes thought to be restricted to a limited number of church-related situations, not to everyday life. Principals may have good reason to avoid utilizing values in some situations; sometimes, they are convinced, it is more important to be successful than to show concern for one's fellow human beings. Or, to borrow a term from a philosopher, "moral weakness" prevents them "from acting in accordance with clearly recognized principles in circumstances to which they are clearly applicable" (Körner, 1976, p. 190). The moral and legal implications of situationism cannot be easily or glibly ignored (cf. Cross, 1968). We thus emerge with a vivid description of why we live in an imperfect world and why skepticism concerning appreciable improvement in that world is unavoidable.

Skeptical Note: Is there a difference between being opportunistic and responding to situations?

7.3 EXCEPTIONS

Proposition: Unanticipated unusual situations, conflicts in values, and incompatible replies to probing questions often require exceptions contrary to salient values or intentions.

The existence of exceptions, breaches of imperative values, departures from the habitual offer another reason to be skeptical concerning the possibility of achieving perfection. A principal has no inclination to murder another human being, every aspect of his background disapproves of murder, but suddenly he kills someone in self-defense or in order to save another person he cherishes. Who, even when he proclaims his devotion to telling the truth, would not protect a "good" person in hiding by giving false or no information to his potential "evil" murderer who asks his whereabouts? The exception that tests the rule may not be straightforward: any exception requires another judgment stemming from a different value and hence is derived from a previously existing or an emerging hierarchy of values. Some reason can be found, therefore, to alter rules and duties, however strict they apparently are.

In contrast, games have rules that cannot be modified. Someone like an umpire or a referee is given the power to enforce them and not to tolerate exceptions. When necessary, but not during a game, a new rule is added to which the players then must conform: in a chess tournament a specified time is allotted for each player to make his next move. Life, as a philosopher might say, however, is not a game.

The most notable and perhaps frequent reason for intending an exception occurs when two values are incompatible. Many principals in modern countries seek "uninterrupted peace among nations" and also "unfettered sovereignty of nations" (J. F. A. Taylor, 1966, p. 153). One of these values must be sacrificed; an exception to it becomes necessary. Trivial, apparently nonmoral conflicts plague us almost every hour of the day: should we eat what appeals to us or what promotes health? I presume you do not have the freedom to shoot your neighbor when his television keeps you awake at night, however much I would encourage you to do so; and he in turn does not have the right to punish his child by beating him unconscious, however much you and he cherish freedom for all. A principal may kill in self-defense if from a legal standpoint he can prove that his life was being threatened; in time of war soldiers may receive commendation, raises in rank, and honors for killing persons temporarily called enemies; counterillustrations for any imperative value can be discovered with careless ingenuity *(Meandering 7.1: Coping with Exceptions)*.

Again and again in Western society we are admonished not to make exceptions or at least not glibly to do so. A truly moral person always adheres to his principles (that is, values) and tolerates no exceptions;

he avoids the sin of "inconsistency" (Brandt, 1959, pp. 16–18); he should be an "absolutist," not a "situationist" *(Proposition 3.6)*. Perhaps such a view itself is a utopian fiction designed to discourage exceptions. It is unrealistic, however, to imagine that principals can forever adhere to their values. On the other hand, in our society the ability to compromise—that is, to cast aside a value or objective in favor of a temporary gain or the resolution of a conflict—is usually considered a virtue, not a defect. Not to abandon a value in favor of one less than ideal is thought to be a symptom of rigidity; but abandoning it reveals weakness under pressure. Whether two principals in conflict can achieve, through interaction or negotiation, not a compromise but a resolution or integration of their disagreements is one of the challenges of our era, as one views conflicts between married people, labor and management, or nations.

Principals are able, perhaps too easily, to find and then plead extenuating or mitigating circumstances to justify exceptions. As a result of ingesting a drug, an otherwise normal principal cannot resist an uncontrollable impulse he normally represses and he then insults or injures another person, an action that would not have occurred, it is presumed, if it had not been for the drug. Is he responsible for that action or, if not, is he responsible for having taken the drug? Who is responsible for making the drug available, for making him succumb to using the drug? The very notion of mitigating circumstances raises again the intriguing question of responsibility from the standpoint of observers *(Proposition 9.3)*. Those living in the complex societies of the West, which do not provide ready-made solutions to numerous problems and challenges of everyday life, have at their disposal many reasons for finding exceptions to values. The alibis or rationalizations, if they be such, moreover, may not be fully conscious: the individual may be convinced that he must deceive or lie for the benefit of some noble formula. Little wonder that many principals are not absolutists but tend to be situationists or somewhere in between *(Proposition 3.6)*.

The political scientist whose six categories of metaethical beliefs have been previously outlined *(Meandering 3.5)* has sought to rescue himself and mankind from subjectivism and relativism. According to him, an imperative value that would be objective must claim, roughly in the writer's own words, to be rationally unquestionable, without exception, applicable to any moral problem, justifiable according to an unbiased observer, consistent with conscientious moral decisions, and applicable with strict impartiality (Fishkin, 1984, pp. 45–81). After considerable soul-searching and critical attacks upon others toiling in the identical vineyard, he argues that the belief concerning "considerations that anyone should accept, were he to view the problem from what is contended to be the appropriate moral perspective," enables a principal to rescue himself from subjectivity and to be objective. That alternative, he points out, permits exceptions, but otherwise it satisfies all the other claims. The bow to exceptions is the significant point here; but, as will be emphasized later *(Proposition 13.6)*, the abstract criteria for general values do not provide mankind with a concrete, morally complete program.

Deceiving and lying, therefore, can easily be justified. Principals know they cannot tell the "whole truth" because such a truth is out of reach. They may not be aware that they are lying; perhaps they deceive themselves. They tell white lies because they fail to reflect, because they wish to be sociable, because they would exhibit themselves in a favorable light. In the West they know that lying can be expedient when they are asked to write a letter of recommendation for an acquaintance or to express judgment in front of someone they would not offend. A psychologist who has examined lying both clinically and politically wonders what would happen in our society "if we could never lie, if a smile was reliable, never absent when pleasure was felt, and never present without pleasure." In fact, "life would be rougher than it is, many relationships harder to maintain. Politeness, attempts to smooth matters over, to conceal feelings one wished one didn't feel—all that would be gone" (Ekman, 1985, p. 283). Lying and deceptions as well as the closely allied practice of secrecy are thus woven into the web of a principal's personality and his society.

The challenge always exists: when are there extenuating circumstances that justify a lie? Should the physician tell the patient with cancer that his disease is incurable and that his life expectancy is definitely limited and thus becloud whatever time remains for him? Should foster parents tell their adopted child at an early age, whether or not he asks them, that they are not his biological parents? Should a man in our society tell his beloved wife that in his opinion her beauty is beginning to fade? In time of war should the commander of an army reveal the current casualty figures among his soldiers and thus run the risk of allowing the enemy to acquire valuable information? Is not bluffing permissible in poker? May not a football player mislead the opposing team concerning the next play?

The very expression "white lies" suggests that principals believe some lies to be harmless, perhaps even laudable because of their ends. Samples of American undergraduates quite consistently rated a series of lies on a continuum ranging from "extremely wrong" to "permissible." Least permissible was telling "a lie that hurts someone else, so that you can gain"; most permissible was telling "a lie to save others from minor hurt, shame, or embarrassment"; somewhat in between was telling "a lie that will influence others in an official position in such a way that you will gain by their response to you, but they will not be harmed" (Lindskold and Walters, 1983). The ranking of lies seems to have been made on the basis of the motives and intention attributed to the liar, whether selfless or selfish.

A more general and trenchant analysis of lying and deception as exceptions to an otherwise strict morally complete judgment favoring honesty has been provided by a philosopher whose thesis seems to be—with some misgivings—that both misrepresentations are inevitable exceptions to telling the truth, especially when they are encouraged by society or when some principals are unable to act otherwise. She indicates again and again, most convincingly, the dangers of lying for both the liar and his victims, yet she is forced to admit that circumstances provide liars with "the strongest excuse for their behavior"; therefore she cannot support the "absolutist rejection of all lies," even though "line-drawing is a hard task once one leaves the domain of the clear-cut life-threatening crisis." Lies should be, however, limited in scope and often eliminated by effective ethical codes *(Proposition 13.4)* for industry and other institutions and of course through education. Her final hymn: "trust and integrity are precious resources, easily squandered, hard to regain" and "they can thrive only on a foundation of respect for veracity" (Bok, 1978, pp. 118–19, 248–49).

Deception may have future consequences not intended by the principal *(What would the consequences be?)*. If it is unmasked, the deceived person may behave differently in the future. A customer who has been misled to expect merchandise to be first-rate subsequently does not patronize the shop. The owner who instructs the clerk to lie may secure a momentary gain while anticipating that the future loss either will not occur or will be of no concern to him.

Secrecy is a negative form of lying: you do not tell another person what you know or believe to be true. Only a spy reveals to the enemy a secret military plan or significant item of intelligence. Unless he wishes to damage another person or simply engage in gossip, a principal does not communicate a defect of that person to others; he respects privacy. Unless he would lose his own sense of integrity, he does not express, perhaps even to his spouse or best friend, some of his repressed impulses. Unless there is some very good reason, the physician, the psychiatrist, or the ordinary mortal does not convey to others secrets that have been given him in confidence. Lies, all lies: information in all these instances is being withheld from someone else. Again, it is presumed, the holder of the secret would suffer from not keeping that secret, inasmuch as "control over secrecy and openness gives power; it influences what others know, and thus what they choose to do" (Bok, 1982, p. 282). A secret is not kept when the principal would disturb the integrity of his relation with the secret giver or the group to which he belongs. A distinction, however, must be drawn between the welfare of the secret giver and the others: a principal who is told in strictest confidence by a deranged terrorist that he has planted a bomb in an open marketplace or in airplane baggage will—and should—have no qualms about informing the police. And so secrecy may be violated—an exception is made. But of course the spy who commits treason by betraying his country may be convinced that his exception will redound eventually to the benefit of mankind as well as to the foreign country that hires him.

Self-deception is difficult to unravel: the principal seemingly makes an exception to utilize for himself the best or most accurate knowledge available to him. He may be unaware of what he is judging or doing, as when he rationalizes a decision. Or he may deliberately prevent himself from acquiring certain knowledge—so called constructive ignorance—for fear that relevant information will make it difficult to function as he wishes to function. On occasion an American lawyer prevents himself from knowing all there is to know about his client, for such knowledge he believes would act upon him as a constraint (Taylor, 1983). Some ignorance is unavoidable; if we knew in detail the experiences suffered by starving people, we might be unable to eat our own meals with any gusto.

The skeptical conclusion to this discussion of lies and deception, white and otherwise, must be that no value can possibly cover all contingencies for virtually every principal. Conceivably one might think of superordinate or universal values for which exceptions are very few in number—to thyself be true, my interest comes first, anything the priest says must be true and good—but even then the particulars are missing and some of them may require exceptions. To thyself be true: is the principal truer to that self when on one occasion he is selfish and on another generous? Both selfishness and generosity may be embraced by the self, yet then the value leading to judgment and action is not unequivocal. Or even a broad and highly respected value in the West, that of tolerance, can guide behavior only up to a point—a point that is reached undoubtedly when one's own body, kin, community, or nation is threatened.

Skeptical Note: When and why is one value so compelling that it requires an exception to another value?

7.4 REASONED JUDGMENT

Proposition: Reasoned judgments may be passed when habits do not resolve conflicts between replies to one or more of the probing questions.

A reasoned judgment can be the penultimate outcome of the responses to the preceding probing questions: it is a kind of cognitive judgment considered necessary under the circumstances; the principal weights the knowledge and values interacting within himself. If he has never stolen in the past and never even contemplated stealing, whatever judgment he makes need not be reasoned: the habitual reaction suffices; his response in effect is mandatory, not optional. When alternatives appear possible and after weighing all the factors he considers to be relevant, the principal says to himself, this is what I wish to do and I have good—or sufficiently good—reason for doing so. A reasoned judgment is not necessarily moral from the standpoint either of the principal or of the observer.

Some judgments are made instantly, others are delayed. Merely contemplating the wanton killing of a child or the commission of a "sin" generally requires little reflection before feeling or expressing disapproval. Nobody presumably likes the reality of death, but the initial judgment may be cast aside: "Horror at the sight of death," it was once said, "turns into satisfaction that it is someone else who is dead" (Canetti, 1962, p. 227). When Americans are asked by a pollster their opinion of the president, they may delay their response to weigh his good and bad points. Without deifying reason or deprecating habits, it is at least possible to imagine that hesitation and reasoning may help the principal achieve some insight into himself and his own predispositions so that he can avoid the kinds of evil resulting from failure to understand himself or from his own impulsiveness (Doob, 1978, pp. 86–87).

The outcome of a reasoned judgment is likely to be a statement of intention by the principal either to himself or to others: I intend to be a good citizen; I intend to tell the whole truth for the following reasons. But complications arise. A young child, when questioned, may claim that he intended a particular action and hence declares himself responsible; but then adults or courts of law may assert that the very fact of his age means that the judgment behind his act could not have been fully reasoned and therefore he cannot or should not be punished at all, or punished as severely as an adult would be after committing the same act *(Proposition 9.3)*. Then a principal may be, as the phrase goes, "well intentioned," but he may be concealing from himself his true intentions, true in the sense that some of his motives may be unconscious and some of the anticipated consequences unforeseeable: his reasoning has been faulty. Or he may provide himself beforehand with a rationalization: if they catch me, I shall tell them that I did not mean to do it, it was an accident. Some actions, though carefully and honestly reasoned at the outset, cannot possibly be the result of reasoning when they turn out to be truly accidental. A driver who intends for very good moral or nonmoral reasons to reach a destination on time collides with another car; certainly he did not intend the collision, which, however, becomes the consequence either of his original intention to get to work (cf. Fincham and Jaspars, 1980; Sabini and Silver, 1982, pp. 65–67) or, of course, of his having driven too quickly or carelessly. For that matter, a motorist certainly does not intend to contribute to the traffic traveling along the same road or to the companies profiting from the gasoline his car consumes. Also inadequate knowledge inevitably produces inadequate reasoning. A parent cannot possibly know precisely how he will affect in the long run the child he praises or scolds. Knowledge within the society may not have diffused to a principal: he knows he is ill but believes he is not a health menace to others if he takes certain precautions that happen to be ineffective.

Eventually, as one philosopher has suggested, "a chain of practical reasons" provided by a principal "must come to an end when one reaches an ultimate reason for which no further reason can be given; at this point one can only say: 'I cannot give any reason for performing actions of this kind; I just happen to approve of the performance of such actions.' " I am giving money to that beggar because I don't want him to starve; I don't want him to starve because I would prevent unnecessary suffering; I would prevent unnecessary suffering because I want to do so (cf. Norman, 1971, pp. 8–9). Perhaps philosophy has arisen in order to halt this infinite regress or at least to make its end point seem abstractly profound, reasonable, or respectable.

In various ways and for various reasons the principal may convince himself that a judgment is unavoidable (Stevenson, 1963, pp. 139–46). Other persons directly or through institutions give him no alternative—allegedly. He may admit that at the outset options were available but, having begun to smoke or to be dependent on someone, thereafter he has had no other realistic option. He may subscribe to an overall fatalistic philosophy and thus convince himself that destiny or the gods themselves have removed other options. He may truly have been unable to anticipate all possible consequences in detail. As ever, rationalizations are easy to come by.

At least on a conscious level principals determine their judgments by balancing, weighting, and revising the bases for their judgments. The reasoning may include all the factors potentially or actually contributing to the judgment, such as the values applicable to the situation (is it more important to be loyal than to be truthful?), the person or persons to be affected by the ensuing action (will this person be pleased, that person disturbed?), and the principal's own responsibility in the situation (is it really necessary to pass judgment or to take action?). The ways in which children and, less so, adults arrive at such judgments have been assiduously studied by numerous investigators. What often emerges, not without debate and certainly not unanimously, has been the view that principals go through various "stages" as they mature (cf. Graham, 1972, pp. 180–91). At each stage the reasoning is different, and some principals in modern societies and many elsewhere never reach a so-called higher stage. One observation cannot be too strongly emphasized: the children and adults who have been investigated perforce provide information about their reasoning only when they are questioned by an investigator; ordinarily they may habitually pass judgment without cataloging their reasons. It is thus assumed that, as they formulate and carry out their own intentions, they reason similarly either privately or in relevant situations. Maybe yes, maybe no, the skeptic must add, but probably yes.

The outpourings on the problem of stages are so numerous that only the salient issues can be discussed in a separate meandering which in this instance is most aptly named *(Meandering 7.2: The Pursuit of Moral Stages)*. The flavor of the cognitive research is best conveyed here by citing the schema most frequently quoted, abbreviated slightly but in one of the shifting versions provided by the author himself:

Stage 1. Punishment and Obedience
    Content: literal obedience to rules and authority, avoiding
        punishment, and not doing physical harm

Perspective: egocentric; [judging actions] in terms of physical
consequences rather than [the] psychological interests
of others

Stage 2. Individual Instrumental Purpose and Exchange
Content: serving one's own or other's needs and making fair
deals
Perspective: Individualistic; [separation of] own interests and
points of view from those of authorities and others

Stage 3. Mutual Interpersonal Expectations, Relationships, and
Conformity
Content: playing a good (nice) role, being concerned about
other people and their feelings, being motivated to
follow rules and expectations
Perspective: the individual in relationship to other individuals,
the "concrete Golden Rule," putting oneself in the
other person's shoes

Stage 4. Social System and Conscience Maintenance
Content: doing one's duty in society, upholding the social order, and maintaining the welfare of society or the
group
Perspective: [differentiation of] societal point of view from interpersonal agreement or motives

Stage 5. Prior Rights and Social Contract or Utility
Content: upholding the basic rights, values, and legal contracts
of a society, even when they conflict with the concrete rules and laws of the group
Perspective: aware of values and rights prior to social attach-
ments and contracts

Stage 6. Universal Ethical Principles
Content: guidance by universal ethical principles that all humanity should follow
Perspective: moral point of view from which social arrangements derive or on which they are grounded (Kohlberg, 1976)

Somewhat flamboyantly the author calls stages 1 and 2 "precon-
ventional," 3 and 4 "conventional," and 5 and 6 "postconventional
and principled" (Kohlberg, 1983, pp. 209–12). From the standpoint
of the analysis in this book the shift from an essentially nonmoral
stage 1 to the later stages that become morally more complete rep-
resents less concern for rules and duties *(What may I do? What must
I do?)* or the anticipation of consequences for the principal himself

(What would the consequences be?) and greater concern for the anticipation of consequences for others and especially for general values:
the process of passing judgment becomes increasingly complex. The
progenitor of the schema reports that none of his subjects in the
United States, Israel, and Turkey apparently has reached stage 6
(Kohlberg et al., 1983, p. 60), but a few have attained an even higher
seventh stage. At that stage principals identify themselves "with the
cosmic or infinite perspective" and "value life from its standpoint";
they have "most distinctively religious experiences of union with deity, whether pantheistic or theistic" (Kohlberg, 1983, pp. 345–70).

Details concerning the stages may be missing, the techniques may
be imperfect and not standardized, and most probably many principals, especially English and American students, fall between the
stages and may frequently flit from one stage to another in judging
different situations (Fishkin, 1984, pp. 5–9; Kohlberg and Higgins,
1984), but this conclusion is inescapable: "reasoning" (so measured)
to reach morally complete judgments emerges slowly, it is not a genetic or god-given talent, and it varies considerably from person to
person and from society to society. We must be skeptical, therefore,
concerning any attempt to assume that principals are inherently good
or bad or that we can find prescriptive values they "instinctively" acknowledge. They possess the capacity to change—to reach a "higher"
stage, if you insist—but the progression is not inevitable.

Skeptical Note: Should a character in a Russian novel be believed
when he states that "reason had never had the power to define
good and evil, or even to distinguish between good and evil,
even approximately; on the contrary, it has always mixed them
up in a disgraceful and pitiful way"? (Dostoyevsky, 1936 ed., p.
254)

7.5 FEASIBILITY AND PROCRASTINATION

Proposition: Under varying conditions reasoned judgments do not
give rise immediately to appropriate behavior; procrastination
has advantages and disadvantages.

The principal may wonder whether he should or can carry out his
reasoned judgment to behave appropriately. Desirable consequences
may well have been anticipated before an actual judgment, but then
other conceivable consequences are taken into account *(What might
the consequences be?)*. New information becomes available. Conditions

in the society change. Other prophets appear and offer different rewards and punishments. Means are lacking, it is discovered, to implement the intention *(What can I do?)*. The principal begins to wonder
whether he is capable of reaching the goal. He may empathize with
victims—say, whales or seals being slaughtered for commercial reasons
(Shelton and Rogers, 1981)—and he may be horrified by what is
happening to them, but he will not signify his intention to assist them
unless he or someone makes him acquainted with practical actions
he might conceivably take *(What do I do?)*.

The principal may be convinced that it is his duty to lead people
out of the wilderness and away from sin, but simultaneously he realizes he lacks authority, the resources that accompany authority, indeed most of the necessary demographic attributes that facilitate
leadership *(What can I do?)*. He is convinced he cannot realize his
dream.

Nonfeasibility as well as other inhibitions prevent principals who
call themselves good Christians, Jews, Muslims, or members of any
other great religion from realizing the values they profess because of
their affiliations with these denominations. They believe they would
be ridiculed if they followed the tenets of their creed, or the required
self-sacrifice would interfere with the attainment of more personal
goals.

The consequences of temporarily postponing a judgment or action
after an initial reasoned judgment to act vary from sterility to creativity. A principal is not likely to delay or postpone either one when
past habits prevail; then, as has been repeatedly emphasized, he leaps
from perception to behavior via habit without making an intervening
judgment *(Proposition 4.2)*. Delays, however, can be desirable and
useful for many reasons. Opponents of the apartheid regime in South
Africa, including some black lawyers, have had little enthusiasm for
trying to reform the legal system in order to improve the justice accorded blacks, for they have believed that they thus would acknowledge the existence of a system they would radically change; they have
been willing to make sacrifices in the present for the sake of a future
existence they themselves may never live to enjoy. More generally,
a delay may enable a principal to gather additional, relevant information. Options may be carefully weighed. Clarification can be
sought. The impulse to base present decisions on past experience may
be resisted, and thus one form of the naturalistic fallacy can be
avoided: the principal does not select an imperative value on the basis
of precedent or the status quo *(Proposition 11.1)*. Advice can be sought,

and there may be an opportunity to interact with other persons, perhaps thereby achieving a creative solution to a pressing problem. He who hesitates is lost in only a small number of situations; usually it is wiser to follow another adage and to count, quickly or slowly, to ten before deciding or acting *(Proposition 13.1)*.

In our time, perhaps in all times, for most persons the pursuit of peace is a value incomparably more compelling if not salient than that of engaging in war, but the means to live in harmony with one's neighbors or other nations are elusive; judgments remain incomplete. To find suitable means, planning is needed, and planning means gazing into a pending or far-flung future. Will deterrence, for example, prevent war?

The greatest challenge facing a principal arises when the means to carry out his intention are only partially or completely unknown; he may then feel discouraged if he has confidence in the value to be achieved *(Proposition 5.6)*. As an individual, for example, he may seek to have harmonious relations with all mankind, including his spouse; to be successful but not at the expense of others; to make a significant contribution to the welfare of mankind; to contemplate his own mortality without fear or regret. Together with his peers he would attain peace and eliminate war; abolish or at least mitigate poverty in his own and other countries; elect competent persons to public office; preserve the natural environment, including endangered species and wilderness areas. He may intuit first steps to resolve these problems and thus attain the values at the foundation of his moral judgment, but no one—unless he sincerely and deliberately believes in one of the panaceas offered by some psychiatrists and some political leaders—knows in detail how such objectives can be attained and retained. For many of the challenges thus facing groups, engineers and scientists offer selected means or technologies, but the solutions always transcend their particular competence and interests. In addition, values conflict, and the principal and his peers must choose, for example, between certainty and risk, with the former offering little change and the latter perhaps significant change. Little wonder that the principal who does not know how to achieve his goal may indeed alter his intention and become cynical or disenchanted.

Possibly, perhaps, maybe: the adverbs imply skeptical restraint regarding the translation of judgments into actions, and yet principals do carry out their intentions. Unless the action is habitual, there are scores of reasons why judgments are difficult and why they do not inevitably lead to appropriate action. Values are often insufficient, nevertheless; somehow they must lead to action.

Skeptical Note: How can feasibility be determined? Just when is procrastination sensible?

Envoi: Although hesitation is inevitable, although momentary impulses triumph, and although miscalculations occur, *nevertheless* it is often possible to carry out intentions successfully.

MEANDERINGS

7.1 Coping with Exceptions

In my fallible opinion, it is not difficult to discover, without burdensome search, a defense of exceptions in the writings of most philosophers who appear disturbed that they have been unable to unearth values applicable in virtually all situations. An astute member of the profession, after criticizing one of his predecessors as well as teleologists, suggests that action is "good" when it can be said to "fulfill some impulse of human nature"; *but* then he immediately states that some impulses, such as hatred and jealousy, should not be "indulged." He also believes that there must be a respect for human rights or, in his words, the "potentiality for good that ought not to be repressed"; *but* this right to freedom must be limited by "the public good" (Blanshard, 1966). Another modern philosopher even admits that any ordering of priorities "will not stand the test of instances"; thus when wondering whether keeping a promise is more important than helping others, he can say only, "Sometimes it is and sometimes it is not" (Melden, 1977, p. 17; cf. Everett, 1918, pp. 7, 187).

A valiant effort may be made to deny that exceptions are really exceptions. A philosophically inclined physicist argues that "conflict arises . . . from incompletely stated and unqualified imperatives." The fifth commandment, "Thou shalt not kill," must be "properly formulated"; it must be "subjected to the qualifications by which our society actually restricts its application," and principals must be "taught the circumstances under which the imperative is to be suspended" (Margenau, 1964, pp. 267–69). The author is certainly correct when he thus preserves the commandment, but the restrictions and the circumstances are the exceptions lifted to a formal level. Other philosophers argue somewhat similarly (cf. Körner, 1976, p. 117). One conclusion concerning the "right not to be killed and a corresponding duty not to kill" adds that in "scarcity situations" (when millions are starving or malnourished in Africa and elsewhere) "there cannot be an absolute duty not to kill persons . . . but only a commitment to kill only for reasons." The essay considers two possibilities for situations on the hypothetical lifeboat of philosophers: a well-equipped one with enough provisions to last until the six survivors are rescued, and an underequipped one with inadequate provisions for all of them to survive. Then, the story goes on, various events may occur on either boat. On the well-equipped boat one of the occupants threatens to throw over the fresh water because he is hostile or deranged and cannot be persuaded not to do so; or five of them for no good reason decide to withhold food from the sixth person and he eventually dies. On the underequipped boat, one person is very ill and requires extra water, the others refuse to let him have the scarce water, and he dies; or since there is water for only four of the six persons, two of them are chosen by lot and allowed to die; or either those two are asked to be shot or they rebel and then are shot (O'Neill, 1977). Quite obviously the situations are different: the morally incomplete judgment is different and the responsibility of the surviving principals is different; but in all of them exceptions to the original rights are made. Should they be made?

Good friends of philosophers, including humanists and some social scientists, are likewise troubled by exceptions; for example: "Suppressing a hundred opponents is surely an outrage, but it may have meaning and a reason; it is a matter of maintaining a regime which brings to an immense mass of men a bettering of their lot" (Beauvoir, 1948, p. 146). Unsurprisingly a psychologist skirts the problem by asking whether it is true that "it is always better to help than not to help, to share than not to share" (Blasi, 1980).

7.2 The Pursuit of Moral Stages

The earliest and for decades the most stimulating investigations of stages have been conducted among children in French Switzerland by the gifted, sensitive psychologist Jean Piaget. Young boys and girls of varying ages, for example, play a game of marbles according to existing rules among children; they are asked by the investigator to explain the rules as well as the reasons for them and how they might be modified *(What may I do?)*. In this situation four stages have been distinguished. At first, the child cannot verbalize the rules or conform to them; then later he tends to give an egocentric explanation that disregards other players—he is playing only for himself *(What will I do?)*; when still older, he observes his partner in the game, and he wants to know and obey the rules *(What must I do?)*; and finally, even later, he masters the rules and likes to discuss and apply them (Piaget, 1965, pp. 15–76). Rigidity thus gives way to the possibility of modification, egocentricity to deference for the welfare of others (Hoffman, 1977) *(cf. Proposition 6.2)*. The child learns the rules; he knows he must follow them if he is to participate with his peers; hence he wishes to obey them under most but not all circumstances. Simultaneously he characteristically moves from a stage of egocentrism to one of more or less blind obedience to adults, and finally to one in which he seeks to compare and evaluate rules favored by himself and adults (cf. Boyce and Jensen, 1978, pp. 95–96). His norms thus change, so that justice consists no longer of obedience but first of equality and then equity. Individual differences in response to the questioning are frequent. When asked to give examples of judgments they considered unjust, one Swiss child age six mentioned "children who make a noise with their feet during prayers," but another of the same age replied "giving a big cake to one and a little one to another." These salient values guiding behavior are transmitted to children as they are socialized; they are altered and elaborated during play and other informal contacts (Piaget, 1965, pp. 96, 190, 314), so that there is seldom a complete one-to-one relation between what is taught and what is learned *(Proposition 4.5)*.

The most extensive cognitive research in the same tradition has been conducted by the American psychologist whose six or seven stages are cited in the text. He has obtained quantifiable data from both children and adults, especially from undergraduates and graduate students, by using the typically American method of interviewing principals by means of a more or less standardized questionnaire. Usually his reports are based on cross-sectional responses obtained at a given moment; much less frequently they include longitudinal studies over time; they are almost always accompanied by copious quotations from the informants and by interesting if wordy and rambling interpretations. The principal is confronted with a dilemma facing a fictitious character in a specified situation: he is challenged to decide what the character should do or what he would do in the somewhat unlikely event that he himself was in that situation; and then he is asked, sometimes at considerable length, to give reasons for his judgment. The well-worn example: should a husband steal an expensive drug from a druggist in order to save his wife's life when he cannot afford to buy it? In this example and in the others composing the scale, the principal is in conflict: he must choose between two courses of action. The presumption is that he projects upon the dilemmas his own "moral theories" related to problems of this type that are "not for the moment" his (cf. Wright, 1971, p. 171). Or when he is asked what he himself rather than a hypothetical person would do in a contrived situation, he must base his judgment upon an imagined observation of himself (cf. Rest et al., 1974). The unavoidable tenuousness of this method has been demonstrated by the responses of Australian students who were confronted with hypothetical situations in which the characters were portrayed as males or females: the women were not affected by the sex of the fictitious characters, but the men had a tendency to react like the women only when the characters were female but at a different or higher level when they were males (Bussey and Maughan, 1982).

According to this schema, the progression of moral judgments is from rules and duties *(What may I do? What must I do?)* to a consideration of values concerning other persons and society *(What would the consequences be?)*. With increasing development, the principal confronts himself with more of the probing questions until the values become prepotent and replies to the remaining questions are less important. Even with this detailed analysis of morally incomplete judgments, however, the investigator states that he has most deliberately confined the analysis to "stages of justice reasoning, not of emotions, aspirations, or action" (Kohlberg et al., 1983, pp. 17, 20), so that some of the factors that can affect moral judgments in real life—capability *(What can I do?)*, aspects of anticipation *(What would the consequences be?)*, other significant values such as *agape,* which he translates as "charity, love, caring, brotherhood, or community" *(What ought I do?)*, and the effects of past actions *(What did I do?)*—are omitted. Constituents of moral development, such as the child's use of the criteria of intention and consequences, require investigation in their own right and have motivated specific studies (Moran and O'Brien, 1983). Finally, although the original investigator documents the fact that "moral *action* usually takes place in a social or group context and that context has a profound influence on moral decision-making" (Kohlberg et al., 1983, pp. 53–59), he himself makes no systematic effort to investigate the background of his informants, he alludes only casually to the zeitgeist in which they are reporting their judgments, and he offers the hypothetical situations in a neutral vacuum. The development from so-called stage to stage, therefore, is affected by the age of the principal, experiences in his milieu, and the situation at hand.

The postulated stages and the importance of the problem itself have inspired a flood of studies among children, especially Americans, concerning their moral judgments (cf. Staub, 1979, v. 2; Page and

Bode, 1980). Perforce almost all have employed a similar, somewhat artificial technique: subjects have been asked to pass judgments concerning the same or other hypothetical situations presented to them by the investigator. A notable and praiseworthy exception is more realistic: first, the children were unobtrusively observed as they interacted with one another; then afterward they were asked whether they had observed transgressions and, if so, what their judgments were (Nucci et al., 1983). Since the studies to date have employed slightly or markedly different techniques, the responses have been classified in various ways, if only thus to demonstrate the originality of the particular investigator. One study suggests that morally incomplete judgments and behavior may have one of five "types" of orientation: toward the self, authority, peers, or collectivities (that is, enduring group goals), or the orientation may be objective (that is, "functionally autonomous," responding "on the basis of principles rather than on the basis of orientations toward social agents"). Presumably children begin with the first orientation and then move up the ladder without necessarily reaching the higher rungs (Garbarino and Bronfenbrenner, 1976; cf. Percival, 1979). Another investigator has derived a fourfold classification based upon two sets of variables: the tendency to judge in terms of teleology (emphasizing consequences) versus deontology (emphasizing the nature of the actions themselves) and the use of extrinsic versus intrinsic standards. True, when the schema is operationalized by means of hypothetical paper-and-pencil situations, differences appear among Mormons, Peace Corps applicants, members of fraternities, delinquents, coeds at different kinds of colleges, Catholics, Protestants, and Japanese in Japan and in America (McCord and Clemes, 1964). Now, what? One reply is an aside concerning the practical implications of the research: its originator has attempted to utilize his principal findings in a practical way by devising curricula to facilitate development to higher stages, an attempt that has met with varying degrees of success but has been severely criticized (cf. Sommers, 1984).

The existence of different schemas to describe moral development is a convincing illustration of the complex nature of judgments: investigators dip into those judgments in various ways and emerge with their own abstractions. There is no reason to believe that one schema is superior to another: each simply extracts different processes either because the investigator has evoked different ones or because he has chosen to mention only ones of his own selection. Obviously differences may be marked when values or modes of thinking with different techniques, especially in real-life rather than hypothetical situations, are employed (for example, Wahrman, 1981). The rationale behind these so-called instruments has been called biased: they are accused of being individualistic, rationalistic, liberal, and androcentric (Kohlberg et al., 1983, pp. 104–62). The masculine bias has been mentioned above and has been repeated by other investigators (Kurtines and Greif, 1974), but the author patiently denies the charge (Kohlberg et al., 1983, p. 25). Giving the hypothetical characters Muslim or non-Muslim names, however, affected the moral judgments of Nigerian secondary school boys (Maqsud, 1977). The method of scoring the replies to the dilemmas and its reliability have also been attacked in general terms as well as specifically for using norms based upon males. American college women, it has been shown, tended to base moral judgments less frequently upon justice and more frequently on "care as the most adequate guide to the resolution of conflicts in human relationships" than do males (Gilligan, 1982, pp. 18, 105).

It is legitimate to ask whether we have been dealing only with "normal" Americans or Swiss as the various schemas are promulgated by their proud progenitors. Tentatively but with hesitation the reply may be negative (cf. Gibbs, 1977). The sixfold classification cited in the text has been utilized almost sufficiently and successfully inside the Western orbit (Israel, Mexico, Turkey) as well as outside (Bahamas, Belize, Japan, Taiwan, Zambia) (Kohlberg, 1968). The investigator also asserts that the evidence collected by himself and his students reveals "no important differences in moral thinking between Catholics, Protestants, Jews, Buddhists, Muslims, and atheists" as well as in non-Western societies; yet he also indicates that he is referring not to the content of the judgment (particularly the anticipated consequences) but to abstractions concerning the forms of the judging that emerge from the six-stage schema as measured in a particular way (Kohlberg, 1971). Impressive as the cross-cultural data are, when the ethnocentric nature of most social science research is noted, it is premature to argue that in all societies similar or identical aspects of moral judgments are to be found and that therefore the developmental schema possesses "cultural universality" (Kohlberg, 1971). In fact, the number of societies perforce is limited: we do not know whether similar results would be obtained in the hundreds of other societies throughout the world. Differences appear even in the restricted sample of societies, which may or may not invalidate the universality of the stages. In Belize, for example, the responses of eighty-four boys between the ages of ten and sixteen could be squeezed into the same frame of reference, although only one child could be scored above stage 2. Age was related to this restricted range of the two stages and mixtures thereof; and boys in urban areas tended to score higher than those in isolated villages. The investigators believe that the latter difference may have resulted from the need to make moral decisions more frequently in cities than in villages (Gorsuch and Barnes, 1973). The evidence at hand does not justify the original author's claims, as one of his critics has culled from his writings, that the sixth stage "defines the right for anyone in any situation"; or that the stages form an "invariant sequence" and represent for the entire human race hierarchies of "cognitive difficulty" and of "moral adequacy" that are always perceived and preferred by all principles everywhere and forever (Fishkin, 1984, pp. 151, 158). Instead it seems more reasonable to conclude that the stages reflect the demands of society everywhere: to live with his family and his peers the developing principal must learn not to cater to his own whims most egocentrically *(What will I do?)* and instead to consider their interest and responses *(What would the consequences be?)*: he must acquire "an increasingly complex and well-informed view of the way the world works" (Easterbrook, 1978, p. 207).

If the six or seven or any number of stages are interpreted in terms not only of development but also of judgment, then the additional problem arises concerning the stability of the "higher" stage reached by a principal. Do the different modes of passing judgment persist? The principal proponent of the stages believes that lower stages persist but that they are "reintegrated at a higher level" (Kohlberg, 1971; Davison, 1979). For a while, after examining longitudinal data obtained from university students, he seemed loath to accept the possibility that principals may retrogress to a lower stage with the passing of time (Kohlberg, 1983); but later he accepted and sought to account for such an allegedly backward shift (Kohlberg and Higgins, 1984). The challenge, therefore, is not to classify a principal at one of the six or seven stages but to answer the question "To what extent and under what conditions does a person manifest the various types of organization of thinking?" (Rest, 1979, p. 63) as he passes morally complete or incomplete judgments; can we determine the precise reasons principals in general or a particular principal moves or fails to move from one stage to another? The "stage" may indicate one tendency for a principal to be consistent; yet there is no compelling reason to anticipate that every informant so categorized will be consistent in all situations.

In view of the fact that so many studies of this sort have been conducted, it is not surprising that relations between so-called stages of development and aspects of personality have also been investigated. Maybe some of the relations could have arisen by chance, but it is highly likely that such a complicated process as moral judgments springs from a large variety of predispositions within even young children, again an indication of the complexity of the judgments. With one instrument, for example, the level of judgment was more closely related to education than to age; subjects from the American South or affiliated with conservative religious groups tended to have lower scores than those, respectively, from other regions or affiliated with liberal groups; scores tended to be more highly correlated with tests of verbal ability than with general aptitude tests; the principals' sex and paper-and-pencil values appeared, at least among these subjects, to be unrelated to their modal ways of passing judgments. In the same body of research the stages had such fluctuating and unimpressive relations with various measures of behavior (such as cheating or competing versus cooperating) that the proud, energetic investigator concluded that these judgments interact with so many "other factors" that "simple, linear correlations cannot be expected" (Rest, 1979, pp. 170–95, 250–51, 260).

"Cognitive development," a concept that has inspired a raft of investigations in a psychological tradition opposed to orthodox behaviorism, is a form of skill that presumably increases with age. It has been considered to be, like IQ, "a necessary but not sufficient condition for ego development," certain features of which in turn are thought also to be similarly related to the "development of moral structures (Kohlberg, 1976). The upshot of the research at present is not clear: some association between cognitive development and moral judgments exists (Aronfreed, 1976), although the precise effects of experience (as measured by chronological age) and intelligence (as measured by the standard tests) are uncertain (cf. Kahn, 1983). If anything, loose associations between conventionally measured intelligence and more or less systemically assessed moral development crop up again and again because skill affects the individual's ability to anticipate consequences of his actions *(Proposition 5.2)* or because in turn it is related to the ability to think abstractly and thus consider many or some of the probing questions (Graham, 1972, pp. 237–45).

Different studies cut themselves loose from the stages and grope for other relations. American undergraduates scoring high on a semi-projective test and therefore called "mature" with respect to moral judgments concerning the sanctity of the individual and society as a whole, the spirit rather than the letter of the law, and the ability to see both sides of an issue appeared slightly more sensitive to injustices, to be better socialized and more empathic, and in general to be more independent; they also tended to be more approving of an intuitive rather than a rational approach to morality than those scoring low on the same test (Hogan and Dickstein, 1972). Except for the last tendency, which the authors themselves call "puzzling," the findings do not violate common sense but scarcely improve upon it. Then a baker's dozen of studies of American children have revealed a connection between "cognitive transformations" (in less ostentatious language: modes of reasoning) and the "stages," but that interaction is also affected by the "social experiences" of the young principals (Keasey, 1975).

From a practical as well as from a theoretical standpoint a crucial problem centers on the relation between the stages and action. Only a "weak" relation between moral development and compliance with the terms of mandated restitution of money to the victims by convicted criminals could be ascertained, and no relation was found between the developmental stage and the criminal records of the men who had been convicted (Van Voorhis, 1985). For a sample of American undergraduates some relation existed between volunteering for stuffing envelopes in behalf of a charity, and actually appearing to do just that, and their scores on two standard moral development questionnaires; combining the latter increased the predictive value (Tsujimoto and Emmons, 1983). In fact, a compelling, impressive review of American studies indicates "considerable support for the hypothesis that moral reasoning and moral actions are statistically related." All the studies did not determine whether the subjects behaved consistently in diverse situations; rather they were queried in interviews or questionnaires concerning their "fundamental criteria for right and wrong" and their "reasons for their moral decisions." The reviewer reports that he encountered frustrating difficulties in his attempt to synthesize the research: different techniques were employed to determine the respondents' subjective values, different operational definitions of moral actions were invoked, and frequently no effort was made to determine whether the principals themselves considered their values to be salient in the behavior being examined. In addition, even the statistical relation between the development "stage" revealed by the mode of moral reasoning and the actions varied with the problem being considered. In the majority of the studies delinquents tended

to be at a "lower" stage than nondelinquents, even though delin-
quency was variously defined and the nondelinquent controls were
variously selected. In contrast, little support emerged for a connection
between development and the ability to resist pressure to conform
(Blasi, 1980). Imperfect as these studies are and imperfect as is the
relation between the shifting operational definitions of rationality and
actions even in the best of them, we have here sufficiently encouraging evidence that behavior may on occasion (or often?) stem from
moral reasoning, and therefore a change in a principal's values of
which he is aware will affect his behavior, but—ah me, there are other
problems I must politely postpone *(Meandering 9.1: Omnipresent Value
Judgments)*.

Let us end this prolonged discussion of stages on a gentle, skeptical
note: in view of the ever complicated relation between personalities
and their environment, it is too much to anticipate that a definitive
schema concerning the stages of moral development will ever emerge
for all time and for all principals. The conscientious efforts to locate
and then validate such stages have revealed some uniformities in development. We have useful guides that must be employed cautiously.

CHAPTER 8

Behavior

The eighth and final probing question considered in this chapter is double-edged: not only does the principal experience his own actions during their occurrence *(What do I do?)* but he is also likely to remember those experiences in the future as he judges dissimilar and especially similar situations *(What did I do?)*. Good intentions and all other propitious replies to probing questions may or may not produce action, and when they do, the action may or may not be satisfactory for the principal. As anticipated from the complicated, precarious relation between predispositions and behavior *(Proposition 3.6)*, a review of systematic studies investigating the relation between judgments and behavior reveals some connection that is, however, complex and not clear-cut, not only because more or less identical behavior may be linked to different judgments, but also because the judgments interact "with other situational and personal dimensions" before affecting behavior (Rothman, 1980; cf. Blasi, 1980; Social Science Research Council, 1984). Such a hiatus means, for example, that the effect of the "stage" at which a principal allegedly tends to make his judgments, if there be an effect—or for that matter if there be a stage—does not inevitably lead to appropriate action. When a judgment is or is not expressed in action, the principal is likely to be influenced in the future by what has or has not occurred or by ripples therefrom.

Be it noted, very quickly in passing, that some philosophers deliberately avoid the problem of behavior; for example, "the ethical character of an act is determined by the *way* in which an act is willed rather than by the nature of the act itself" (Girvetz, 1973, p. 234). In contrast, what might be called a behavioral approach concerns itself only with outcomes and does not necessarily investigate the judgmental factors mediating the behavior; such an incomplete approach may face difficulties when almost identical outcomes have resulted from different replies to one or more probing questions.

8.1 INACTION

Proposition: When replies to one or more of the probing questions are negative, reasoned judgments may not be implemented.

Negative replies to the probing questions range from rules prohibiting the intended action *(What may I do?)* to consequences anticipated to be unfavorable *(What might the consequences be?)*, from inadequate skill *(What can I do?)* to realistic or unrealistic grounds for procrastination *(Proposition 7.5)*. When an imperative value is salient, it may not guide behavior: it may be declared irrelevant to the situation at hand; it may be rejected; or it may be modified to fit some other situation (cf. Körner, 1976; Doob, 1983). Thus attitudes and beliefs may be salient without affecting behavior; other conditions must first be present.

A principal may have sublime imperative values without acting upon them. Someone utterly opposed to nuclear weapons and favoring a freeze may simply be unable to find a satisfactory outlet for his conviction: belonging to an antinuclear organization or even voting for candidates with a similar viewpoint may seem inconsequential, and therefore he or she is reduced to hopeless despair or tries to ignore the threat to mankind's existence. On a humbler level American undergraduates in two laboratory studies were tempted to cheat either when alone or when a peer (the experimenters' confederate) tempted them to do so; and indeed more than one-third of them in the first situation and over 80 percent in the second did in fact cheat. There was, however, no relation between their general stance concerning the value of honesty or even their attitude toward cheating (as determined by questionnaires) on the one hand and their cheating behavior on the other hand (Forsyth and Berger, 1982). In short, the lofty judgments did not necessarily lead to appropriate action.

Obviously inaction may be frustrating: the principal experiences, as it is sometimes phrased, dissonance within himself. He may feel guilt, for example, when he has the impulse to help another person and does not do so. Every action, including inaction, affects the self, which is yet another way to phrase the assumption that all behavior is motivated *(Proposition 3.2)*: each person dwells within himself, but this does not mean his selfishness, his egotism, his conscience eliminates the possibility of helping or harming other persons.

Principals are moved to take appropriate action when they believe their "rights" are threatened or violated; they themselves may provide a definition of those rights. Americans may think of their own eighteenth-century revolt from England, which occurred, at least in part, when some of the elite were convinced that they were being deprived of various rights, such as having a voice in the levying of taxes. Two caveats, however, would suggest that a threat or deprivation does not inevitably produce action. The aggrieved principals may also anticipate that action will be fruitless or more punishing; then they remain quiet and allow their resentment to smolder and remain unexpressed. Second, they may not ascribe the rights to themselves; the ascription may originate among observers. Slaves may not rebel, even when disinterested parties deeply believe that their human integrity is being abused.

Skeptical Note: Are not many actions ill prepared and ill reasoned?

8.2 RISK

Proposition: Action is likely when principals believe, if and when they reason concerning their intentions, that potential gains outweigh possible losses.

This proposition considers one of the factors determining whether a reasoned judgment leads to action: the risks associated with that action as a result of knowledge acquired in the past or from perceiving the situation at hand. Few actions can be undertaken without some risk, however trivial. What are the dangers of riding a bicycle, marrying a beloved, or building a nuclear power plant? At least in theory the principal seeks to balance anticipated benefits and injuries from an action, but what he considers upon reflection or feeds into a computer must be a potpourri of facts, hopes, experiences, and guesses (Gardner et al., 1982). An unfathomable but necessary calculus concerning consequences or trade-offs occurs *(What would the consequences be?).* On occasion the principal may simply act against his better judgment when inactivity is too frustrating or when he is thrilled by the possibility of winning against odds. He may know he will be punished, but his motives or values prevent him from doing otherwise.

Leaders in modern complex societies must constantly make decisions concerning both the risks involved in technological change and the reactions of potential victims to those risks. Technological "progress" has increased potential dangers as a result of the complexity produced by the interactions of persons concerned with the functioning of airplanes, nuclear power plants, ships at sea, petrochemicals, and thrusts into space; these risks threaten us, it has been pointed out, not only because of the possibility of human error, the absence of adequate safety devices, or faulty administration but also because parts of a system of machines or devices and the human beings who supposedly control them may be so tightly "coupled" that accidents become almost inevitable or at least virtually impossible to prevent (Perrow, 1984, chap. 3). Systematic knowledge, however, may make both leaders and followers aware of problems they had not previously known. Pollutants from industrial plants were once thought to be harmless or simply nuisances, but now research and experience have demonstrated their undesirable, even lethal effects upon bodies of water, plants, animals, and human beings. When potential risks have been ascertained, leaders may try to determine the ones their followers in fact are willing, or say they are willing, to tolerate by observing or asking them—or by keeping them ignorant. They themselves may calculate the risks on the basis of models, experimentation, or what they believe to have been the experience of the society (Douglas and Wildavsky, 1982, pp. 67–82). In any case, perception of risks varies from principal to principal, and therefore leaders' decisions about tolerable risks for their followers are themselves fraught with risk. Does experience help? It may indicate that the risks or the benefits were previously exaggerated or underestimated; but it may also motivate principals to acquire new knowledge or to use different techniques, which then affect future anticipations.

Skeptical Note: Can risks be accurately estimated?

8.3 REWARDS AND PUNISHMENTS

Proposition: Actions are rewarding and/or punishing in varying degrees.

It is now assumed that action occurs, as a result of which the principal has a rewarding or a punishing experience, or both. These behavioral rewards and punishments are administered by other persons and by the principal himself. They include literal or symbolic experiences such as, respectively, food or a beating and a gold medal or a tongue-lashing. They may be anticipated, accurately or not, as a reasoned judgment is made; thus the incentive of a reward may push the principal into overt behavior. To be rewarded is obviously gratifying, to be punished just as obviously frustrating. A psychoanalyst defines morality exclusively in terms of such behavioral consequences: "ideals to be attained, restraints to be exercised, guilt to be felt, and punishment to be endured" (Flugel, 1945, p. 240). Behavior experienced as neutral may be nonfrustrating or—when viewed in terms of other consequences—even gratifying. Punishment may be viewed as gratifying and pursued when a principal would express remorse or assuage a sense of guilt.

Whether gratification can ever be complete, whatever the definition of the concept, is a challenge best dismissed as moot. The principal who helps another person, who resists temptation, or who fights the good cause in behalf of justice may feel happy as a result; thereafter he may be tempted or he may actively seek to repeat the experience without passing another judgment. Often the behavioral outcome of a judgment is not unambiguous. What has been anticipated to be rewarding turns out to be punishing or at least not as attractive as previously expected. Then the joy of attainment may be mixed with sadness; or what was thought previously to be only bad contains some elements of the good. Thus a student of the devil's history suggests that among the first prophets he was not only the source of evil but also "Lucifer, the bearer of light, the spur to curiosity and thus to knowledge" (Woods, 1975). Even such a scholarly dissection of the devil evokes ambivalence in us when another writer suggests that "we" associate darkness with evil in the major religions and hence we contrast darkness and light. In the Judeo-Christian tradition, however, "the Devil is a by-product of the goodness of God and emerges from within the religion of Yahweh, primarily as a result of reluctance to attribute evil to God" (Cavendish, 1975, pp. 87–89, 184). Confused? Exactly so, except for the fact that almost all animals, including us, sleep in darkness, but we dream—often brightly or vividly—when we are asleep.

Behavior considered moral within a society is rewarded, and the rewards vary widely, ranging from riches and honors to the promise of eternal life. Behavior branded immoral also produces a galaxy of punishments beginning with a verbal reproof and ending with the threat of eternal damnation. The existence of taboos and sanctions in every society suggests that human beings are not inherently good or bad: they must acquire their values during socialization and thereafter from those who wield power and authority, such as parents and educators, their own peers, or members of some outgroup.

Skeptical Note: Can rewards and punishments be anticipated or assessed in the long run?

8.4 FUTURE EFFECTS

Proposition: Virtually every past or present action is likely to have future repercussions.

The experiences of the past become part of the principal's personality; they are stored as attitudes or beliefs, which, when salient in the future, affect the goals he seeks *(What will I do?)*, the anticipated effects of repeating or not, modifying or not the behavior *(What would the consequences be?)*, and the moral or nonmoral judgments likely to be passed when a similar or dissimilar event occurs in the future. The fashionable word is feedback: the lessons from the past, anticipated or not *(Proposition 5.5)*, largely depend upon whether the principal has found or finds that behavior itself to have been or to be rewarding or punishing, or both, but not neutral. Criminals presumably are punished so that they will not repeat their crimes. A principal may possibly appreciate his own inadequacies and adequacies as a result of experience. He may make the assumption that a similar outcome will occur in the future. Or he simply wonders: Could I have done something different from what I did? Did I do the right thing? But of course he himself may change, and so may conditions in the future. The effect of the present and the past upon the future is epitomized by guilt, the least constructive effects of which are self-punishment or denial. In other situations or with other principals the effect of nonsuccess or punishment is to provide an incentive not to shun the action in the future but to redouble the effort to succeed, especially perhaps if the individual feels responsible for the failure and if another opportunity presents itself (cf. Brazerman et al., 1984).

In general, however, gratifying action tends to be repeated, often habitually unless the principal thereby experiences regret or some other form of punishment inflicted by himself or others. Frustrated or frustrating behavior is very often followed by compensation in the immediate future and by nonrepetition or avoidance in the extended future. The principals who do not achieve their goals are dissatisfied with what they have done, or they may be punished by others. But, continuing to live, they must somehow cope with the frustration.

If the principals themselves have committed what they consider to be an injustice or if an injustice has been committed in their behalf or is communicated to them, they may wish somehow to retain a previously held "belief in a just world." A psychologist who has conducted and inspired an impressive series of experiments reports the view of some Americans that victims usually "get what they deserve." The undocumentable conviction that they live in such a fantasy world, however, may be affected by events in the real world, yet they have many ways to retain their faith in such justice, ways that range from seeking to prevent injustice and compensating the victim to preventing themselves from learning of injustices or denying their existence (Lerner, 1980, chap. 1). The just-world belief may also vary with principals' religious background and convictions (Zweigenhaft et al., 1986). Immediately after World War II, what could Nazis and non-Nazis in Germany say about the Holocaust with which they had been previously acquainted or which then had been brought to their attention? The answer in one fat sentence seems to have been: "with few exceptions, the Germans interviewed during the de-Nazification campaign stood at a distance from the Nazi crimes, feeling personally uninvolved or unconcerned, or they denied the facts or they projected their guilt on others or they rationalized and justified the atrocities or they simultaneously engaged in several or all of these maneuvers, little inhibited by logical inconsistency" (Opton, 1971). They thus kept their just world undisturbed (Meandering 8.1: Aggression and Guilt). We must remind ourselves, too, that many of the devices employed by principals after the fact may also be employed in advance: he deserves what is going to happen to him.

After having been rewarded or punished as a consequence of his behavior, a principal may pass judgment on the persons who have affected him and alter his attitudes toward them accordingly. He thus also becomes, as it were, an observer, for he may question their intention. Certainly their mode of administering the rewards and punishments and their personalities may affect him. With increasing age larger percentages of American children approved the behavior of a fictional father on videotape who punished his son for fighting aggressively with a peer (Eimer, 1983).

A principal who achieves his goal and believes he has behaved morally may find that he is ignored, reprimanded, or otherwise punished by his parents, peers, or authorities (Proposition 5.4). Whether the behavior is then repeated or becomes habitual depends upon his attitude toward those observers. If he views them unfavorably—and particularly if the hurt from them is tolerable—he may nevertheless repeat the behavior, though perhaps with some hesitation. If he views them favorably, the flavor of his behavior may well change from positive to negative. As phrased in a platitude, it takes a strong character to ignore one's contemporaries.

The effects of a principal's actions are not likely to be completely reversible: never the same river, once again. Praise may be followed by reproof, yet some of the pleasure from the former may remain or the discrepancy between the treatments may create a lasting effect. Ruthless exploitation of natural resources may give way to conservation, although some of the losses may never be regained. The principal, wittingly or unwittingly, judges whether to be delighted or guilty concerning his own behavior, and thus the future is affected. For example: "Blaming oneself," one writer has suggested, "is quite a different matter from blaming other people," as a consequence of which "a special word"—remorse—refers to self-blame (Winch, 1972, p. 185).

The effects of past behavior may be transmitted not only by the principal to himself but also to other persons in the future. Some, perhaps most of what parents and others communicate to children stems from past experiences, not of themselves, but of previous generations. Experiences become embedded in tradition. During a given historical period, for example, members of group A whose ancestors were once maltreated by members of group B are likely to resent the descendants of group B, even though those in group B at the present time, of course, are not responsible for the original actions and may in fact truly regret they happened. More than a century after the American Civil War some hostility toward northerners still exists in the South. Among the arguments marshaled by blacks in South Africa concerning the injustice they have experienced is the assertion that present-day Europeans, who in fact have been born in the country, have no right to the land since Africans migrated to what is now South Africa before the arrival of the first Europeans. Traditions, however, tend to be transmitted only when they continue to serve a present function. The descendants of ancestors may thus be experiencing not hollow images from the past but real benefits or deprivations. For this reason differing socialization practices can be traced to differing experiences within societies. In Israel, for example, fifteen-year old children were once asked to judge the behavior of characters in sixteen short stories. Those who had been born and hence socialized in the Soviet Union and who had been in Israel a relatively short time (two weeks to six months) tended, in the words of the investigators, to be more "realistic" and less relativistic than their comparable peers who had been born in Israel (Ziv et al., 1975). Presumably socialization practices differed in the two countries: in the Soviet Union it had been wiser to conform to prevailing legal and social norms than it had been in Israel where judgment at that time could be less rigid.

If the reader has the patience to cast another glance at the Morality Figure in chapter 3, he may possibly appreciate its circular form. The occurrence of a habit, of a moral or nonmoral judgment, and especially of an action is not the end of a story; rather it is an episode likely to have an effect upon the personality now and hereafter. Round and round go judgments, behavior, and hence morality: the future comes from the past and then eventually influences yet another future.

Skeptical Note: Once again: can repercussions be appreciated?

Envoi: Although reasons not to carry out reasonable judgments exist, *nevertheless* actions occur.

MEANDERING

8.1 Aggression and Guilt

Frustration may give rise to aggressive behavior, which can assume many different forms ranging from hostile actions against the person or object allegedly or actually producing the frustration to self-accusations or even suicide. The frustration of immediate concern here is one resulting from a failure to achieve the goal of a moral judgment, especially when others are hurt. A probable reaction then is to feel guilty, the experiencing of which may have far-reaching effects so that, for example, the guilt-producing behavior is not repeated. A principal may also anticipate guilt before he acts in a manner he believes to be antisocial; and he may be equally disturbed when damage is inflicted not by himself but by someone else.

On the basis of experiments, almost exclusively with American undergraduates, it has been suggested that a principal "may react in several different ways after injuring another: he may attempt to make restitution, he may justify his harm doing, or he may engage in self-punishment." The technique he selects depends upon whether he feels distressed as a result of his actions, whether he feels he can restore "equity to his relationship" with the other person, and whether he believes a technique is available; he may combine, however, compensation and self-punishment (cf. Walster et al., 1970).

To allay guilt or remorse, the principal must somehow absolve himself (cf. Freedman, 1970). He may invoke the "just world hypothesis" and convince himself that the victim deserves the hurt he has received; he then attributes derogatory characteristics to him (cf. Staub, 1978, v. 1, pp. 151–70). He may believe he did not or could not anticipate the consequences of his own behavior. He may accept the blame and punish himself. He may believe the damage was necessary or justified generally—the view of victorious principals in battle and in war. He may enjoy hurting the other person: many sports sanction violence; convicted criminals are punished humanely or savagely. He may think he has evidence indicating that the victim has not been hurt or prefers to be hurt. He may minimize the hurt that has been inflicted. He may apologize and express regret. He may try to seek amends in the future by compensating the victim or by helping him in a related or unrelated context; for example, he may comply with one or more of his requests. His motive for restitution or reparation may stem from one of his own values, such as equality or equity, or—less loftily—he may fear that the other person will seek revenge. In trite terms, he must somehow live with his conscience.

Revenge or retribution—both forms of aggression—are generally disapproved in Western society. It is not surprising, therefore, that a sample of American male undergraduates was less likely to hurt someone who had frustrated them in the presence of an observing audience than those who were not being observed. Laboratory setups sometimes offer a somewhat unexpected twist: the tendency just mentioned occurred only if members of the observing audience themselves had witnessed the original frustration (Baron, 1971). Other students, also in a laboratory experiment, tended to be more aggressive if they felt less rather than more responsible for the punishment they believed they were inflicting upon others; but their aggressiveness also depended upon whether or not those others had been made to appear attractive or unattractive (Bandura et al., 1975).

Considerable evidence in American laboratories and also in contrived but naturalistic situations on the streets indicates that principals who themselves have transgressed conventional behavior are more likely to engage in "prosocial behavior" than comparable persons who have not broken a so-called ethical code, especially when another person or persons other than the victim benefits (Tedeschi and Riordan, 1981). Their reasons for doing so may be the same as the host of reactions listed above, particularly to allay guilt. In addition, when principals are seeking to make direct amends to the victim, they may thereby wish to demonstrate their power over him or at least to improve their own image in his eyes, almost a public-relations gesture. Subtler may be a tendency not to help or compensate the victim but to confer a benefit on someone else. Perhaps the American robber barons of the nineteenth century, after building their fortunes in part upon the inadequate wages of the poor, unscrupulous land deals, and cutthroat disposal of competitors, attempted to make amends by establishing foundations whose aim has been to promote health, education, and research.

PART 3

OBSERVERS

CHAPTER 9

Roles and Inferences

Part 2 of this book was devoted almost exclusively to principals. It should be reasonably evident that initially and later their morally complete or incomplete judgments result from their personalities and perceived events, which have induced them, unless habits suffice, to seek answers to one or more of the probing questions. In this part we turn away from principals, although they cannot be ignored completely, and concentrate upon those who observe them. Whether it is more or less difficult to know thyself than others I do not know; do you?

An intriguing, exasperating attribute of all human beings is their inaccessibility by outsiders. No one can ever know another person; in important and unimportant respects he is, if I may give the concept a psychological twist, solipsistically encased. Yes, a mother knows her child; old friends know what to expect from each other; an experienced physician can make an accurate prognosis concerning his patient—but surprises may always occur. The joy or the pain you experience is yours, not mine, even when you tell me about it and I am able to see your radiance or suffering. Observations inevitably are imperfect if only in minor detail; they make inferences concerning principals, and often they must resort to intuition.

The judgments an observer passes upon principals may be related to their morality. He may call them good or bad when he approves or disapproves of some constituent of their judgment or action. Or he may label the judgment or behavior right or wrong in terms of whether he thinks they have or have not discharged an obligation (cf. Boyce and Jensen, 1978, p. 14). The principal also employs the same verbal language or a nonverbal one in observing himself: he evaluates his judgment or behavior with the label of good or bad by smiling or grunting.

9.1 OBSERVERS' MOTIVES

Proposition: Motives for observing principals are incidental, practical, theoretical, or moral.

Perchance an observer notes the action of a principal and quickly labels it good or bad; unwittingly or not, he then stores that judgment and later trusts or distrusts him. Or he deliberately observes him since he knows he will have further contact with him and that he will find it useful to appraise him. The prototype of an observer with a theoretical interest is the anthropologist who would determine the values of the society he investigates, the possible explanation for their persistence or change, and their transmission and reinforcement from generation to generation. He takes precautions, usually but not always successfully, to ensure that his presence does not affect the ways in which the people express themselves and behave; he hopes, therefore, that he can emerge with a set of data as valid as if he himself were not there to collect them. Leaders in general, and especially those in politics, concern themselves with the descriptive values of their followers, but it is clergymen, theologians, philosophers, and some activists who not only make note of such values among their followers or audiences but also would impose prescriptive values upon all or most human beings (cf. Paton, 1947, p. 26). Judges in courts of law observe defendants and litigants in the course of presiding over trials; they ascribe intentions to them or instruct juries concerning possible ascriptions.

It is unnecessary to search very far in modern society to discover persons whose primary goal is to observe others and to pass moral judgments upon them. Any leader with authority has such a responsibility, or he assumes it for its own sake in order either to retain power or, as a judge or supervisor, to discharge the duty of his office. The problem is acute when risks and benefits from a proposed procedure are assessed. A military or industrial staff may foresee the benefits to society or themselves from a prospective judgment, but they must also assess the casualties or costs to be borne by others— the soldiers, workers, or ordinary citizens. It is especially difficult while observing an opponent, whether a personal competitor or the leaders and people of a hostile country, to secure "a realistic understanding of the thoughts and feelings" of him or them; such cognitive empathy is to be distinguished from affective sympathy (White, 1983).

It is well to realize that merely attributing beliefs or attitudes to others may imply, wittingly or unwittingly, a reasoned judgment by an observer. When a modern man or woman states that most women in our society tend to be subservient to men, he is doing more than describing objectively a relation between the sexes. He himself may be expressing disapproval or approval of women's role, or he may be wishing or provoking others to do so *(Meandering 9.1: Omnipresent Value Judgments)*.

Mankind everywhere seeks an observer who is not fallible and hence should be unhesitatingly obeyed. Sometimes such authorities are worldly men like political leaders or jurists whose judgments are considered final. The power and wisdom of influential kings and churchmen may be ascribed to divine or semidivine sources. Philosophers believe they have more than a touch of this authority: they do not wince or blush when they read in Plato's *Republic* that philosophers should be kings (and hence presumably sagacious), and they may be prone to attribute especially profound insights to some members of their own profession, now dead and hence less vulnerable, such as one of the ancient Greeks, Leibnitz, or, within certain cliques, a Marxist or existentialist. In modern times scientists possess so much prestige that often they are accorded similar respect in connection with knowledge and values unrelated to their disciplines or competencies. Even classical gods had their foibles; only monotheism postulates a perfect god—and the followers of that god are sometimes perplexed and skeptical when they note the evil he permits to flourish.

Skeptical Note: Which observers are competent to observe either generally or in specific situations?

9.2 SOURCES

Proposition: Original sources of information concerning principals come from the observer himself or from others.

Direct or indirect observation provides information concerning the principals of interest to an observer. If he can actually perceive them, at a very minimum he then knows or thinks he knows what they are doing, how they are behaving. But of course there are difficulties. According to an old saw, nobody lies like an eyewitness, which is to say that an observer almost always must be somewhat selective. When the information comes via a second person, the possibility of error may be greater. The informant may also perceive selectively, his recollections may be faulty, and additional errors can creep in as information is communicated. The bill of particular reasons why the inferences of observers may not be valid is presented at very great length in the next chapter.

Skeptical Note: Do or can observers reveal the sources of their judgments?

9.3 RESPONSIBILITY

Proposition: Observers assign responsibility to principals on the basis of their own general theories and interpretations of the intentions of those principals.

The problem of whether a principal assumes responsibility for his own action has been previously faced in connection with rules and duties *(Proposition 4.6);* here attention is directed to observers who may or may not assign responsibility to him for the same action. Why, the observer asks himself, did that principal do it—is he responsible or is someone else responsible? Some observers have a general theory concerned with causation; others rely on the alleged intention of the principal (cf. Bulloch et al., 1982). The problem is compounded when thousands or millions of principals are judged. Hunger and poverty can be the unhappy illustrations. No one, including even philosophers who deplore the naturalistic fallacy *(Proposition 11.1),* presumably wishes to starve or live below the poverty line. Who should be blamed? In a developing country the final cause may be a natural drought or a slump in the world market, which consequently purchases less of its exports or pays lower prices. In a developed country like the United States, discrimination against underprivileged blacks, Hispanics, and other minority groups results in shrinking opportunities for employment and for education. The external circumstances, however, may not be completely responsible for the plight of these people. Alleviating poverty can be in large part the responsibility of government leaders who prefer to allocate scarce resources to their own countrymen or to constituents. The victims, because they may remain unorganized, do not exert pressure upon authorities. Slum dwellers may be offered opportunities to improve their lot (for example, in the United States through schools teaching English to Hispanics who thereby increase their job opportunities), but for understandable reasons they may not take advantage of them: are they themselves responsible? We are faced once again with an infinite regress, and hence we might draw the skeptical conclusion that the problem is hopeless. But no, real persons are affected, so that an arbitrary point must be established and appropriate action taken.

Some observers subscribe consistently to an extreme doctrine of determinism or fatalism, the consequence of which can be to absolve principals of all or most responsibility. Principals are thought to be responding to conditions and events over which they have allegedly no "control"; hence punishment in any form, for example, is not mandated (cf. Baier, 1966). The behavior of even a convicted criminal is believed to have been unavoidable: he cannot be held responsible for his crime because he was inclined not to be law-abiding as a result of the cruel way in which he had been socialized by his parents who therefore are responsible for his crime; but they in turn were cruel to him because of the way they were socialized by their parents who therefore are ultimately responsible; and the two sets of grandparents in turn—well, here is still another infinite regress, which must end and hence begin with Adam. Adam's behavior, however, was determined by Eve and the serpent for whose behavior the Almighty may have been partially responsible. Obviously on pragmatic grounds a halt in such a sequence must be called at some arbitrary point, which is the reason other doctrines of responsibility are invoked and some behavior or some judgments are considered controllable. In the skillful language of a philosopher, observers draw a line, on one side of which they declare that responsibility can be assigned *as if* the principals were to have free will and on the other side responsibility cannot be assigned *as if* determinism reigns (Baier, 1966). Surely a decision to make a selfless sacrifice is different from choosing chocolate rather than strawberry ice cream. Presumably even the most extreme fatalistic parent punishes his child who misbehaves and thus indirectly blames him for his naughtiness.

The distinction just made and indeed the issue of determinism itself are not simply occupational conceits of academic observers but concern all societies. Although the gods may be considered to be the primal cause of all human actions and hence to have unlimited power over all persons, at some point in most, perhaps all creeds a doctrine of free will creeps in: we are responsible for at least some of our deeds. Vietnamese thinkers of the eighteenth and nineteenth centuries struggled with the problem of whether "moral doctrines" were more important in producing social and political change than "Heaven, at least Heaven as represented in non-human forms" and than astrological influences (Woodside, 1982). In many societies, including ear-

lier ones in the West, principals called witches are said to be responsible for the misdeeds of other persons, a milder and less mysterious form of which is to maintain that a principal has been unduly
or perversely influenced by a contemporary *(Meandering 9.2: Responsibility and the Law).*

Other theoretical distinctions concerning responsibility are about as
numerous as snowflakes during a blizzard, and perhaps as significant.
A philosopher has suggested that responsibility can be viewed in three
ways, each of which may be positive or negative. The principal may
be held responsible for an action he did or did not carry out: he is
responsible for his child's character; he is responsible because he did
not encourage him or her to be self-reliant. The action may be contemplated in the future: he becomes a father; he must function as a
responsible parent; he must avoid passing judgment before he has
the facts. Or he himself is not involved: an event in which he might
have participated took place before he moved into his present neighborhood (Becker, 1973, pp. 129–30). Some responsibilities between
persons imply contracts, whether they are expressed in legal documents or in informal promises: it becomes the duty of the principal
who makes a commitment to carry out the appropriate action, even
as the principal to whom the commitment has been made usually
has the right to have his expectation fulfilled. Why? Legally the principal may simply be required to discharge his obligation. A principal
has the duty to keep a promise—he places himself under an obligation
(cf. Grice, 1967, p. 46)—because otherwise contact between persons
would be unpredictable and hence either unpleasant or impossible;
or the principal making the promise may fear that he will be punished
either directly or through nonreciprocation in the future. Reciprocation suggests problems in its own right, such as whether a principal
must return a favor he himself did not originally ask for. You may
or may not agree that no hard-and-fast generalization emerges; I
myself am skeptical—I see none.

In fact, observers may assign responsibility on the basis of the principal's potential or actual behavior *(What do I do? What did I do?),* but
they also take into account his ability or inability to respond to the
probing questions as well as his relation to themselves and his success
or failure (cf. Finney and Helm, 1982). A principal may clearly be
the cause of an event and hence be responsible for it, but his degree
of responsibility depends upon the intention ascribed to him *(What
shall I do?).* The child or adult who accidentally stains a precious rug;
the youth who joins companions in a game that perchance leads to

the injury or death of a thoroughly innocent bystander; the motorist who, despite his best efforts, cannot prevent his car from hitting another on a slippery road; the well-trained guardians of a control panel who make a wrong decision that results in a disaster at a nuclear power plant: these persons are believed to be responsible for a consequence they certainly did not intend and for which they may then be excused.

Ordinarily principals are not considered to be responsible for actions in which they have played no role whatsoever either because they were not consulted and might have passed a different judgment (a pacifist whose country goes to war) or because they were not yet even alive (Germans born after 1945 with reference to the Nazi Holocaust). The observer may then assign ultimate responsibility not to the principals at hand but to others; yet do we or do we not inherit the sins of our fathers? According to Catholic doctrine, sins are distinguished on the basis of intention or will: an original sin is inherited from Adam who erred, but actual sins are traced to the intention of the principal. Mortal and venial sins do not necessarily differ with respect to seriousness: the former involves an intentional attack upon authority; the latter does not. The principal's intention thus affects the responsibility assigned to him as well as the possibility of divine forgiveness.

"An action that is judged to have been executed intentionally and by choice is regarded as having been freely willed" (Easterbrook, 1978, p. 19); "in a civilized system only those who *could have* kept the law should be punished" (Hart, 1968, p. 189, italics his)—statements like these assume that the principals are able to pass almost morally complete judgments. An insane person who kills someone is not responsible for his crime either because he could not anticipate the murder *(What would the consequences be?)* or because he could not pass "rational" or moral judgment *(What ought I do?)*. Principals with an extremely strong motive such as jealousy *(What will I do?)* may be temporarily in the same condition as the insane, but they may be held responsible for their motivation and hence for their actions. Responsibility may be assumed, moreover, even in the absence of a direct link with the ensuing action. "Ignorance of the law is no excuse"; here the individual may not have deliberately flouted the regulation *(What may I do?)*, but it is assumed he has had an opportunity and hence the responsibility to become acquainted with it. A young child who damages the property of another person is the cause of the damage, but his parents are more likely to be held responsible for the deed. Formally it is said that the parents are responsible for what the child does because of their relation to him (cf. Fincham and Jaspars, 1980); but in another sense they can be called the cause of the misdemeanor: they have failed somehow to socialize the child "properly." According to a common and incorrect stereotype that has also emerged in hypothetical situations posed in research, women who are "attractive," who dress themselves attractively, and who act seductively are judged to be somewhat or at least partially responsible for being raped; they are believed to have deliberately provoked the rapist even though they may have had no conscious or even unconscious desire to be raped (Seligman et al., 1977; Kanekar and Kolsawalls, 1980). But the subjects in such experiments would have known that some women are more beautiful than others as a result, let us assume, of their genetic constitution; should the beautiful have been held more responsible for being raped than the ugly? Ultimately, perhaps not; yet it might also have been reasoned that these women could make themselves appear less attractive, could they not? Why should they do that? Why should they ever be concerned with the possibility of rape?

Little may be gained by asking a principal directly whether he intended or intends his actions and then assessing responsibility. Many persons seek to avoid responsibility for their judgments or actions, for example, by offering excuses (Snyder et al., 1983, p. 46) *(Meandering 9.3: Just Who Is Responsible?)*. Even simple declarative sentences can imply an intention. "He became a monk and lived a simple life"— surely he intended to do just that. Or it has been suggested that an action harming another person cannot be called aggressive when it is in self-defense, when it has been provoked, when no other alternative appears available—or when it is not intended (Brown and Tedeschi, 1976). What must be ever remembered is that the observer's judgment eventually stems from his own values and preconceptions concerning intentions and responsibilities. It follows, therefore, that a "morally good deed can be done without the slightest intent on the part of the agent to promote social good" (Brennan, 1973, p. 55): in this instance it is the observer and not the principal who passes judgment.

Responsibility is double-edged when the principal functions as an observer and also feels impelled to judge whether he himself or someone else is responsible for an action. In a series of experiments employing American students as subjects and requiring that they cooperate with another person in order to solve a crossword puzzle successfully, it was found that a principal tended to attribute responsibility for the success to the partner when he was asked to assign responsibility immediately after completing the task and he believed his reply would be seen by someone else; but he tended to take the credit when questioned three days later or when he was tricked into believing that what he really believed could be ascertained (Burger and Rodman, 1983).

Skeptical Note: Ultimately and on what bases do observers assign responsibility?

Envoi: Although we ourselves cannot observe all the principals we consider, for example, responsible for their actions and although therefore we are dependent upon others, *nevertheless* we can find competent observers whom we trust.

MEANDERINGS

9.1 Omnipresent Value Judgments

Praise or condemnation can be heaped upon a meal, a painting, a landscape, or the actions of a wild animal. Similarly the actions of a principal can be evaluated as good or bad when he has climbed a mountain, swallowed four cocktails, or obtained a divorce from a third spouse. A judgment concerning an object or animal has no effect on the referent unless action by the observer or another human being ensues, but that concerning a person may have an effect upon him when he knows or imagines what the judgment has been.

One philosopher makes a distinction between the observations that a man "had a good life" versus that he "led a good life." In the first instance, the man allegedly was happy or satisfied; in the second his life, presumably as a whole, had been "morally good, or useful, or virtuous" (Frankena, 1963, p. 62, italics omitted). It is not necessary, I think, to make such a distinction; it is more parsimonious to assert that the first man achieved the value of happiness and that the second one, in the view of someone making the observation ex post facto, was guided by many values that may or may not have included happiness. In either case the person is being evaluated positively.

When an economist speaks of values, he may be referring either to the desirability and scarcity of a good or service or to the labor required to produce the good or service. Again, he himself as the observer is describing a value, and he assumes that the value is either descriptive or prescriptive for producers and consumers. The value of air may be high, but ordinarily its market value is low because it is plentiful. In contrast, a scarce object like diamonds or an item requiring raw materials and labor like a television set may be variously valued but may have a high market value. The value, market or otherwise, is not inherent in the goods or services, but is ascribed to them by observers and principals.

Many social scientists now agree with a statement appearing in the introduction to a collection of essays by members of their profession and humanists: "ethical orientations are present, disguised or not, everywhere in the enterprise of social science" (Haan et al., 1983, p. 8). Values are assumed or required before or after a problem is investigated; even when an author claims to be nihilistic, the values of principals or processes are probed or appraised; values necessarily are reflected in the language investigators employ to communicate their findings. Perhaps the extension of hermeneutics into inquiries outside of literature and the resulting or desired "deconstruction" compels the investigators and their audiences to become aware of the problem of values and hence morality.

9.2 Responsibility and the Law

A practicing attorney, also well versed in social science, considers that "consciousness of behavior" and hence intent can be conceptualized along an eight-point continuum, which varies from "pure accident" to "conscious action with conscious intent." In between are what he calls reflex action, action under hypnotic suggestion, action interrelated with social transactions (social suggestion), and action in which the consequences are foreseeable. His analysis of how the concept of intention is employed in the law and especially by judges and juries suggests that in theory but not always in practice principals are considered responsible for their actions and hence subject to prosecution and conviction only when the "consequence is foreseeable" or there is "conscious intent." Drug addiction and chronic alcoholism are instances in which individuals, driven by uncontrollable impulses, presumably cannot foresee the total consequences of their actions and hence perhaps do not intend them. There are, however, complicating assumptions. Thus Oliver Wendell Holmes once wrote that "the test of foresight is not what this very criminal foresaw but what a man of reasonable prudence would have foreseen." According to this view, I add, the assigning of responsibility is allocated to an observer who makes a statistical or reasonable assumption on the assumption of available evidence. Often, however, it is difficult for such an outsider to determine whether an action is accidental. If a child throws a stone that breaks the window of a passing car, for example, his action could be accidental, but frequent repetition of that action is likely to be considered intentional. As the same author points out, however, "the very repetitiveness of deviant behavior—as by the shoplifter, the arsonist, and the rapist—may be evidence that there is no freedom of choice, no intent, but the compulsion of a neurosis." A principal, consequently, may know that an action is unlawful and that punishment will ensue, but he may be unable to control his behavior. Finally, a principal may be held responsible for an action that he did not intend but that, as in the case of a bank robbery resulting in the killing of someone by another accomplice, occurs in the course of a related action (Marshall, 1968, pp. 6, 72, 108–09, 133–34, 159). This behavioristic approach to responsibility is not likely to survive a confession or the expression of intent by a modern terrorist.

9.3 Just Who Is Responsible?

Borderline situations immediately arise when the principal himself is questioned concerning his own responsibility (cf. Heider, 1958, pp. 112–14). If he states, "I intended to do it and I did it," presumably he is responsible for what has occurred. But why did he want to do it in the first place? A paranoid or a person fulfilling a posthypnotic suggestion may make such a claim, but the assumption by the observer must be that his verbal utterance, though true enough in an existential sense, is only the last link in a series of previous experiences over which he has had no control and hence—and hence has he no responsibility? Or, from another viewpoint, should the mentally ill have the right to refuse medication prescribed by competent physicians who are the observers of the disease? Should these principals or their observers assume responsibility for the welfare of patients (cf. Applebaum, 1982)?

Suppose a principal supplies a reason for his behavior; may it be assumed that he has thus expressed his intention? Philosophers sometimes distinguish between reasons and causes (Toulmin, 1970). And a psychologist has suggested that a cause is "that which brings about a change," a reason "that for which change is brought about " (A. R. Buss, 1978). Clearly there may be a difference when the principal provides a reason for acting as he does at a particular moment, or when an observer, such as a calm psychiatrist, believes he has evidence that the purported reason is a rationalization or an excuse and hence that the behavior springs from present and past causes of which the principal himself cannot or will not be conscious. Or a young child may not be able to provide a reason for his discomfort and his parent may be so skillful that she or he quickly eliminates its responsible cause.

The principal's position in the chain of events affects the responsibility attributed to him. At the time of the Nuremberg trials of Nazis associated with crimes throughout Europe, it was stated that persons of lower status should not be held responsible for obeying orders resulting in criminal actions unless they had "voluntarily" participated in an evil organization (Marshall, 1968, pp. 101–02). Probably most observers would agree that an enlisted soldier should not be punished for being in a firing squad that kills an innocent person when his commanding officer has ordered him to join that squad. But the officer was commanded by his superior and that superior by another superior: where can or should the line be drawn? A great learned philosopher, I think, offers us no assistance: "when we see a man doing something which does not conform with the universal, we say that he scarcely can be doing it for God's sake, and by that we imply he does it for his own sake" (Kierkegaard, 1968, p. 81).

The experimental investigation of assigning responsibility has thrown some light on the problem, but as ever the variable is intertwined with other attributes. The judgments of American middle-class children were affected not only by the consequences or damage they attributed to principals but also by the intentions they ascribed to them. Both factors, however, were also influenced by their own age as well as by the order in which the two factors had been communicated to them: either one tended to have more effect when it reached them last (recency) rather than first (primacy) (Nummendal and Bass, 1976). In passing, it is of interest to note that the American psychologist whose studies of children's moral development have been most widely publicized places great emphasis upon what he calls "role-taking" as a prerequisite to development (Kohlberg et al., 1983): perhaps to understand another's intention, the child as observer must first experience that concept within himself by assuming the role of the other person. Wisps of contrary evidence, however, suggest that there may not be such a direct relation between role-playing ability and prosocial behavior (Kagan and Knudson, 1983); perhaps the two develop at different rates.

CHAPTER 10

Fallibility

This chapter is devoted exclusively to the fallibility of observers, whether they are ordinary persons, social scientists, historians, scientists, or philosophers. My skeptical barbs have already suggested that they commit errors, they seek and do not find elusive, prescriptive or imperative values, and they obviously do not agree with one another. They are inescapably handicapped for two unavoidable reasons: they are doomed to be both egocentric and ethnocentric. No matter how conscientiously they try, they cannot jump out of their own personality and their milieus. "A man cannot know what a mother means by the word 'childbirth,' " it has been said, "any more than a congenitally blind person can understand the significance of colour" (Czartoryski, 1975, p. 65). Aristotle also could not escape: he was a Greek living in a particular society, Athens, at a particular time, and therefore his philosophy, however brilliant and influential it appears now to Western thinkers, cannot be universal; and this must be said even when we fail to find "better" morally related propositions anywhere, including, I quickly add, among Platonists.

On a completely intellectual level there is always the danger of committing two types of errors. The first rejects a proposition that is true; the second accepts one that is false. Interacting with these logical sources of error are psychological tendencies. According to Descartes, "it is the part of prudence not to place complete confidence in that by which we have once been deceived." Thus the modern philosopher who cites his predecessor suggests that "the prudent man" who "always avoids drinking from the well which once gave him indigestion" (Rescher, 1980, p. 177) is either negatively conditioned against the well as a result of his unfavorable experience (the sight of it upsets him) or he does not wish to risk a second bout (why take a chance?). But of course, unknown to him, the pollution that led to his indigestion may have been removed in the interim and the water may be perfectly safe.

The fallibility of observers must be examined in some detail since it is they who pass judgment upon principals and judge them to be moral or not. They assemble information concerning human beings, information most relevant to the probing questions. How else are we to become better or systematically acquainted with human capabilities (*What can I do?*), the rules governing societies and groups (*What may I do?*), and so on down the whole list? Observers provide reasoned judgments and exhortations to adopt prescriptive values: they would save our souls or our society. In effect we are concerned, as we must be (cf. Hogan and Emler, 1978), with the sociology of knowledge: some observers are better equipped than others to trnscend their culturally imposed limitations, even though we have convincing evidence that everyone is enmeshed in the values of his society and cannot emerge completely therefrom (Mannheim, 1936, pp. 237–80). It is very, very doubtful whether an observer can "objectively" designate the value allegedly behind a principal's action without intentionally or unintentionally expressing or implying approval or disapproval.

Judgments slip into vocabularies even through the use of single words—*fine, contemptible, admirable, worthwhile*—although the individual himself is not aware of the moral judgment being passed (Edel and Edel, 1968, p. 109). When once an observer plasters a verbal label upon a principal—such as honorable or dishonorable—he is likely to judge his future behavior in a manner congruent with that designation (cf. Wyer et al., 1984). The label containing the value judgment, moreover, almost always implies a prediction. You call him generous because he has been generous in the past according to your definition of generosity, and therefore you anticipate that he will behave similarly in the future. Of course your prediction, like any other prediction concerning persons, may be wrong: later he is no longer generous because he has had a traumatic experience or has lost his money in a company that has gone bankrupt (cf. Sabini and Silver, 1982, pp. 146–47). But by and large principals do not wipe out their reputations conveyed by the ways they are described in words and sentences.

Certainly, it must be hastily added, emphasizing only fallibility is itself one-sided. Some observers can make valid, verifiable judgments, particularly when they are scientists seeking to codify observable conditions having impact upon their senses. Our human condition might be even worse than it is now, were this not so. But a forceful note of cautious skepticism must be repeated: observers and specialized others are likely to be imperfect.

10.1 LAY OBSERVERS

Proposition: All observers tend usually if not always to be fallible because they are human, lack adequate information, and can make only inferences concerning other persons and themselves.

It is easy to assert that competent observers are needed to pass morally related judgments until questions are asked concerning the definition of competence in this context. We must immediately agree that there are no seers in whom all of us can have complete confidence. Some observers obviously have prestige with some principals: the word of the parent or the clergyman is sacred, respectively, to his child or to a member of his parish. But their observations cannot be universalized outside the family or the church. A competent physician or, better, a team of competent physicians can make a trustworthy and probably reliable prognosis concerning a patient's disease, but not concerning actions that also include nonmedical goals and values. The parents, the priest, and the physicians are able to judge answers to one or possibly more of the probing questions, but not all eight.

Observers, regardless of their roles, are human beings and hence inevitably have preconceptions or theories concerning the principals they observe. We must constantly remind ourselves that nobody ever perceives an event or another person with a blank mind: he comes to the situation with his own predispositions that willy-nilly affect his judgments (cf. Brewer and Nakamura, 1984). On the basis of experience or prejudice he anticipates that principals with certain attributes will behave in a particular way and hence must be judged accordingly. The attributes may be demographic (for example, he is a white or a Swede) or personal (he is an extrovert or a miser) and therefore—most persons, to our sorrow, can complete such a sentence. The salient experience or prejudice from the past may be affected by the observer's own mood at the moment of observation. From one standpoint it makes sense for a "good" or a "bad" action to be attributed to a principal previously judged, respectively, to be "good" or "bad": in actuarial terms, such a judgment is sensible, for it assumes that the present or future resembles the past (cf. Eiser and Van der Plight, 1984). But, of course, certainty is not guaranteed, exceptions are possible if not probable; common sense thus leads to error.

When observers pass judgment simultaneously on more than one principal, as is frequently the case, they are likely to have preconceptions as well as biases concerning those persons. It is necessary only to consider pairs of principals who perform a given act to infer that the observer's judgment concerning each principal will differ: adult versus child, leader versus follower, employer versus employee, ethnic A versus B, stranger versus friend, foreigner versus countryman, famous versus unknown person. In each instance the two principals evoke different attitudes and may be assigned different degrees of responsibility for a joint or similar action. In the moral dilemma already mentioned (*Meandering 7.2*) and favored by American researchers, sometimes principals are asked to pass judgment not only upon the husband who would steal a drug to save his dying wife but also upon the druggist who sells that drug at a high price (Kohlberg and Higgins, 1984). An individual observing several principals, moreover, may alter his judgment when they interact; then he can note whether one is, for example, more altruistic, outgoing, dominant, generous, happy than the other.

Discrepancies between the values of principals and those of observers may be evaluated in their own right (Nelson, 1968). The principal knows or thinks he knows his own needs better than an outside observer, once again for solipsistic reasons that render his inner processes private and inaccessible. From another standpoint, however, the observer's judgment may be "better" than that of the principal. The child craves food rich in sugar or carbohydrates (*What will I do?*), but the nutritionist knows—and can prove in passing if not for eternity—that a balanced diet is more certain to promote his health and general well-being (*What might the consequences be?*). A choice must be made, and either party may be in error—from some standpoint.

The observation of an observer, therefore, may be correct for him but not for the principal. He may judge a principal to be thoroughly moral when that person obeys the demands of a standardized code, whether legal or religious, without having passed a judgment other than one referring to only one of the eight probing questions—*What must I do?*—in terms of that code. Should praise be showered upon German Christians who usually at great peril saved Jews from the Nazis? The impulse of observers is to reply affirmatively, but without detracting from their admirable bravery, reference must be made to a post hoc investigation of a sample of them and of the persons who had been rescued: some were thrilled by the adventure, others were paid, and "almost all . . . tended to have very strong identification with parents, usually more with one parent than the other, but not necessarily with the same-sex parent" (London, 1970). Was their behavior morally deficient because it stemmed in part from conscious or unconscious motives (*Proposition 3.2*)? Most persons find it easier to follow a code with only the flip of a habitual judgment; hence some philosophers such as Kant judge an action to be morally complete not only because of its outcome but also with reference to the principal's motive. Saving a drowning person is to be considered good only "if it is done for the right reasons," which do not include vanity or a desire to be considered heroic (Roubiczek, 1969, pp. 194–95). The observer, however, is more likely to judge the action than the action-and-motive because the action is more accessible to him than the motive.

Observers may be unaware of the ways in which values are related to one another when they make what they believe to be a clear-cut, isolated value judgment. Should not water, pure water, be easily available? Of course, but:

> To expect people to prefer tap-water to well-water because it is cleaner and easier to draw assumes a whole host of shared values which simply are not shared by all cultures. It assumes that getting water from a well is purely instrumental to having it; that saving a little time is more desirable than taking time for friendly interchange and gossip, even courtship, for which village wells or fountains commonly afford opportunity. It assumes that having more water or cleaner water is obviously a common goal, forgetting that the extent to which we value cleanliness today is far from obvious to people who do not share our theories of disease. And it overlooks, too, other moral questions of a different sort that may relate to water-supply: economic dislocation of the water-carrier, or possible offense to a djin in the fountain, or the polluting effect of having people of different social classes or different religious affiliations drawing water from a common source. The possibilities are endless. (Edel and Edel, 1968, p. 80)

Similarly, virtually any social-psychological textbook or journal is likely to contain an illustration of the tendency for individuals, whether principals or observers, to be affected by the attitudes and beliefs of others and by their own predispositions as they pass judgment or behave (*Propositions 5.4 and 6.2*); a contrary or contradictory opinion by someone may affect the confidence with which a belief is held but not the attitude toward that other person when he is believed to be superior in some respect (cf. Wagner, 1984).

Inferences are expressed in words, the subtle connotations of which may be different for principals and observers. Even when both have the same mother tongue, the referents and the feeling tones of their concepts, especially abstract ones, depend not only on dictionary "meanings" but also on their own previous experiences. You and I may designate the same animal with the word *gazelle*, but—unlike you—I have a special feeling for the word ever since my dish of spaghetti was covered with a sauce whose principal ingredient was gazelle meat, which was once my experience in an outpost of an African country when my hosts honored me with their prized delicacy. Observers and principals who exchange sentences and belong to different groups may attach similar denotative meanings to a word such as *justice* or *truth* but quite different values at a given moment or over time. In the modern world, for example, *segregation* clearly means keeping groups apart. Principals on one side may oppose the practice because they believe it leads to discrimination and exploitation or because they think that the less powerful group, having acquired only some of the society's privileges, should be given the opportunity to acquire more of them. Those favoring segregation may be as firmly convinced that they must protect their own system of values or that each group, by being separated from the other, can thus retain and develop its own values.

No observer can be omniscient: he is likely to lack certain crucial facts concerning the principal he is observing and judging. Persons married for years suddenly discover gaps in their knowledge of each other. Leaders' decisions are seldom if ever based upon adequate information. Their decisions have moral implications when they determine the goals principals seek (*What will I do?*) and the rules they must follow (*What must I do?*). A declaration of war assumes that followers will cooperate with government or can be forced to do so. The difficulties encountered when observers would comprehend the predispositions and values of a single principal are necessarily compounded when thousands or millions of followers (for example, the citizens of a country) are the principals. Leaders may utilize information about those followers provided by their own agents, by public opinion surveys or their equivalent, by reactions of the mass media, and by their own limited observations, but to these must be added sagacious or foolhardy intuition. The intuition may be valid when the leaders, being also members of the society, can find within themselves attitudes or beliefs that for traditional reasons they can ascribe to followers with some confidence.

Even when an observer has adequate facts at his disposal, he must judge which ones are essential and which are trivial—and another observer may not agree with his definition of what is indispensable. The editors and journalists associated with the mass media, for example, know very well that often they must decide whether to be guided by what they believe to be the truth or by what they are convinced will boost circulation or the size of the listening or viewing audience. For this reason responsible observers grope to establish codes regulating their output; they are "continually torn between the responsibility to give a balanced presentation of contradictory views and the desire not to confuse their audiences by cluttering up a story" (Friendly, 1982).

A principal's behavior may be directly observed (*Proposition 9.2*), but his predispositions—his motives, beliefs, attitudes, skills, as well as his values—cannot be conceived; they must be inferred. No X ray can immediately peer into these mediating or cognitive variables. Instead the observer must use his intuition or make inferences from the information at his disposal, including the principal's behavior and again his demographic attributes. Under these circumstances it is no small wonder that little agreement exists among philosophers, social scientists, or scholars from those disciplines concerning both the content of their inferences and the manner of determining them.

Other complications exist, especially when the information of the observer is indirect or secondhand. The recipient of another observer's observation—the observer of an observer—may be unable to infer the intention of the first observer. Let me distort slightly an example provided by a venerable philosopher who indicates in effect a basic difference between calling one person the *enemy* of another and judging that person to be *odious*. In the first instance, the description arises from the "particular circumstance and situation," in the second, from the conviction that other observers share a similar value and will accept the designation (Hume cited in Frankena, 1963, p. 108). The first name-calling observer is concerned with values; the second observer receives unfavorable information concerning the principal, which he then must evaluate.

An observer is likely to project his own values upon others. In the primary or in the last analysis, he is likely to ask himself secretly, what would I do or have done in that situation (*What do I do?*)? If he values his own family tremendously or if he never contemplates committing suicide, he will condemn others, respectively, who are nonchalant about their wives and children or who threaten to take their own lives. Psychologists and others take advantage of this frequent tendency to project in order to ascertain the principal's own values as he judges others. One of many pitfalls in the use of a projective technique may arise when the observer is more tolerant of others than he is of himself: though I would not do it, I have no objection to his doing it. Such tolerance admits exceptions for others and provokes another morally complete judgment.

A frequent discrepancy occurs between the principal's behavior and the observer's inference and evaluation concerning the motive for that behavior. A Swedish philosopher has suggested that the same actions may be performed for praiseworthy or justifiable motives or for selfish ones. Should a teacher give a pupil a low grade because he deserves it or because he strongly dislikes him? Should a journalist write a sensational article about famine in Bangladesh in order to induce wealthy countries to increase their aid or because he knows he will thus advance his own professional career? By and large both the philosophers and eight educated, philosophically unsophisticated informants once approved actions such as these. They tended to believe, however, that the truly praiseworthy actions should stem from the first but not from the second motive; in the first example it was considered obligatory and in the second one desirable that the motive be the other-centered rather than the self-centered alternative (Malmström, 1980, pp. 119–29). Ordinarily observers are not informed concerning principals' motives: this exercise merely suggests that knowledge or inferences concerning motives may be evaluated in their own right even when they lead to similar actions.

An exposition of observers' fallibility cannot conclude without repeating what has been said at the outset of this section: some observers are in fact or are considered better than others, no matter how "better" is defined. Acceptable judgments, for example, are those which are made by observers who are impartial and competent (cf. Brandt, 1959, pp. 172–76, 249–50). The action of a thief is judged differently by a fellow thief than it is by a policeman or a judge. Impartiality can be appraised, although often the biases of an observer are unknown or difficult to detect. Competence is another matter. Clearly there are authorities in a society who are assumed to be competent and whose judgment is supposed to be almost automatically accepted. May philosophers, who disagree so violently with one another when they discuss values and morals, be so categorized? Politely, let the question be merely rhetorical. In the West, courts of law, as it were, observe defendants and litigants and then pass judgment. In those courts that use juries, observers are supposed to be selected who are impartial; otherwise any person of normal intelligence and possessing demographic characteristics (such as ethnicity) not at variance with the litigants is considered to be qualified to pass judgment. It is known, however, that some judges are very competent, others less so; and decisions of courts or juries may often be appealed to another set of observers such as a higher court or an executive. The Supreme Court of the United States, for example, is supposed to have the final word. Competence also includes momentary attributes, such as having at one's disposal or deliberately seeking all relevant information and being, as the cute phrase has it, of sound mind. On the basis of societal experience, which they may or may not evaluate correctly, both legislators and jurists judge whether specific laws in the past have achieved their objectives and therefore should or should not be continued.

Skeptical Note: Are not human weaknesses inevitable?

10.2 SOCIAL SCIENTISTS AND HISTORIANS

Proposition: Social scientists and historians are fallible.

According to some critics, social scientists are unable to offer adequate answers to important, unanswerable questions, such as one angrily posed by a revolutionary social philosopher: "Who can quantify and who can compare the sacrifices exacted by an established society and those exacted by its subversion" (Marcuse, 1966)? With few exceptions, however, the pride they take in their theories and data is justified; controlled observation and hard work are usually better than splendid intuition. At the same time, it is essential to acknowledge that errors are likely to arise from the fact that the investigators, as one iconoclast has indicated, are expressing and communicating their beliefs about events and persons in the external world (Habermas, 1983). For this reason and in the present context reference must immediately be made again to the fallibility of the disciplines.

Almost always empirically established generalizations are admittedly only trends with exceptions; deviations from central tendencies are virtually inevitable, which is one of the reasons statistical analysis is usually essential. "Bellicosity" in a society carefully defined, for example, is associated with certain childhood practices, personality traits, sexual activities, and social institutions; but the most pronounced tendency accounts for only slightly more than half of the variability (Doob, 1981, pp. 94–95). Social science observers, therefore, know they are dealing not with certainties but with probabilities as they make inferences concerning principals or as they seek to comprehend their own observations. Whether social sciences in general or a particular social science progresses as mountains of research appear in books and journals only a nonskeptical fool would dare assert. It is impossible, nevertheless, not to mention the somewhat unstable foundations provided to observers: fashions in social science change, and more often than not each investigator would demonstrate his own originality by making a devastating or petty criticism of his predecessor. According to one writer in the early 1980s, "Not since they first appeared upon the scene as an institutionalized, professional status group in American life some fifty years ago have social scientists been quite so self-reflective and so deeply perplexed about the philosophical status of their work, the proper standards with which to assess the competing theories and approaches they offer, and their own proper social and political roles as intellectuals" (Jennings, 1983).

Social scientists are torn between what a philosopher in the middle of the last century called a nomothetic and an idiographic approach: the former seeks to transcend the particular by unearthing general principles; the latter claims that the particular is unique and hence cannot be transcended (Windelband, 1844; cf. Kenrick and Braver, 1982). In passing, very quickly, I would say that it seems fruitful to be as nomothetic as possible but always with the reservation that in each situation the idiographic will appear. In my view, however, no matter how "reductionistic" a piece of nomothetic research, a cautious scholar or observer can almost always salvage at least a minor insight from it (*Proposition 1.1*). In addition, social scientists seem to realize more and more that the model of natural science may not be applicable to human affairs as a result of changing conditions and other circumstances. From a quantitative standpoint, surveys or their equivalent represent the best imitation of science social scientists have been able to devise to measure predispositions, values, and activities. Allow me unobtrusively to summarize some of the problems (*Meandering 10.1: The Imperfections of Social Science*).

Whether quantification in some form can rescue historians from half-cocked characterizations (cf. Tilly and Rule, 1965, pp. 44–49, 86–87), concerning institutions and events is problematical: they may lack adequate information, or the quantitative data may be biased; perforce they are guided by their own values and the zeitgeist. Although it is true that all or at least most aspects of value must be assessed in their historical context, it is also true, I think, that the lessons to be inferred from history are fuzzy. If we are to learn from human choices in the past, we must first know what those choices have been. Like survey results and social science generalizations, the interpretations of past events—whether valid or not—can affect those who influence present and future events and who subscribe to the notion that there are lessons to be learned. Some, perhaps most historians believe that each event is unique in some respects and hence that "history" never repeats itself; but then the same scholars may also say that "history" teaches us something or other, without being able to specify any more clearly what those lessons are, even as psychologists and social scientists cannot provide definitive answers. In addition, their observations are based upon documents from which they seek to infer the nature of the events that have transpired. They would identify and locate the principals in those events, sometimes to account for their motivations and the consequences of their actions. Usually but not always they clearly indicate whatever evidence they can find and they distinguish that evidence from their own interpretations. Like the rest of us, they also are human and therefore they cannot be completely trusted: their accounts of events may be affected by their own conception of what is important as well as by their own values. Perforce by definition the historians begin their analyses by knowing beforehand the outcome of an event, however unlikely that outcome may have appeared in advance: it is perhaps easier to explain what one already knows than to forecast the future, even if the conlusion is drawn that the event itself is so specific that it is not likely to be repeated.

Through no fault of their own, what historians write is incomplete because all relevant evidence may be lacking or new evidence may be subsequently unearthed. Without doubt past events are frequently described or explained differently by each generation of historians in response either to new evidence or to the spirit of the times in which they live; as a distinguished historian once wrote, "the historian cannot eliminate the personal equation" (Becker in Snyder, 1958, p. 56). Historians may do the best they can in view of the personal and factual constraints with which they must contend, yet they cannot provide a solid basis for detecting the descriptive or the prescriptive values of the past. They remind us, deliberately or not, that the present is built upon the past, which therefore affects our values, judgments, and actions; but, even as all of us recall events from our childhood, our memory of the past tends to be selective in terms of current pressures.

Although it may be true, as only a theologian would be inclined to suggest, that "social science cannot finally disavow or eliminate metaphysical issues" (Muelder, 1983, p. 201), that collection of disciplines is in the same predicament as history with respect to prescriptive values. They, as well as psychiatry and psychology, seek to explain the basis for descriptive values in terms of the principal's or the observer's life history and the pressures placed upon him. Indeed they and all sciences are themselves not value-free, even when the investigators are only dimly aware of their values or maintain that their "basic research" eventually will produce fruitful action by someone else (cf. Sieber, 1982; Leary, 1980). Traditionally economists avoid—or try to avoid—the problem of value since for them the utility of an object or service is the ability to supply some human need whether, as a philosopher has phrased it, that need is "brute animal hunger or a religious hunger for salvation" (J.F.A. Taylor, 1966, p. 126). What emerges from the behavioral sciences is a vague notion of normality and deviations therefrom; but such insight, however valuable in its own right, provides only clues to prescriptive values. One philosopher has hurled a charge against psychologists that, though just, is also applicable to his own discipline: "unfortunately, psychological theories do not provide a uniform answer" to whatever moral questions are raised. No matter how completely or convincing a theory of learning is, for example, the question remains, as another philosopher has written, "Who decides what is 'desirable' and 'undesirable' behavior" and "by what authority do they decide and implement the decisions?" (Brennan, 1973, p. 215).

The behavioral sciences, nevertheless, again and again are confronted with the problem of prescriptive values, which they usually try to resolve by utilizing values unrelated to their own discipline. Classical, liberal, and other economists hold the view that permitting the market to operate without interference will satisfy the needs of most persons, which itself is a value judgment stemming from but not part of the analysis. Often in the West, moreover, they also observe that the costs of free competition or of supply and demand are too great in certain areas such as the employment of minorities or the allocation of medical care. At this point they may decide that the value of eliminating the undesirable consequences is more important than that of maintaining a free market; again the judgment comes not from economics but from the economist's own set of values. Equally or more complicated are the values inherent in psychotherapy: what kind of a person does the therapist wish his patient to be? Here the value comes either from the patient who would be less anxious or less compulsive or from the therapist who possesses some kind of ideal arising from his own philosophy but not from psychiatry or psychology. The challenge is the same as that confronting all parents and educators who would influence those in their charge.

Social scientists keep trying to find universals both in general and in connection with specific schemas such as the so-called stages of moral development (*Meandering 7.2*). Even the most orthodox Freudian who subscribes to the master's own progression from oral to anal to genital would not and could not claim that the principal at any one of these stages inevitably is confined completely to the stage in all situations; admittedly, moreover, Freudian thinking prescribes the genital stage as the desirable mode of behavior and looks with sympathetic disfavor on those fixated upon an earlier stage. Evidence supporting any system of stages, therefore, exists, but it is not sufficiently overwhelming to serve as the basis for universal prescriptive values.

It is impressive and perhaps an indication of their universality when values survive from previous eras or appear in many societies. The incest taboo, beliefs in the supernatural, some form of love-thy-neighbor are easily produced as illustrations. At the same time less desirable, obviously immoral forms of behavior also pass the same test: war, jealousy, ruthless ambition. The problem of evaluation, consequently, is unavoidable; no simple Darwinian solution is evident.

So be it; as two critics have suggested, "every theoretical model" has "value implications" because "that is the way nature is constructed and the human mind operates" (Hogan and Emler, 1978). I fear, I know that the only conclusion to be drawn about the social sciences and history is that they cannot be blindly trusted. So great is their quest for new knowledge about persons and so tremendous is the pressure to find or present something new and startling that evidence has been or could be accumulated to "prove" almost anything, although—as someone else has remarked—no one so far has contended that there must be a society somewhere in which men and not women give birth to children.

Skeptical Note: What can laymen expect when so-called experts are not always expert; what can experts expect from laymen who prefer to ignore them?

10.3 SCIENTISTS

Proposition: The achievements of scientists are only indirectly related to morality.

Scientists, as has been said, establish the truth or falsity of propositions, not their values, just as social scientists may seek to explain why principals have motives and values but not whether they should possess them (cf. Russell, 1935, p. 249). The greatest challenge of the present era has come from those scientists whose theory and engineering have produced nuclear weapons (*Proposition 5.2*). The question of whether these weapons should have been dropped on two Japanese cities in 1945 or should be employed in a future war is not of course answered by a reference to this scientific, technological advance. Or indeed the useless perplexity as to whether the weapons should have been created in the first place can be settled only by invoking nonscientific values and evaluating their consequences. Clearly, too, applied science supplies means to achieve ends. We know, for example, that chemical fertilizers increase the growth of crops at least in the short run; whether the greater yield now is more important than the possible depletion of the soil in the future is not always the direct responsibility of the soil chemist. Often, when very reputable scientists turn to the problem of values, it would seem that their efforts are more likely to ease their consciences than to provide information for other than one of the probing questions: *What can I do?*

Two contributions of science, one general and the other specific, cannot be neglected. The method of science—objectivity and the validation of findings—can be of service to test the effectiveness of an ethical code, for example, even as scientific hypotheses are tested; and then the investigator conducting the test is likely to be a social scientist who uses or tries to use scientific criteria. That the scientific method seldom functions in the realm of human affairs is not the fault of scientists. As has been effectively noted (Brandt, 1959, p. 184), however, moral judgments and behavior cannot be directly observed in the manner of science: it is impossible to appeal directly to the senses or to symbols to determine whether they are good or bad; the evaluation does not come from science.

Scientists seek to explain unanticipated surprises by formulating the premises from which they could have been anticipated beforehand. They have their problems, too, even as social scientists find it remarkable after the fact that a great man could have arisen and exerted profound influence. Within recent years the doctrine of evolution has had to be modified: instead of gradual changes in the development of living matter, including mankind, it has become necessary to find explanations for sudden spurts in the evolutionary process. The theory of chaos seeks to restore order to complicated events (Woodcock and Davis, 1978, chaps. 1 & 2) and hence may be able to improve social science in its descriptive role.

Significant insights into the bases of human behavior are obtained from scientific disciplines like physiology, biochemistry, biology, and endocrinology. As a result valid knowledge concerning the functioning of the body, and especially of the brain, also contributes facts directly related to descriptive values. The responsibility of a principal with a brain tumor, for example, is judged differently from that of an individual with a "normal" brain. Experienced physicians, undoubtedly more frequently than not, make valid diagnoses and prognoses. The existence of variability in connection with a scientific or medical generalization does not invalidate the generalization; it gently suggests skeptical caution.

Skeptical Note: But are not scientists also biased?

10.4 EXPERTS CONCERNING ETHICS

Proposition: Philosophers, theologians, and other experts are especially fallible.

Present-day society is teeming with a variety of conflicting values, a state of affairs appreciated by many principals even in authoritarian countries. There are no experts to whom such persons can turn as they do when they consult a competent plumber to repair a leaky pipe or a certified accountant to balance their accounts. Yes, self-styled experts concerning ethics exist, but they are critical toward one another and they usually pride themselves on the distinctions they make. Among Christians and other adherents of the great religions, ecumenism makes slow progress: differences include varying emphases upon values as upon beliefs and rituals. A high church official has declared that "it is the business of our theologians to reinterpret the faith to each age of cultural change" (Wedel, 1963), so that here, too, uncertainty and reserved skepticism exist, if not among the reinterpreters, then among their adherents. There is no standard textbook to be offered eager students who seek guidance and truth. Conventional distinctions in ethical treatises, such as idealism versus realism, reappear as slightly different verbal guides, and there is no end in sight to terminological and deep-seated controversies. No matter how alluring a system of morality, it is subsequently demolished even by the same generation of thinkers. Without rancor it is fair to point out again (*Meandering 1.3*) that philosophers provide no new replies to the same questions that our ancestors raised and that we and our descendants seem doomed also to raise. The great among them, particularly Aristotle and Kant, are revered, elaborated, criticized, or ignored. No wonder philosophers fail to gain universal respect when some of their loose statements are contemplated, such as the following from a notable, courageous theologian who eventually was murdered by the Nazis: "It is true that it can never be admirable to act against one's own conscience" (Bonhoeffer, 1964, p. 211). Never? Before ending his book with the phrase, "without opening the door to universal skepticism," a Victorian philosopher stated that "the Morality of Common Sense may still be perfectly adequate to give practical guidance to common people in common circumstances," in spite of "its inevitable imperfections" from a systematic standpoint (Sidgwick, 1962, pp. 361, 509). Whose common sense? Such complaints merit and receive considerate elaboration (*Meandering 10.2: The Values of Experts*).

Skeptical Note: To whom should we turn?

Envoi: Although experts are elusive, *nevertheless* some observers may not be far from providing accurate observations that necessarily must include some anticipated deviation.

MEANDERINGS

10.1 The Imperfections of Social Science

Of crucial significance is the basis employed by observers to pass judgment upon principals. An Israeli philosopher quite properly points out that, with exceptions, philosophers tend to employ, as "the proper object of moral judgment," the criterion of "motives and reason" or that of "the beneficent consequences" resulting from the action, whereas "common sense" and also some social scientists stress the relation between "overt behavior" and "moral norms and duties" (Kleinberger, 1982). A translation: the two groups concentrate upon different probing questions.

It is not necessary to look outside social science and consult humanists, scientists, and journalists to uncover devastating criticisms of modern social science. Some social scientists have flayed their own discipline as their ranks and publications have swelled. One trenchant criticism embodies most of what others have declaimed. The efforts of social science, especially in connection with public policy, are said to "appear intrinsically more controversial than those of the natural sciences" for the following five reasons; in the authors' own words:

1. The social sciences entertain a greater range of permissible, even conflicting conceptualizations because there are few widely accepted theoretical models.
2. They also allow a greater range of permissible research designs and methods.
3. Weaker ethical guidelines exist in the social sciences.
4. There is also a weaker "norm of skepticism."
5. There is far greater difficulty in achieving true empirical replication that can act as an effective peer review mechanism.

The same writers believe—and they deplore the alleged fact—that "the advocacy position" of social scientists who report their own policy research "will often not be judged as if it were advocacy but rather [as if it] represented 'scientifically' derived results" (Warwick and Pettigrew, 1983).

Another devastating and stimulating criticism begins by indicating that frequently social science is no more valid or useful than "ordinary knowledge" acquired in everyday life and without the assistance of social scientists. The careful analyses of the latter often look "more like reporting than science." In real life "various kinds of social interaction are necessary to social problem solving," an obvious fact that must be overlooked when careful or controlled analyses are made by professionals. The findings of social science often diverge and quickly become obsolete. Little wonder, then, that most policymakers do not find the conclusions of social science to be "authoritative," with the result that by and large social scientists have little effect upon policy decisions and actions (Lindblom and Cohen, 1979, pp. 11, 12, 42, 83). By and large, I gain the impression that anyone who surveys the whole field of social science is likely to be critical and iconoclastic unless of course he advocates a system of his own which perforce he knows—doesn't he?—is superior to all others.

Let me become more specific. Suggestions concerning modes of making inferences about principals are supposed to emerge from the social sciences. Perhaps an individual employs different standards in assessing himself and others (*Proposition 5.4*). It is however, difficult, I think impossible to salvage from current research the "best" or the-most valid theory to recommend to observers who would improve their judgments concerning principals. All that can be said is that, in order to secure a balanced conception of behavior both in the present and in the past, it is necessary to consider not only the cognitive structure of principals (for example, the current fashion in much of psychology that struggles to free itself from "objective" behaviorism) but also the reality impinging upon them—and that reality is likely to be mediated by groups (cf. Sampson, 1981). And there is no sure-fire method to determine or isolate the influence of these two sets of factors.

Consideration may now be given to the specific methods of social science, particularly the behavioral sciences. The principal imperfec-tions of public opinion surveys can be summarized in a long sentence: no sample is completely representative of its population or universe; the content and order of questions can affect informants' replies; the characteristics of the interviewer (such as his race), the nature of the interview or written schedule, and its auspices may also be influential; and a variety of other circumstances, well known to the pollsters themselves and admitted by most of them, can introduce additional errors. It is scarcely necessary to mention the possibility that a prin-cipal may deliberately or unconsciously deceive a particular observer or persons in general by not telling the truth, by posing, or especially by ingratiation. My experience in various African countries, especially during and shortly after colonial times, suggests that many, not most Africans made the response they thought I wanted to hear, not be-cause they wished to deceive me, but because they sought to please me or at least to live up to what they thought were my expectations. And yet it is necessary also to emphasize an important lead provided by surveys: the fact that respondents do in fact reply to pollsters' questions suggests that descriptive values become momentarily salient as a result of the questions. It is useful for many purposes to observe these descriptive values, provided no inference is made concerning their usual role in the awareness of principals and provided the easily "measurable" values are considered only one basis for prescriptive values and not their equivalent. Simultaneously, however, it is es-sential to realize that almost all polling data are collected in a manner to which respondents ordinarily are not accustomed: the investigator poses the problem or the question to which an immediate response is required, whereas usually there is give-and-take between conversationalists before a value is expressed (cf. Sievers, 1983).

In recent decades, however, the mounting sophistication of pollsters and others who conduct social surveys in the quick one-two-three tradition has increased the accuracy of what is publicized and may therefore affect what policymakers as well as ordinary persons think and do. In the United States major and minor political leaders, especially during election campaigns, are guided to an increasingly greater extent by what the surveys reveal. If a theme of a speech increases one's standing in the polls, then give 'em more of the same. Whether there may be a so-called bandwagon effect from published polls (stick with the leaders) or the opposite result (fight harder if you are behind) may be debatable, but it is probable that so-called exit polls—sampling opinions of persons leaving the polling booth— affect those who have not yet voted, and hence voices have been raised advocating that such information be suppressed until everyone has voted. Here is an instance in which a social-psychological technique helps perpetuate or change principals' descriptive values.

Actually there are currents within the social sciences, especially among social psychologists, which suggest that these disciplines should not seek to use the natural sciences as a model. For, it is said, "in essence, the study of social psychology is primarily an historical undertaking"; therefore that discipline is "essentially engaged in a systematic account of contemporary affairs" (Gergen, 1973; cf. Cronbach, 1975). Indeed, "any given action may be subject to multiple identifications, no one of which is inherently superior"; "virtually any experimental result used as support for a given theory may be used as support for virtually any alternative theory" (Gergen, 1982, p. 72, italics omitted). All that can be accomplished by conscientious research is to seek enlightenment concerning "the range of factors potentially influencing behavior under various conditions"; or, in the words of yet another rebellious psychologist, if one makes "the outrageous assertion that . . . all hypotheses are true," the task of empirical social science is "not to test which of the opposite formulations is valid but rather to explore and discover the range of circumstances in which each of the opposite formulations holds" (McGuire, 1980). In addition it is stressed—with reference not only to polls but also to all generalizations—that human beings, unlike objects in the environment, can be influenced by the investigator, try as hard as he would to be unobtrusive and to be momentarily blind to the hypotheses he is testing; nevertheless, "scientific conduct is thoroughly suffused with value choices" and hence scientific findings themselves function as "an active agent in social life" (Gergen, 1982, p. 29). In brief, the discipline is said to be in a "crisis" from which it shows no inclination to emerge (Rosnow, 1983). A historian is similarly and more vigorously pessimistic about psychology: "any attempt to bring ethics within the field of psychology . . . would necessarily and always result in failure." Not unexpectedly, he adds that "a better understanding of human affairs" and hence of human values is perhaps attainable only "by studying history" in the manner he advocates; Freud's contributions, he thinks, "sank beneath contempt when they treated of ethics, politics, religion, or social structure" (Collingwood, 1978, pp. 94–95). These gloomy voices have been noted here because of their gloom. What they say clearly fortifies the skeptical view that clear-cut solutions to moral problems are not emerging from social science; yet they leave the door open a slight crack when they admit the possibility that social science—and history?—may offer tentative, historically limited generalizations.

The greatest handicap of all for the observer interested in a principal is his inability to measure directly what transpires within that person. He can observe him and make inferences from his behavior; but as indicated, they are only inferences and hence subject to error. He can ask other persons about him, but their reports may also be fallible. He can interview him directly, but the reply may not be truthful. The existence of the so-called bogus pipeline is symptomatic of the desperate measures psychologists and others have evolved in order to circumvent the principal's tendency to appear respectable or worthy: subjects are hooked up to an impressive-looking, ostensibly electrical apparatus, which, they are falsely told, can record whether they are telling the truth; what they say, after believing the investigator, nevertheless, may not be different from what they report in the absence of the gadget (Jones and Sigall, 1971). Psychoanalysis is a tedious technique through which the analyst over a prolonged period of time wins the confidence of the analysand who then allegedly reports the truth about his past and present life, including his emotions.

Problems, therefore, arise whenever observers ask principals directly to reveal their values instead of relying on their own risky inferences. It seems sensible to agree that "no one has a right to the truth, generally and without qualification." A parent must have adequate information from his children in order to discharge his function adequately, but such information need not be communicated to outsiders unless there is a "legitimate" reason for doing so (Melden, 1977,

p. 20). Each profession has or is supposed to have its own code of ethics, from which departures presumably are not tolerated as essential information is gathered. An attorney does not communicate information given him by his client in strictest confidence, but—unlike a priest who has heard the confession of a parishioner—he may have second thoughts when his client has revealed illegal or fraudulent action.

Every principal in some situation, therefore, considers his thoughts or feelings private and not to be passed on to others. The right to individual privacy is one of great significance, whether or not it is respected by others. In systematic research, subjects are requested or forced inadvertently to utter a word or phrase, or rank a series of words and phrases. Are they telling the truth? To be sure, investigators make every effort to improve the validity of their so-called instruments, but doubts remain. Projective methods are also employed, such as the Thematic Apperception Test (TAT) which requires the respondent to report what he sees in a drawing or to construct a story on that basis; but then the investigator must infer the values from the words of the principal.

In addition, for solipsistic reasons ranging from the inadequacy of language to shyness or inexperience, it seems true, as a philosopher has asserted, that "we can never express all we know about our experience" (Becker, 1973, p. 16). Even an ostensibly personal and private diary may be slanted consciously or unconsciously with a view to the reaction it may conceivably produce in some unspecified readers in the immediate or distant future. No observer can expect to know all the details that go into the judgments passed by any principal. Observers do what they can; they break down some barriers, but others remain.

Social science is also deficient with respect to predicting future events or, rather, the consequences of utilizing specific means to achieve specified moral ends. Nobody would deny that families may affect the values of children and perhaps also the adult personalities who eventually emerge, but a competent survey of our present knowledge concludes that "there is a considerable range of opinion as to what factors in the 'family constellation' seem to be important for moral development and as to how such factors operate" (Graham, 1972, p. 158) (*Proposition 4.5*). Economists may have had as much success in predicting how and whether specified measures will prevent or mitigate a depression as psychologists who forecast the psychological state and behavior of patients after therapy. It has been said that even a physicist is not likely to be able to forecast the location of a Ping-Pong ball a few months after it has been tossed into an ocean. But there are limits to fallibility and infallibility: the Ping-Pong ball will not land on the moon, and we may be able to anticipate, on the basis of existing principles concerning ocean currents and winds, where approximately the ball will be. Similarly social science can be of some assistance—perhaps.

Social scientists continually attempt to circumvent some of the difficulties confronting them. They know, for example, that a well-designed questionnaire or interview usually determines the respondent's values by his response not to a single question or item but to a series; this is the procedure that ascertains the reliability of the instrument. Similarly a single observation of a principal's behavior may not be reliable or sufficiently reliable to warrant ascribing a value to him. What is needed is a number of observations that indicate whether he responds or behaves consistently, at least according to the observer's criterion, in those situations. Then, perhaps only then, can a central determining tendency or a value be inferred. Even so, doubts may arise not concerning the consistency of the behavior but concerning the relation of the postulated value to the individual's own consciousness. Is he aware of such a value? If not and even if the postulated value provides insight into him in terms of increasing the ability to predict his behavior, may one speak of unconscious values?

New ways to secure insight into a principal's personality and hence his private judgments and values are constantly being sought. A seemingly objective method has been to consult the stars at the time of the individual's birth, and different ways of interpreting astrological information linger on. More recently another technique to circumvent the barriers between us and them is ethnomethodology, a discipline that studies "the stock of knowledge at hand among ordinary persons." Such knowledge consists of "recipes, rules of thumb, social types, maxims, and definitions." When that knowledge is available, it is claimed, an observer can discover how persons use cryptic and apparently imprecise expressions in conversation and yet be understood; how they are likely to reason; how they describe their own motives; and how the "meaning of a situation" to them can be defined. The observer thus tries to assess behavior, and then perhaps he describes "how people use rules and other elements of culture" (Leiter, 1980, pp. 1, 12, 63, 192, 232, 234; cf. Garfinkel, 1967), and therefore the bases for their values and morality.

10.2 The Values of Experts

The discipline of ethics, sometimes called the science of morality, would discover and advocate values that are both universal and prescriptive. A quick or laborious survey of that discipline provided by any encyclopedia or textbook, however, reveals that this pursuit is as futile as the search for universal descriptive values (*Meandering 1.3*). Philosophers and other expert scholars hurl devastating or quibbling disagreements at one another. Indeed it appears both fair and just to maintain again that ethics, a "trite" subject according to a nineteenth-century philosopher (Sidgwick, 1962, p. 9), has made no appreciable progress throughout the ages. A note of discouragement, discernible among these writers as they seek prescriptive values and means to achieve them, is perhaps best expressed by an existentialist: "Ethics does not furnish recipes any more than do science and art" (Beauvoir, 1948, p. 134). Other doomsayers among philosophers are not difficult to uncover. "It is rather depressing," one of them has remarked, "to find so many conflicting views" among those who write treatises on ethics (Greet, 1970, p. 12). Another: "Western ethical thought has made little progress since the days of the Greeks" (Weiss, 1952). The moans are endless; but just one more, which is the first sentence of a book with the title of *For an Ontology of Morals:* "Could it be that contemporary ethics has just about reached a dead end?" (Veatch, 1971, p. 1). Nevertheless, tons of books—which no man or woman possibly can or actually should read—testify to the unquenchable human desire to find the true or the better pathway to morality. At least we and they keep trying, particularly in the modern world when confronted with new problems produced by pollution, energy shortages, and nuclear warfare (Mader, 1979, pp. 9, 201–05).

Disagreements concerning prescriptive values and the resulting problems that arise when such values are postulated can be quickly illustrated in skeletal form:

1. The seven deadly sins: pride, covetousness, lust, anger, gluttony, envy, and sloth. Possibly only their extreme form is to be avoided, for milder expressions may embody positive prescribed values: a healthy ego (pride), goal seeking (covetousness), love (lust), indignation (anger), appetite (gluttony), role modeling (envy), and relaxation (sloth). At what point does the action shift from the desirable to the undesirable?
2. The "ethics" of the Old Testament, namely, "conformity to

the will of God" (Barclay, 1971, p. 14). Ascertaining that will is not straightforward, as every principal can testify who has read the books of the Bible or who has consulted biblical scholars.

3. "Intuitive insights" such as pleasure, happiness, knowledge, rationality, rational belief, beauty, aesthetic excellence, moral worth; and also the "doubtful candidates" of self-perfection, friendship, courage (McCloskey, 1969, p. 163). "Hardly anybody will deny," another philosopher has asserted, "that courage, nobility, or firmness are admirable," although "there may be disagreements, in particular cases, as to their actual presence or absence" (Roubiczek, 1969, p. 240). Such disagreements refer to problems of measurement (*Meandering 10.1*).

4. "Traits of mind" that "enhance the realization of other goods in life," such as "courage, self-discipline, wisdom, respect for and thoughtfulness about the welfare of other conscious beings, fairness and impartiality, conscientiousness (concern to fulfill one's obligations), veracity, kindliness, prudence, honesty, reliability, and tolerance": "The importance of these traits has long been recognized" (Brandt, 1959, p. 345). Have they really been "long recognized"?

   A. The same philosopher cited at the end of the previous section (if with an apology I may cite him out of context) states that only truth, beauty, and goodness are "absolute values" because "there are three—and only three—major operations of thinking which make us accessible to the impact of the absolute" (Roubiczek, 1969, pp. 272–74).

   B. Values having "personality utility" such as perseverance, self-control, punctuality, and accuracy (Ossowska, 1970, p. 177).

5. Values allegedly at the core of different systems of ethics; in the words not of a philosopher but a psychologist:

   Hedonism: pleasure is good for man and pain is bad.
   Utilitarianism: good [is] that which is useful. . . . objects are good which better the social condition of man.
   Religion: good and evil are defined by revelation and prescribed by religion.
   Organismic ethics: good is what is healthy for the biological and psychological organism; bad is what leads to organic or psychological disturbance.

> Relativism: good and bad depend on the individual and on
> the situation to which they are applied. (Wolff, 1950, p.
> 49)

Admittedly I have been deliberately meandering among philosophers who criticize themselves and the discipline of ethics. Indeed, a friendly outside observer like me often has the impression that they enjoy battling with one another: they can thus assert their own egos and enlarge the regions of thought they consider within their domain. A devastating hymn to skepticism emerges from one of their number, a distinguished British philosopher: "it is impossible to find a criterion for determining the validity of ethical judgments." The reason? Sentences that "simply express moral judgments do not say anything. They are pure expressions of feeling. . . . They are unverifiable for the same reason as a cry of pain or a word of command is unverifiable— because they do not express genuine propositions" (Ayer, 1946, p. 108).

By profession philosophers as observers are supposed to be able to anticipate *all* the consequences of a moral judgment, the value behind which they then designate as descriptive or prescriptive. According to popular stereotypes, they have a sense of detachment from their society and their fellows, enabling them to anticipate such consequences. Also it is imagined they can sit back and survey descriptive values and then, to the best of their knowledge and skill, summarize their impressions and recommend changes. Whether any person, including philosophers, as one of them candidly admits (Stevenson, 1963, pp. 3–4), can jump out of his own skin and acquire such a perspective is perhaps doubtful since it is evident—with or without assistance from sociologists of knowledge (Mannheim, 1936, pp. 264– 311)—that insights are limited to the time and society in which they are acquired. This characterization applies to the present analysis and this writer.

In such a vein, one philosophical historian argues that, even when philosophers deal with apparently similar ethical problems and employ apparently identical concepts, it is misleading to compare them: they have both thought and written in different historical contexts that are themselves not comparable (Collingwood, 1978, pp. 58–62). Indeed any writer is obviously a creature of his time; why should more credence be given to Kant whose system inevitably was distilled, consciously or unconsciously, from the experiences of his childhood and the values existing in his society? He affirmed the existence of a categorical imperative, which, as might be expected from a Prussian and the philosophical traditions of that period, proffered absolute unconditional commands. Empirically it may be true that men obey some commands, such as those of ruthless dictators, as if they were indeed categorical in Kant's sense, but this does not make them compelling over and beyond the point in historical time in which they are enforced. Kant himself was a human being as are other philosophers and experts who derive their values from some teleological assumption concerning nature or the universe. For this simple and obvious reason no doctrine can transcend the person who has formulated it, and no person can transcend completely the age in which he formulates his doctrine. Like it or not, there is no one authority, no single expert who can claim that he has enunciated the values mankind must follow now and for all time (once again: *Meandering 1.3*): exceptions arise, interpretations are inevitable. Principals, observers, and observers of observers may seek eternal certainty, but they are doomed not to achieve this objective *unless* they postulate a deity as the source not only of these values but also of whoever decides whether they are executed or obeyed. But even then human principals and observers usually disagree concerning their interpretation of the will of God; the leaders of any religion issue statements amending or revising principles or their execution. Any theory about values, therefore, must be cautiously evaluated, which is not to say that all aspects of philosophical doctrines should be carelessly dismissed as cultural or time-bound artifacts; for this reason I am now about to offer part 4, even though I cannot quash my own skepticism.

PART 4

MORAL PERSONS

CHAPTER 11

Dreams and Reality

Not only responsibility, according to an "Old Play" cited by a poet (Yeats, 1956, p. 97), but also reality begins in dreams. I entreat both you and myself for the moment to cut ourselves loose from the restraints demanded by cool rationality and analysis and to try, however vainly, to envision *moral persons*. Moral persons? Yes, they are principals who seek adequate replies to all eight of the probing questions and almost always guide their judgments and actions by salient imperative values that are prescriptive. A useful, if unrealizable ideal is being deliberately postulated. A precedent comes from economists who have advanced the theory of their discipline by assuming that persons pursue only their own economic interest, although of course they do not always do so. A similar procedure has been followed in attempting to distinguish between good and evil persons as well as to contrast a homo pacificus and a homo maleficus in analyzing war and peace (Doob, 1978, 1981). Philosophers also seek moral persons. Plato entrusted his ideal Republic not to politicians but to philosophers presumably because they conscientiously pursue and implement prescriptive values. A modern writer proposes that moral persons satisfy three criteria that embody some but not all of the probing questions: they try to do "the right thing . . . for the right reasons"; they have a "disposition" to do so; and they have been "tested" in action (Becker, 1973, pp. 184–87, italics omitted).

The very expression "moral person" raises the question of who is making the designation: the principal himself or an observer? The two may or may not agree; thus we have a statistics-like table with four cells, in which both agree that he is or is not a moral person; or the two disagree, with one using the designation and the other not. Then either may be referring to the principal's behavior with no or few exceptions, or else either or both may be referring to specific or general forms of action. In addition, usually more than one principal and more than one observer makes the evaluation so that mixtures of designation appear. Within a given group or society the modal evaluation as moral or nonmoral may be of special interest because ordinarily it constitutes one of the significant components of what is referred to as culture. The minority view, however, may turn out to prevail in the longer run, so that it becomes the prescribed value.

Many thinkers and writers dream about a society in which the prescriptive values they prefer are realized without concern for the remaining seven probing questions. According to the American Declaration of Independence, human "inalienable rights" include "life, liberty, and the pursuit of happiness," echoed in the French Revolution as "liberty, property, security, resistance to oppression." Nightmares, or the negation of these rights, should be avoided, especially by leaders of modern governments who should not engage in "violations of the right to life and physical integrity, such as systematic torture, and . . . arbitrary arrest or the perversion of the judicial process, as well as policies that create misery or deprive citizens of health and frustrate their basic needs for things such as food" (Hoffmann, 1984).

Dreams concerning prescriptive values are forever salient among both principals and observers. Principals would realize the dreams for themselves and also for whoever affects them. Observers dream when they ascribe values to principals and would have them change their values and behavior.

In seeking to describe prescriptive values as dreams, a kind of perfection is postulated. Throughout the history of mankind glimmerings concerning the perfectibility of persons and their society keep appearing again and again. Although gloom, imperfection, and skepticism pervade the modern world, there remain not only the conviction that more perfect principals once existed in some earthly or heavenly paradise but also the hope that greater perfection is achievable now or in some distant future. These ideals, these dreams suggest at the very least dissatisfaction with the present state of man and his society. Something has gone wrong, something is wrong; even in this chapter it is impossible not to criticize the dreams instead of awaiting more detailed criticism in the next chapter. Sophisticated or unsophisticated skeptics may hold ideals in low esteem and declaim that perfection, however defined, is unattainable; yet others are convinced that the very existence of ideals functions as a goal to desirable change and hence is useful. Many Christians, for example, may pay only lip service to the prescriptive values provided by the Decalogue and the Sermon on the Mount, which, however, serve as a reminder of the attainable or the unattainable and offer appropriate inspiration. More than a touch of faith is required, and therefore, as will be noted, rude reality intrudes upon the dreams of human perfection. In what other ways can we dream? In the writing of philosophers and others the usual confusion and profusion have been reported (*Meandering 10.2: The Values of Experts*); unavoidably I shall now follow in their tradition and propose prescriptive values with names identical with or similar to theirs. But my dream allegedly comes from social science; yes, the word must be "allegedly."

11.1 NATURAL NATURALISTIC FALLACY

Proposition: The naturalistic fallacy is natural; it cannot and should not be completely dismissed or deplored.

A persistent perplexing problem with which philosophers are quite rightly concerned, as suggested in the first chapter (*Proposition 1.3*) and as repeatedly indicated throughout these pages, is posed by the so-called naturalistic fallacy, namely, deriving the *ought* (or *should*) from the *is*, obtaining prescriptive from descriptive values. Anyone satisfied with the status quo either of himself or of his society is committing the fallacy if he proclaims that perfection has already been achieved for all time. "Tension" between any two values may give rise to change; it is somewhat doubtful, as has been also asserted, that " 'should' is always richer than what 'is' " (Melsen, 1967, pp. 67–69, 107). One principal's prescriptive value is another's descriptive value, even as leaders in developing countries, rightly or wrongly, have striven to attain some of the alleged benefits of the West which those in developed lands take for granted.

A philosopher begins his discussion of ethics with what appears to be an ambiguous banality: "What is good depends to a great extent on what tends to promote the *flourishing* of individuals and communities." The word I have italicized seems to beg the question. But after reviewing some of the influential scientists of the modern era— Laing for psychiatry, Lorenz for animals and man's genetic structure, Marx for society, and Freud and Jung for personality—he concludes that "man cannot be treated . . . as though almost any overall pattern of behavior was open to him." The naturalistic fallacy in this sense is unavoidable, but no single *is* by itself can give rise to an *ought;* all of the *is*-derived criteria must be taken into account before an action can be called morally "good," "ambiguous," "bad," or "indifferent." For this reason, too, exceptions must always be anticipated (*Proposition 7.3*) (Meynell, 1981, pp. x, 63, 101–02, 166, 175). Many other modern writers, moreover, likewise survey at great length the scope and findings of the biological and particularly the social sciences before they propose their own system of values (cf. Gillet, 1973); it looks as though philosophers are tending to prefer systematic data of this sort rather than ingenious hypothetical anecdotes of their own. They do not avoid completely the first five probing questions nor the two behavioral questions while concentrating upon imperatives (*What should I do?*) (*Meandering 11.1: Coping with the Naturalistic Fallacy*).

Encouragement for believing that some of our dreams are buttressed in reality and that the bugaboo of the naturalistic fallacy cannot and should not be completely avoided is a modern viewpoint worthy of praise and not disdain. It has been expressed by the psychologist frequently cited in these pages: "any conception of what moral judgment ought to be must rest on adequate conception of what it is" (Kohlberg, 1971). Parts 1 and 2 of this book, especially part 1, have been devoted to conceiving what *is* in terms of human predispositions and behavior. Thus, as I have frequently emphasized with no touch of originality, we have to eat and sleep, to use our feet to walk or run but not to fly, to interact with peers, and to try to make sense of existence— these are undeniable, "uncontrollable" human predispositions accompanied by appropriate descriptive values. Actions are often motivated by prescriptive values that may also be salient (for example, rules of etiquette affect the way we eat) and that stem from an unknown or unknowable source. The clearest refutation concerning the bugaboo of the naturalistic fallacy is provided by the physical environment and its ecosystem: unless some kind of adaptation is made to that environment as it exists in its natural state, forests are destroyed, soil is leached and eroded, endangered species of animals become extinct, traditional societies are decimated, agricultural costs are likely to rise, and people everywhere are deprived of the aesthetic thrills and satisfactions associated with nature. And whoever can deny that, in spite of heating and air-conditioning, some adaptation has to be made to climate and prevailing weather? In brief: respect the naturalistic fallacy; don't be afraid of it; assume inevitable and desirable infractions.

Skeptical Note: Is it not natural, often sensible to praise what is?

11.2 SOCIAL UTILITY

Proposition: Pursued should be the happiness or satisfaction not only of the individual principal but also of the society or mankind.

The proposition suggests again that the dream embodied in a prescriptive value should include other persons besides the principal (*Proposition 5.4*). Similarly, though on a descriptive level, economists who mention the utility or marginal utility of a product are referring to the individual as well as the buying or selling judgments or actions of consumers and producers of that product in a particular market. The value of social utility faces two stimulating challenges. First, the goal of happiness or satisfaction, whether of a principal or the larger number of principals constituting the group, cannot be easily measured; and the concrete embodiment of the achievement is likewise elusive. One has, however, the vaguely formulated conviction, in the absence of a hedonistic calculus, that somehow the achievement of goals produces momentary or enduring conditions within the principal or his group to be contrasted with nonachievement, and also that each achievement is accompanied by a quantitative or qualitative difference in pleasure. A fine wine, a gourmet meal, a Bach concerto, a snow-covered landscape, a loving human relation—they all usually bring pleasure, happiness, or contentment to principals in the West, yet they cannot be directly compared or distinguished. Then, second, utilitarian doctrines describe only end products; they do not suggest concretely, except in passing, how those products are to be attained. It may be asserted that democratic regimes bring more happiness to greater numbers and hence have greater social utility than police or authoritarian states—and perhaps the contention is valid or we hope it is—but completely convincing evidence is lacking, or at least it is needed to propose within a context the concrete measures to obtain the alleged benefits. A huge dose of skepticism should be showered upon any principal, leader or follower, who maintains that his society is more perfect than any other.

If a principal seeks happiness exclusively for himself, he may be secretly admired but publicly condemned as selfish or even "immoral." Social utilitarianism seeks to meet this charge by postulating the value of the greatest happiness for the greatest number. The last phrase is important, for it disposes of statements such as "pleasure in the pain of others seems thoroughly bad" (Paton, 1947, p. 36): of course such pleasure is bad since it is enjoyed only by the principal and not by the hurt person or persons. Suppose someone steals an expensive pen from a large department store whose owners or investors are not at all or seriously injured by the trivial loss. According to one philosopher, the theft cannot be considered in isolation; it must be judged in terms of "the pattern of life to which the act belongs" (Blanshard, 1966). For the ultimate benefit of all, theft is intolerable, inasmuch as any action has the potentiality of affecting others.

This necessarily speedy discussion of social utility reveals a profound truth: no matter how compelling a value appears in its own right, it cannot be considered alone but must be related to other values. Social utility may adequately supplement a crude doctrine of hedonism, but in turn it requires a companion for two reasons. The value itself remains crudely numerical—you add the happiness together to determine whether the maximum has been attained—but the challenge of distributing the joy remains; hence another value, that of justice or equity (*Proposition 11.4*) is required. Thus the value cannot be expressed without a qualification, such as "generally" or "almost always"; and here again the challenge of exceptions arises (*Proposition 7.3*).

Skeptical Note: Can ordinary principals be induced to show concern for society or mankind?

11.3 LOVE

Proposition: Priority should be given principals' positive feelings regarding other persons.

Subsumed under love are the attractive social emotions ranging from parental and sexual warmth and affection to an appreciation of all mankind. Even the antonym *hate* may often, but not always imply love: one hates a rival or an enemy as a way of benefiting or loving oneself or one's associates; or one should learn to love them, which must mean that only certain of their qualities should be hated, not their total personalities. It is noteworthy that, in the Sermon on the Mount, Jesus revised some of the Ten Commandments: He advocated a positive rather than a negative form of love. The dream of love is, therefore, universally extolled whether in poetry, literature, psychiatry, or religion. One bishop has written that "the moral precepts of Jesus are not intended to be understood legalistically, as prescribing what all Christians must do whatever the circumstances, and pronouncing certain courses of action universally right and others universally wrong. They are . . . illustrations of what love may at any moment require of anyone" (Robinson, 1963, pp. 110–11). Other hymns praising love, any kind of love, are commonplace: "The basic principle of ethics" is "devotion to life resulting from reverence for life. And this manifests itself in a devotion of the self to others" (Schweitzer, 1952). No one in his right or wrong mind, therefore, would dare utter an unkind word about love, even if—always a qualification—the emotion is designated so differently as is quickly suggested by the fact that in Greek four different words can be employed: *eros,* passion or sexual love; *philia,* friendly feeling or social empathy; *storge,* love in family circles; and *agape,* unconquerable goodwill or selfless, spontaneous love. A sociologist who once called ethics "a wasteland on the philosophical map," was convinced, however, that the only "rule" to be justified is the Golden Rule of doing unto others as you would have them do unto you (MacIver, 1952).

A philosopher is quick to remind us of an injunction within the commandment concerning the need to love one's neighbors: it is "basic," and "it says something definitive about our attitudes, but not what we ought actually to do in any particular situation, and thus it can come into conflict with other, more specific principles which then acquire equal weight" (Roubiczek, 1969, p. 132). The full implications of love as a value, therefore, must be comprehended. Clearly its application can be extended in ever-widening circles. Warm, overpowering feelings are first felt for parents who provide nurture and affection. Later are included the family, perhaps the neighborhood, then larger areas until, as the phrasing goes, the principal loves his country, he is patriotic. At some point, however, the value becomes less concrete and it loses some of its denotative meaning: ordinarily patriotism leads to actions quite different from those directed toward parents or lovers. In addition, love usually does not extend to strangers or to members of some outgroup; such persons evoke different values relating to hostility, protection, and fear. The great teachers have said over and over again that love must be extended to all human beings, perhaps even to animals: love your enemies as yourself; forgive them their sins. Perhaps, therefore, love is a useful metaphor that covers a broad range of feelings extending from one's spouse or "friend" and children to generations yet unborn. Can one really love all the peoples of this planet?

The motive for love may be concern for the beloved or for the principal himself. The beloved, it is felt, merits affection, or else undesired reciprocity may be anticipated. Sometimes the loved one is an abstraction or nonexistent: a donation is made to a cause or an action is carried out (saving money or preserving the natural environment) for the benefit, one says, of one's children (*Proposition 5.4*).

The problems and challenges arising in connection with love are infinite, so infinite that much of literature and poetry concentrate upon the divine passion or at least deal with it in passing. I would here mention one negative practice, that of scapegoating. Or is it negative? Surely for the principal locating a scapegoat may be a very satisfying experience: he absolves himself of responsibility for an action (his own or another person's) meriting his disapproval, or he obtains satisfaction from being able to affix responsibility upon someone else. But if his value is that of love, he will not hurt another person—or at least he will not do so deliberately. The catch turns on the meaning of "deliberately," for he may not be aware that he is scapegoating and hence he is convinced that he keeps his value of love unscathed. Love, ah love, in short, has its complications when principals do not or cannot love one another (*Meandering 11.2: The Tragedy of the Commons*).

Skeptical Note: Love?

11.4 JUSTICE

Proposition: The value of justice should be salient whenever the conflict between self and others arises.

"Justice," it has been eloquently stated, "is the first virtue of social institutions, as truth is of systems of thought" (Rawls, 1971, p. 3). Those institutions, I must repeat, are composed of persons, and therefore this imperative value refers to the hope that, to survive and to be happy and also to be capable of love, principals require a just share—however justice is defined—of the world's goods and services (cf. Mikula, 1980a, p. 11). The value of justice is likely to be salient when the principal himself or another person is suffering some kind of deprivation or when either person is not receiving the rewards to which, according to some principle of equity or equality, he is supposed to be entitled (cf. Lerner, 1977). In short, the cry of justice arises when there are "conflicting claims" (Harvey, 1973, p. 97), or at least when one of the parties in conflict believes there is such a claim (*Proposition 6.2*). A principal makes sacrifices or runs risks in behalf of a value he believes to be threatened: he gives money to a charity, he volunteers to fight for his country in order to rectify a state of affairs he considers unjust. Other persons should receive what they deserve, and what they deserve may in turn be thought to depend upon various norms within the society and upon what they have contributed to an enterprise in comparison with the principal's own contribution.

In every society observers are designated to ensure, actually or allegedly, that justice is impartially achieved (Leventhal et al., 1980). Formal courts were supplemented by informal modes of arbitration and mediation by the early settlers in colonial America and then later by utopians, employers, unions, and churches (Auerbach, 1983, chap. 2). When a principal believes that justice has miscarried or when he has failed to achieve what he considers to be equity, he has suffered a frustration (cf. Austin and Hatfield, 1980), the response to which can also be most varied. Like revolutionaries, he may strike out against those allegedly inflicting the injustice or in fantasy imagine that he is doing so. At the other extreme he may rationalize the state of affairs and try to believe he merits his fate. Up to a point an ethical code seeks to establish limits concerning a victim's permissible actions.

Then there are also informal codes applicable to those benefiting from injustice. The beneficiaries usually take steps to forestall or diminish both the victim's hostility and their own sense of guilt. They may modestly deny that they are privileged (cf. Schwinger, 1980). As previously indicated (*Proposition 8.4*), they may consciously or unconsciously allocate responsibility to the victims in order to retain their own "belief in a just world." They may claim to have used as guides permissive rules of their society. In some situations they may distribute goods and services equally even when they themselves merit a greater share; they thus believe they can promote harmony with their peers (cf. Leventhal et al., 1980). The "general opposition to any form of discrimination" (Melsen, 1967, p. 64), whether of an individual or a group, suggests the possible universality of the dream of justice.

On a phenomenological level, many, perhaps most principals possess a sense of justice that, in the paraphrased words of an ancient Latin jurist, is "the ever present will to give everybody what is due to him" (cited in Körner, 1976, p. 152). This urge, this definition contains an ambiguous abstraction: aside from being able to survive or to survive above a subsistence level, what is an individual's due? If a principal desperately contracts a large debt, one that "objective" observers judge to be "unfair," does "justice" demand that he repay that loan when it is "due"? According to one writer, equity "has been

viewed as consisting in the treatment of all people" in terms of one
or more of the following criteria: the principals' inputs, needs, abilities,
or efforts; their opportunity to compete equally; and concern for the
common good, a specified minimum for everyone, and the supply
and demand of the marketplace (Deutsch, 1975). These splendid
words represent a heterogeneous mixture of predispositions, behavior,
and social abstraction. Obviously, therefore, the value of justice has
many meanings and even as a dream is most variously achieved
(*Meandering 11.3: What Is Justice?*). When the cry of justice is heard,
the principal is seeking a distribution of some service or commodity:
the concept is being operationalized.

In the spring of 1983, a presidential commission in the United States
concluded that "society has an ethical obligation to insure equitable
access to health care for all" and such access "requires that all citizens
be able to secure an adequate level of care without excessive burdens"
("Presidential Panel . . .," 1983). Why? Presumably need was the
value guiding the commission in this instance: sick persons must have
medical attention, regardless of their status or financial condition.
Even so, subtle problems can arise. What does "adequate level of
care" mean? Some physicians are more capable than others, and they
are more likely in American society to be consulted by wealthy persons who can afford to pay their fees, whereas poor persons dependent upon socialized medicine may be unable to afford those fees
or perforce may go to less-qualified members of the medical profession.

The reference to need, therefore, by no means provides a solution
to all the challenging problems of justice. Both in psychophysics and
in classical economics attention is called to the fact that equal incre-
ments do not have the same effects upon situations or persons. A
single candle is clearly visible in a dark room, but may go unnoticed
in one that is highly illuminated. The utility of a glass of water to an
extremely thirsty person obviously is greater than it is to someone
whose thirst has been adequately satisfied. The moment genetic factors
are mentioned, justice becomes entangled with other values. If we may
use a harmless and noncontroversial illustration, that of musical talent,
it is unquestionably true that exceptional musical talent is inherited.
Should those with such talent (provided it can be ascertained at an
early age) be given greater opportunities to be trained musically than
those without it? Similarly "justice" may require that the victims of
prejudice and discrimination—such as blacks or women in the United
States—be offered special privileges, but then the puzzling question
of reverse discrimination arises, namely, "unjust" treatment of whites

and men who may be better "qualified" for a position but who are discriminated against for the sake of those for whom in the name of justice redress is cultivated. Should the privileged be made to suffer for sins that not they but their predecessors committed? As often happens, Aesop provides a bit of wisdom: "When the hare addressed a public meeting and claimed that all should have fair shares, the lions answered: A good speech, but it lacks claws and teeth such as we have" (cited by Bass, 1960, p. 221).

Perhaps the most puzzling and plaguing problem of this dream is evoked instantly by the phrase "just war." The roll call of those justifying war includes Aristotle, Cicero, the crusaders of the Middle Ages, St. Thomas More, John Calvin, Hugo Grotius, and any leader (whether Napoleon, Lincoln, Hitler, the two Roosevelts) who has ever led his country into war (Doob, 1981, pp. 209–16). Not to resort to war under specified circumstances, it is asserted, will produce or perpetuate greater evils than those occurring during and after the conflict. In contrast are those who oppose violence in any form, particularly war; they assert that the consequences from the use of force inevitably are worse than the gains from employing nonviolent means. Here indeed is an eternal tussle (*Proposition 13.6*).

Finally, the dream of justice concerns persons. The principal may seek justice for himself or for others, or for both. Perhaps justice for others is more likely to be salient when the person or persons are vividly or realistically perceived and not viewed as abstractions; thus the photograph of one malnourished child may evoke more compassion than a report concerning millions who are perishing from starvation. The principal may demand justice for himself, yet pride or some other ego-oriented impulse may cause him either to deny that others, even those in the same category as himself, are suffering from injustice or to claim that they are being treated well (Crosby, 1984). No wonder the quest for justice, skeptics correctly say, is so elusive—and yet either now or later the cry against injustice is constantly raised by principals, scholars, statesmen, and the rest of us.

Skeptical Note: Does not injustice pervade society?

11.5 TRUTH AND PREDICTABILITY

Proposition: Principals should be truthful; otherwise their behavior is unpredictable.

The two values are intertwined. The need to pursue truth ruthlessly in science is obvious; if not, theories and propositions could not be tested and verified. Truth in human relations, though often more elusive, is equally necessary. Unless persons keep their promises and are "true to their word," unless they report or indicate the truth about themselves, unless they speak and behave sufficiently consistently so that principals and observers can know what to predict, social life becomes impossible, difficult, frustrating, or chaotic. Surprises may be gratifying, provided they do not occur too often and provided they bring joy and not shock or trauma.

A politician who does not carry out his campaign promises after being elected is condemned as an opportunist or a liar; or else with a cynical sneer he may be simply dismissed as playing politics. Legal phrases such as "the rule of law" and "due process" mean, among other things, that citizens have the right to be able to predict what will happen and how they will be treated if for any reason, regardless of their status within the society, they are accused of breaking the law.

The "often noted paradox" displayed by Ronald Reagan as president lay in the fact that "such an upright, likable fellow" could "initiate policies entailing such cruel results," especially for the underprivileged in American society. For him and for many other principals, leaders and followers alike, there has been, there is "a lack of connection between private and public ethics" (R. H. Williams, 1982). The genial private president or the considerate loving parent at home seems inconsistent with his ruthless behavior, respectively, in public office and in a competitive trade: the whole truth about him is not known by observing his role in only one situation. Consistency giving rise to predictability, however, is not always an indication of truth: a rogue may be utterly consistent and hence predictable—he is always a rogue—and is thus deceitful, hence not truthful.

Skeptical Note: If the truth is not known, how can one be truthful?

11.6 BEAUTY

Proposition: Beauty should be cultivated, however indefinable the value in any universal sense.

This value has numerous referents and evokes or is evoked by the most varied judgments. The appearance of human beings as well as the ways in which they are portrayed in paintings, sculptures, and literature; buildings and landscapes; speech and music; movements in walking, running, and dancing; the list of ways in which persons and their environments are judged and can be made aesthetically attractive is interminable. Clearly there are fashions in art within a society, and artistic standards differ from society to society: but the craving for beauty in a form demanded by principals is undeniable and requires no meandering documentation. Indeed tribute is paid to this self-evident value by its brief treatment here.

Skeptical Note: And what is beauty?

11.7 PERFECTION

Proposition: Principals should be as perfect as possible with respect to normality, rationality, the possession of faith, and the avoidance of evil.

Dreams can be realized only when the dreamers, the principals, approach perfection. Yes, you would have me declare, perfection is impossible to define in detail. Yes, each principal is unique and hence must embody perfection differently. Two supplementary observations, nevertheless, are crucial. First, the perfect principal must possess values and demonstrate actions corresponding to the values fleetingly mentioned above and in chapter 6. He requires other attributes or capacities in order to have those values and to act in corresponding ways. The attributes and capacities are difficult to specify because no one, certainly not this writer I say for the nth time, can escape his own ethnocentric mold and indicate or foresee what they must be.

Perhaps we find consolation and a bit of wisdom by noting that every philosopher, educator, theologian, and psychotherapist wittingly or unwittingly postulates or glimpses the dream of perfect persons. As I have already noted (*Meandering 10.2*), would that they could agree, which they do not; yet agreement is impossible and, to avoid monotony and conformity, undesirable. Perfect persons cannot be cataloged: extroversion is an asset to one man, a liability for another. But noble have been the efforts to create an inventory of traits. More or less at random, some of these traits can be nominated. Perhaps, for example, self-esteem is highly desirable; one study suggests that in a clinical population of adult Americans self-derogation was found to be statistically related to the severity of psychopathological symptoms (Harder et al., 1984), which is not to say that self-derogation produces or is produced or augmented by mental disorders. No, the search is interminable. Instead let us skeptically plunge in and with humility discuss briefly the four traits in the proposition as prototypes: normality, rationality, the possession of faith, and the avoidance of evil.

If the first be *normality,* one must immediately ask about geniuses who allegedly have at least a touch of abnormality: are they not desirable, and should they not pursue desirable ends? Once more the abstract attribute of a value raises a semantic problem: the simple answer must be that most geniuses are within the range intended to be specified. That range ordinarily excludes pathology: the psychoses as well as some of its symptoms, such as paranoia, sadism, and masochism. The psychopath usually is unhappy and incapable of love, of acting sincerely, and of reporting truthfully. In contrast, a normal person has a set of values likely to function in appropriate situations and to be accompanied by relevant responses. Persons who are too offbeat are a nuisance; yet admittedly the line between normality and abnormality is unclear and wavers. Perhaps I have the courage to say that a reasonably well-integrated or organized person is desirable. Or, on a more optimistic note, the nonpsychopathic person may be considered "creative" with respect to his own development and existence (cf. Wolff, 1950, pp. 50–51). Even with the license permitted in dreaming, however, it is impossible to reel off the attributes of normality: there are or could be too many, and they vary considerably according to the norms and fashions of the society. In this context I cannot resist the temptation to refer again to a fact of history, as historians might say: the ever-changing nature of values and hence of the criteria for normality over time (*Meandering 11.4: Shifting Normality*).

Normal or not, principals should be as *rational* as possible in order to be able to reply validly to the probing questions and then to improve their judgments and actions. Use your head, we are advised in effect again and again. Certainly, if Kant's dictum concerning responsibility to all mankind is to be realized, principals may not ordinarily respond impulsively. Anticipating consequences demands reflection, which requires that time be available. But often time is not available: a decision must be made at the spur of the moment; in crowded societies, such as those in the West, principals and observers are kept so busy that they lose the capacity and the will to reflect. Whatever relation exists between cognitive and moral development (*Proposition 7.4*) supports the view that rationality is associated with moral persons. Philosophers may disagree concerning the precise role of "reason" in the judgments and actions they advocate, but they agree that principals must be rational in some respect, whether in connection with assessing motives (*What will I do?*), values (*What should I do?*), or means (*What would the consequences be?*) (*Meandering 11.5: Pro Rationality*).

Is *faith*, faith in the meaningfulness of existence, rational? Perhaps the question is foolish, for clearly faith is needed because frustrations are inevitable: children are disciplined; even the most successful experience some failures; everyone—including those with a confident belief in an eternal afterlife—is aware of ultimate and unavoidable death. No society is perfect: cruelty, shortages, spells of inhospitable weather, evil contemporaries exist and persist everywhere. It is important, therefore, to restore some semblance of equanimity in the absence of evidence that can be directly perceived. In spite of being sensibly skeptical, principals and observers should believe that somehow conditions will change and improve and that there can be if not everlasting, then at least longer enduring bliss. The presence everywhere of what persons in the West call religion (though the people themselves may not place their system of beliefs in such a category) suggests the many functions that internalization of beliefs can serve, ranging from the cosmological to the affirmation of justice. Faith in what is sometimes called progress, in the existence of a loving and forgiving god, and in possible immortality becomes essential.

Although faith may not be supported continually by the kind of evidence common sense and science demand, adequate substitutes are sometimes available. The authority, power, and guides to judgments and actions provided by religions all require faith. Buttressing the faith are miracles that the faithful or persons of little faith claim to have perceived directly with their senses. A belief in the mysterious brings its own personal relief and satisfaction reinforced by the procedures and rituals almost any religion provides. Having faith in perfectibility while recognizing inperfectibility may often be difficult but comforting.

When once an acceptable, seemingly valid basis for faith exists, principals then have a point of departure for their values from which, in theory at least, deviations are less likely to be tolerated. The Holy Bible of the Christian world, particularly the New Testament, is a case in point. Those who believe that its account of the ancient prophets and particularly of the commandments and actions of Jesus is accurate have or should have no difficulty accepting the edicts of their church. It has been decreed from on high that one should not work on the Sabbath and therefore . . . "This is my body," "This my blood," and therefore . . . Associated with Jesus are the values of . . . Good Christians and some non-Christians can complete sentences such as those.

Equivocal evidence supports faith in the possibility that over the centuries the actions of human beings have "improved," even as the ability to understand and to some extent to control nature and natural forces has increased. Perhaps there is less cruelty of a physical sort than formerly: even though men still torture and mutilate victims in police states, at least lip service is paid to international agreements such as the Geneva Convention regarding the treatment of war prisoners; and atrocities tend to be deplored almost everywhere. Organizations like Amnesty International seek to protect and promote human rights whenever they are violated. But the persistence of wars, terror, and other evils again raises the specter of skepticism and solidly punctures any optimistic view of changes in morality, even if more persons may have become aware of the need to formulate golden rules for conduct. It is to be doubted that the followers of those great religions are more devout today than they were in the ancient days of the founders. Possibly, at least in some nations—better perhaps not to try to name them—leaders and followers wish and demand, respectively, to have material goods distributed more equitably. And certainly advances in medicine have prolonged life expectancy in some but not all countries, so that perhaps it is true that the value behind this growth of knowledge has become more firmly anchored in human motives.

Our paragon, the perfect person, finally *avoids evil,* however evil is defined. In every society some actions are taboo; they are called evil and hence are supposed to be avoided (cf. Doob, 1978, chap. 1). It is difficult, however, to discover universal evils when attention is focused upon details. Indiscriminate murder, for example, may never be tolerated, yet the definition and the circumstances under which the killing of other persons inside or outside the principal's own society is permissible certainly vary considerably. Incest? Well, sometimes relatives considered "close" in Western society are not sexually taboo, although nowhere does a girl "marry" her father except perhaps in a ceremonial sense. In any case, evil, however culturally defined, is to be avoided.

Skeptical Note: Can a principal's reach exceed his grasp?

11.8 UTOPIA

Proposition: Principals should strive to create utopian conditions in their society.

The concept of utopia is a way of alerting us to the fact that most dreams, more often than not, can be realized only when adequate opportunities are provided within the society, when the "right patterns of behavior" are offered (Mannheim, 1943, p. 111). Every principal at some point in his existence is patriotic and is devoted to his neighborhood and country of birth since he has been socialized there; rejection of this social base signifies an imperfection in that base or in the principal himself. Any dream is realizable only with some assistance from reality: justice is administered by the state; beauty is more likely to be appreciated in the presence of objects or persons the principal considers beautiful; perhaps a personality trait like "self-esteem" is facilitated by "self-government" that provides "a sense of being the co-master of the rules under which one lives" (Bay, 1968). In constructing utopian institutions, it is difficult if not impossible to project upon them the passing values of our own era. Persons with a so-called liberal philosophy and supporters and members of labor unions believe that principals affected by decisions should play an active role in arriving at the decisions: who among them would dare dispute that moral proposition? Not I for one; but, skeptically I immediately tell myself, I am reflecting a democratic bias, and I also recognize that some principals prefer to have decisions made for them to avoid either responsibility or the travail of participation.

Sociologists and especially writers with Marxist inclinations are ever ready to point out that existing and potential moralities depend upon the society in which they are formulated and promulgated. Illustrations abound; I select one from a modern East German writer whose views reflect and express that tradition most eloquently: "Only on the basis of socialist conditions of production is it possible for political power and humanistic socialist morality to agree; indeed they are inseparably bound up with each other because under socialism the social, collective, and personal interest are in agreement" (Eberhard Fromm, 1970, p. 153). The great prophet himself, Karl Marx, however, expressed what I must call skepticism concerning such complete utopian determinism: "Men make their own *history,* but they do not make it just as they please; they do not make it under circumstances chosen by themselves, but under circumstances directly encountered, given, and transmitted from the past" (Marx, 1953 ed.). Substitute "morality" for "history" and note the dent principals make upon the restrictions and opportunities of their milieu.

Skeptical Note: Have utopias ever existed?

Envoi: Although dreams are dreamy, *nevertheless* they come from human beings and hence reflect and affect reality, however dimly.

MEANDERINGS

11.1 Coping with the Naturalistic Fallacy

One philosopher points out that this so-called fallacy has produced "persistent and intractable" arguments and that "at present there is no orthodoxy or even anything like a dominant view" (Nielsen, 1979). If anyone is luckily innocent concerning the fallacy, let him examine the "series of statements" one philosopher employs to illustrate his contention that the "ought" can be derived from the "is":

1. Jones uttered the words "I hereby promise to pay you, Smith, five dollars."
2. Jones promised to pay Smith five dollars.
3. Jones placed himself under (undertook) an obligation to pay Smith five dollars.
4. Jones is under an obligation to pay Smith five dollars.
5. Jones ought to pay Smith five dollars (Searle, 1964).

If the reader is intrigued and believes the author has or has not accomplished the objective of squeezing an *ought* out of an *is*, let him read the rest of the argument; and then let him study the volume in which the essay has been reprinted and note how other philosophers seize the above statements and squirm and squirm to refute or support the reasoning (W. D. Hudson, 1969). The author himself introduces what he calls a rider between most of the above statements: other things must be equal, certeris paribus. An "institutional fact" must thus be assumed before the fact of the promise (the *is*) and the prescriptive value can emerge: in the society of Jones and Smith there exists a value that promises must be kept; and the certeris paribus clause presumes there are no other conflicting values, such as Jones's inability to discharge his debt because he needs the money to prevent his wife and seven children from starving to death. To determine the prescription of obligation from the fact, it is necessary to reply to only one of the probing questions (*What must I do?*) and to presume that other values are irrelevant or unimportant.

A simpler illustration from another philosopher:

Fischer wants to mate Botwinnik.
The one and only way to mate Botwinnik is for Fischer to move the Queen.
Therefore, Fischer should move the Queen (Black, 1964).

The inescapable value appears in the original premise: Fischer is motivated to win (*What will I do?*). Of minor significance but still relevant is that both players are willing to follow the rules of chess (*What may I do?*). In short, I agree, but for different reasons, with a pair of philosophers who criticize the philosopher from whom the first illustration above has been borrowed (Thompson and Thompson, 1964): a prescribed value cannot be derived from a fact unless other values are inserted.

A modern Hungarian philosopher deliberately argues against the naturalistic fallacy and anticipates "emphatic opposition" since that argument "opposes the firm prejudices of the prevailing trends in bourgeois philosophy." His reasoning seems to stem from an admittedly Marxian conception of change. Perhaps his clearest statement— in an opaque translation—appears in the following sentence: "the inner unity of 'what is good and right for us' is determined by the ideal; the final answer to the question 'what is good for us?' and 'what ought we to do?' is determined by 'what has to be according to our opinion' " (Makai, 1972, pp. 7, 83). Perhaps, then, if we know a trend is inevitable, the fact of that trend (the *is*) inevitably prescribes the *should*. But can we be that certain of the trend? Are human or social tendencies as certain as gravity?

My impression is that almost all philosophers spend their excess or limited energies trying to refute the naturalistic fallacy. The philosopher cited at the outset of this meandering comes close to the position advocated in the present analysis, but then skips away, or tries to: "There is . . . the possibility of founding morality on the nature of man and . . . for establishing by analysis systematic connections between value and the nature of man and the world, while still preserving the insight . . . that (a) value and fact, norm and existence, the *is* and the *ought* are all distinct and (b) . . . no categorical moral statements can be derived from the cold facts, including the facts of human nature" (Nielsen, 1979).

11.2 The Tragedy of the Commons

The title of this meandering is a compelling metaphor that appropriately suggests one of love's complexities (Hardin, 1972). When the grazing land of a community is open to all its members, each principal can secure maximum benefit for himself by having as many of his own cattle as possible feed upon the public land. If everyone pursues his own gain, however, the commons will be overgrazed and all will suffer. Under these conditions, love for others becomes a necessity: it is to the advantage of everyone to reach an agreement to limit the use of the commons by each citizen so that the public land is not overgrazed and the common good is promoted. Every person makes a sacrifice ultimately for his own good as well as out of consideration or love for his contemporaries. In modern societies the effect of a principal's loveless, selfish actions are not always as easily noticeable, but the tragedy of noncooperation or the absence of love may be less apparent though nevertheless real. The smoke from a coal-burning factory appears to disappear when in reality the exhaust produces acid rain upon the crops and persons of other regions; pollution of this kind is curable at a sacrifice by the factory owners, who pay extra to buy cleaner coal or to install expensive equipment in order to prevent the noxious by-products from entering the atmosphere. We are, therefore, interdependent; as the same writer has suggested with another imposing, convincing metaphor, "the earth is a spaceship" on which we cannot avoid affecting one another. Once pollution has occurred, the pollutants will not disappear but must be allowed, for example, to drift to another part of the continent. We have limited resources to distribute; if principals exercise freedom without regard for the consequences, eventually they will experience the tragedy of the commons: their cattle will overgraze and the commons as well as everyone will suffer (Hardin, 1972, pp. 109–40). We have here a statement of the problem without a solution. How, for example, can the expanding growth of population be controlled so that all people can be adequately fed, housed, clothed?

11.3 What Is Justice?

A quick aside concerning the looseness with which most discourse relating to values, especially justice, is employed. According to one philosopher, "love and justice are the same, for justice is love distributed, nothing else" (Fletcher, 1966, p. 87). Nothing else, really and truly, nothing else? When a judge in a court decrees that a convicted criminal is to die, is he expressing love for the criminal? Or love for the citizens of the community who will no longer be endangered by the man or who, if capital punishment acts as a deterrent, will not be attacked by other potential murderers? In most Western societies wealthy persons are taxed more heavily on their incomes than poor people; is such a policy a by-product of love or a conviction concerning ability to pay? In contrast, on the basis of his own research concerning the development of moral values in children and young adults, a psychologist concludes that "only principles of justice have an ultimate claim to being adequate as universal, prescriptive principles" (Kohlberg, 1971). But he has also admitted that justice may be admired more by men than by women, for perhaps—and I would emphasize perhaps—women are more strongly motivated by a "wish not to hurt others" and to resolve conflict (Kohlberg et al., 1984, pp. 122–24, 139; cf. Gilligan, 1982, p. 65).

The concept of justice is more frequently applied to institutions than to individuals. According to Aristotle, "the law is wisdom without desire," by which he means that judgments can be passed without the "passions" characterizing individual decisions (Aristotle, 1944 ed., p. 265). Actually that "law" is administered everywhere by human beings who may or may not be able to curb their passions; often when they do not succeed, they are accused of "bias." The analysis of justice thus quickly passes over into the realm of freedom which has its own tangles. In that context many are the additional challenging statements that must be digested and appraised, such as "No alternative to in-equality has yet been found that is consistent with freedom" (Mason, 1970, p. 326). It is well, however, never to forget that the sense of justice is always within persons and therefore must be learned like almost every other value. At the outset, as Piaget has indicated, the very young child may believe in "immanent justice" or the "expiatory punishment" that occurs almost automatically whenever he engages in behavior disapproved by adults even in the absence of the pun-ishing agent (Piaget, 1965, pp. 251–62), but eventually he applies standards both to others and to himself.

The importance principals place upon equity has been repeatedly demonstrated when that value is salient or is made so. In a hypo-thetical paper-and-pencil situation German secondary school students were asked how they would allocate money that two hypothetical persons had earned: both had made equal contributions to earning the money, but the need of one was supposed to be greater than that of the other. The needier person was allocated a greater share, re-gardless of the hypothetical relation between the two, when the equity value had been made salient by the investigator who told the boys to "perform the allocation in such a way that in your opinion it is as just as possible." When that value had not been made salient, however, need determined the distribution only under one additional condition: the two recipients had been portrayed as friends and not as superficial acquaintances (Lamm and Schwinger, 1983). When participants judge they have been treated equitably, their judgments and behavior may be favorably affected; for example, American col-lege couples were more likely to have "intimate" and hence presumably satisfying contacts with another person when they judged their relationship to be equitable (Walster et al., 1978).

A key question in the dream of justice is to determine the conditions under which this value becomes salient and, when it is, whether equity or equality results. A sample of German students considered the ability of another person to be less important than the effort he expended when they allocated hypothetical gains and losses (Lamm et al., 1983). American students had a slight tendency to share equally a sum of money with a peer, even though they ostensibly contributed more to the task at hand, when they had affective bonds with that person than when those bonds were lacking (Bagarozzi, 1982). Apparently new factors emerge in almost every experiment when different variables are manipulated by the investigator; for example, Australian students in passing judgment concerning hypothetical situations involving the allocation of rewards to two persons reacted differently in part as a function of the context: more equitable distributions were approved when the two persons were said to be employed by the same company than when they interacted in noneconomic situations (Boldero and Rosenthal, 1984). Justice, or at least the factors determining the form it takes, is elusive.

In the West the concept of justice is frequently associated with the courts, which are supposed to administer it. The meaning of the concept in a judicial context is diverse and ranges from the view that legal regulations must protect "society" from criminals to the conviction that all persons accused of crimes must be given a "fair" trial regardless of their status within the society. In more general terms, the judgment of just depends not only upon the individual or action being judged but also upon the participant's own conception of justice and other predispositions (cf. Staub, 1978, v. 1, pp. 179–80). It is futile to assert, therefore, that murder is murder and therefore the accused is treated the same whether the victim is a king or a hobo. Justice is too complex to be handled with a cliché.

A modern philosopher suggests that two principles guide institutions as they would realize the dream of justice; in his own words:

1. Each person is to have an equal right to the most extensive total system of equal basic liberties compatible with a similar system of liberty for all.
2. Social and economic inequalities are to be arranged so that they are both (a) to the greatest benefit of the least advantaged, consistent with the just savings principle [justice between generations], and (b) attached to offices and positions

open to all under conditions of fair equality of opportunity.
(Rawls, 1971, p. 302)

These are brave principles, but—and the buts in practice are numerous, without deprecating those principles. In connection with the first principle, for example, the author notes that "a less than equal liberty must be acceptable to those with the lesser liberty." How is this to be achieved? How are the persons "with the lesser liberty" to be convinced that they should suffer the deprivation and that their deprivation will "strengthen the total system of liberty shared by all"? The author recognizes that "other fundamental social problems, in particular those of coordination, efficiency, and stability" must also be solved (p. 66). In addition, more or less in the tradition of the psychologists previously cited (*Proposition 7.4*), he suggests that "moral development" progresses or should progress through three "stages" called "authority," "association" (the values of the principal's groups), and finally a reliance upon "principles" such as those quoted above (pp. 458–79). The principles themselves appear less helpful when one glances at the modern world and perforce notes that all or most government officials, whether they preside over systems labeled democratic, communist, authoritarian, and even fascist, are eager to subscribe to the phrasings; perhaps they truly are groping to achieve justice as they view it. A skeptic must say that they are considering only a particular group or class as they enact legislation they consider just, while they themselves, cynically or not, may truly believe they are seeking justice for everyone.

11.4 Shifting Normality

A glance at almost any phase of mankind's history immediately provides copious illustrations of changes in values (*Proposition 4.3*) and hence in the definition of normality, whether one considers the shift from hunting and gathering to agriculture and herding in prehistorical times or an event like the French Revolution. In his own lifetime the individual principal may be confronted with evidence that his behavior is not consistent with some of his values (*What ought I do?*); that one of his values cannot be realized because it is incompatible with another value (*What shall I do?*); that a value has consequences of which he himself may not approve because of its relation to other values and other persons (*What would the consequences be?*) (Ball-Rokeach and Tallman, 1979). Equally important is the possibility that he may be forced or force himself to acquire new values as a result of changed circumstances in his life, as when he marries, has children, changes his occupation, or migrates (cf. Feather, 1979). The dream applicable to a normal principal is that he will react positively to such inevitable changes and adapt "satisfactorily" to them.

And his positive reaction should be, the dream continues, not to fall back upon a habitual action—jumping from perception to habit to behavior, as the Morality Figure suggests—but to pass moral judgments that take into account, as far as possible, all eight probing questions. His behavior should be predictable up to a point without having him become a bore to himself and others. Within himself he seeks to comprehend the conflict between the old and the possible new. He is wary of his own emotions at this point. For he may be having what has been called a "peak experience" in which an "*is*" becomes the same as *ought*" and "*fact*" becomes the same as *value*" (Maslow, 1963, italics his). Glorifying the naturalistic fallacy, as it were, in this fashion results from the enthusiasm of the moment, the conviction that one's feelings must be valid. At the same time the principal knows that living could be robbed of some of its glories if the spontaneous joy associated with such experiences were to be eliminated.

A normal person, either immediately or upon reflection, is able to decide what is appropriate, proper, or permitted in a given situation. Who should try to rescue that man who has been so frequently drowning throughout these pages? Here is a situation that is equivocal for most persons because they may be uncertain whether it is necessary or desirable for them to risk their own lives. That question, however, does not arise for a policeman who is expected to be heroic, and it most definitely does not occur to that lifeguard on a beach who sees a swimmer in distress beyond the breaking waves. Again and again, therefore, in unstructured situations the principal wonders whether he is his brother's keeper and then he arrives at a well-balanced, a normal decision. Really? Skepticism is merited.

11.5 Pro Rationality

Most philosophers who discuss morality and almost all classical economists assume that principals make or are capable of making rational choices and that they are therefore aware of the alternatives confronting them and of the consequent need to weight them (*What might the consequences be?*). Kant himself has issued the challenge when he stated that "only a rational being has the power to act in accordance *with his idea of laws,* that is, in accordance with principles" (cited by Paton, 1947, p. 39, italics his). Aristotle, however, in advocating a golden mean first argues that "reason" usually does not govern men's actions: "anybody can become angry—this is easy, and so it is to give and spend money; but to be angry with or give money to the right person, and to the right amount, and at the right time, and for the right purpose, and in the right way—this is not within everybody's power and is not easy; so that to do these things properly is rare, praiseworthy, and noble" (Aristotle, 1934, ed., p. 111). But later he suggests how reason should operate to achieve the highest good. For principals begin with a "major" or "universal" premise—or "opinion"—which is the value or principle. The minor or "particular" premise is a "perception" of the situation at hand. When there are conflicting major premises, "desire" (that is, motive) selects one rather than the other; in either case the conclusion and hence the action follow reasonably from the major premise that is selected and from the minor premise (Aristotle, 1934, ed., pp. 391–93). In contrast, Freud has made most educated persons in the West conscious of the unconscious and hence of the difficulties that arise when they seek to be rational; his method of therapy, psychoanalysis, would enable many of these unconscious impulses to become conscious and it contributes perhaps to rationality.

American psychologists concerned with the development of moral judgments characterize their highest stage as a rational one: it is "the belief as a rational person in the validity of universal moral principles, and a sense of commitment to them," one of them postulates (Kohlberg, 1976). Another: "principles . . . so presented that rational, equal, and impartial people could choose them as the governing terms of their behavior" (Rest, 1979). And yet two others: "the individual responds to situations on the basis of principles rather than on the basis of orientation toward social agents" (Garbarino and Bronfenbrenner, 1976).

CHAPTER 12

Constraints

Dreams, as bravely and cautiously stated at the beginning of the last chapter, may affect and change reality, but they can also be wrecked by the intrusion of reality. Perfection is not being achieved, is perhaps unachievable. Why? The question is asked formally here and answered not by principals about themselves but by observers about principals. One view is clear: it is not helpful to assert that human beings are inherently good or bad. Perhaps they are quite capable of becoming villains or saints under circumstances that do or do not, can or cannot exist in their society. Nor does it advance knowledge, except perhaps in an important metaphysical or theological sense, to believe that they are born in sin: it is not the newborn babe, but his parents or ancestors who are largely responsible for the values he originally acquires or does not acquire. Better, then, to concentrate upon the constraints preventing perfection. Skepticism moves to the forefront, after being not particularly shy throughout the previous discussions.

12.1 DISAGREEMENT AND UNREALITY

Proposition: Observers, as well as principals, almost always disagree concerning the nature and realism of their own dreams and especially those of others.

Superficial evidence for this proposition can be acquired merely by asking individuals what they mean when they refer to the good life or some equivalent banal phrase. One man's meat is another man's poison: the platitude describes the difference between an honest man and a thief or, according to Marxians and other opinionated observers, entrepreneurs and workers. Even discovering, as a matter of fact, the modal values within a society is no easy task, as has been repeatedly emphasized *(Proposition 1.3)*. What emerges, then, is only a collation of descriptive values, perhaps also a few prescriptive values, in the form of largely unrealizable dreams. Minorities and deviants are ignored, even though their views in the long run may prevail. Such persons, to be sure, engage in behavior considered morally deficient by conforming observers, but they may be suddenly labeled moral when they also perform heroic deeds. And so the very concept of perfect persons may be misleading in the sense that such persons cannot be delineated; yet that is true of all dreams—obviously.

As every parent and educator in Western society acknowledges when challenged, there is little agreement concerning the positive traits to be cultivated in children as they are socialized: the models are so diverse. Even when candidates as prototypes are confined to the great religions—Jesus, Buddha, Confucius, the prophets, the saints—it seems clear that, although they share traits like compassion and humility, their personalities differ in many respects. And the heroes and heroines who transcend their own eras—do they share common traits? Before seeking an answer to that question, it would be necessary to identify universal heroes—and who would they be?

In societies less complicated and diverse than those in the West, it ought to be feasible to postulate the personality traits considered desirable, at least in a particular society. A philosopher turned anthropologist, in order to acquire the perspective afforded by immersion in a totally different culture, believes that the following "traits," in the language he himself has chosen, characterize the "good" Hopi Indian: a family man who is agreeable in social relations, not dangerous, cooperative, generous, honest, modest, quiet and unobtrusive, cheerful, manly and brave, a good worker (Brandt, 1954, p. 138). Perhaps the dreams of societies more complicated than the Hopi can be thus ascertained, but our values are too diverse to be easily codified, even by a philosopher. When a glance is cast at us, we find Plato advocating philosophers as kings, scribes in the Middle Ages extolling absolute monarchs, and Benjamin Franklin finding bourgeois values dear to his heart (cf. Ossowska, 1970, pp. 124–82). Here is yet another compelling reason to search for variables that might account for the diversity among principals and hence for their diverse values, but unanimity cannot thereby be achieved.

Again and again, since the time of the ancients, good persons report their dreams. In an address before the Pontifical Academy of Sciences, Pope John Paul II declared that "truth, freedom, justice, and love" are the cornerstones of science and of the life of civilized society (John Paul II, 1983). Concepts like these can easily be expressed and they lend an appealing tone to such an appeal or to any statements concerning the goals of mankind, but they remain almost in the category of slogans—or dreams—until they are embodied in and applied to a specific social context or to specific actions. It is heartening, nevertheless, that men and women of good will at least utilize the same or similar concepts, slogans, or clichés even though their definitions are varied.

Was Hitler a moral person? Of course not, but why not? According to the twisted definition of millions of German observers who approved of him and subscribed to his dictates, he was certainly a morally complete hero during the periods when he sought and then held power. His judgments were based on replies to all the probing questions, and through skillful propaganda he was able to raise the supporting forces that made him the leader of his nation. He possessed values that justified the murdering of his opponents and the events leading to World War II. But other observers—opponents of his regime including some Germans, the leaders and peoples in the lands that defeated him, and undoubtedly future generations—do not consider his behavior moral because they do not approve of the goals he sought and the imperative values guiding him.

A swift turn from the ridiculous and the wicked to the sublime and the more permanent: heroes arise and persist with every society. A small minority may view them as role models, but the vast majority who lack the necessary skills and status respond to them either as dream figures or as powers requiring conformity. Observers over time pass different judgments upon them, for especially in the West great originality is supposed to be demonstrated by writers and gossips who unearth flaws in the characters of the famous. Perhaps only very great religious figures survive as heroes, for one reason because historical documentation in the modern sense is lacking and what has remained are only accounts provided by their admirers and disciples.

Skeptical Note: Why worry about consensus?

12.2 HUMAN FRAILTIES

Proposition: Principals are human and hence prone to be frail.

No elaboration of this proposition should be necessary other than to list the skeptical notes within the half dozen chapters devoted to the principals and the envois at their conclusions (chapters 3 through

8). The frailties tax the patience of Lucifer. Let me gently note those defects most relevant to moral judgments and actions. On occasion, principals are selfish, unreflective, rationalizing, and prone to make false judgments. They may be so completely driven by their own motives that they ruthlessly ignore the welfare of others: presumably then they lack the inhibitions provided by a strong conscience either because they have been inadequately socialized or because they have learned through experience that such behavior frequently is not punished and may even be rewarding *(Proposition 6.1)*. They may or may not consider themselves morally deficient, even when they realize they are violating acceptable modes of behavior. The tragedy of the commons previously mentioned *(Meandering 11.2)* is a metaphorical lesson concerning the human dilemma of selfishness versus the good of society. According to one stimulating, tour-de-force analysis, principals and observers everywhere—yes, everywhere—are able most ingeniously to find villains or scapegoats to account for their miseries or to justify behavior otherwise considered immoral; among other consequences, "social change has been hampered and distorted" (Lauterbach, 1983). No one expects anyone other than a god or a demigod to be completely consistent—consistent in terms of his own values or of a trait ascribed to him *(Proposition 7.3)*. Perhaps a German literary writer is correct when he asserts that every principal has the potentiality of becoming a traitor when he lives under a regime that does not meet his approval (Enzensberger, 1967, pp. 49–50); temptation is possible under some circumstances. Another human frailty, almost too obvious to mention, is a proclivity to be mentally slovenly; one repeats that we live in a land of opportunity and hence that every child has the possibility of becoming wealthy or successful and forgets that the principal from an underprivileged family is less likely to realize that opportunity, which therefore is for him only a hypothetical one.

Were society or groups and persons less complicated, it may be guessed with some confidence, the social sciences, psychology, and psychiatry—and their precursors or equivalents in other societies—would not have developed and would not be consulted to gain insight into their functioning. These disciplines stress the complexity of their subject matters. Thus the concepts of manifest and latent have been employed by a sociologist to refer, respectively, to the adjustments or adaptations "intended and recognized by participants in the system" and to those "neither intended nor recognized" (Merton, 1957, p. 51). The same terms appear in Freud and other psychoanalysts to describe the conscious and the unconscious, especially in connection with dreams. Thus the sociologist and the analyst assume that they rather than the principals themselves have the expertise to uncover or help uncover the latent.

When a group of principals is observed in everyday life or functions as subjects for research, deviations appear that have implications for changing prescriptive values. In any group, including relatively homogeneous families, individuals react differently to the same communication after being exposed to it or after actually perceiving it. When the lives of writers who were brothers are surveyed, for example, it can be seen that some of the siblings were friendly and cooperative (Julian and Aldous Huxley), others very unfriendly and nonsupportive (Heinrich and Thomas Mann), and still others fluctuating and ambiguous (James and Stanislaus Joyce) (Kiell, 1983). Some children obey adults in response to threatened punishments, others when provided with a rationale for doing so (cf. Kurtz and Eisenberg, 1983). To cope with deviations, different routes to conformity are usually offered.

Reference must be made again *(Proposition 3.6)* to the frequent discrepancy between judgments and intentions on the one hand and behavior on the other hand. Often principals tend not to practice what they preach to themselves and to others; why? Other motives may be stronger: they may genuinely wish to help the unfortunate even when demands from their immediate family are more pressing. Ghetto children and adults may share the value of honesty with middle-class Americans, but as a result of "differences in social perspective and situational opportunities" they may find it more difficult to execute the implications of that value (Kohlberg, 1971). Often the "categorical" attitude or belief as measured in a questionnaire may remain intact and precious, but other attitudes or beliefs function in particular situations (cf. Milner, 1984); thus the high ideals of his religion may bring great satisfaction to a businessman, yet are perhaps abandoned when he competes with another firm for a contract. From an opposite standpoint, morally almost complete behavior may occur even though the principal has no really compelling values promoting that behavior, inasmuch as many values may be pure verbalism. And so, for example, "individuals at different stages [of moral development] can exhibit the same behavior using different types of reasoning, whereas individuals at the same stage can exhibit different behaviors using the same type of reasoning" (Kurtines and Greif, 1974).

Moral judgments must be made again and again, even when the principal is not always prepared to do so. If honesty is the best policy, one honest action occurs not in isolation but as the prelude to numerous other actions, provided somehow the principal finds honesty a rewarding experience in the widest sense and provided he can be consistent when and if that value is salient in all relevant situations. The hereafter quickly becomes the new present and the pending future.

Little wonder that both principals and observers often employ vague criteria to decide whether actions are good or bad. They may say their judgments are based upon intuition, which is a way of affirming their correctness without offering any or sufficient supporting evidence. They resort to analogy and claim their judgments are as quick and correct as when they avoid oncoming danger or use correct grammar without reflection. Probably such analogies are misleading: a principal who claims he can instantly make moral decisions may be reporting the truth as he introspects; what he reports, however, provides no criterion independent of the values that he has acquired in the past and that now function without an immediately conscious trace.

Not only may the principal lack the experience or skill to anticipate the consequences of an action *(What would the consequences be?)*, but he may be unable also to evaluate the outcome of the action he is performing *(What do I do?)*. He reacts nobly, but does not know whether the accomplishment has been really significant or whether the action has been appreciated by the recipient *(Proposition 5.4)*. He does not know, he may never know what the consequences for himself and others would have been if he had not performed that act or had performed some other act. Under these circumstances he makes certain adjustments in his attitudes or beliefs which themselves, though humane, may lead him into further error. He may experience guilt and then be faced with the problem of coping with that guilt; what happens in the future depends on how successful the coping turns out to be. He may repress what has happened, try to forget it; here his behavior in the hereafter will depend on processes deep in his unconscious. He may resolve in the future to compensate for an action in the past by attempting the opposite. Or he may rationalize what he has done, so that the behavior appears positive to him; then repetition in the future becomes more probable. Thus, as has been indicated *(Proposition 11.4)*, there are two ways to achieve the dream of justice and equity in society. One is objective: the principal conducts himself in such a way that the other person is rewarded in a manner conforming to that principal's conception of the value at stake. The second is subjective: the principal somehow convinces himself that the other person has been dealt with justly or equitably even when no change in his situation has necessarily occurred. Rationalization may be provoked by a dream that later has nightmarish results.

In exactly the same context the reaction to injustice may be viewed as a frailty by an observer and as a strength by the victim. The observer believes that the principal should combat the injustice he is enduring, that he should seek to "restore the state of equity." Instead, from the observer's standpoint, he is weak because he diminishes his stress by finding some explanation for the injustice, such as self-blame or some other rationalization (Mikula, 1984) *(Meandering 11.3)*.

Human fallibility reappears when the naturalistic fallacy is committed and when it is not committed *(Proposition 11.1)*. Not committing it presents no problem in connection with blatantly morally deficient behavior: murders ought not be encouraged because they are committed. But at the other extreme it may be good in some sense to try, however vainly, to correct faults by trying to achieve the perfection of the moral person. To draw any kind of line between necessary and desirable behavior, however fuzzy, is difficult in situations less extreme than murdering and sleeping. In short, some relation between descriptive and prescriptive values, I say again, is unavoidable; as one writer convincingly argues in favor of a "fusion" between science and "ethics," adjustments in values must be made to "new factual information" (Sperry, 1983, pp. 19, 71–72).

Skeptical Note: Can human frailties be overcome, whether serious or trivial?

12.3 LIMITED JUDGMENTS

Proposition: Judgments are usually incomplete because principals rely on one or several but not all the replies to the probing questions.

The need to consider all eight questions has been previously stressed, perhaps overstressed; the understandable reasons for not doing so have been mentioned in the last proposition. Principals may embark on a praiseworthy enterprise, and then, because they have ignored one of the highly relevant questions, they find themselves on a slippery slope leading them to the basest of evils (cf. P. Singer, 1979, pp. 153–57). The limitations, therefore, must be considered one by one.

The first limitation comes from the environment: the prevailing climate and natural resources *(What can I do?)*. Some tasks can be performed more easily in daylight than in the dark; crops require optimal sunlight and rainfall. To prescribe even morally incomplete actions contrary to such restrictions would be to doom the results to failure. This limitation cannot be exaggerated even when it is remembered that through technological advances (such as irrigation) principals have been able to overcome many but not all such handicaps. Similarly "nature" imposes certain limits upon every principal: we can endure only a certain amount of pain, disappointment, or frustration; without assistance there are limits to the weights men and women can lift in rescuing another person. These limits, however, can also be stretched, as martyrs and others have demonstrated.

Assuming various responsibilities is unavoidable and hence duty becomes another constraining limitation *(What must I do?)*. When a child is born, parents must tacitly agree both with themselves and with the state to care for, and to raise him or her, even though they cannot possibly anticipate all the details parental responsibility entails. A physician assumes responsibility for a person he accepts as a patient. Nowadays in the United States he may share that responsibility by consulting other physicians before deciding on a diagnosis or treatment, or he may have the patient participate in the decision. He may protect himself from malpractice suits through insurance; he thus places some responsibility, as it were, upon the insurance company, but he cannot completely gainsay it.

Principals are limited by the fact that the achievement of private goals *(What will I do?)* may be satisfying but one-sided. On a provocative psychiatrist's paper-and-pencil test that sought to measure "purpose-in-life" (with items such as "I am usually bored," the responses to which could vary on a continuum ranging from 1, "completely bored," to 7, "exuberant, enthusiastic"), normal Americans scored higher than those assigned to various psychiatric categories, and among the normals the apparently successful also scored higher than the indigent (Crumbaugh, 1968). Principals with a clearly formulated system of values may well find that life for them is meaningful, but their values may be morally deficient from the standpoint of observers or those they affect. A Central American dictator may be exuberant and enthusiastic, but he is not considered to be a morally perfect person. Two investigators, after surveying and seeking to influence large samples of American undergraduates, concluded that their subjects were "selective about the direction of value change that they say they are willing to tolerate" and actually did tolerate; the students were maintaining in effect that they would not modify their values unless they were or could be made to feel dissatisfied with them (Rokeach and Grube, 1979).

It is easy to assert that so-called basic needs must be satisfied if the principal is to survive or even if he is to appreciate the beauty of a sunset *(cf. Proposition 3.2)*. The moment the derived or secondary needs are contemplated, however, the task of ranking their value becomes difficult if not impossible (Narr, 1983). Who is to say whether having access to a sunset should have a lower or higher priority than being able to listen to chamber music played by a gifted quartet? Or is a short, joyous life preferable to a longer, duller one? Knowledge required to reply to probing questions such as these must always be limited because by its nature it offers no way to select alternatives. If there were hedonic units enabling the principal or the observer to quantify the satisfaction derived from a sunset and a quartet, a decision might be feasible—but such units do not exist *(Proposition 6.3)*.

Poets, psychiatrists, and most principals stress that every person is embedded in an intricate network of other persons, so that almost any action of his must have repercussions not only upon those close associates but also conceivably upon a wider range of persons now living or yet to be born *(What did I do?)*. Sometimes it appears as if a single action does not have such consequences when, for example, principals in our society make decisions concerning animals, plants, and land; they legally or legitimately control them and what they do with them is their own affair. In fact, however, the changes cannot be judged in isolation: what happens to these nonhuman resources may affect other persons both now and later. In circumstances like these, either principals may be ignorant of the consequences or else— if permitted—they deliberately and selfishly ignore them.

The search for means to achieve ends is often a limitation if only because both the principal's capability *(What can I do?)* and relevant rules *(What may I do?)* are involved *(Proposition 13.5)*. The problem is a favorite of philosophers, but sometimes their solution is more glib than helpful; for example, " 'If the end does not justify the means, what does?' The answer is, obviously, 'Nothing!' " (Fletcher, 1966, p. 120). According to the present analysis, the confusion arises when the eight probing questions are not asked with reference to *both* the ends and the means. Should that frequently mentioned hypothetical person steal the drug to save his wife or should he not steal it and risk having her die? So crudely stated, the dilemma is between the values of honesty and life. Applying only one of the questions to the

means *(What can I do?)* could stimulate the poor husband to find another solution besides that of stealing; he might be able to borrow
the money from a friend or—nowadays in the West—he could apply
to a government agency for financial assistance. Waging a war considered "just" has ever been a challenging thorn in men's conscience:
with well-equipped and well-trained fighting forces such a war has
been previously feasible, and no compelling international rules have
prevented it, but—consider the consequences of any war. When all
the aspects of waging and not waging war are estimated in terms of
the eight questions, a solution other than war might be achievable.
In any case the consequences, the values, and all the rest must be
weighted for both means and ends before a moral decision can be
rendered.

The beneficiary of an action who can be the principal himself, other
persons, or humanity in general likewise limits the actions of principals *(What would the consequences be?)*. This limitation is especially
relevant when assistance is to be rendered or to be required. Among
Canadian nurses, helping or receiving help was associated—somewhat, but not dramatically—with demographic factors (age, education, income, experience, and status), but not with attributes of their
personalities (Burke, 1982). The principal's own motive may be decisive *(What will I do?)*: he may wish to be ostensibly generous because
he anticipates a reward, because he would conform to one of his own
values or that of his group, or because he feels sympathetic toward
the other person (cf. Staub, 1978, v. 1, pp. 42–45). He thus weighs
the costs to himself of helping versus not helping.

Implementing prescriptive values may be limited by the fact that
they are difficult to achieve *(What can I do?)* or that their implications
are not sufficiently taken into account *(What would the consequences
be?)*. Nirvana, it should be realized, can seldom be achieved in a single
leap. "To each according to his need, from each according to his ability"—capability has been thus featured as an explicit goal in communist thinking and to a certain extent whenever philosophers of
ethics and clergymen become practical or realistic. Immediately apparent are the difficulties arising when the critical words *need* and
ability are operationalized. Basic needs, yes: a grown man needs more
food than his infant son or daughter. A sick individual needs more
personal care than someone who is healthy. But otherwise needs are
so elastic that they cannot constitute the ultimate or the only basis
for moral judgments. One person claims to need water, another milk,
another red or white wine, another beer with his principal meal each

day: should each be granted his wish simply because he possesses the need, even if it is assumed that without the desired beverage the meal would appear less satisfactory? The taste for wine or beer, if not for water and milk, is obviously an acquired taste and therefore there is no inherent reason why it should be satisfied simply because for good reasons, either beyond the individual's control or not, it has been acquired. The concept of "ability" also abounds in complexity *(What can I do?)*. Yes, clearly the physician and not the mason should be called upon to attend the ill, and the skilled musician rather than the atonal amateur should play in the symphony orchestra. The difficulty decreases when the status quo of abilities is accepted. Or does it? Some physicians are more conscientious than others. The person with the ability to do what is considered to be the dirty work of society—usually a disagreeable or dangerous task such as collecting garbage or working with asbestos products—may have this ability through no fault of his own but only because, being unfavorably placed within the hierarchy of society by reason of his birth, he has had little choice except to accept the occupation. He has the ability in spite of himself, and under other circumstances that ability might have been quite different. "To each according to his need, from each according to his ability," therefore, is a slogan that refers only to the status quo of principals derived from avoidable or unavoidable experiences in the past, and it ignores their present and future potentialities.

Moral judgments are limited when they stem from inadequate or false information *(Proposition 3.3)*. A principal may think he can follow an ethical code without investigating the difficulties he must resolve. He may simply be inexperienced. Or data may be lacking, so that his judgment is incomplete; at this moment, for example, mankind does not know precisely what would transpire if a nuclear war between the Soviet Union and the United States were to occur, and additional knowledge may not be acquired for decades to come. In many studies, we know, apparent sex differences appear, but we are uncertain whether all of them can be attributed to cultural rather than biological or genetic factors. In the meantime, it is impossible to reply to some of the probing questions for the two sexes, such as the one pertaining to capability *(What can I do?)*.

The final limitation concerns the relation between the genetic constitution of principals and their culture. On the one hand it is clear, I say once again, that certain basic needs require satisfaction: principals must breathe and eat, and there are perhaps other biological propensities that cannot be denied. On the other hand it is equally evident that the needs and propensities are modifiable by culture. We cannot examine human nature and proclaim that prescriptive values are derivable therefrom, although aspects of that nature must guide the values—and the guide must come from the constituents of culture *(Proposition 11.1)*. Principals can be neither completely egocentric nor selfish. Glibly but trenchantly expressed, some aspects of human nature must conform to culture, but others can correct culture (cf. Salkever, 1983)—the optimum combination is elusive.

The foregoing limitations require us to emphasize that rationality or complete rationality is probably impossible *(Proposition 11.7)*. It may be comforting to assume that each individual principal is able under ideal conditions to consider all the factors relevant to a judgment, to weight them properly, and to make a wise judgment. In some instances these assumptions may be valid, as when one must choose between lamb or duck for dinner or between contending candidates for the chairman of a small committee, but the possibilities of moral irrationality are legion. The principal may be driven by unconscious motives or by habits that prevent him from considering all relevant information. Much of what he thinks he knows and believes to have been "voluntarily" and "rationally" obtained in fact may have originated from outside sources not without prejudice. In any case his information is limited. If he seeks help in order to reach a decision, he may consult others who are also biased or ignorant. If he participates in a group to reach a collective decision, he may be influenced by prestigious peers. Little wonder that rationality must be included among the dreams and that we, you and I, must be skeptical concerning the possibility of realizing any dream.

Skeptical Note: Conceivably can judgments be improved?

12.4 COMPLEXITY

Proposition: Complexity resulting from the nature of society as well as changes and conflicts within it increase the difficulties of principals as they pass moral judgments.

Judgments cannot be rigid; exceptions are necessary and inevitable *(Proposition 7.3)*. The relation between judgments and behavior, also as previously indicated *(Proposition 3.6)*, is not invariant. Whereas some values endure over generations, others need to be revised and adapted to changing conditions *(Proposition 4.3)*. The very nature of human existence is perplexing and hence the dreams based on faith persist *(Proposition 11.7)*. With the possible exception of very isolated societies, a constant struggle occurs between persons advocating

change and those upholding tradition. Principals straying from conventional values are punished when they do not conform or when
they are otherwise induced to do so. Medicine men and priests provide the instruction, particularly with reference to religious actions.
In Christianity what is called original sin is an abstraction that must
be taught because no principal ever witnessed or experienced that sin;
and the same kind of tutelage is needed again and again when members of the faith are expected to appreciate the sins that bring grief
to a Heavenly Father in whose existence they have intuitive faith.

Moral persons, nevertheless, cannot always depend upon their
habits to regulate behavior; in spite of constraints, they must seek to
concern themselves with many of the probing questions as they pass
moral judgment *(Proposition 12.3)*. They must first process their immediate reactions to events; as previously indicated *(Proposition 7.3)*,
they are likely to be not absolutists but situationists. On the one hand,
a situationist approach or its equivalent has rightly been called "a
needed corrective for overemphasis upon laws, codes, rules, and
principles" (Barnette, 1968); on the other hand, a proponent of a
more absolutist approach claims that "whatever is the most loving
thing in the situation is the right and good thing" (Fletcher, 1966, p.
65), which would appear to be only a restatement of the problem by
means of the ambiguous concept of "loving" *(Proposition 11.3)*.

The interaction of values and social conditions adds to the complexity. "Poverty, sickness, and sudden disaster were . . . familiar features of the social environment," it is reported, at the time of the
Reformation. Perhaps, therefore, people then felt the need for some
kind of help with "their daily problems," which they formerly had
sought, for example, at "the healing shrines of the Catholic saints"
and which they now believed they could obtain through magic and
astrology. Similarly there was at that time an increase in beliefs concerning witchcraft, ghosts, fairies, omens, and good and bad luck associated with various temporal periods. Religion, however, eventually
triumphed and these beliefs and practices declined, although they did
not completely disappear (Thomas, 1971, pp. 17, 631–39). Thus a
change in theology first led to a change in values associated with
magic and the like and then later inspired a modification of the original religious system.

Unlike principals in so-called nonliterate societies, those in modern
lands live in an era of changing values. During World War II a sociologist noted correctly an "increasing demand for social justice" and
an "antagonism of values . . . linked up with the labour process"
(Mannheim, 1943, pp. 6, 19). Alternative styles of living ranging from

conformity to rebellion exist, from which adolescents and even adults
are sometimes compelled to make a selection. It is often impossible
to adhere strictly to the values that have been learned at home and
in school because either they have changed or else one's appreciation
of them has become different *(Proposition 4.3)*. The decrease in the
length of the workweek, for example, has or should have challenged
most of us to discover how "best" to spend the increased leisure.
Disputes concerning the nature of the good life abound, and even the
established religions are compelled to reconsider some of their traditional cherished beliefs and practices.

Consider quickly the ingredients of utopian dreams *(Proposition
11.8):* how should the perfect society be organized? Obviously, mankind has never reached agreement on this score; for this reason so
many different utopias have been advocated—on paper. Marx proposed societal arrangements to avoid exploitation, but Lenin almost
immediately after securing power had to modify the plan. A psychologist suggests that the following conditions, more or less in his
own words, are required for a society to survive: civil order; defense
against outside attack; production and availability of material goods;
a safe and healthful environment; values transmitted from generation
to generation; opportunities to pursue and achieve happiness; stability,
but encouragement to examine prevailing practices and traditions and
to experiment with new ones; moderate but not too rapid change
(Skinner, 1971, pp. 152–53). Such a list is a stimulating one, yet it
cannot easily be transformed into a reality that is not utopian.
Whether a society's survival should be considered a desirable value
is obviously debatable; the Nazis wanted their own regime to survive.
If a society is considered "good," then it must have defense forces;
but the existence of such forces may provoke others to provide for
their own defense, and thus the arms race has escalated since the end
of World War II. The list, however, is a fruitful challenge, but the
details are elusive.

Should the millions of hungry persons throughout the world be
allowed to starve? Should many or any of them perish in infancy or
later? Of course not. That is an immediate reply: human life is both
sacred and precious. But there are puzzling questions effectively raised
in a collection of essays by philosophers (Aiken and La Follette, 1977):

Do people everywhere have "the right to be saved from starvation"?
Are we really living on the spaceship earth and hence the com-
     monweal is of supreme significance?
Is the supply of food limited?

Should persons in affluent countries become vegetarians in order to increase the available supply of grains?

Should those who do nothing to solve the problem of starvation be condemned or punished?

Should weaker people be allowed to die since, as on a lifeboat, all cannot possibly survive before being rescued?

Should benefactors require beneficiaries to restrict population growth as a condition for receiving assistance and thus "diminish the amount of suffering in the long run"?

Should fertilizer be used by golf courses in prosperous countries when it could increase the agricultural productivity of developing countries?

Should the rich make meaningful sacrifices, resulting in damage to their pursuit of acceptable values in science, education, and art, in order to help the needy; should they render assistance only when they believe they are not "sacrificing anything of comparable moral importance"?

Should food be given only to friendly and not unfriendly countries; should food be used as a political weapon to further political ambitions?

Should animal pets be eliminated so that their food can be sent to the hungry?

Should assistance be given when it is needed even at the expense of diminishing supplies in the future?

Is there a special obligation to help starving millions when no one else will or can render aid?

Should help be given only to those needy whose plight is known and advertised and thus neglect others in dire distress whose plight has not been publicized?

Do governments in affluent countries have a greater responsibility to be helpful than those in less affluent lands; is there a "means test" for potential benefactors?

If food is shared—equally or not—should "*all* the necessities of life" then also be shared?

Should generous impulses be tempered—even curbed—by considering the possibility, perhaps the probability that "most of those who are poor and could use some of the money possessed by the rich would have been unwilling to part with their money, had they been in the position of the rich"?

We are being asked, in short, to make complicated moral judgments concerning both the starving millions and ourselves. What response should be made to the challenge, "how many people an acre can feed depends on whether the land is used to *feed people directly or to feed livestock*" (Lappé and Collins, 1977, p. 4, italics theirs)?

Decisions concerning facts and relevant legal regulations do not necessarily lead to unequivocal moral judgments. A dramatic illustration is that of biomedical research. As a result of advances in knowledge it is possible to predict in advance the sex of an unborn child, to fertilize an egg in a test tube, to impregnate a sterile woman with the sperm of a man who may or may not be her husband, to freeze and then store fertilized eggs for short periods of time, to enable a woman to bring to term a fertilized egg that originates in another woman, and to carry on experiments with fertilized eggs that exist only in test tubes. Should these practices be encouraged? The nature of human life, the desire of married couples to have children, the edicts of a church, the legal ordinances of the society, the nature of matrimony, the benefits from research—these are only some of the issues that are relevant to any one of the problems at hand and that cannot be easily resolved. Even if they are momentarily resolved, new information in the future may make them obsolete or inappropriate; in addition, the values in the society are bound to change and affect evaluations.

Again and again principals, therefore, are torn between complicating alternatives and are uncertain concerning which ones they should select. Leaders who propose or vote upon a specific bit of legislation may recognize that it implies both a "political" and a "moral" dimension. The political would satisfy practical demands of the moment, practical from the standpoint of fellow politicians or constituents; the moral, a value they know to be important in the longer run. On a humbler level the individual layman, when a choice is available, somehow compares the values of a position that pays well but brings little satisfaction with one that pays lower wages but is more satisfactory and desirable.

Few if any principals have the ability to pierce through the complexity of modern society in order to comprehend and anticipate events and thus be able to make enduring moral judgments *(What would the consequences be?)*. Some employ a macro, or global, approach and attempt to fathom the overall situation in which they find themselves; others resort to a micro, or detailed, examination of immediate problems. What usually emerges is an informal analysis to which the current buzz word *hermeneutical* might be applied (cf. Bauman, 1978), and in which the goal is not prediction or forecasting but the belief that somehow the complex events are intelligible. Possibly it is no exaggeration to repeat that seldom if ever do principals have all the information they need or desire in order to make sagacious decisions—or so it seems after making the decision with all the wisdom that retrospection provides *(What did I do?)*.

An important difference in emphasis is or should be evident at this point. On the one hand, social scientists stress how readily beliefs and values may be changed (cf. Cohen, 1974, p. 82); and their evidence is very convincing when one considers, for example, how attitudes toward slavery as an institution have been drastically altered in the West since classical times. On the other hand, philosophers and theologians with equal passion point out that some values, like those embodied in the creeds of the great religions, continue to guide behavior for centuries, although of course they "always have to be experienced anew, if they are not to become a dead letter" (Roubiczek, 1969, p. 61). The views of these two disciplines concentrate upon different probing questions—the social scientists on the rules and duties *(What may I do? What must I do?)*, the humanists on the imperative values *(What should I do?)*.

Skeptical Note: Can such complexities be overcome?

12.5 INELASTICITY

Proposition: Principals and therefore their values and institutions tend to be inelastic.

The very word *habit*—the shortcut from perception to behavior which thus avoids judgment in the Morality Figure—would suggest the stability of judgments and behavior: what has been learned in the past and has proven satisfactory resists change *(What do I do?)*. Existence would be more difficult than it is for most persons if they could not rely upon past experience. Conforming to values may be an admirable trait, but simultaneously it is clear that exceptions are both inevitable and desirable as a result of changing conditions, changing values, or changing circumstances *(Proposition 7.3)*. When hell or high water comes, adaptation is needed and principals may be loath to change.

Just as it was once said (but it is no longer true since World War II as a result of contacts with British and American soldiers as well as the dependence of the West German economy on its former enemies) that "the German language" was resistant to borrowed foreign words and expressions (Sapir, 1921, pp. 194–95), so it seems that some values tend to be relatively impervious to change. When those values have closely related beliefs and attitudes, any proposal to alter them is likely to be rejected with strong conviction. Conservative Catholics' reaction to abortion, devout Marxians' to abandoning the concept of surplus value, orthodox Afrikaners' to racial equality, Kantians' to the philosophy of William James are hostile and involve both the issue in question and its relation to the principals' own systems of values or philosophy. Closely knit systems of this kind linger after the conditions producing them have changed. The conception of "honor" in the American South, which arose in the days of slavery, continues in somewhat modified form to the present day. It is important, however, not to misunderstand the significance of what is being said: the German language or any other social system does not have a life of its own. Just as it was not the German language that resisted foreign words and expressions, but individual Germans, so it is individual Catholics, Marxians, Afrikaners, and Kantians who find it difficult, disagreeable, or impossible to alter part of their theological, intellectual, or emotional system. Within their group they may be influential leaders or they may constitute a minority or majority; in any case the opposition comes not from a vague institution or philosophy but from the reactions of principals. These persons interact with others; they or the interactions may not be easy to locate *(Proposition 2.2)*, and therefore once again the shorthand metaphor of referring not to them but to their overall views is employed.

Inelasticity crops up at expected and unexpected times. Not surprising is the tendency of most persons to prefer and reject certain types of food and never or seldom to alter their diet. Other preferences linger within some persons in a society and are expressed unexpectedly. The given function of the technique of amniocentesis is to determine whether the fetus is normal or abnormal, but occasionally it has also been employed in the United States for quite a different reason: "even when the fetus is normal, a disproportionate number of mothers abort female children" (Krimmel, 1983), presumably as a result of a lingering prejudice favoring boys rather than girls.

For other reasons *(Proposition 12.3)* rationality as an imperative *(Proposition 11.7)* appears irrational and unrealizable. Both before Freud and for decades after, psychiatrists, poets, and novelists have uncovered within themselves and their patients and others the irrational workings of the unconscious. Human beings cannot be completely rational. The fact that some psychologists previously cited *(Meandering 7.2)* postulate rationality as their top stage is not surprising since they are all Americans struggling in a society where irrationality is prevalent. The modern dependence upon computers, especially in the area of artificial intelligence, indicates in part that we do not or cannot trust our own rationality in the face of growing complexity. The psychologists and others in stressing rationality are in effect also warning against being rigid and compulsive.

For there are also advantages, even moral ones, that accrue from being irrational on occasion. The joy of being spontaneous merits lisping approval, though Mrs. Grundy immediately adds that impulsiveness should not lead to immoral action. Then some values may be so heavily reinforced that the principal can leap without reflection from perceiving an event to acting upon it. Clergymen and others who originally and deliberately acquire and then practice embracing systems of values may gradually behave habitually in a manner no different from what would transpire if they delayed and reflected upon all or most of the probing questions. In any society, however, no matter how isolated or how apparently stable, changes occur that render habitual behavior perhaps no longer suitable, perhaps no longer moral. For this reason, the moral person is ever alert to the need to reexamine the bases for his behavior, to make a moral judgment and not simply to pass a habitual one. Well might we be skeptical concerning the possibility of a complete assessment or overhaul.

Other dangers lurk beneath elasticity. The principal who ruthlessly pursues his own goals in a profession but who is highly moral in relation to his immediate family can maintain that he is adapting one set of standards to a hostile, competitive milieu outside and another inside his home. Sociologists who have long maintained in effect that principals are situationists in the sense that they vary the role they play from situation to situation (for example, Goffman, 1961, pp. 85–152) are also calling attention to the variable judgments and values being employed, not all of which are completely moral.

Skeptical Note: Can there ever be basic change?

Envoi: Although disagreements are inevitable, *nevertheless* consensuses are not forever doomed.

CHAPTER 13

Struggles

Principals must constantly struggle when they wish to become moral persons, and observers must likewise struggle whenever they would determine whether principals have approached that unattainable objective. The greatest challenge of present concern includes the efforts of both principals and observers to perfect their judgments and behavior. On and beneath the surface the outlook is not bright, yet we dare not give way to complete skepticism.

The outlook is not bright because almost always, as I have been saying again and again and again, even the foremost scholars, like ordinary mortals, neglect some or many of the probing questions while concentrating upon their own favored dicta. Kant's most crucial assertion, for example, regarding the universalization of his particular maxim, necessarily assumes that the principal has sufficient knowledge to be able to anticipate the universal consequences of his actions *(What would the consequences be?)*. Such knowledge, I repeat, is hard to come by and usually impossible to secure. The injunction, however, may suggest an unrealizable ideal that at the least inhibits the principal from reacting exclusively in terms of his own goals or intentions.

Sometimes the moral judgment and its underlying value may be clear, but a principal for purely practical reasons simply does not know how to achieve his objective *(What can I do?)*. The paths to peace are numerous, hence uncertain. They are symbolized by concepts like disarmament, negotiations, deterrence, inspections, freeze; yet obviously there is no certain way to attain peace.

At other times the struggle can be traced to the principal's own predispositions *(What will I do?* or *What do I do?)*. The sublime is postponed as a result of an urgent present need. Should one read a book that requires effort and possible gratification in the future, or instead view a television program that brings immediate superficial gratifi-

241

cation? Any principal experiences conflict regarding competing or contradictory values not only within himself but also in relation to other persons, no matter how dear or deadly they appear to him. Freud undoubtedly was expressing almost the whole truth when he suggested that the taboos of society are "directed against the most powerful longings to which human beings are subject" and that this desire to violate them "persists in their unconscious" (Freud, 1950, pp. 34–35). And mortal observers are themselves bound by similar constraints: is that principal guilty or innocent, responsible or irresponsible, good or bad?

To emerge a little beyond skepticism, it is absolutely essential—no, let's tone that not down but up and say possibly necessary—to offer guidelines that may help achieve the nonattainable goal of becoming moral persons living in a state of utopia.

13.1 AWARENESS

Proposition: Awareness of the probing questions and the implications of replies are essential.

Habitual reactions to events, though essential to carry on a normal existence *(Proposition 4.2),* may not have been the outcome of moral judgments. Any predisposition, including the most imperative of values, moreover, cannot be influential unless it is salient, and therefore the struggle is ever to keep salient the replies to relevant questions. And salience means that, although the principal or observer is conscious of the need to decide, he suspends judgment until he is able to survey and evaluate all factors relevant to the judgment.

Being conscious of alternatives and perplexities is perhaps the most prized of human attributes (whether animals are conscious is one of those tantalizing but moot matters). As a result, the principal, although self-conscious, is likely to have some insight into himself, and insight is often the first step to wisdom. Perhaps improved moral judgments can be passed and moral actions carried out only when the principal challenges himself or is challenged to justify his judgment or behavior. The challenge in turn may result from the uncertainty associated with the options confronting him or, as has been experimentally illustrated, either when he believes that his behavior runs contrary to his own values *(What ought I do?)* or to those of others or when his responsibility is clear *(What must I do?).* For most principals moral judgments usually require deliberation and reflection if all eight questions are to be considered and if the irrationality to which we are all sometimes doomed *(Proposition 11.7)* is to be—well, not overcome but appreciably diminished. Human beings have the equipment to be rational: they are provided with linguistic symbols to appraise reality and themselves; they can employ the rules of logic and mathematics to enable them to reach decisions; and they can verify those decisions through the use of science or its informal equivalent (cf. M. B. Smith, 1969, pp. 375–79). Privacy and time to reflect, however, are prerequisites to reasoning, both of which may be difficult to achieve in the midst of the bustle of family life everywhere and the societal pressures upon most of us. It requires courage, as has been proclaimed, to be "reasonable" and to lay aside "the accidental in us" (Tillich, 1952, p. 13); awareness is undoubtedly the accompanying prerequisite.

Intellectuals in particular continuously raise questions concerning values, especially when referring to political objectives. The debates may be endless and inconclusive, but at least they make the discussants aware of additional questions besides that of personal gain. This awareness, as one blandly says, is "consciousness-raising" and can be the first step to improvement: merely calling an issue or a doubt moral thus leads to hesitation and requires a more inclusive judgment. Again and again throughout these pages various philosophers have been almost caricatured because they do not have definitive answers to crucial questions or because they do not agree with one another when they provide answers, but here it must be said that they at least raise crucial questions and stimulate awareness of the inexorable moral issues. For example: should officials in any branch of government, especially in democratic countries, function as servants or leaders of their constituents, or should they try to combine both functions and be agents who interpret the interests of those constituents according to some compelling value (cf. Newton, 1981)? Or when the costs and benefits of actual or proposed legislation are determined, how can responsible leaders reach morally complete decisions (cf. Braybrooke and Schotch, 1981)? The gadfly role of philosophers in such contexts merits only praise; and the same is true of any group that performs such a function *(Meandering 13.1: Prescriptions for Awareness)*. Ultimately, no definitive answers to the moral problems of our times may be procurable, but the hope must be that awareness at least of alternatives with reference to issues ranging from abortion to transplants facilitates broader, even "better" judgments and actions.

To make a temporal choice *(Proposition 5.3)*, a principal must be aware of the consequences of his judgments and actions *(What would the consequences be?)*. Children have difficulty postponing an immediate gain for the sake of a greater one in the future, and adults frequently have the impulse to seize the moment especially when the future appears uncertain or precarious. But planning of any kind requires that long-term interests be taken into account. Similarly other human characteristics praised by clergymen and philosophers—conscientiousness, self-sacrifice, weighing of means and ends—do not spontaneously arise but require careful reflection.

Whenever a philosopher proclaims the characteristics of a moral person, he may be assuming that any principal cannot possibly consider all the probing questions unless he is aware of the replies and their interactions. The following is a typical statement:

> A man is effectively free . . . so far as he is able to attend to a wide range of evidence available to experience on any topic; so far as he is able to envisage a wide range of explanations by which that experience might be accounted for; so far as he is able to make a judgment of fact or value by selecting the possibility most in accordance with the evidence; and so far as he is able to judge accordingly. (Meynell, 1981, p. 177)

Freedom demands a multifaceted response, not a conditioned reflex.

Even with complete awareness, however, judgments may not be completely moral. Socrates must have been too optimistic when he stated in effect that "if a man knows the good, then he cannot choose evil" (paraphrased by R. Taylor, 1970, p. 51)—really, why not? With such knowledge, principals may be prone to justify themselves or otherwise rationalize a disturbing state of affairs (cf. Gibbs, 1977); principals, moreover, have manifold ways in which to deceive themselves (Goleman, 1985, pp. 97–124). At the very least, it may be argued, they must be aware of what is considered evil within their own society *(Proposition 4.4)*: whatever is so designated must be intelligible to them and be communicated in such a way that the sanctions for transgressing are also salient (Doob, 1978, chaps. 4–6). Awareness may require a belief that the world and hence human beings and their affairs are amenable—forcibly, if need be—to rational appraisal and understanding *(Proposition 11.7)*. Consistency is assumed whether the phenomenon be the rising and the setting of the sun, the change in the seasons, or the predictability of the behavior of others and of oneself. Even those who consider "reality" too complex to be grasped and hence are inclined to subscribe to a doctrine of irrationality must believe, nevertheless, that segments of their existence are rational— otherwise they would not even brush their teeth. Or else they hope eternally that more of existence can be forced to appear rational (Perrow, 1981).

It could well be that the moral person is so aware of the probing questions that his values are organized into a coherent, consistent system. His principal judgments and behavior then are guided by that system so that, somewhat like a saint or a compulsive neurotic, his life is well organized. The moral judgment of the observer relates not to the coherence of the system or the consistency of its principal but to the values it embodies. Just as cultural elements in a society either seem or do not seem to be necessary conditions or inevitable con- sequences of one another (Goldschmidt, 1951), so personality traits and their accompanying values may or may not cling together into moral systems. A truly devout Christian, it may be assumed, is not likely to become a thief or a murderer, but his attitude toward many political measures may be unrelated to his central beliefs.

Finally, a skeptical note concerning the value of awareness: no matter how self-conscious a principal is, he is more likely to provide a reason for his judgment and his action rather than to be able to uncover the cause as postulated by an observer (cf. A. R. Buss, 1978). He may be eager to justify or rationalize what he contemplates or does, and he may therefore offer a distorted explanation even privately to himself. The observer may be more objective but not without bias. What version is more correct, the principal's reason or the observer's cause? It is even difficult to guess.

Skeptical Note: Aware and unaware of what?

13.2 INTERPERSONAL SENSITIVITY

Proposition: Interpersonal sensitivity is essential and inevitable.

Save for hermits, principals must live together and interact. Even when parents believe they know the values they wish their children to learn, they are never certain whether the response will be favorable or rebellious *(What would the consequences be?)*. The value of love is achievable only when the principal is sensitive to the moods and needs of others *(Proposition 5.4)*. Whether or not the pursuit of privacy is universal, it is clear that some persons, especially in a mass-media- oriented modern society, believe they require opportunities to be alone and to meditate: truly sensitive friends and acquaintances do or do not recognize that need and do or do not intrude, especially with telephone calls.

Again there is no magic formula for developing sensitivity. Mothers become sensitive to the needs of their infants, an ability more or less reciprocated by the children as they mature. Experience with other persons facilitates an appreciation of the desires and moods of others, whether or not the principal has selected them or they have been forced upon him. Perhaps membership in diverse groups broadens the area of sensitivity.

Within the past few decades a specialty called "sensitivity training" has become popular in American and British circles. Under the guidance of so-called trainers, principals are made aware of some of their own blockages and of ways to understand others (Bradford et al., 1964). They may be instructed, for example, to play in front of an audience the role of another person they either like or dislike; lest they make fools of themselves, they try to act genuinely as if they were that other person; thus for the time being at least they internalize some of his attitudes and beliefs. Together with colleagues I have attempted to employ this technique in the real conflict situations of the Horn of Africa, Northern Ireland, and Cyprus on the assumption that being sensitive to the predispositions of the other side might enable the principals to achieve understanding and then possible solutions to some of their problems; the achievements have been less than modest (Doob, 1981, pp. 235–36).

Any form of psychotherapy, by reducing the patient's tensions and perhaps helping him partially resolve some of his conflicts, invariably increases insight into himself and into the others within the milieu who allegedly have contributed to his troubles. The social sciences, particularly anthropology, psychology, and sociology, try to suggest directly why persons behave the way they do, and hence, although pitched abstractly and relying usually upon illustrations beyond the immediate experience of the student or reader, they offer principles applicable to specified kinds of human beings. For some observers, linguistics can be most helpful: comprehending how the individual himself and others use language as well as some of the pitfalls resulting therefrom offers valuable clues. The humanities, including history and all forms of creative art from painting to poetry, would augment sensitivity by portraying the best and the worst, the most brilliant and the most mediocre human beings and human actions. You may never know anyone as wavering and profound as Hamlet, but an acquaintanceship with that character affords additional knowledge of persons clearly or remotely resembling him and his contemporaries. As ever, these disciplines, especially the social sciences, may be biased and communicate error. Nowadays much of literature and art is shoddy and not produced by first-rate persons; the motive is often commercial and directed toward popular appeal—and thus bogus sensitivity is trumpeted.

Skeptical Note: Must not sensitivity to others be restricted?

13.3 CAUTIOUS INDOCTRINATION

Proposition: Indoctrination is usually essential but difficult to plan and implement.

Admittedly the word *indoctrination* has an unpleasant connotation; it suggests the kind of communication and restraints of fascist and other authoritarian regimes, the methods of the church or, generally, the organizations to which one does not belong, and the degrading standards of commercial advertising as well as too many but not all the features of the modern mass media of communication. But indoctrination is essential if the struggle of moral persons is to be satisfactorily pursued. Parents try to prevent their children from associating with delinquents not because delinquents are incurable but because for the moment they do not wish their own children to be indoctrinated with asocial values. Again the importance of models must be stressed, whether they be parents, peers, or distant advice givers; it is not surprising to learn that in American society the success or failure of individuals from the standpoint of "mental health" has been found to be associated with "sustained relationships with loving people" in their early years (Vaillant, 1977, pp. 337, 350). Obviously the right kind of indoctrination is sought, not the wrong kind. Caution is essential, otherwise we may try vainly and stupidly to build a kingdom of supermen, as Hitler and his associates proclaimed, that will last a thousand years.

Indoctrination, moreover, may well flounder when its contents are considered: exactly what should be taught? Perhaps the probing questions once again can be a guide. Thus the rules of the society must be learned, and they perhaps are easiest to obey or certainly easier than the Golden Rule *(What may I do? What must I do?)*. The rub comes when consideration is given to inculcating good habits generally so that personalities with "good character" will emerge

(Proposition 4.2). There is agreement only concerning the need to instruct, educate, or indoctrinate. It is as if an entrepreneur were to assemble raw materials and tools without knowing the precise nature of the product he wishes to manufacture; both he and the workers would be perplexed. One indignant philosopher complains that her college students have been "ill served" by the "moral education" they have previously received: they have been taught to "clarify" their own and their society's values and to evaluate current problems, such as capital punishment, abortion, DNA research, without acquiring a profound knowledge of what she calls "the traditional virtues" (Sommers, 1984). Do you agree with her?

The challenge to one who would change the values or behavior of a principal is both moral and psychological. It is moral because presumably the proselytizing observer is propagating an imperative value and its appropriate behavior that are "better" than those of the principal; otherwise he would not strive to produce the change—or else he is simply pursuing his own interests. It is psychological, as any learning theory suggests, because generally or specifically some reward, punishment, or explanation must be offered if principals are to be influenced. Even among children, sometimes but *not* always, a rationale may be more effective than a prohibition or the threat of punishment, and the appeal to a personal emotion like guilt or empathy may be more effective than shame (cf. Kurtz and Eisenberg, 1983).

Effective indoctrination must be adapted to the groups or principals who are to be influenced. There is no sure-fire route to success. The sensitivity to nuances advocated in the previous section is essential. The fact that similar behavior can result from dissimilar judgments and that similar judgments can give rise to dissimilar behavior may increase the difficulties of predicting in either direction, as previously indicated *(Proposition 3.6).* These varying linkages, however, can be advantageous when individual differences are taken into account: a similar objective can be accomplished variously, depending on the principal's own predispositions. The optimum method need not be rigid: sometimes obvious rewards and punishments such as material gifts or ostracism suffice; at other times less obvious incentives are provided such as a warning that the second coming of a messiah (Handy, 1977, pp. 155–56, 191–92) or of a judgment day requires adherence to the rules and values of a church. A strongly held and somewhat validated view in democratic societies is that individuals who are consulted about a decision or participate in making the decision are more likely to be cooperative than if a commandment reaches them from on high. In spite of tendencies for members of groups to be adversely affected by their own interaction, they also may stimulate one another and arrive at decisions superior to ones that all or most of them would have reached if functioning alone.

It is known that education is effective because values, the right or wrong kind, are acquired in the home and the school. A journalist reports that the "teaching of old-fashioned values is making a comeback in public schools" in the United States; the values being promulgated, he believes, include honesty, friendship, fair play, and civility; and he notes that the American Federation of Teachers has prepared "five specific curriculum guides on the themes of honesty, loyalty, responsibility, compassion, and courage" (Maeroff, 1984). Caution suggests that there is no guaranteed way to improve moral judgments by inducing principals, whether children or adults, to consider, as often as possible, all eight probing questions; they may consider them but give the wrong replies. When a philosopher refers to the "peculiar primitiveness of the Nazi regime, the extent to which a people who had prided themselves on their culture" had "degenerated into the lowest form of barbarism" (Passmore, 1970, p. 265), it is too easy to say that not all Germans were that primitive—and yet they tolerated their rulers and thus perhaps gave the lie to education as the ultimate remedy. Principals being educated also respond to pressures within their milieu, as the Germans responded to their traditions and the severe economic depression in which they were engulfed, enabling the Nazis to campaign successfully and eventually assume power.

Verbal communications, however, remain essential. Quite obviously they must be comprehended and remembered if they are to be effective *(Proposition 4.4)*. In modern society slogans satisfy these criteria, but principals are constantly bombarded with so many smart statements, especially by advertisers, that communications frequently are recognized but not recalled, as a result of which their behavior is not appreciably affected. Again perhaps activity may be necessary, and activity presupposes that the audience is motivated to learn the value and also carry out its implication. The parables in the New Testament are ideal models. Originally they were told by a great teacher, Jesus, to disciples and others eager to listen. For them and for all subsequent persons their lessons—the moral judgments—were not immediately clear or applicable to their own lives: they require interpretation and hence reflection rather than a habitual response; obviously, too, they must be appreciated as stories that might guide judgments and actions.

Understanding the past presumably enables us to try to improve the future. It is thus clear that the Nazis or at least some Nazis were responsible for the Holocaust, but the challenging problem decades later is to discover the means to prevent such ghastly deliberate murder from ever recurring. Presumably people everywhere must be enlightened or indoctrinated: they must learn that the leaders of a civilized society could perpetrate such evil. But how best to communicate the documented facts? There exist, for example, videotapes in which survivors describe in moving detail what they experienced in the extermination camps or while in hiding. Should these tapes be shown to American children in schools, and if so, will they simply be perceived in the same category as the staged violence to which they are accustomed as they view ordinary television?

Indoctrination and its twin called communication are so pervasive that a long meandering is necessary and is therefore provided (*Meandering 13.2: Indoctrinators and Their Methods*).

Skeptical Note: What are the best methods of indoctrination?

13.4 ETHICAL CODES

Proposition: Ethical codes are difficult to devise as well as to obey and enforce.

Argument upon argument, alleged fact upon alleged fact have been assembled to pass moral judgments and to improve moral behavior. Even moral persons are too often confronted with situations compelling them to select "higher" imperative values. Again and again they seek help from some authority, and that authority may or may not be present or known. Perhaps only courts of law can be of assistance, but even they often feel compelled to consult experts before rendering decisions. Who should decide whether a patient in an incurable coma should be allowed to live in a vegetative state until he finally dies: the court, the physician, the clergyman, the individual's own family?

It has been repeatedly stated that philosophers and theologians cannot always settle moral problems when options are offered. Once more: should Heinz steal the drug to save his ill wife or should he remain honest and let her die? Social science can only state that principals make a choice and perhaps the reasons for doing so can be investigated. A principal believing himself to be a moral person can assert that human life is always more precious than honesty or that honesty must have precedence even over human life, but such an assertion is his conviction and cannot be proved as a scientific hypothesis is validated. Thus it is clear why the utilitarians have attempted to apply the metaphor of a hedonistic calculus to the problem of choice: if we could truly measure the happiness for ourselves and mankind as well as the damage resulting from two choices, then the computer could supply the answer. Almost wherever one turns in society, alternatives arise and a choice must be made.

One easy solution to this predicament is to control behavior through the use of taboos, which exist in every society and which usually are transmitted from previous generations. At a given moment in time, ethical codes are established to guide judgments and behavior. But is this a solution? The code may furnish a reply to one or more of the questions but not to others that may be highly relevant. Someone who sincerely says he guides himself by the Ten Commandments is answering one question, *What should I do?* But "the commandment not to covet one's neighbor's wife" must then be interpreted as "the commandment not to follow one's desire, and to do one's best to make it vanish if one has it, as well as to do one's best to prevent its emergence if one does not have it" (Körner, 1976, pp. 144–45); in short, other probing questions must be answered if the commandment is to be implemented *(What can I do? What must I do? What will I do?).*

A prime requirement of an ethical code is that it be intelligible to those destined to use it. Since the code is expressed in language, difficulties inevitably arise: words may be ambiguous or variously interpreted by different principals. In modern society some codes are so incomprehensible or inconsistent that specialists are trained to interpret them. Laymen, for example, consult attorneys who then may themselves be uncertain or challenged by other attorneys, with the result that another group of specialists—judges or arbitrators—are called upon to adjudicate the problem.

The complexity of modern society increases the number of codes. In the United States, corporations, principally the larger ones, have devised codes to supplement some of the recent legal requirements that hold them accountable for "safe products; high quality and service; honest advertising; safe working conditions for employees; equal opportunity for all employees; fair prices; and detailed information for consumers about products, activities, and finances" (G. A. Steiner, 1974). Great advances in medicine, such as the use of transplants for human beings, raise difficult problems: is the knowledge gained for the benefit of future patients more important than the patients who at the moment are the subject of experimentation? Conflicting values require codes to resolve disputes through mediation or compulsory arbitration. The emerging codes may suggest who is responsible and legally entitled to pass judgment *(Proposition 4.6 and Meandering 9.2)*.

Changing standards also create confusion. If mankind's dreams include beauty *(Proposition 11.6)*, then it is disappointing though not surprising to note that those exercising aesthetic judgments, particularly scholars and critics, are at loggerheads when they define what they consider to be beautiful. Treatises on aesthetic criticism reach no firm conclusion. One on *Literary Theory*, for example, spends an introductory chapter giving various answers to the tantalizing question, "What Is Literature?" and then devotes the rest of the book to outlining the various theories of literary criticism ranging from common sense and phenomenology to psychoanalysis and deconstructionism (Eagleton, 1983). Without doubt a principal may ignore good or bad art, but the criteria he employs when he passes judgment have an effect upon how he judges artists and perhaps himself. Even such an embracing code of conduct like Christianity is not a complete guide and must forever be interpreted. On grave matters of policy Christians themselves very frequently disagree; many modern problems, a devoutly Christian philosopher suggests, "had not even been dreamt of when Christ was alive" and therefore principals are warned "to guard against the kind of arrogance which assumes that Christians know all the answers" (Greet, 1970, pp. 64, 114). Then, too, even when moral or legal codes are formulated to meet a specific problem or challenge, the exigencies of every situation cannot be foreseen or taken into account. One principal's freedom of expression may affect others adversely; codes seek, however vainly, to achieve a balance.

A physicist agrees with clergymen and social scientists that "when complete assurance is sought, it is easiest to rely on divine revelation" (Margenau, 1964, pp. 148, 168–80, 280). No code formulated or attributed to human beings, unless they be kings claiming the divine right to rule, is likely to possess such prestige and to command unswerving obedience. And yet, the observation must be repeated again and again, rarely do all the adherents of any religion always obey. The same writer, moreover, suggests that "ethics is an empirical science": its values are ever tested by experience; therefore values constantly change or may be abandoned and replaced; we have "empirical validation through living." The empirical element, however, usually applies to means rather than to the values themselves; thus ethical codes to ensure a value such as justice shift as societies become more complex, but the goal or value remains unchanged. One would have to believe in "progress" with reference to moral values if one were to have faith that mankind "experiments" with values and then finds "better" ones. An additional complication results from the fact that the trials and errors, whether with reference to means or ends, involve not a single principal who is seeking a better existence but many persons in the society who usually have different goals and always have different personalities *(Proposition 2.1).* How "progress" can emerge from such an interaction is not easy to anticipate and provides an additional reason to be forever skeptical, in the long if not in the short run.

In most societies, furthermore, the values in codes are more likely to come from the powerful than from the weak. Philosophers and others may claim that the vox populi, whoever the people happen to be, perpetuates descriptive values and does not evolve prescriptive values and hence cannot commit the dreaded naturalistic fallacy *(Proposition 11.1).* Maybe so, but there is no other way to continue the struggle to reach perfection, although a skeptic can be convinced that perfection can never be achieved. Ideals are embodied in documents proclaiming human rights and expressing noble sentiments. Examples of codes abound; only some of the additional puzzling problems associated with some of them can be briefly discussed *(Meandering 13.3: Informed Consent).*

Men of goodwill keep groping for ethical codes that will be adequate under modern conditions. Perhaps typical is the book of a German clergyman. Without hesitating he returns again and again to the words of the Bible but finds tthat what he calls the dogma derived from God must be combined with other values. He believes that his own religion and other major religions also consider their dicta inadequate. He may be commanded never to kill, he says, but has a German mother the right to kill her eight-day-old daughter born without arms and with crippled feet, and doomed to a life of misery? How can or should sexual relations and political revolutions be evaluated? The Sermon on the Mount cannot possibly provide the details of a code. We might cultivate certain values such as tolerance, personal integrity, and seeing oneself in perspective; but again certainty is not thereby achieved. What does this good theologian conclude? Like the philosopher cited above, he refers to the historical context: "the question can be raised whether the time has come today for Christians to be in a position, as Jesus could not at the time say to them, to be able *now* to grasp, to work through, and to cope with the new and that which had not been previously present" (Gerlitz, 1971, p. 188). Such thoughts and hopes must arouse sympathy for us who, as the writer also says, are faced with the possibility of nuclear annihilation, but any one code is not a means to safety or salvation.

Formal codes embodied in governmental legislation would also resolve conflicts inherent in the tragedy of the commons *(Meandering 11.2)*. Unless the public lands are to be overgrazed, the contending parties must be prepared to make sacrifices. Should all of them make equal sacrifices, or should some principle of equity be invoked so that those able to endure greater losses will make larger sacrifices than those less able to do so? The graduated income tax is also a case in point: the higher the income, the larger the percentage of it that is supposed to be taxed. From one standpoint the principle seems unjust until it is recalled that the wealthy, although they may be called upon to pay a higher proportion of their earnings and other income, are likely to be compelled to sacrifice fewer necessities and luxuries of living than poorer persons who pay a smaller share. Also a practical matter arises: the rich probably have more legal loopholes than the poor. The pros and cons of a tax program, however, cannot be debated indefinitely: legislation is adopted and a code in the form of a tax schedule goes into effect.

An ethical code, in this instance a criminal code, exists in any society to specify the conditions under which an action may be called criminal, the nature of a hearing or trial, and the permissible or mandatory punishments. The aim is to establish the distinction between the "controllable" and "uncontrollable" attributes of the behavior thus specified *(What shall I do?)*. Has a crime been premeditated? Premeditation means that before the deed the principal consciously reached a decision to behave as he in fact behaved, that he could have "controlled" his behavior but chose to ignore the anticipated consequences of what he did. When legal authorities maintain that ignorance of the law is no excuse for violating it, they assume that all persons have had ample opportunity to learn its content, or should have done so, and hence they are responsible for acquiring the necessary knowledge—except for morons and very young children who could not have done so *(What may I do? What must I do?)*. The criminal code changes, especially with reference to punishments; thus capital punishment in some societies or states is permitted, then found inhumane, and later sometimes restored. Any punishment may or may not fit the crime according to the prevailing code.

Skeptical Note: Can ethical codes be satisfactory, and, if so, for whom?

13.5 SEARCHING FOR MEANS

Proposition: The search for means to achieve moral ends is everlasting and ever incomplete.

Such a search occurs wherever we look. A married couple in conflict with each other is uncertain as to how they can avoid divorce and be happy; what should they do? It has become unsafe to walk the streets in many modern cities because of the increase in the number of muggings; what should the police, the schools, the churches do? An epidemic of an identifiable disease is anticipated; what should health centers and individuals do? Noted is the fact that there are answers to such rhetorical questions, but the answers vary in terms of certainty. Innovation always involves a risk, a leap into what is not completely known. The search, however, goes on; in words attributed to Pascal, "all the good maxims have been written, it only remains to put them into practice" (cited by Margenau, 1964, p. 293).

I cannot resist an urge to offer at some length one scholarly attempt to locate the means to achieve carefully specified ends *(Meandering 13.4: Laudable Means for Laudable Ends)*. There it is possible to observe the reasoning of an anthropologist who labors conscientiously from ends to means. Obviously his proposed means may be effective or ineffective, and they may or may not affect the goals he would have us attain, but at least he struggles to be concrete and practical in terms of what he believes to be the best of existing knowledge. I must add, both cynically and skeptically, that his well-reasoned treatise has not changed the course of politics or nations years after its publication. What do serious students of principals and their societies accomplish? What indeed?

Social science, history, or any science often is able to provide suggestions concerning the means that have been or might be employed to achieve particular ends. In many instances the failure to employ their insights lies not with them but with policymakers and officials who do not utilize solidly grounded knowledge. Such knowledge is ignored for a variety of reasons: the individual with power may be prejudiced against the discipline for valid or invalid reasons; he may have to make an immediate decision and be unable to be patient and await the passing of time necessary for careful scholarship, inquiry, or experimentation; consciously or unconsciously, he may be prejudiced in favor of his own intuition and hence believe that so-called experts need not be consulted. Sometimes, however, when political leaders heed scientists employing a vocabulary different from their own and hence unintelligible to them, their "moral fiber" may be in danger of being "coarsened"; being exposed, for example, to "endless tabulations of income levels, rates of recidivism, cost-effectiveness of artillery fire, and the like" inclines them to "cease to think of their fellow citizens *as* fellow citizens" with distinctive personalities and other attributes (Rorty, 1983, p. 164, italics his).

Skeptical Note: What happens when there are apparently alternative means to achieve the same or a similar end?

13.6 ETERNAL TUSSLE

Proposition: We can find no final solution to the human effort to attain perfect morality; we strive and strive and strive.

No one can doubt the fact that individual human beings vary and keep changing. We may be no closer to everlasting truth than were the ancients, but within certain spheres—such as those in the holy scriptures of the great religions—we keep experimenting to achieve the ideals more completely (cf. Roubiczek, 1969, pp. 62–63). The tussle involves the search for moral traits, for means to express them, and for a society that encourages the traits and helps provide the means.

The assumption must be that moral persons possess certain desirable or even necessary traits. What are those traits? And the answer must be that they are elusive. One philosopher may portray them convincingly on an abstract level (cf. Becker, 1973, pp. 180–90), but then we turn to another writer who uses different concepts and also sounds convincing *(Meandering 13.5: Locating Moral Traits)*. The difficulty arises from the fact that, since each society has ideals concerning the kind of person or persons considered desirable, the variability from culture to culture is too great to enable the most astute philosopher or social scientist, no matter how abstract he strives to be, to extract a characterization that transcends the place and the time of the formulation. Just a glance at the kinds of heroes and heroines, especially within a modern society, is sufficient to fortify our skepticism. If forced at gunpoint to name a trait that appears in every society and in every—

or almost every—list emitted by philosophers and social scientists, it might be that of interpersonal sensitivity *(Proposition 13.2)*: interaction with one's fellows is inevitable, hence necessary and related to morality.

The analysis throughout this book, especially when references have been made to the bugaboo of the naturalistic fallacy *(Proposition 11.1)*, has stressed the almost complete certainty that dreams about moral traits are not misleading when they are realistic, and that they are realistic when they have a basis in human needs or motives. No one will argue with the fact and the value, I say again, that crops should be grown if people are to eat and survive. The difficulty arises when the motive is essentially cultural. Reference has been made to dreams concerning faith *(Proposition 11.7)*, the embodiment of which may be organized religion. Joining a church can be justified and realized on metaphysical grounds, but can other dreams also be similarly fulfilled? The belief exists that being religious may diminish the anxiety many persons have concerning death, since most religions suggest the possibility of an afterlife following inevitable death. The evidence of the connection between church membership and death anxiety, at least among Americans, is not clear-cut; possibly such anxiety is diminished thereby among young adults but not among older persons (cf. Richardson et al., 1983).

An additional difficulty in selecting moral traits results from the fact that any particular trait is associated with attitudes, beliefs, or other values, which then must be evaluated in their own right. Should moral persons, for example, believe that the world is basically a just place? On a priori grounds the argument might go either way: the believers might wish to keep the world just, the nonbelievers to rectify its injustices. Which is the more compelling value? To reply, available research is of little assistance, principally because it does not address the question. Among samples of American college students and nurses, in comparison with the nonbelievers in a just world, the believers tended to esteem the fortunate and to derogate the victims, to be more religious, authoritarian, and internally (rather than externally) oriented, and to admire contemporary leaders and existing social institutions (Rubin and Peplau, 1975). These tendencies emerged from replies to a questionnaire concerning the just world and from other paper-and-pencil measures of the indicated attributes. Even if the assumptions are made that the research method is more valid than it claims to be, that the statistical tendencies are more convincing than in fact they are, and that generalizations can emerge from such limited and atypical samples, the observer must then decide whether those tendencies associated with believing or not believing in a just world are themselves desirable or moral.

Frequently, however, the desirable traits or values are self-evident and beyond dispute; then it is, again, the means to achieve the ends that create the tussle. The view of Aristotle is clear-cut and eternal: "we deliberate not about ends, but about means. A doctor does not deliberate whether he is to cure his patient, nor an orator whether he is to convince his audience, nor a statesman whether he is to secure good government. . . . they take some end for granted, and consider how and by what means it can be achieved" (Aristotle, 1934 ed., p. 137). For example: in moments of gloom and of hope men turn to revolutionary means whether they are considering their traditional religion or the existing social order. They would have, as one writer has declared, "a change in the view of evil," they would have the "world . . . seen from a different vantage point" (Gunnemann, 1979, pp. 29, 223). But then afterward, after the victory and the apparent change, other problems arise and there is no solution lasting even for their lifetime, much less for eternity. Here is the challenge, and there are good reasons, too many of them, to believe that such a challenge can never be adequately met. For this reason moral decisions are always tentative; they must be tested in practice to determine whether they can be realized among the principals for whom they are intended (cf. Held, 1984, pp. 265–68).

Perhaps the greatest tussle of all involves efforts to survive on this planet. There is general agreement concerning certain facts that suggest circumstances mitigating against survival: wars, hunger and disease, expanding populations, depletion of natural resources, terror and crime. Out of such conditions positive means must be discovered that will reverse the trends. Actually, during personal or societal crises, moral judgments and practices may be found inadequate and hence are more likely to be revised, even though the changes may turn out to be shortsighted and hence counterproductive. Utopia cannot be achieved in a full swoop; all that we can hope for, as one scientist suggests, is improvement in our condition *(Proposition 11.8)*. He may be right in maintaining that human beings ignore the sweep of evolution that continues and that inevitably affects the values that guide us; he considers this our new theology (Sperry, 1983, pp. 8, 46, 72, 115).

What is needed and what remains elusive are values that can produce unity and shared enthusiasm on this planet. These are not hollow phrases when one thinks how beliefs and faith have united millions of persons within each of the great religions—but not between those religions. Differences must remain—differences among principals within the same family, neighborhood, region, and nation as well as among nations, cultures, and religious groupings. We are struggling to find and phrase, yes, common denominators. Everywhere, in spite of the differences, we all want to live and be happy. Some may seem to prefer death rather than life when they sacrifice themselves for a common cause; yet be it noted that they must be persuaded or compelled to make those sacrifices by believing that they will thereby win life eternal either in a hereafter or in the minds of those they love—yes, it is life in a different form.

To feel discouraged is unrealistic; nothing apparently perfect or satisfactory remains forever. Love's first blush endureth not. After the most delightful meal, hunger eventually reappears. A good night's sleep may be followed by a zestful day, which then gives way to a craving for sleep. The greatest accomplishments of a life terminate in death. We know all this, even without reminders supplied by priests, poets, and scientists. But the struggle to retain our joys as long as possible is both feasible and desirable.

Skeptical Note: If we are uncertain concerning the nature of perfect persons, then must not the tussle be teeming with uncertainty?

Envoi: ?, nevertheless we must try.

MEANDERINGS

13.1 Prescriptions for Awareness

The Institute of Society, Ethics, and the Life Sciences, known from its location in New York State as the Hastings Center, conducts discussions, seminars, workshops, and courses on perplexing problems confronting persons and groups. It also publishes a series of books and a bimonthly magazine. It was founded in 1970 and has concerned itself with the following broad topics: birth (abortion, conception, gestation), care of the dying, genetic engineering, health policy, behavior studies, and applied and professional ethics.

The masthead of its journal notes the "increase in public and professional awareness of public issues"; every number contains cogent articles that reflect and would increase such awareness. Listed below are a dozen miscellaneous quotations from a sampling of those

articles; they are ones that have caught my fancy, and to symbolize
the arbitrary selection, they are listed alphabetically by author. When
possible, I have also extracted pertinent, provocative questions out of
context.

1. I am . . . told that I have the right to fashion my moral life
   and shape my own moral goals. But how do I go about
   doing that (Callahan, 1984)?
2. Cadaver organ donation is, whether we like or not, a family
   matter. Families should be given every opportunity to act
   upon their desire to transform the tragedy of death into the
   gift of life. But they must be asked (Caplan, 1984).
3. Why should we suppose that the reproductive barriers between humans and "lower" primates are inseparable? The
   fact that experimentation along these lines seems unthinka-
   ble or distasteful is no basis whatever for believing that it
   will never happen (Dixon, 1984).
4. Today an . . . important boundary issue is being raised with
   respect to medical technology: what are the legitimate
   boundaries for medical intervention—and how shall these
   boundaries be delineated? . . . Upon what basis can one person know what is best for another (Green, 1984)?
5. Any move to encourage or discourage the development of
   sex choice technologies brings into conflict at least two contemporary societal trends, namely the move towards increasing the equality of standing between the sexes and the
   growing assertion of the privacy of discussions regarding re-
   production (Lappé, 1974).
6. When we can know that a person is at risk for a major dis-
   abling or costly condition long before he or she manifests
   symptoms (for example, when we do a prenatal test for
   hemophilia), does society have a right to evoke prepayment,
   taxation, or other schemes to offset the inevitable cost of the
   disease (Lappé, 1984)?
7. Given the power of the media to evoke imitative behavior—
   as seen not only in suicides but also in the Tylenol poison-
   ings, bomb threats, hostage taking, and other violent
   events—what, if anything, ought to be done (Levine, 1983)?
8. A prisoner in jail has few options to influence those in authority, but one—a hunger strike—is a powerful weapon.
   The prisoner's refusal to eat creates a dilemma: shall the
   medical personnel force-feed the prisoner to save his life or
   allow him to die (Levine, 1984)?

9. Do the "deserving poor" ever have claims to be provided with medical care, in addition to food, clothing, and shelter (Sher, 1983)?
10. The police cannot presume the innocence of everyone and still do their job (Sherman, 1984).
11. In spite of vigorous [and costly] treatment . . . the survival rate for these tiny infants is relatively low and among survivors the neurological outcome is often poor. . . . none of the various arguments to the effect that physicians should withhold aggressive treatment of very low birth weight infants has proved satisfactory (Strong, 1983).
12. Do parents have a duty to avoid bearing children with serious genetic defects if this is feasible (Twiss, 1974)?

Most of us have no easy answers to the questions and problems raised by those statements, but merely raising them clearly and illustrating them dramatically may lead to an awareness of the need to pass moral judgments.

Let us abruptly turn to Aristotle, our usual source of wisdom, for hints concerning the cultivation of awareness. In discussing the "three states of moral character to be avoided," he indirectly suggests that moral judgments require awareness when he includes, in the translation being employed here, "unrestraint" as one of the trio (the other two are "vice" and "bestiality"). The "unrestrained man," according to him, "is so constituted as to pursue bodily pleasures that are excessive and contrary to right principle without any belief that he ought to do so" and therefore he is "like people who get drunk quickly, and with a small amount of wine, or with less than most men" (Aristotle, 1934 ed., pp. 375, 419). Such a person presumably is temperamentally incapable of evaluating options and of considering all the factors related to moral judgments.

In general it is a fair question to ask whether awareness is increased by consulting philosophers who hope to guide the rest of us. Each of them, in my opinion, however, seeks to make an original contribution; why else would he, like me, attempt yet another treatise on the subject? One plows through book after book, and one is always able to salvage something, a new thought or a twist to an old one; but final, definitive answers to the probing questions remain elusive. And yet being thus stimulated or inspired is a contribution, however minor, to increased awareness.

Unless he is a philosopher, clergyman, or an unusual social scientist, the lay observer may pass judgment when he praises, condemns, or seeks to change a principal. As previously indicated *(Proposition 12.3),* there may be disagreement especially in the changing West concerning the best methods of rearing children (cf. Staub, 1979, v. 2, p. 89), but being aware that there are alternatives and that this problem exists may be the first step to improving practices. Perhaps it is the deviants with respect to socialization and other practices who by challenging the status quo make themselves and others aware of the imperfections; hence the struggle for improvement continues.

A philosopher suggests that a "person is of good will if he adopts the moral point of view as supreme." That point of view, among other attributes, consists of examining the facts in terms of his own beliefs, and of not following his own self-interest but relying on principles and on roles applicable, in the Kantian tradition, to "everybody" (Baier, 1958, pp. 185–204). He will be unable to satisfy such criteria if he is impulsive; rather he must reflect, he must be sure of the factors contributing to his judgments. Similarly, he must justify his decision or action, especially if he is to follow some modification of a golden rule and not self-interest; he must consciously challenge his own motives and place them alongside his moral values (P. Singer, 1979, pp. 9–10).

It is not surprising that the search for ways to make principals aware of their own descriptive values and especially of observers' judgments and commands is an ancient one and appears whenever one person would affect another. Appeals and documents that have proven effective can be located. The Sermon on the Mount, the Magna Charta, the Declaration of Independence, the Communist Manifesto, the Four Freedoms of Roosevelt and Churchill—these have been statements that, embedded as they were in the needs of contemporary principals and observers and also of others not yet born, would not and cannot be ignored. Possibly the great advances of science and even social science, which continually demonstrate that the material world and aspects of human behavior can be controlled, alert us all to the possibility and hence increase awareness in this respect; the study of what is called ethics may have the same salutary effect (cf. Garcia, 1971, p. 92).

In almost any normal existence the principal is confronted or confronts himself with a problem that compels him to challenge his own values. I recommend to sophisticated persons a consideration of our treatment of animals, especially the higher ones or mammals. Should we kill them for food? Should we raise them efficiently on animal farms where they are crowded together and hence presumably suffer or at least are unable to develop the potentialities we know they pos-

sess? Should we use them as beasts of burden? Should we exploit
them for our enjoyment as in bull and cockfights or races? Leave aside
the fact that there possibly would be enough food for the starving or
malnourished peoples in developing countries if Americans were
vegetarians and did not inefficiently use 87.5 percent of their grains
and other vegetables to feed animals (Rachels, 1977) *(Proposition 12.4).*
Forget, too, for the moment the permission granted by Holy Scripture
to dominate animals (Gen. 1:29, 9:1–3). Under these conditions, try
to answer two questions:

1. Is there a sharp difference between animals and human
   beings? Cannot animals learn, discriminate, remember, suffer,
   reciprocate affection? They do not have speech in the manner
   of persons, but they communicate with one another and with
   us.
2. How can we justify our treatment of animals?

The details relevant to the first question are supplied by ethologists,
psychologists, and anyone who has had experience with pets. The
darts for the second have come effectively from philosophers; here is
a sample from two of them:

> To give preference to the life of a being simply because it is a mem-
> ber of our species would put us in the same position as racists who
> give preference to those who are members of their race. (P. Singer,
> 1979, p. 76)

> To protest against the rights view that justice applies only to moral
> agents, or only to human beings, and that we are within our rights
> when we treat animals as renewable resources, or replaceable re-
> ceptacles, or tools, or models, or things—to protest in these terms
> is not to meet the challenge the rights view places before those who
> would reject it. (Regan, 1983, p. 399)

13.2 Indoctrinators and Their Methods

The role of the indoctrinator, the observer who advocates values and
ways of behaving, is specified within a society: parents, clergymen,
teachers, in Western countries whoever controls the media of communication. Roles change; for example, many responsibilities for
transmitting both knowledge and values have been transferred from
the family to—well, to whom or what? Modern television is important
in molding attitudes and beliefs, even though its main function by
and large in the United States is commercial and not the promotion

of a more moral society or of moral persons. Much depends upon the prestige of the source of the communication. Even when the ultimate authority is a supernatural source, someone in the society must indoctrinate principals with its, their, his, or her presumed existence and importance.

Indoctrination by doing rather than through verbal instruction has a long pedagogical tradition associated with many educators, especially John Dewey. Closely related is the view that a stronger impression is likely to be created by persons who are present rather than by those whose existence is known only symbolically and hence must be inferred. A starving individual who is visible probably, but not always, has greater impact than a report, possibly even a televised view, concerning malnourished thousands or millions in a faraway land.

There is, however, no sure-fire way to inculcate values or to strengthen or weaken them. In a contrived experiment, for example, cheaters, in comparison with noncheaters, tended to be more severe in their general attitude toward cheating, especially when their temptation to cheat had been light and also when the reward from not doing so had been relatively high (Mills, 1958). Other combinations of temptations and rewards were less clear-cut; indeed it would be foolhardy to predict lasting effects from this investigation, even though the variables that were manipulated are of more than passing interest.

Principals belonging to an established association do not necessarily absorb its values. A sample of American students was once divided into believers and skeptics on the basis of their replies to a written questionnaire. More of the believers than the skeptics reported that certain "antiascetic actions" that allegedly have only general effects (gambling, drinking, and nonmarital sexual relations) were "wrong," and fewer of them claimed to engage in such activities; but the two groups did not differ with respect to condemning or reporting participation in "antisocial actions" that affect other persons (such as shoplifting and lying), and their reports also were similar with respect to whether or not they had violated their own values (Middleton and Putney, 1962). The antiascetic actions presumably were more closely related to religious doctrines than the antisocial actions, which are more likely to be common in American society. Even with this atypical sample and with a questionnaire of uncertain validity, clergymen might have anticipated that the teachings of their church would affect both sets of values and actions. Somewhat similar results have been obtained with a sample of English grammar school students between the ages of seventeen and eighteen and with a slightly different measure of reported religiosity (Wright and Cox, 1967).

The ways in which children are indoctrinated are numerous. One very competent, conscientious summary of research on socialization, almost exclusively among Americans, indicates a host of "influences" upon moral actions ranging from "warmth and affection" of parents to the "distribution of authority" in the environment (Staub, 1979, v. 2, p. 252). The same writer concludes that every learning theory in modern psychology has inspired research tentatively demonstrating that prosocial values can be acquired. Developmental theories of learning implicitly foster values associated with indoctrination: a participant is judged retarded and hence perhaps "bad" if he fails to progress from one postulated stage to another or when he moves backward to an earlier stage. Such a value judgment, it is suggested, is especially prominent in Freudian theory where "fixation" at one stage or "regression" back to another is thought to be psychiatrically abnormal and hence, except under very special circumstances, to be deplored (Gergen, 1982, pp. 171–72). Indoctrination, therefore, whether subtle or direct, is all-pervasive.

Examples of systematic indoctrination in experimental settings are profuse because attitude change has been a popular topic among social scientists during the last four decades. The findings need not and cannot be reviewed in detail; rather any haphazard choice reveals the need for extreme caution and skepticism in interpreting the results and hence the consequences of indoctrination. In one investigation, for example, a control group of American smokers was only asked to stop smoking and keep records of their smoking rates. A comparable experimental group was also made aware of the value they placed upon broadmindedness and self-discipline and of the similar values of those who quit smoking; in addition, they were made self-conscious concerning their own dissatisfaction with smoking. More of the experimentals than the controls, it was found, markedly reduced the number of cigarettes they smoked daily, at least during a sixteen-day period, and slightly so for six months (Conroy, 1979). American children in a Sunday school spent an hour in twelve sessions and adolescents in a junior and senior high school spent two hours per week for nine weeks listening to their instructors discuss various alternative judgments that were possible in biblical or hypothetical situations, as a consequence of which they changed their standards of judgment (Blatt and Kohlberg, 1975). Similarly a college course in ethics, in which the instructor deliberately avoided the moral dilemmas that served as the before-and-after measures, seemed to produce significant changes, although both this experimental group and a not completely adequate control group not enrolled in such a course revealed "a great deal of consistency" over this ten-week period (Page and Bode, 1980). In an understandably and hence excusably imperfect study, a tendency for juvenile delinquents to "improve" their judgments (as measured by a standardized paper-and-pencil questionnaire) occurred after discussing dilemmas in six sessions, each of which lasted an hour and a half (Fleetwood and Parish, 1976). Even though individual differences as ever appear, experiments such as these at least demonstrate the obvious: successful indoctrination is feasible.

In addition, such experiments provide a somewhat tenuous guide to the optimal method of indoctrination. One investigator, for example, conducted two studies among American kindergarten and sixth-grade children to determine whether prosocial behavior (giving additional money to a charity rather than keeping it for themselves) would be encouraged by the actions of an adult. In both studies the older children were more generous than the younger ones. In the first study, however, the younger but not the older children were affected by the actions of the adult; whereas in the second, neither age group was affected, and it also seemed to make no difference whether the adult set an example or exhorted them to be generous. Although in both studies the money at the disposal of the children resulted from playing the same game and although the charity was identical, there were slight differences with respect to details. The model in the first experiment was a female, in the second a male; under one of the control conditions, the "selfish" model gave nothing in the first study, one quarter of his earnings in the second; instructions concerning the opportunity to give money to the charity were given by an adult male who was present in the first study and via videotape in the second (Lipscomb et al., 1982, 1983). These slight differences in the procedure evidently produced differences in behavior; in real life, procedures are also not uniform and hence similar differences always appear. Even with such restricted samples of American children there is no sure-fire route to success.

A competent review of more than two dozen studies reveals that either in a natural setting or in the laboratory young American children became more "prosocial" after viewing various kinds of television programs. Whether the increase in "generosity, helping, cooperation, friendliness, adhering to rules, delaying gratification, and a lack of fear" endured for any length of significant time, however, is not indicated; and the reviewer himself, while extolling the positive potentiality of television, perforce also points to the contents of many programs that certainly cannot be called prosocial (Rushton, 1981). In addition, the situation is both encouraging and discouraging when the investigator seeks to increase the number of high school or college students who will help another person apparently in distress (for example, a confederate is sprawled on the floor) after being given a lecture or seeing a film encouraging altruism of this sort. In comparison with controls not exposed to such indoctrination, more of the experimental subjects helped immediately in one study (Beaman et al., 1978), more helped after the passage of time in another study (Schwartz and Gottlieb, 1980), and no greater number helped in yet a third study (Katzev and Averill, 1984). The ingenuity of the investigations is praiseworthy, of course; for example, a mass media campaign against shoplifting in a university bookshop increased students' intentions to report those committing this petty crime, but no larger number actually did so, whether the culprit (a confederate) appeared to be a fellow student or not (Bickman, 1975). Not unexpectedly, the exposure of American students and adults to commercially available or edited films having "violent and sexual content" increased "aggressive-sexual fantasies, acceptance of aggression, beliefs in rape myths, and aggressive behavior" immediately following exposure as well as "several" days later (Malamuth and Donnerstein, 1982). Deliberate indoctrination, in short, may or may not be influential, for better or worse—and it depends on the problem, the persons, and the situation.

Two other writers, after demonstrating that children can be directly trained "to reason about morality more maturely," criticize their own research for failing to enable the subjects to reason independently of "adult or external sanctions." They then change their method and review the efforts of others, with the result that they favor "an indirect method" which they believe to be

> perhaps the primary condition free of contradiction and conducive to effective moral growth. The most critical and significant aspect of this exposure to moral dilemmas, or differing opinions, is perhaps best obtained in the family. Moral maturity is enhanced, first, by creating a general condition of horizontal, cooperative interaction, and second, by the parents' own autonomy and discussion of fundamental aspects of morality. (Boyce and Jensen, 1978, pp. 133–75)

Again, therefore: principals can be influenced but not always in predictable ways (cf. Tipton and Browning, 1972).

13.3 Informed Consent

Let us concentrate largely upon a relatively or seemingly simple problem, that of human subjects in research. Current practices in the sciences vary somewhat, but in the United States codes exist requiring investigators to protect the welfare of human subjects, to avoid possible risks, to strive for objectivity in the design of the research, and not to embarrass or libel anyone when publishing the results. Above all, when recruiting subjects, the investigator must obtain what is called their informed consent—and here numerous moral problems arise. Codes provide that human subjects in experiments be told the general nature of the experiment in which they will participate as well as the risks and the possible benefits to themselves and to science or society. Even when details of the research are disclosed (such as the names and addresses of the researchers and the sponsors) and even when subjects are given the opportunity to withdraw from the research and are guaranteed confidentiality, additional challenging problems remain. The investigator himself may be unable to anticipate all the consequences of the research, even when to the best of his ability and knowledge he provides subjects with the most promising educated guess. Being enthusiastic concerning the contemplated investigation, he may unwittingly or egocentrically overestimate or exaggerate the alleged benefits. Deception may be necessary in many experiments, or otherwise subjects behave unnaturally: deliberately or not, they may provide or not provide the data being sought or they may simply be affected by knowing what is transpiring. A substitution for deception may be difficult to find, and debriefing at the end of the experiment does not always relieve possible psychic damage. Merely attempting to recruit subjects or, later, publishing the outcome may be an invasion of privacy, certainly a negative value in our society. Perhaps written rather than oral consent by adults is preferable; yet the procedure may provide only the investigator with legal security (cf., for example, Conner, 1982; Campbell and Cecil, 1982; Diener and Crandall, 1978, chap. 3; Geller, 1982; Hartley, 1982; Tanke and Tanke, 1982).

A most heartbreaking challenge, particularly in experiments with drugs and other forms of therapy, involves the treatment or lack of treatment of a control group in an experiment. Giving these subjects a placebo is a deception, a necessary one from a methodological standpoint. Even though they are randomly or otherwise assigned to that group, the individuals perforce cannot reap whatever benefits accrue to the experimental group; of course, they may also avoid whatever damage, if any, the experimental group endures. The most challenging question is whether the benefit to "society"—which means other persons not participating in the experiment—is more important than the damage to the control subjects. Responsibility is shifted only in part from the investigator to the subjects by obtaining their informed consent, but again they may agree to participate without comprehending the hazards when or if those hazards are known to the investigator.

A psychologist, after demonstrating to his own satisfaction that a combination of his theory and its practical application as measured by scales of his own design has enabled him to change the values of undergraduates, has forthrightly worried about the "ethical implications" of his research. He is well aware of the fact that educational institutions as well as "parents, ministers, and military men" are "in the business of shaping values." He consoles himself with the smug status-quo view that changing values in the course of research is "ethically permissible" only when he himself and competent colleagues conclude that the changes are "compatible with the basic assumptions of a democratic society and, even more important, in the interest of all humanity." He thinks that decreasing the values of "freedom, equality, a world at peace, or a world of beauty would not be ethically permissible" (Rokeach, 1973, pp. 335–37, italics omitted). That is one view, a socially acceptable one in the light of the values of one conscientious man and his society.

More generally, it is usually assumed that the person who is asked to give his consent is both able and willing to do so. This assumption clearly was not true of the human guinea pigs in Nazi concentration camps who were subjected to inhuman experiments sometimes resulting in death. It may not be true for prisoners in a penitentiary, the mentally deficient, children in a classroom, or respondents deceived by pollsters. Can patients in general fully comprehend the risks and benefits from a drug or a form of therapy even when it is explained to them patiently by a conscientious physician (Abram, 1983)? At any rate, the obligation of researchers and physicians to obtain consent, whether informed adequately or perfunctorily, at least makes both parties aware of the problem, which may be the laudable benefit of the necessarily imperfect ethical codes toward which we grope.

A somewhat similar problem arises in modern society when an employer compels employees to undergo risks to health or life (in return for compensation), or when he subjects them to those risks without their prior knowledge or consent. Should a worker, for example, be allowed or compelled to work under conditions that are hazardous to his or her health or that of children unborn or even not yet conceived? In this instance both the principal and the other persons have conflicting values. The employer seeks to continue his industry profitably, but may not wish to be accused of inflicting damage upon his employees; the worker wishes to earn a living, but is troubled by a health problem. One solution to both conflicts can be to supply, if it is possible and there is time, information or an authoritative statement to the effect that no hazard is involved; either party, however, may seek out false information or engage in wishful thinking to avoid admitting the hazard. Often, therefore, it is government that must play the active role and either prohibit or regulate the conditions under which work occurs, in which case the ethical code is imposed from above and undoubtedly requires skeptical assessment.

13.4 Laudable Means for Laudable Ends

Raoul Naroll begins a brilliant analysis of *The Moral Order* by postulating four "core" values, each with two or more subvalues: peace (universality, order, stability), humanism (scientific empiricism, mankind's happiness), decency (brotherhood, health), and progress (wisdom, variety). These values, their formulator frankly and disarmingly believes, he himself shares "with almost anyone who is likely to look" at the human situation; they are "the chief values of European humanism." After summarizing partially in his own terminology what he considers to be the assets and defects of relevant research methods, the author dwells upon the following problems that prevent the achievement of those values: mental illness, alcohol abuse, suicide, family breakdown, child abuse, youth stress, maltreatment of old people, subordination of women, and sexual difficulties. Each problem he examines in detail, supplying whatever data he can find from the world societies, including those that are traditional or developing; some of his data are shaky, but they are the best available. For each ill, too, he suggests specific means to mitigate the conflicts and unhappiness they produce, and he provides costs and benefits for the remedies. When all the statistical information is gathered for each country, according to his precisely described mode of reckoning, Norway emerges as "the model country."

Here is an approach derived from postulated values derived from the goals the author assumes (with documentation) human beings everywhere have been attempting to achieve or avoid. It deliberately and explicitly commits the naturalistic fallacy by basing programs on human nature as perceived by science (largely social science) and interpreted by this particular writer, and it then prescribes means to attain those values. The specific programs require a book in their own right, but I would quote a sample of the way in which five of the ills and the worst evil of all are handled *in part:*

1. To reduce the risk of mental illness, these family life styles are implied by the studies I have just reviewed: People—especially women—need to marry someone they can trust with their secret thoughts and fears, someone they can confide in.
2. [To] avoid trouble with alcoholism . . . [your] home needs to be tied in with at least five other friend-family homes, with whom you often meet to share a meal socially.
3. If they work, give heavy support in the future to day care centers for all mothers of young children and to Mothers Anonymous, as well [as] for mothers in trouble for child abuse.
4. If political and legal equality of women is to be gained where it is wanting or be maintained where it now exists, it [is necessary to] give women equal access to formal education, in order that their services may be equally needed and so in time equally valued.
5. If unmarried people have sex, they should take care to use safe and effective contraception.
6. We need a worldwide arms control and disarmament program to banish the threat of atomic holocaust that might destroy us, and to free 400 billion dollars a year for better uses. To attain that, we need an effective mechanism to keep peace worldwide. (Naroll, 1983, pp. 29, 44, 48, 72–75, 178–79, 195, 254, 336, 369, 409)

13.5 Locating Moral Traits

There has been an eternal struggle to locate the traits to be cultivated by parents and other socializers of children who would create moral persons. According to one modern philosopher, Plato "and other Greeks" advocated four traits: wisdom, courage, temperance, and justice. Christianity, he thinks, stressed seven: faith, hope, love, prudence, fortitude, temperance, and justice. He himself believes that traits such as those can be "derived" from benevolence and justice, but then he immediately suggests that there are desirable "second-order" virtues: honesty, fidelity, conscientiousness, moral courage, integrity and goodwill, wisdom (or practical wisdom), "moral autonomy," and "the ability to realize vividly, in imagination and feeling, the 'inner lives' of others." Later in the same treatise a survey of what philosophers mean by the "good" produces an even longer list beginning with "life, consciousness, and activity" and ending with "good reputation, honor, esteem, etc." (Frankena, 1963, pp. 63–70, 88–89). It is impossible not to extol every single one of these traits; undoubtedly they are steps in the direction of the goal of human perfection. But are they the best traits toward that end? Are all of them compatible with one another? How can they or some of them be embodied in imperfect principals? Skepticism is not included in the list; perhaps it should be.

A slightly different but related approach also seizes upon human predispositions and suggests the traits that might be considered desirable. A French philosopher has concentrated upon what he calls "moral attitudes" because he thinks "they can give me the illusion of being a person." What he then does is to point out in separate chapters what he considers to be the moral implications of good and bad faith; seriousness and humor; scrupulousness; suspiciousness and slander; patience and impatience; resolution and compassion; and generosity and benevolence. His analysis, however, consists only of stimulating opinions without documentation or justification: for example, "the patient man is a reformer who knows that innovation comes into existence slowly in the course of history; an impatient person is a revolutionary who believes in innovating values arising from the transgression of laws and prohibitions" (Mehl, 1971, p. 76).

A psychologist has tried valiantly and incisively to dredge out of intuition, psychology, psychoanalysis, and the humanities compelling criteria for the "healthy personality." He finds that "their" paths toward that end contain different concepts and also different goals. There is no agreement even within each of the fields; thus since Freud—or for that matter even during his lifetime—divergent viewpoints have existed concerning, for example, the etiology of the neuroses. The final summary is modest and hence not very satisfactory. For psychological health, the personality must be viewed "as continuous change, rather than as the establishment of fixed systems." For dynamics, there must be "a progression from the primarily biological functions of the organism to the direct utilization of such resources by the ego." More specifically, with reference to dynamics, the individual does not repress impulses but permits them to govern behavior; he engages in "constructive rather than defensive tactics to produce socialized acts" which are "satisfying, meaningful, and enjoyable in their own right"; he is able to profit from experience and flexibly modify his behavior (Vinacke, 1984). These words and the summaries are not merely clichés: they purport to reflect the "unified" values of different disciplines. As such they perhaps function as a prelude to the problem of groping toward the moral person.

It is pointless to continue the roll call of authors who postulate their dreams as desirable traits (for example, Flugel, 1945, p. 242; Wilson et al., 1967). In view of the emphasis this book has placed upon skepticism, it seems only honorable or appropriate to wonder whether skepticism is a desirable trait. One staunch defender of skepticism has surveyed some of the conventional attributes of mental health and concludes that "there is no good *a priori* or general reason to suppose that a sceptic cannot stand up" to those criteria; if such an individual fails to achieve such stability, the explanation is to be found in another consequence of his ethical philosophy, namely, his refusal to accept dogmatically the demands of his society that he conform to its beliefs and regulations (Naess, 1968, pp. 66–67).

I give the final word to a German philosopher who immediately before his death in 1973 completed a noble defense of skepticism. He ended his treatise by producing a somewhat Germanic inventory of perfect traits he considered achievable. He began by postulating the "radical question" of the "basic attitude" *(Grundeinstellung)* that results in "basic behavior" *(Grundhaltung)* and in turn in various forms of "behavior" *(Haltungen)*. The two behaviors have three divisions each of which has subdivisions—together they are the inventory:

1. Frankness *(Offenheit)*
   a. Veracity *(Wahrhaftigkeit)*
   b. Objectivity *(Sachlichkeit)*
   c. Compassion *(Mitleid)*
2. Distancing *(Abschiedlichkeit)*
   a. Renunciation *(Entsagung)*, modesty *(Selbstbescheidung)*, humility *(Demut)*, and self-directedness *(Selbstaufgabe)*
   b. Self-control *(Selbstbeherrschung)* and cautiousness *(Besonnenheit)*
   c. Bravery *(Tapferkeit)* and frankness *(Freimut)*

    d. Generosity *(Grossmut)* and kindness *(Güte)*
    e. Relaxation *(Gelassenheit)* and patience *(Geduld)*
3. Responsibility *(Verantwortlichkeit)*
    a. Solidarity *(Solidarität)*
    b. Justice *(Gerechtigkeit)*
    c. Loyalty *(Treue)* (Weischedel, 1976, pp. 188–220).

Where, oh where can one find such a person? No doubt psychologists, especially Americans, can design scales to "measure" each of these eleven components, and then what? They will find that each person has some of the attributes and not others, that the mode varies from society to society.

CHAPTER 14

The Future?

When we humbly and genuinely think about our isolated earthly spaceship and even only about ourselves, it is difficult or impossible not to feel gloomy. Although this book tries to push us slightly beyond skepticism and therefore ends each chapter with a "nevertheless" introducing the main clauses of an encouraging envoi, I confess I feel the need for an unpedantic, undocumented, and above all happier summary of what I have written. Perhaps the reader has a similar feeling. It is all very well to have criticized philosophers, social scientists, and others and to offer relevant evidence. But now what? Where are we?

Except for higher powers concerning which or whom we hold respectful beliefs, no authorities can offer definitive guidance to morally complete judgments or particularly to enforceable, worldwide, morally complete actions. We are alone. What must we think, what can we do?

There are good reasons to be discouraged, as the sixty-five Skeptical Notes throughout these pages have unsubtly suggested. From recorded time men and women have been seeking to improve themselves and the societies they create. They continue to grope, and the best and worst thoughts of the supposedly wise—the oracles of holy men and the specialists usually called philosophers—have not changed; rather, over the ages they have been expressed slightly differently in a manner more or less intelligible to their audiences. Misunderstandings persist among persons and groups, whether they be principals or observers. We have learned more, albeit perhaps not significantly more, about our own behavior and the probable consequences of individual and social actions. At the moment, possibly at any moment, the everyday technological and political risks confronting us are tantalizingly difficult to assess. Selected sages of yore have been as perspicacious as

contemporary social scientists. We cannot, we dare not delude ourselves with the wishful conviction that we have "improved" ourselves,
our way of life, or our morality since the days of the fourth century
B.C. Any scholar—whether humanist, philosopher, or historian—can
fondly imagine or point to some other era he believes to have been
"better," more "civilized," or more "advanced" than his own.

On the other hand—yes, on the other hand—good reasons can also
be found not to feel discouraged. Undoubtedly technology and science
have progressed: potentially we have greater and more certain control
over aspects of our environment. Some urban developments, sufficiently reliable and speedier modes of transportation and communication, a landing on the moon, satellites in space, perhaps nuclear
power, the tasks assigned to computers and robots, the discoveries of
medicine that prolong life—each of us can provide a list of continuing
accomplishments over time. Although multitudinous gaps remain, we
can plan further ahead than our ancestors did. We are better acquainted with some, if not all the dangers inherent in our common
existence. A search for values has become more deliberate, and possibly revered values are more frequently salient than formerly.
Whether these compelling if tentative achievements are utilized for
good or evil or have benevolent or malevolent consequences is another matter.

In addition, we take courage from the fact that traces of universal
values are more or less evident, even though almost all values vary
and are modifiable. We are able to realize some but not all of these
values. As human beings we have admirable traits and proclivities,
which I would suggest once more by condensing into one long sentence and in slightly different form the thirteen independent clauses
following each "nevertheless" in the envois. We struggle on, we make
useful judgments, we understand ourselves and others somewhat, we
enact sufficiently satisfactory rules that we feel obligated to obey, we
anticipate aspects of the future, we catch glimpses of compelling values, we may intend to act and actually sometimes do act morally, we
are often observed and are helpfully criticized by competent and
trustworthy observers, we have dreams concerning morally complete
values, we often achieve consensus with our fellows, and above all
we keep trying.

As a model in some but not all respects we have science, an un-
questioned advantage of which is that immediately or eventually any
proposition or hunch can be verified by those competent to repeat
experiments or to make their own empirical observations, regardless

of their language, nationality, religion, ethnic background, or personal prejudices. In contrast, although moral judgments and actions cannot be so rigorously verified, segments thereof can be held up to scrutiny. For example: when consequences are anticipated or sought as a result of morally complete judgments, it may be possible to determine, if with less precision than that of science, whether the employed means have been successful or unsuccessful.

However—a variant of nevertheless—too often our knowledge and our advances have been compartmentalized or segregated from their immediate or ultimate values. The proclaimed or self-proclaimed experts on morality and moral development bite off only segments of what in this book I have frequently called the eight probing questions. Morally deficient rather than morally complete judgments guide us. We may, we must forgive the inadequacies and failures of scientists, scholars, and ourselves to be morally complete because we have neither the time nor the talent to grasp reality in its entirety. For this reason we cannot ever reach eternal truth, eternal in the sense that values and knowledge become valid or useful for all persons, in all societies, or forever over time. We may praise brilliant analyses and apparently new discoveries or methods without losing sight of the fact that they are defective or temporary and will be supplanted by different, not necessarily better—or worse—versions.

Reasons for being eternally skeptical are thus abundantly clear. Disagreements and uncertainties are inevitable. Rather than belittle the naturalistic fallacy, we should remember that we are what we are; some of what we are we must retain; other aspects of us can change if only within limits.

We can impel ourselves slightly beyond skepticism. Men and women may continue to disagree concerning the nature of complete morality, yet they keep trying to make their audiences sensitive to the quest. The modern mass media, especially television, may be permeated with superficial trifles. Still, in some ways, they also supplement widening educational efforts to make persons everywhere better acquainted with themselves and others, so that a consciousness of one world spreads even when enthusiastic allegiance to it is lacking. Few groups or societies remain isolated except those their inhabitants would deliberately keep separate. More and more persons know the dangers confronting us, although their awareness produces no compelling solutions. The social and behavioral sciences may overflow with piffling distinctions and statistical neo-nonsense, but their insights, however unoriginal, have diffused widely to many audiences.

Great men—both good and bad—arise from time to time, and their influence, especially those considered "good," does not fade; rather, they continue to affect the moral judgments and actions of contemporaries and descendants.

Although moral persons are difficult to find or define, the search is not abandoned. Whenever we discover clues to their personality, we may be confident that within limits most individuals can be somewhat resocialized or socialized accordingly: they can be sufficiently elastic, they can exercise the potentiality of carrying out their own intentions, and they can behave sufficiently consistently in a variety of situations. In spite of variability from individual to individual and from society to society, we are dimly aware not only in our dreams but also in reality of the attributes of moral persons. Let those attributes be derived from the probing questions and let them be expressed in the first person:

1. My judgments reflect my total personality; I can establish priorities among my values at the moment or in the longer run.
2. I am potentially capable to act upon the judgments I make or highly value.
3. My actions are completely or somewhat in harmony with the significant groups in which I live and to which I owe allegiance.
4. Among my judgments and actions I recognize obligations to groups to which I belong or which must not be ignored.
5. To the best of my experience and knowledge, I clearly and reasonably anticipate the many or at least the significant consequences of actions I undertake.
6. Whenever possible I pass judgments and act on the basis of morally complete rather than morally deficient values.
7. Barring accidents, I do what I intend to do in the hope that the action will be morally complete.
8. How I behave is not only satisfying but, as frequently as possible, also morally complete, especially with reference to my fellow human beings.

I conclude that our situation is neither hopeful nor hopeless. We must be generally skeptical, yes—I say once more—quite skeptical about skepticism. It would be folly to anticipate sheer bliss—setbacks for us and our society are unavoidable. Everlasting truth and complete morality we shall not attain, yet improvement in our lot is both possible and feasible. Trials and errors are inevitable. Again: how can some kind of world unity be achieved in order to avoid nuclear warfare and to evolve the complete morality that has always been the eternal dream of human beings?

Desperately, we say, perhaps a soul-stirring document *(Proposition 13.1)* can move persons, so that they will remember its phrases, which will then affect their behavior. *(Meandering 14.1* is my attempt to reply spontaneously to a Pakistani foundation official who politely challenged scholars in various countries to comment briefly on "the moral bankruptcy which is so rampant today" and on the danger to "peace and the moral lapses.")* Maybe even the guilt from malpractices will motivate us forward. Yet again we must remain skeptical because at some time every conceivable action, including those we may consider most evil or atrocious, has secured approval by someone or in some society. The model of scientific achievements points the way, as it were, to our salvation, although science by itself is insufficient. We must combine science with what we know or think we know about ourselves from our experiences in the past and, yes, from social science as well as the humanities and religion. Nirvana or utopia will never arrive; we cannot all behave like saints. But perhaps, perhaps, perhaps we can marshal our creative capacities and come a trifle closer.

MEANDERING

14.1 A Declaration

There is no one compelling explanation of the moral bankruptcy that pervades too many persons and groups; there is no one panacea that can relieve this state of affairs and eliminate forever the scourge of conflict and war. In fact, one of the reasons for our present plight may well be the belief that evil can be understood by glancing at one entrenched doctrine or that evil can be combated by relying upon a single cause. Moral bankruptcy, we are told, is due to the ways in which we have been reared as children; to the failure of religious leaders to be more convincing or to be heeded; to mistaken or unfounded faith; to the exploitation and selfishness of the elite and the consequent poverty and latent or bursting aggression of the masses; to demagogues and other ruthless leaders who pursue their own selfish ends; to the mass media which seek profit and one-sided objectives—the list staggers on and on. Wars, our mentors say, result from imperialism, sovereignty, nationalism, power, weakness, frustration, wickedness, propaganda, alliances, misunderstanding, patriotism—again the list is long and perhaps endless.

It is not easy to abandon a favorite theory concerning moral bankruptcy or conflict and war, and there is no reason for doing so. We need only realize that every theory, including ours, contains a partial truth; every theory requires assistance from almost all the other theories—at some time, at some place, for some persons, for some countries—to provide more complete insight. Moral bankruptcy and war are thus too complicated and too heterogeneous to be grasped by a single idea, philosophy, or science.

Such eclecticism, however, need not end in nihilism. This man, those men, this nation tends to be bankrupt because of poverty, but that other man, those other men or nations suffer because of lack of faith. This war occurred when the country's leaders felt insecure, that war when they were driven by a desire to be free and independent from a dominating power.

In addition, men and women everywhere, no matter how different they and their culture appear, share one attribute: they are human beings and their cultures spring from the needs with which they are endowed and which they acquire. Their bankruptcies and their wars, therefore, always—yes, always, always—stem from and are related to that indisputable fact. Without succumbing to a single explanation or theory, we may cut through the surface variability that is so heavily reinforced: human beings without exception wish to live; they wish to live satisfactorily; they do not wish to kill or exploit unless they have been previously warped by unfortunate hurting experiences.

But it has never been easy to find the ways "to live satisfactorily" because—and here the variety of explanations and theories already mentioned is most relevant. One but not the only imperative is reasonably clear: individuals cannot be rescued from moral bankruptcy and war unless they play a significant role in finding practical, innovative solutions for their plight. They do not seek misery or conquest; they are fundamentally decent and humane. When they can be brought together in small meaningful groups in which they may express their open and hidden cravings without fear and with trust, and when in consequence they break down substantially the solipsistic predicament in which they are encased, they themselves may well be able to leap, however slowly, in the direction of their own salvation (Doob, 1985).

REFERENCES

INDEX

References

Abelson, R. P., Kinder, D. R., and Peters, M. D. (1982). Affective and semantic components in political person perception. *Journal of Personality and Social Psychology, 42,* 619–30.

Abram, M. B. (1983). Ethics and the new medicine. *New York Times,* June 5, sec. VI, pp. 68, 69, 94, 100.

Abramson, L., Seligman, M. E. P., and Teasdale, J. D. (1978). Learned helplessness in humans. *Journal of Abnormal Psychology, 87,* 49–74.

Aiken, W. (1977). The right to be saved from starvation. In W. W. Aiken and H. La Follette (Eds.), *World hunger and moral obligation* (95–102). Englewood Cliffs, N.J.: Prentice-Hall.

Aiken, W., and La Follette, (Eds.) (1977). *World hunger and moral obligation.* Englewood Cliffs, N.J.: Prentice-Hall.

Ajzen, I., and Fishbein, M. (1980). *Understanding attitudes and predicting social behavior.* Englewood Cliffs, N.J.: Prentice-Hall.

Amato, P. R. (1983). Helping behavior in urban and rural environments. *Journal of Personality and Social Behavior, 45,* 571–86.

Applebaum, P. S. (1982). Can mental patients say no to drugs? *New York Times,* March 21, sec. VI, pp. 46, 47, 51, 54, 58.

Arendt, H. (1964). *Eichmann in Jerusalem.* New York: Viking.

Aristotle (1932). *Rhetoric.* Englewood Cliffs, N.J.: Prentice-Hall.

———. (1934). *The Nicomachean ethics.* Cambridge: Harvard University Press.

———. (1944). *Politics.* Cambridge: Harvard University Press.

Aronfreed, J. (1976). Moral development from the standpoint of a general psychological theory. In T. Lickona, (Ed.), *Moral development and behavior* (54–69). New York: Holt, Rinehart & Winston.

Arthur, J. (1977). Rights and the duty to bring aid. In W. Aiken and M. La Follette, (Eds.), *World hunger and moral obligation* (37–48). Englewood Cliffs, N.J.: Prentice-Hall.

Atiyah, P. S. (1981). *Promises, morals, and law.* Oxford: Clarendon Press.

Auerbach, J. S. (1983). *Justice without law?* New York: Oxford University Press.

Austin, V. D., Deane, N. R., and Trabasso, T. (1977). Recall and order effects as factors in children's moral judgments. *Child Development, 48,* 470–74.

Austin, W., and Hatfield, E. (1980). Equity theory, power, and social justice. In G. Mikula (Ed.) *Justice and social interaction* (25–61). New York: Springer-Verlag.

Ayer, A. J. (1946). *Language, truth, and logic.* New York: Dover Publications.

Bagarozzi, D. A. (1982). The effects of cohesiveness on distributive justice. *Journal of Psychology, 110,* 267–73.

Bahm, A. J. (1979). *The philosopher's world model.* Westport, Conn.: Greenwood Press.

Baier, K. (1958). *The moral point of view.* Ithaca: Cornell University Press.
——. (1966). Responsibility and freedom. In R. T. DeGeorge (Ed.), *Ethics and society* (49–84). New York: Doubleday.

Ball-Rokeach, S. J., and Tallman, I. (1979). Social movements as moral confrontations. In M. Rokeach (Ed.), *Understanding human values* (82–94). New York: Free Press.

Bandura, A., Underwood, B., and Fromson, M. E. (1975). Disinhibition of aggression through diffusion of responsibility and dehumanization. *Journal of Research in Personality, 9,* 253–69.

Barclay, W. (1971). *Ethics in a permissive society.* New York: Harper & Row.

Barnett, M. A., Feighny, M., and Esper, J. A. (1983). Effects of anticipated victim responsiveness and empathy upon volunteering. *Journal of Social Psychology, 119,* 211–18.

Barnette, H. H. (1968). The new ethics. In H. Cox (Ed.), *The situation ethics debate* (121–40). Philadelphia: Westminster Press.

Baron, R. S. (1971). Aggression as a function of audience presence and prior anger arousal. *Journal of Experimental Psychology, 7,* 515–23.

Bass, B. M. (1960). *Leadership, psychology, and organizational behavior.* New York: Harpers.

Battin, M. P. (1983). The least worst death. *Hastings Center Report, 13*(2), 13–16.

Bauman, Z. (1978). *Heremeneutics and social science.* New York: Columbia University Press.

Baumer, F. (1960). *Religion and the rise of skepticism.* New York: Harcourt, Brace.

Bay, C. (1968). Needs, wants, and political legitimacy. *Canadian Journal of Political Science, 1,* 241–60.

Beaman, A. L., Barnes, P. J., Klentz, B., and McQuirk, B. (1978). Increasing helping rates through information dissemination. *Personality and Social Psychology Bulletin, 4,* 406–11.

Beauvoir, S. de. (1948). *The ethics of ambiguity.* Secaucus, N.J.: Citadel Press.

Becker, L. C. (1973). *On justifying moral judgments.* London: Routledge & Kegan Paul.

Berkowitz, L. (1972). Social norms, feelings, and other factors affecting helping and altruism. In L. Berkowitz (Ed.), *Advances in experimental social psychology* (Vol. 6, 63–108). New York: Academic Press.

Bettelheim, B., and Zelan, K. (1982). *On learning to read.* New York: Knopf.

Bickman, L. (1975). Bystander intervention in a crime. *Journal of Applied Social Psychology, 5,* 296–302.

Biderman, A. (1966). Social indicators and goals. In R. A. Bauer (Ed.), *Social indicators* (68–153). Cambridge: MIT Press.

Bidney, D. (1963). The varieties of human freedom. In D. Bidney (Ed.), *The concept of freedom in anthropology* (11–34). The Hague: Mouton.

Black, M. (1964). The gap between "is" and "ought." *Philosophical Review, 73,* 165–81.

Blanshard, P. (1966). Morality and politics. In R. T. DeGeorge (Ed.), *Ethics and society* (1–23). New York: Doubleday.

Blasi, A. (1980). Bridging moral cognition and moral action. *Psychological Bulletin, 88,* 1–45.

Blatt, M. M., and Kohlberg, L. (1975). The effects of classroom moral discussion upon children's level of moral judgment. *Journal of Moral Education, 4,* 129–61.

Bok, S. (1978). *Lying: Moral choice in public and private life.* New York: Pantheon Books.

———. (1982). *Secrets.* New York: Pantheon Books.

Boldero, J., and Rosenthal, D. (1984). Equity, compromise, and competition effects of situational variables and type of allocation pool. *Journal of Social Psychology, 123,* 207–21.

Bonhoeffer, D. (1964). *Ethics.* New York: Macmillan.

Boyce, W. D., and Jensen, L. C. (1978). *Moral reasoning.* Lincoln: University of Nebraska Press.

Bradford, L. P., Gibb, J. R., and Benne, D. D. (1964). *T-group therapy and laboratory method.* New York: Wiley.

Brandt, R. B. (1954). *Hopi ethics*. Chicago: University of Chicago Press.

————. (1959). *Ethical theory*. Englewood Cliffs, N.J.: Prentice-Hall.

Braybrooke, D., and Schotch, P. K. (1981). Cost-analysis under the constraint of meeting needs. In N. E. Bowie (Ed.), *Ethical issues in government* (176–97). Philadelphia: Temple University Press.

Brazerman, M. H., Giuliano, T., and Appelman, A. (1984). Escalation of commitment in individual and group decision making. *Organizational Behavior and Human Performance, 33*, 141–52.

Brehm, S. S., and Brehm, J. W. (1981). *Psychological reactance*. New York: Academic Press.

Brennan, J. G. (1973). *Ethics and morals*. New York: Harpers.

Brewer, G. D. (1978–79). Operational social systems modeling. *Policy Sciences, 10*, 17–69.

Brewer, W. F., and Nakamura, G. V. (1984). The nature and function of schemas. In R. S. Wyer, J. Wyer, and T. K. Skull (Eds.), *Handbook of social cognition* (119–60). Hillsdale, N.J.: Erlbaum.

Brown, A. L. (1975). The development of memory. In H. W. Reese (Ed.), *Advances in child development and behavior* (Vol. 10, 103–52). New York: Academic Press.

Brown, R. C. J., and Tedeschi, J. T. (1976). Determinants of perceived aggression. *Journal of Social Psychology, 100*, 77–87.

Buber, M. (1953). *Good and evil*. New York: Scribner's.

Buldain, R. W., Crano, W. D., and Wegner, D. M. (1982). Effects of age of actor and observer on the oral judgments of children. *Journal of Genetic Psychology, 141*, 261–70.

Bullock, M., Gelman, R., and Baillargeon, R. (1982). In W. J. Friedman (Ed.), *The developmental psychology of time* (209–54). New York: Academic Press.

Burger, J. M., and Rodman, J. L. (1983). Attributions of responsibility for group tasks. *Journal of Personality and Social Psychology, 45*, 1232–42.

Burke, R. J. (1982) Personality, self-image, and situational characteristics of effective helpers in work settings. *Journal of Psychology, 111*, 213–20.

Buss, A. H. (1983). Social rewards and personality. *Journal of Personality and Social Psychology, 44*, 553–63.

Buss, A. R. (1978). Causes and reasons in attribution theory. *Journal of Personality and Social Psychology, 36*, 1311–21.

Bussey, K., and Maughan, B. (1982). Group differences in moral reasoning. *Journal of Personality and Social Psychology, 42*, 701–06.

Callahan, D. A. (1984). Autonomy: A moral good, not a moral obsession. *Hastings Center Report, 14*(5), 40–42.

Campbell, D. T., and Cecil, J. S. (1982). A proposed system of regulation for the protection of participants in low-risk areas of applied social science. In J. E. Sieber (Ed.), *The ethics of social research* (97–121). New York: Springer-Verlag.

Canetti, E. (1962). *Crowds and power.* New York: Viking.

Caplan, A. L. (1984). Organ procurement. *Hastings Center Report,* 14(5), 9–12.

Cavendish, R. (1975). *The powers of evil in Western religion, magic, and folk belief.* New York: Putnam's.

Childs, B., and Hickman, F. (1983). Human genetics. *Daedalus,* 112(2), 189–209.

Cohen, A. (1974). *Two-dimensional man.* Berkeley: University of California Press.

Collingwood, R. G. (1978). *An autobiography.* Oxford: Oxford University Press.

Conner, R. F. (1982). Assignments of clients in social experimentation. In J. E. Sieber (Ed.), *The ethics of social research* (57–77). New York: Springer-Verlag.

Conroy, W. J. (1979). In M. Rokeach (Ed.), *Understanding human values* (199–209). New York: Free Press.

Costanzo, P., Cole, J. D., Farnill, D., and Grumet, J. F. (1973). A reexamination of the effects of intent and consequence on children's moral judgment. *Child Development, 44,* 154–61.

Cronbach, L. J. (1975). Beyond the two disciplines of scientific psychology. *American Psychologist, 30,* 116–27.

Crosby, F. (1984). *Before and beyond anger.* Informal talk, Yale University.

Cross, W. O. (1968). The moral revolution. In H. Cox (Ed.), *The situation ethics debate* (146–70). Philadelphia: Westminster Press.

Crumbaugh, J. C. (1968). Cross-validation of purpose-in-life based on Frankl's concepts. *Journal of Individual Psychology, 24,* 74–81.

Czartoryski, A. (1975). *Education for power.* London: Davis-Poynter.

Damon, W. (1983). *Social and personality development.* New York: Norton.

Danieli, Y. (1981). On the achievement of integration in aging survivors of the Nazi holocaust. *Journal of Geriatric Psychiatry, 14,* 191–201.

Darden, D. K. (1983). Values and policy. *Basic and Applied Social Psychology, 4,* 29–37.

Davis, K. E., and Jones, E. E. (1960). Changes in interpersonal perception as a means of reducing cognitive dissonance. *Journal of Abnormal and Social Psychology, 61,* 402–10.

Davison, M. L. (1979). The internal structure and the psychometric properties of the defining issues test. In J. R. Rest (Ed.), *Development in judging moral issues* (223–45). Minneapolis: University of Minnesota.

Dawson, C. (1959). Notes on culture and ethics. In L. R. Ward (Ed.), *Ethics and the social sciences* (43–50). Notre Dame: University of Notre Dame.

Deutsch, M. (1975). Equity, equality, and need. *Journal of Social Issues, 31*(3), 137–49.

Dewey, J. (1920). *Reconstruction in philosophy.* New York: Holt.

———. (1922). *Human nature and conduct.* New York: Holt.

———. (1928). Skepticism. In J. M. Baldwin (Ed.), *Dictionary of philosophy* (Vol. 2, 489–91). New York: Macmillan.

Dicks, H. V. (1972). *Licensed mass murder.* New York: Basic Books.

Diener, E., and Crandall, R. (1978). *Ethics in social and behavioral research.* Chicago: University of Chicago Press.

Dixon, B. (1984). Engineering chimeras for Noah's ark. *Hastings Center Report, 14*(2), 10–12.

Doob, L. W. (1961). *Communication in Africa.* New Haven: Yale University Press.

———. (1971). *Patterning of time.* New Haven: Yale University Press.

———. (1972). *The functioning of proverbs among the Twi.* unpublished manuscript.

———. (1975). *Pathways to people.* New Haven: Yale University Press.

———. (1978). *Panorama of evil.* Westport, Conn.: Greenwood Press.

———. (1981). *The pursuit of peace.* Westport, Conn.: Greenwood Press.

———. (1983). *Personality, power, and authority.* Westport, Conn.: Greenwood Press.

———. (1985). Moral bankruptcy and war. In H. M. Said (Ed.), *Voice of morality* (316–18). Naximabad: Hamdard Foundation Press.

Doob, L. W., and Hurreh, I. M. (1970–71). Somali proverbs and poems as acculturation indices. *Public Opinion Quarterly, 34,* 552–59.

Dostoyevsky, F. (1936). *The possessed.* New York: Modern Library.

Douglas, M. (1983). Morality and culture. *Ethics, 93,* 786–91.

Douglas, M., and Waldavsky, A. (1982). *Risk and culture.* Berkeley: University of California Press.

Eagleton, T. (1983). *Literary theory.* Minneapolis: University of Minnesota Press.

Easterbrook, J. A. (1978). *The determinants of free will.* New York: Academic Press.

Eccles, J. C. (1980). *The human psyche.* New York: Springer-Verlag.

Edel, M., and Edel, A. (1968). *Anthropology and ethics.* Cleveland: Case Western Reserve University Press.

Eimer, B. N. (1983). Age differences in boys' evaluations of fathers intervening to stop misbehavior. *Journal of Psychology, 115,* 159–63.

Eiser, J. R., and Van der Pligt, J. (1984). Attitudes in a social context. In H. Taifel (Ed.), *The social dimension* (363–78). Cambridge: Cambridge University Press.

Ekman, P. (1985). *Telling lies.* New York: Norton.

Emerson, W. A., Jr. (1974). *Sin and the new American conscience.* New York: Harper & Row.

Emler, N., Renwick, S., and Malone, B. (1983). The relationship between moral reasoning and political organization. *Journal of Personality and Social Psychology, 45,* 1073–80.

Enzensberger, H. M. (1967). *Deutschland, Deutschland unter anderm Aeusserungen zur Politik.* Frankfurt: Suhrkampf.

Ericson, R. V., and Baranek, P. M. (1982). *The ordering of justice.* Toronto: University of Toronto Press.

Erikson, E. H. (1959). *Identity and the life cycle.* New York: Norton.

Everett, W. G. (1918). *Moral values.* New York: Holt.

Feather, N. T. (1979). Assimilation of values in migrant groups. In M. Rokeach (Ed.), *Understanding human values* (97–147). New York: Free Press.

Fellner, C. H., and Marshall, J. R. (1981). Kidney donors revisited. In J. P. Rushton and R. M. Sorrentino (Eds.), *Altruism and helping behavior* (351–65). Hillsdale, N.J.: Erlbaum.

Fincham, F. D., and Jaspars, J. M. (1980). Attribution and responsibility. In L. Berkowitz (Ed.), *Advances in experimental social psychology* (Vol. 13, 81–138). New York: Academic Press.

Finney, P. D., and Helm, B. (1982). The actor-observer relationship. *Journal of Social Psychology, 117,* 219–25.

Fisher, J. D., DePaulo, B. M., and Nadler, A. (1981). Extending altruism beyond the altruistic act. In J. P. Rushton and R. M. Sorrentino (Eds.), *Altruism and helping behavior* (367–422). Hillsdale, N.J.: Erlbaum.

Fishkin, J. S. (1982). *The limits of obligation.* New Haven: Yale University Press.

———. (1984). *Beyond subjective morality.* New Haven: Yale University Press.

Fleetwood, R. S., and Parish, T. S. (1976). Relationship between moral development test scores of juvenile delinquents and their inclusion in a moral dilemma group. *Psychological Reports, 39,* 1075–80.

Fletcher, J. (1966). *Situation ethics.* Philadelphia: Westminster Press.

Flugel, J. C. (1945). Man, morals, and society. New York: International Universities Press.

Foehl, J. C., and Goldman, M. (1983). Increasing altruistic behavior by using compliance techniques. *Journal of Social Psychology, 119,* 21–29.

Form, W. H., and Nosow, S. (1958). *Community in disaster.* New York: Harpers.

Forsyth, D. R. (1980). A taxonomy of ethical ideologies. *Journal of Personality and Social Psychology, 39,* 175–84.

Forsyth, D. R., and Berger, R. E. (1982). The effects of ethical ideology on moral behavior. *Journal of Social Psychology, 117,* 53–56.

Fowler, H. W. (1926). *A dictionary of modern English usage.* Oxford: Clarendon Press.

Fraisse, P. (1982). The adaptation of the child to time. In W. J. Friedman (Ed.), *The developmental psychology of time* (113–40). New York: Academic Press.

Frankena, W. K. (1962). The concept of social justice. In R. B. Brandt (Ed.), *Social justice* (1–29). Englewood Cliffs, N.J.: Prentice-Hall.

———. (1963). *Ethics.* Englewood Cliffs, N.J.: Prentice-Hall.

———. (1977). Moral philosophy and world hunger. In W. Aiken and H. La Follette (Eds.), *World hunger and moral obligation* (66–84). Englewood Cliffs, N.J.: Prentice-Hall.

Frankl, V. E. (1959). *From death camp to existentialism.* Boston: Beacon Press.

———. (1970). *The will to meaning.* New York: New American Library.

Franklin, R. L. (1968). *Freewill and determinism.* New York: Humanities Press.

Freedman, J. L. (1970). Transgression, compliance, and guilt. In J. Macaulay and L. Berkowitz (Eds.), *Altruism and helping behavior* (155–61). New York: Academic Press.

———. (1978). *Happy people.* New York: Harcourt, Brace.

Freud, S. (1950). *Totem and taboo.* New York: Norton.

Friendly, J. (1982). Editing and ethics. *New York Times,* August 1, p. 22E.

Fromm, Eberhard. (1970). *Politik und Moral.* Berlin: Dietz.

Fromm, Erich. (1941). *Escape from freedom.* New York: Farrar & Rinehart.

Garbarino, J., and Bronfenbrenner, U. (1976). The socialization of moral judgment and behavior in cross-cultural perspective. In T. Lickona (Ed.), *Moral development and behavior* (70–83). New York: Holt, Rinehart & Winston.

Garcia, J. D. (1971). *The moral society.* New York: Julian Press.

Gardner, G. T., Tiemann, A. R., Gould, L. C., DeLuca, D. R., Doob, L. W., and Stolwijk, J. A. J. (1982). Risk and benefit perceptions. *Journal of Social Psychology, 116,* 179–97.

Gardner, H. (1982). *Art, mind and brain.* New York: Basic Books.

Gardner, H., and Dudai, Y. (1985). Biology and giftedness. *Items (SSRC), 39,* (June), 1–6.

Garfinkel, H. (1967). *Studies in ethnomethodology.* Englewood Cliffs, N.J.: Prentice-Hall.

Geertz, C. (1983). Slide show. *Raritan,* no v., 62–79.

Geller, D. M. (1982). Alternatives to deception. In J. E. Sieber (Ed.), *The ethics of social research* (39–55). New York: Springer-Verlag.

Gergen, K. J. (1973). Social psychology as history. *Journal of Personality and Social Psychology, 26,* 309–20.

———. (1982). *Toward transformation in social knowledge.* New York: Springer-Verlag.

Gerlitz, P. (1971). *Die Religion und die neue Moral.* Munich: Claudius Verlag.

Gibb, G. D., Best, R. H., and Lambirth, T. T. (1983). Clients' and therapists' perspectives and reasons for seeking therapy. *Journal of Psychology, 114,* 249–52.

Gibbs, J. C. (1977). Kohlberg's states of moral judgment. *Harvard Educational Review, 47,* 43–61.

Giles, H., and Powesland, P. F. (1975). *Speed style and social evaluation.* London: Academic Press.

Gillet, M. (1973). *L'homme et sa structure.* Paris: Téqui.

Gilligan, C. (1982). *In a different voice.* Cambridge: Harvard University Press.

Girvetz, H. K. (1973). *Beyond right and wrong.* New York: Free Press.

Glazer, M. (1983). Ten whistleblowers and how they fared. *Hastings Center Report, 13*(6), 33–41.

Goffman, E. (1961). *Encounters.* Indianapolis: Bobbs-Merrill.

Goldman, M., Feltham, D. W., and Peters, J. B. (1982). Prosocial behavior and compliance in signing a petition. *Journal of Social Psychology, 118,* 17–21.

Goldman, M., McVeigh, J. F., and Richterkessing, J. L. (1984). Door-in-the-face procedure. *Journal of Social Psychology, 123,* 245–51.

Goldschmidt, W. (1951). Ethics and the structure of society. *American Anthropologist, 53,* 506–24.

Goldschmidt, W., and Edgerton, R. B. (1961). A picture technique for the study of values. *American Anthropologist, 63,* 26–47.

Goleman, D. (1985). *Vital lies, simple truths.* New York: Simon & Schuster.

Gorsuch, R. L., and Barnes, M. L. (1973). Stages of ethical reasoning and moral norms of Carib youths. *Journal of Cross-Cultural Psychology, 4,* 283–301.

Graham, D. (1972). *Moral learning and development.* London: B. T. Batsford.

Green, W. (1984). Setting boundaries for artificial feeding. *Hastings Center Report, 14*(6), 8–10.

Greene, G. (1983). The uneasy Catholicism of Graham Greene. *New York Times,* April 3, sec. IV, pp. 11, 21.

Greet, K. G. (1970). *The art of moral judgment.* London: Epworth Press.

Grice, G. R. (1967). *The grounds of moral judgment.* Cambridge: Cambridge University Press.

Guitton, J. (1970). *Histoire et destinée.* Paris: Declee de Brower.

Gunnemann, J. P. (1979). *The moral meaning of revolution.* New Haven: Yale University Press.

Guttmann, J. (1982). Israeli children's reactions to moral judgment dilemmas as a function of pressure from adults and peers. *Journal of Genetic Psychology, 140,* 161–68.

Haan, N., Bellah, R. N., Rabinow, P., and Sullivan, W. M. (Eds.). (1983). *Social science as moral inquiry.* New York: Columbia University Press.

Habermas, J. (1983). Interpretative social science vs. hermeneuticism. In Haan, Bellah, Rabinow, & Sullivan (Eds.), *Social science* (251–69).

Handlin, O., and Handlin, M. (1961). *The dimensions of liberty.* Cambridge: Harvard University Press.

Handy, R. T. (1977). *A history of the churches in the United States and Canada.* New York: Oxford University Press.

Harder, D. W., Strauss, J. S., Kokes, R. F., and Ritzler, B. A. (1984). Self-derogation and psychopathology. *Genetic Psychology Monographs, 109,* 223–49.

Hardin, G. (1972). *Exploring new ethics for survival.* New York: Viking.

Hardy, H. (1979). *The spiritual nature of man.* Oxford: Clarendon Press.

Harris, E. E. (1966). Respect for persons. In R. T. DeGeorge (Ed.), *Ethics and society.* (111–32). New York: Doubleday.

Hart, H. L. A. (1968). *Punishment and responsibility.* New York: Oxford University Press.

Hartley, S. F. (1982). Sampling strategies and the threat to privacy. In J. E. Sieber (Ed.), *The ethics of social research* (167–89). New York: Springer-Verlag.

Harvey, D. (1973). *Social justice and the city.* Baltimore: Johns Hopkins University Press.

Heider, F. (1958). *The psychology of interpersonal relations.* New York: Wiley.

Held, V. (1984). *Rights and goods.* New York: Free Press.

Herron, W. G., Steyen, R. D., Poland, H. V., and Schultz, C. L. (1983). Moral judgment maturity of process and reactive schizophrenics. *Journal of Psychology, 114,* 21–27.

Hobbes, T. (1946). *Leviathan.* Oxford: Basil Blackwell.

Hoffman, M. L. (1977). Moral internalization. In L. Berkowitz (Ed.), *Advances in experimental social psychology* (Vol. 10, 85–133). New York: Academic Press.

Hoffmann, S. H. (1984). Universities and human rights. *Bulletin, American Academy of Arts and Sciences, 37*(6), 11–33.

Hogan, R. (1970). A dimension of moral judgment. *Journal of Consulting and Clinical Psychology, 35,* 205–12.

———. (1973). Moral conduct and moral character. *Psychological Bulletin, 79,* 217–32.

Hogan, R., and Dickstein, E. (1972). A measure of moral values. *Journal of Consulting and Clinical Psychology, 39,* 210–14.

Hogan, R., and Emler, N. P. (1978). The biases in contemporary social psychology. *Social Research, 45,* 478–534.

Holm, O. (1983). Four factors affecting perceived aggressiveness. *Journal of Psychology, 114,* 227–34.

Hornmuth, S., and Stephan, W. G. (1981). Effects of viewing "Holocaust" on Germans and Americans. *Journal of Applied Social Psychology, 11,* 240–51.

Hospitals turn to philosophers on life issues. (1982). *New York Times,* March 19, pp. A1, B2.

Hudson, W. D. (1969). *The is/ought question.* London: Macmillan.

Inlow, G. M. (1972). *Values in transition.* New York: Wiley.

Irwin, M., Tripodi, T., and Bieri, J. (1967). Affective stimulus value and cognitive complexity. *Journal of Personality and Social Psychology, 5,* 444–48.

Janis, I. L., and Mann, L. (1977). *Decision making.* New York: Free Press.

Jennings, B. (1983). Interpretive social science and policy analysis. In D. Callahan and B. Jennings (Eds.), *Ethics, the social sciences, and policy analysis* (3–35). New York: Plenum.

Joad, C. E. M. (1939). *Guide to modern wickedness.* London: Faber & Faber.

John Paul II, Pope. (1983). Discourse to Pontifical Academy of Scienes. *New York Times,* Nov. 13, p. 36.

Jones, E. E., and Nisbett, R. E. (1971). The actor and the observer. In E. E. Jones, D. E. Kanouse, H. H. Kelley, R. E. Nisbett, S. Valins, and B. Weiner (Eds.), *Attribution* (79–94). Morristown, N.J.: General Learning Press.

Jones, E. E., and Sigall, H. (1971). The bogus pipeline. *Psychological Bulletin, 76,* 349–64.

Jones, L. M., and Foshay, N. N. (1984). Diffusion of responsibility in a nonemergency situation. *Journal of Social Psychology, 123,* 155–68.

Kagan, S., and Knudson, K. A. M. (1983). Differential development of affective role-taking ability and prosocial behavior. *Journal of Genetic Psychology, 143,* 97–102.

Kahn, J. V. (1983). Moral reasoning of Piagetian-matched retarded and nonretarded children and adolescents. *Journal of Genetic Psychology, 143,* 69–77.

Kanekar, S., and Kolsawalls, M. B. (1980). Responsibility of a rape victim in relation to her respectability, attractiveness, and provocativeness. *Journal of Social Psychology, 112,* 153–54.

Kant, I. (1969). *Foundations of the metaphysics of morals.* Indianapolis: Bobbs-Merrill.

Kantola, S. J., Syne, G. J., and Campbell, A. N. (1982). The role of individual differences and external variables in a test of the sufficiency of Fishbein's model to explain intentions to conserve water. *Journal of Applied Social Psychology, 12,* 70–83.

Katzev, R. D., and Averill, A. K. (1984). Knowledge of the bystander problem and the impact on subsequent helping behavior. *Journal of Social Psychology, 123,* 223–30.

Kavka, G. S. (1980). Deterrence, utility, and rational choice. *Theory and Decision, 12,* 41–60.

Keasey, C. B. (1975). Implications of cognitive development for moral reasoning. In D. De Palma and J. M. Foley (Eds.), *Moral development* (39–56). Hillsdale, N.J.: Erlbaum.

Kelley, H. H. (1971). Moral evaluation. *American Psychologist, 26,* 293–300.

Kenrick, D. T., and Braver, S. L. (1982). Personality: Idiographic *and* nomothetic. *Psychological Review, 89,* 182–86.

Kiell, N. (Ed.). (1983). *Blood brothers.* New York: International Universities Press.

Kierkegaard, S. (1968). *Fear and trembling.* Princeton: Princeton University Press.

Kishov, M. (1983). Locus of control and academic achievement. *Journal of Cross-Cultural Psychology, 14,* 297–308.

Klein, P. D. (1981). *Certainty: a refutation of scepticism.* Minneapolis: University of Minnesota.

Kleinberger, A. (1982). The proper object of moral judgment and of moral education. *Journal of Moral Education, 11,* 147–54.

Kluckhohn, F. R., and Strodtbeck, F. L. (1961). *Variations in value orientations.* Evanston, Ill.: Row, Peterson.

Kohlberg, L. (1968). The child as a moral philosopher. *Psychology Today, 2,* 24–30.

———. (1971). From is to ought. In T. Mischel (Ed.), *Cognitive development and epistemology* (151–235). New York: Academic Press.

———. (1976). Moral stages and moralization. In T. Lickona (Ed.), *Moral development and behavior* (31–53). New York: Holt.

———. (1983). *The philosophy of moral development.* New York: Harper & Row.

Kohlberg, L., and Higgins, A. (1984). Continuities and discontinuities in childhood and adult development revisited—again. In L. Kohlberg (Ed.), *The psychology of moral development* (426–97). New York: Harper & Row.

Kohlberg, L., Levine, C., and Hewer, A. (1983). *Moral stages.* Basel: S. Karger.

Kohlberg, L., Ricks, D., and Snarey, J. (1984). Child development as a predictor of adaptation in adulthood. *Genetic Psychology Monograph, 110,* 91–172.

Köhler, W. (1938). *The place of value in a world of facts.* New York: Liveright.

Körner, S. (1976). *Experience and conduct.* Cambridge: Cambridge University Press.

———. (1979). *Fundamental questions of philosophy.* Sussex: Harvester Press.

Krimmel, H. T. (1983). The case against surrogate parenting. *Hastings Center Report, 13*(5), 35–39.

Kunda, Z., and Schwartz, S. H. (1983). Undermining moral motivation. *Journal of Personality and Social Psychology, 45,* 763–71.

Kurtines, W., and Greif, E. B. (1974). The development of moral thought. *Psychological Bulletin, 81,* 453–70.

Kurtz, C. A., and Eisenberg, N. (1983). Role-taking, empathy, and resistance to deviation in children. *Journal of Genetic Psychology, 142,* 85–95.

Lamm, H., Kayser, E., and Schanz, V. (1983). An attributional analysis of interpersonal justice. *Journal of Social Psychology, 119,* 269–81.

Lamm, H., and Schwinger, T. (1983). Need consideration in allocation decisions. *Journal of Social Psychology, 119,* 205–09.

Lappé, F. M., and Collins, J. (1977). *Food first.* Boston: Houghton Mifflin.

Lappé, M. (1974). Choosing the sex of our children. *Hastings Center Report, 4*(1), 1–3.

————. (1984). The predictive power of the new genetics. *Hastings Center Report, 14*(5), 18–21.

Lauterbach, A. (1983). Social change versus perceived villainy. *Journal of Mind and Behavior, 4,* 191–210.

Leary, D. E. (1980). The intentions of Descartes and Locke. *Journal of General Psychology, 102,* 283–310.

Lee, D. (1948). Are basic needs ultimate? *Journal of Abnormal and Social Psychology, 43,* 391–95.

Lefcourt, H. M. (1976). *Locus of control.* Hillsdale, N.J.: Erlbaum.

Leiter, K. (1980). *A primer on ethnomethodology.* New York: Oxford University Press.

Lerner, M. J. (1970). The desire for justice and reactions to victims. In J. Macaulay and L. Berkowitz (Eds.), *Altruism and helping behavior* (208–29). New York: Academic Press.

————. (1977). The justice motive. *Journal of Personality, 45,* 1–52.

————. (1980). *The belief in a just world.* New York: Plenum Press.

Leventhal, G. S., Karunza, J., Jr., and Fry, W. R. (1980). Beyond fairness. In G. Mikula (Ed.), *Justice and social interaction* (167–218). New York: Springer-Verlag.

Levine, C. (1976). Role-taking standpoint and adolescent usage of Kohlberg's conventional stages of moral reasoning. *Journal of Personality and Social Psychology, 34,* 41–46.

————. (1983). Television news and imitative suicides. *Hastings Center Report, 13*(2), 3.

————. (1984). In jail for refusing to testify: Is forced feeding justified? *Hastings Center Report, 14*(1), 2.

Levinson, D. J. (1978). *The seasons of a man's life.* New York: Knopf.

Lewis, C. E. (1955). *The ground and nature of the right.* New York: Columbia University Press.

Lindblom, C. E., and Cohen, D. K. (1979). *Usable knowledge.* New Haven: Yale University Press.

Lindskold, S., and Walters, P. S. (1983). Categories for acceptability of lies. *Journal of Social Psychology, 120,* 129–36.

Linton, R. (1952). Universal ethical values. In R. N. Anshen (Ed.), *Moral principles of action* (645–60). New York: Harpers.

Lipscomb, T. J., Larrieu, J., McAllister, H. A., and Breman, N. J. (1982). Modeling and children's generosity. *Merrill-Palmer Quarterly, 28,* 275–82.

Lipscomb, T. J., Bregman, N. J., and McAllister, H. A. (1983). The effect of words and actions on children's prosocial behavior. *Journal of Psychology, 114,* 193–98.

London, P. (1970). The rescuers. In J. Macaulay and L. Berkowitz (Eds.), *Altruism and helping behavior* (241–50). New York: Academic Press.

London, P., Schulman, R. E., and Black, M. S. (1964). Religion, guilt, and ethical standards. *Journal of Social Psychology, 63,* 145–59.

Luchins, A., and Luchins, E. H. (1984). Primacy effects and the nature of communications. *Journal of General Psychology, 110,* 11–22.

Macaulay, J., and Berkowitz, L. (Eds.). (1970). *Altruism and helping behavior.* New York: Academic Press.

McCloskey, H. J. (1969). *Meta-ethics and normative ethics.* The Hague: Martins Nijhoff.

McCord, J., and Clemes, S. (1964). Conscience orientation and divisions of personality. *Behavioral Science, 9,* 19–29.

McDougall, W. (1923). *Outline of psychology.* New Yorker: Scribner's.

McGlashan, C. F. (1940). *History of the Donner party.* Stanford, Calif.: Stanford University Press.

McGuire, W. J. (1980). The development of theory in social psychology. In R. Gulmour and S. Duck (Eds.), *The development of social psychology* (53–80). London: Academic Press.

MacIver, R. M. (1952). The deep beauty of the Golden Rule. In R. N. Anshen (Ed.), *Moral principles of action* (39–47). New York: Harpers.

MacKaye, J. (1924). *The logic of conduct.* New York: Boni & Liveright.

McKillip, J., and Lockhart, D. C. (1984). The effectiveness of cover-letter appeals. *Journal of Social Psychology, 122,* 85–91.

McKinney, J. P. (1980). Moral development and the concept of values. In M. Windmiller, N. Lambert, and E. Turiel (Eds.), *Moral development and socialization* (201–18). Boston: Allyn & Bacon.

Mader, J. (1979). *Moral, Philosophie, und Wissenschaft.* Vienna: Oldenbourg.

Maeroff, G. I. (1984). Values regain their popularity. *New York Times,* April 10, pp. C1, C9.

Makai, M. (1972). *The dialectics of moral consciousness.* Budapesst: Akadémiai Kiadó.

Malamuth, N. H., and Donnerstein, Edward. (1982). The effects of aggressive-pornographic mass media stimuli. In L. Berkowitz (Ed.), *Advances in experimental social psychology* (Vol. 15, 103–36). New York: Academic Press.

Malström, A-K. (1980). Motive and obligation. *Philosophical Society and Department of Philosophy* (University of Uppsala, Sweden), no. 31.

Mannheim, K. (1936). *Ideology and utopia.* New York: Harcourt, Brace.

———. (1937). The sociology of human evaluation. In J. E. Dugdale

(Ed.), *Further papers on the social sciences* (171–91). London: Le Plan House Press.

———. (1943). *The diagnosis of our time.* London: Routledge & Kegan Paul.

Maqsud, M. (1977). The influence of social heterogeneity and sentimental credibility on moral judgment. *Journal of Cross-Cultural Psychology, 8,* 113–22.

March, J. G. (1978). Bounded rationality, ambiguity, and the engineering of choice. *Bell Journal of Economics, 9,* 587–608.

Marcus, G. E., and Cushman, D. (1982). Ethnographics as text. *Annual Review of Anthropology, 11,* 25–69.

Marcuse, H. (1966). Ethics and revolution. In R. T. DeGeorge (Ed.), *Ethics and society* (133–47). New York: Doubleday.

Margenau, H. (1964). *Ethics and science.* Princeton: Van Nostrand.

Marks, E. L., Penner, L. A., and Stone, A. V. W. (1982). Helping as a function of empathic responses and sociopathy. *Journal of Research in Personality, 16,* 1–20.

Marsden, P. V. (1983). Restricted access in networks and models of power. *American Journal of Sociology, 88,* 686–717.

Marshall, J. (1968). *Intention in law and society.* New York: Funk & Wagnalls.

Marx, K. (1935). The eighteenth brumaire of Louis Bonaparte. In E. Burns (Ed.), *Handbook of Marxism* (116–31). New York: International Publishers.

Maslow, A. H. (1963). Fusions of facts and values. *American Journal of Psychoanalysis, 23,* 117–31.

Mason, P. (1970). *Patterns of dominance.* London: Oxford University Press.

Mehl, R. (1971). *Les attitudes morales.* Paris: Presses Universitaires de France.

Meiland, J. W. (1970). *The nature of intention.* London: Methuen.

Melden, A. I. (1977). *Rights and persons.* Berkeley: University of California Press.

Melsen, A. G. (1967). *Physical science and ethics.* Pittsburgh: Duquesne University Press.

Merton, R. K. (1957). *Social theory and social structure.* Glencoe, Ill.: Free Press.

Meynell, H. (1981). *Freud, Marx, and morals.* London: Macmillan.

Middleton, R., and Putney, S. (1962). Religion, normative standards, and behavior. *Sociometry, 25,* 141–52.

Midlarsky, E. (1971). Aiding under stress. *Journal of Personality, 39,* 132–49.

Mikula, G. (Ed.). (1980a). *Justice and social interaction.* New York: Springer-Verlag.

Mikula, G. (1980b). Introduction: Main issues in the psychological research on justice. In Mikula (Ed.), *Justice and social interaction* (13–23).

———. (1984). Justice and fairness in interpersonal relations. In H. Tajfel (Ed.), *The social dimension* (Vol. 1, 204–27). Cambridge: Cambridge University Press.

Milgram, S. (1974). *Obedience to authority.* New York: Harper & Row.

Miller, J. G. (1978). *Living systems.* New York: McGraw-Hill.

Mills, J. (1958). Changes in moral attitudes following temptation. *Journal of Personality, 26,* 517–31.

Milner, D. (1984). The development of ethnic attitudes. In H. Tajfel (Ed.), *The social dimension* (Vol. 1, 88–110). Cambridge: Cambridge University Press.

Mischel, W. (1974). Processes in delay of gratification. In L. Berkowitz (Ed.), *Advances in experimental social psychology* (Vol. 7, 249–92). New York: Academic Press.

Mischel, W., and Peake, P. K. (1982). Beyond déjà vu in search for cross-situational consistency. *Psychological Review, 89,* 730–59.

Moodley-Rajab, D., and Ramkissoon, R. D. (1979). Internal-external control among South African students. *South African Journal of Psychology, 9,* 145–47.

Moore, G. E. (1903). *Principia ethica.* Cambridge: Cambridge University Press.

Moran, J. D., and O'Brien, G. (1983). The development of intention-based moral judgments in three- and four-year-old children. *Journal of Genetic Psychology, 143,* 175–79.

Morris, C. (1956). *Varieties of human values.* Chicago: University of Chicago Press.

Muelder, W. G. (1983). *The ethical edge of Christian theology.* New York: Edwin Mellen Press.

Mussen, P. H., and Eisenberg-Berg, N. (1977). *Roots of caring, sharing, and helping.* San Francisco: Freeman.

Naess, O. (1968). *Scepticism.* London: Routledge & Kegan Paul.

Naroll, R. (1983). *The moral order.* Beverly Hills, Calif.: Sage.

Narr, W-D. (1983). Reflections on the form and content of social science. In N. Haan, R. N. Bellah, P. Rabinow, and W. M. Sullivan (Eds.), *Social science as moral inquiry* (273–96). New York: Columbia University Press.

Nelson, J. B. (1968). Contextualism and the ethical triad. In H. Cox (Ed.), *The situation ethics debate* (171–86). Philadelphia: Westminster Press.

Nelson, R. R., and Winter, S. G. (1982). *An evolutionary theory of economic change*. Cambridge: Harvard University Press.

Newton, L. H. (1981). Representation: The duties of a peculiar situation. In N. E. Bowie (Ed.), *Ethical issues in government* (41–53). Philadelphia: Temple University Press.

Nielsen, K. (1979). On deriving an ought from an is. *Review of Metaphysics, 32*, 488–514.

Niven, W. D. (1922). Good and evil. In J. Hastings (Ed.), *Encyclopedia of religion and ethics* (318–26). New York: Scribner's.

Norman, R. (1971). *Reasons for actions*. Oxford: Basil Blackwell.

Nucci, L. P., Turiel, E., and Encarnacion-Gawrych, G. (1983). Children's social interactions and social concepts. *Journal of Cross-Cultural Psychology, 14*, 469–87.

Nummendal S. G., and Bass, S. C. (1976). Effects of the salience of intention and consequence on children's moral judgments. *Developmental Psychology, 12*, 475–76.

Olson, R. G. (1967). The good. In F. Edwards (Ed.), *Encyclopedia of philosophy* (Vol. 3, 367–70). New York: Macmillan.

O'Neill, O. (1977). Lifeboat earth. In W. Aiken and H. La Follette (Eds.), *World hunger and moral obligation* (148–64). Englewood Cliffs, N.J.: Prentice-Hall.

Opton, E. M. (1971). It never happened and besides they deserved it. In N. Sanford and C. Comstock (Eds.), *Sanctions for evil* (39–70). San Francisco: Jossey-Bass.

Osgood, C. E., Suci, G. J., and Tannenbaum, P. H. (1957). *The measurement of meaning*. Urbana: University of Illinois Press.

Ossowska, M. (1970). *Social determinants of moral ideas*. Philadelphia: University of Pennsylvania Press.

Ostheimer, J. M., and Ritt, L. G. (1982). Abundance and American democracy. *Journal of Politics, 44*, 365–87.

Page, R. A., and Bode, J. R. (1980). Comparison of measures of moral reasoning and development of a new objective measure. *Educational and Psychological Measurement, 40* 317–29.

———. (1982). Inducing changes in moral reasoning. *Journal of Psychology, 112*, 113–19.

Passmore, J. (1970). *The perfectibility of man*. London: Duckworth.

Pateman, C. (1983). Defending prostitution. *Ethics, 83*, 561–65.

Paton, H. J. (1947). *The categorical imperative*. London: Hutchinson.

Patterson, O. (1982). *Slavery and social death*. Cambridge: Harvard University Press.

Percival, T. O. (1979). Cognitive and motivational parallels in moral development. *Canadian Journal of Behavior Science, 11*, 214–24.

Perrow, C. (1981). Disintegrating social sciences. *New York University Quarterly* (Winter).

———. (1984). *Normal accidents.* New York: Basic Books.

Piaget, J. (1965). *The moral judgment of the child.* New York: Free Press.

Pike, J. A. (1968). *Agapé* is not enough. In H. Cox (Ed.), *The situation ethics debate* (198–200). Philadelphia: Westminster Press.

Plato (1928). *The republic.* New York: Scribner's.

Prather, D. K. (1973). Prompted mental practice and flight simulation. *Journal of Applied Psychology, 57,* 353–55.

Presidential panel says society has an "ethical obligation" to provide equitable access to health care. (1983). *New York Times,* March 23, p. 12.

Prewitt, K. (1983). Scientific illiteracy and democratic theory. *Daedelus, 112*(2), 49–64.

Pugh, G. E. (1977). *The biological origin of human values.* New York: Basic Books.

Rachels, J. (1977). Vegetarianism and "the other weight problems." In W. Aiken and H. La Follette (Eds.), *World hunger and moral obligation* (180–93). Englewood Cliffs, N.J.: Prentice-Hall.

Radcliffe, W. (1952). *The problem of power.* London: Secker & Warburg.

Rawlings, E. I. (1970). Reactive guilt and anticipatory guilt in attitude behavior. In J. Macaulay and L. Berkowitz (Eds.), *Altruism and helping behavior* (163–77). New York: Academic Press.

Rawls, J. (1971). *A theory of justice.* Cambridge: Harvard University Press.

Regan, T. (1983). *The case for animal rights.* Berkeley: University of California Press.

Rein, M. (1983). Value-critical policy analysis. In D. Callahan and B. Jennings (Eds.), *Ethics, the social sciences, and policy analysis* (89–111). New York: Plenum.

Rescher, N. (1980). *Scepticism.* Oxford: Basil Blackwell.

Rest, J. R. (1979). *Development in judging moral issues.* Minneapolis: University of Minnesota.

Rest, J. R., Cooper, D., Coder, R., Masanz, J., and Anderson, D. (1974). Judging the important issues in moral dilemmas. *Developmental Psychology, 10,* 491–501.

Richardson, V., Berman, S., and Piwowarski, M. (1983). Projective assessment of the relationship between the salience of death, religion, and age among adults in America. *Journal of General Psychology, 109,* 149–56.

Robinson, J. A. T. (1963). *Honest to god.* Philadelphia: Westminster Press.

Roemer, J. (1982). *A general theory of exploitation and class.* Cambridge: Harvard University Press.

Rokeach, M. (1973). *The nature of human values.* New York: Free Press.

Rokeach, M. (1979). From individual to institutional values. In M. Rokeach (Ed.), *Understanding human values* (47–70). New York: Free Press.

Rokeach, M., and Grube, J. W. (1979). Can values be manipulated? In Rokeach (Ed.), *Understanding human values* (241–56).

Rorty, R. (1983). Method and morality. In N. Haan, R. N. Bellah, P. Rabinow, and W. M. Sullivan (Eds.), *Social science as moral inquiry* (155–76). New York: Columbia University Press.

Rosinski, H. (1965). *Power and human history.* New York: Praeger.

Rosnow, R. L. (1983). Van Osten's horse, Hamlet's question, and the mechanistic view of causality. *Journal of Mind and Behavior, 4,* 318–37.

Rosser, R. A. (1982). Information use by preschool children in altruistic decision making. *Journal of Genetic Psychology, 141,* 19–27.

Rotenberg, K. J. (1982). Development of the moral judgment of self and others in children. *Genetic Psychology Monographs, 105,* 281–307.

Rothman, G. R. (1980). Between moral judgment and moral behavior. In M. Windmiller, N. Lambert, and N. Turiel (Eds.), *Moral development and socialization* (107–27). Boston: Allyn & Bacon.

Rotter, J. B. (1966). Generalized expectancies for internal versus external control of reinforcement. *Psychological Monographs, 80*(1), n. 609.

Roubiczek, P. (1969). *Ethical values in the age of science.* Cambridge: Cambridge University Press.

Royce, J. R., and Buss, A. R. (1976). The role of general systems and information theory in multi-factor individuality theory. *Canadian Psychological Review, 17,* 1–21.

Rubin, Z., and Peplau, L. A. (1975). Who believes in a just world? *Journal of Social Issues, 31,* (3), 65–89.

Rushton, J. P. (1976). Socialization and the altruistic behavior of children. *Psychological Bulletin, 83,* 898–913.

———. (1981). Television as a socializer. In J. P. Rushton and R. M. Sorrentino (Eds.), *Altruism and helping behavior* (91–107). Hillsdale, N.J.: Erlbaum.

Russell, B. (1935). *Religion and science.* New York: Holt.

Sabini, J., and Silver, M. (1982). *Moralities of everyday life.* New York: Oxford University Press.

Salkever, S. G. (1983). Beyond interpretation. In N. Haan, R. N. Bellah, P. Rabinow, and W. M. Sullivan (Eds.), *Social science as moral inquiry* (195–217). New York: Columbia University Press.

Sampson, E. E. (1981). Cognitive psychology as ideology. *American Psychologist, 36,* 730–43.

Sanford, N., and Comstock, C. (1971). *Sanctions for evil.* San Francisco: Jossey-Bass.

Sapir, E. (1921). *Language*. New York: Harcourt, Brace.

Schafer, S. (1970). *Compensation and restitution to victims of crime*. Montclair, N.J.: Patterson Smith.

Scheibe, K. L., and Spaccaquerche, M. E. (1976). The social regulation of responses to moral dilemmas among Brazilian schoolchildren. *Journal of Cross-Cultural Psychology, 7*, 439–50.

Schlenker, B. R. (1983). Translating actions into attitudes. In L. Berkowitz (Ed.), *Advances in Experimental Social Psychology* (Vol. 15, 193–247). New York: Academic Press.

Schneiderman, L. (1979). Moral judgment and social structure. *Journal of Psychological Anthropology, 2*, 213–33.

Schwartz, S. H. (1970). Moral decision making and behavior. In J. Macaulay and L. Berkowitz (Eds.), *Altruism and helping behavior* (127–41). New York: Academic Press.

———. (1977). Normative influences on altruism. In L. Berkowitz (Ed.), *Advances in experimental social psychology* (Vol. 10, 221–79). New York: Academic Press.

Schwartz, S. H., and Gottlieb, A. (1980). Participation in a bystander intervention experiment and subsequent everyday helping. *Journal of Experimental Social Psychology, 16*, 161–71.

Schweitzer, A. (1952). He that loses his life shall find it. In R. N. Anshen (Ed.), *Moral principles of action* (673–91). New York: Harpers.

Schwinger, T. (1980). Just allocations of goods. In G. Mikula (Ed.), *Justice and social interaction* (95–125). New York: Springer-Verlag.

Searle, J. R. (1964). How to derive "ought" from "is." *Philosophical Review, 73*, 47–58.

Sears, D., Hensler, C. P., and Speer, L. K. (1979). Whites' opposition to "busing." *American Political Science Review, 73*, 369–84.

Seligman, C., Brickman, J., and Koulach, D. (1977). Rape and physical attractiveness. *Journal of Personality, 45*, 554–63.

Selman, R. L. (1971). The relation of role-taking ability to the development of moral judgment in children. *Child Development, 42*, 79–91.

Shelton, M. L., and Rogers, R. W. (1981). Fear-arousing and empathy-arousing appeals to help. *Journal of Applied Social Psychology, 11*, 366–78.

Sher, G. (1983). Health care and the "deserving poor." *Hastings Center Report, 13*(1), 9–12.

Sherman, L. W. (1984). Should police target repeat offenders? *Hastings Center Report, 14*(2), 18–19.

Sides, W. H. (1984). Arthur Galston. *New Journal, 16*(5), 34–41.

Sidgwick, H. (1962). *The methods of ethics*. Chicago: University of Chicago Press.

Sieber, J. E. (1982). Ethical dilemmas in social research. In J. E. Sieber (Ed.), *The ethics of social research* (1–29). New York: Springer-Verlag.

Sievers, B. (1983). Believing in social science. In N. Haan, R. N. Bellah, P. Rabinow, and W. M. Sullivan (Eds.), *Social science as moral inquiry* (320–42). New York: Columbia University Press.

Simmons, C., and Sands-Dudelczyk, K. (1983). Children helping peers. *Journal of Psychology, 115,* 203–07.

Singer, M. G. (1973). Moral skepticism. In C. L. Carter (Ed.), *Skepticism and moral principles* (77–108). Evanston, Ill.: New University Press.

Singer, P. (1979). *Practical ethics.* London: Cambridge University Press.

Skinner, B. F. (1971). *Beyond freedom and dignity.* New York: Knopf.

Smith, J. E. (1963). The moral situation. *Religious Education, 58,* 106–14.

Smith, M. B. (1969). *Social psychology and human values.* Chicago: Aldine.

Snyder, C. R., Higgins, R. L., and Stucky, R. J. (1983). *Excuses.* New York: Wiley.

Snyder, P. L. (Ed.). (1958). *Detachment and the writing of history.* Ithaca: Cornell University Press.

Social Science Research Council. (1984). The development of extraordinary moral responsibility. *Items, 38*(1), 18–20.

Sommers, C. H. (1984). Ethics without virtue. *American Scholar, 53*(3), 381–89.

Sperry, R. (1983). *Science and moral priority.* New York: Columbia University Press.

Staub, E. (1978, 1979). *Positive social behavior and morality.* 2 vols. New York: Academic Press.

Steiner, G. A. (1974). What should schools of business be thinking about business responsibilities? In D. L. Gothie (Ed.), *Business ethics and social responsibilities* (10–23). Charlottesville, Va.: Center for the Study of Applied Ethics.

Steiner, I. D. (1970). Perceived freedom. In L. Berkowitz (Ed.), *Advances in experimental social psychology* (Vol. 5, 187–248). New York: Academic Press.

Stevenson, C. L. (1963). *Facts and values.* New Haven: Yale University Press.

————. (1966). Ethical fallibility. In R. T. DeGeorge (Ed.), *Ethics and society* (197–217). New York: Doubleday.

Strong, C. (1983). The tiniest newborns. *Hasting Center Report, 13*(1), 14–19.

Sullivan, E. V. (1977). A study of Kohlberg's structural theory of moral development. *Human Development, 20,* 352–76.

Swann, W. B., and Hill, C. A. (1982). When our intentions are mistaken. *Journal of Personality and Social Psychology, 43,* 59–66.

Szanlawski, K. (1980). Philosophy of decision making. *Acta Psychologica, 45,* 327–41.

Szasz, T. S. (1966). The mental health clinic. In R. T. DeGeorge (Ed.), *Ethics and society* (85–110). New York: Doubleday.

Tanke, E. D., and Tanke, T. J. (1982). Regulation and education. In J. E. Sieber (Ed.), *The ethics of social research* (131–49). New York: Springer-Verlag.

Taylor, D. M., Watson, G., and Wong-Rieger, D. (1985). Social characterization, justice, and socio-economic status. *Journal of Social Psychology, 125,* 89–109.

Taylor, J. F. A. (1966). *The masks of society.* New York: Appleton-Century-Crofts.

Taylor, R. (1970). *Good and evil.* New York: Macmillan.

Tedeschi, J., and Riordan, C. A. (1981). Impression management and prosocial behavior following transgression. In J. Tedeschi (Ed.), *Impression management theory and social psychological research* (223–24). New York: Academic Press.

Text of declaration by summit conference. (1984). *New York Times,* June 9, p. 6.

Thomas, K. (1971). *Religion and the decline of magic.* New York: Scribners.

Thompson, J., and Thompson, J. (1964). How not to derive "ought" from "is." *Philosophical Review, 73,* 512–16.

Tilker, H. (1970). Socially responsible behavior as a function of observer responsibility and victim feedback. *Journal of Personality and Social Psychology, 14,* 95–100.

Tillich, P. (1952). *The courage to be.* New Haven: Yale University Press.

Tilly, C., and Rule, J. (1965). *Measuring political upheaval.* Princeton: Center for International Studies.

Tipton, R. M., and Browning, S. (1972). Altruism: Reward or punishment. *Journal of Psychology 80,* 319–22.

Toi, M., and Batson, D. (1982). More evidence that empathy is a source of altruistic motivation. *Journal of Personality and Social Psychology, 43,* 281–92.

Toulmin, S. (1970). Reasons and causes. In R. Borger and F. Cioffi (Eds.), *Explanation in the behavioral sciences* (1–48). London: Cambridge University Press.

Tsujimoto, R. N., and Emmons, K. A. (1983). Predicting moral conduct. *Journal of Psychology, 115,* 241–44.

Tulving, E. (1972). Episodic and semantic memory. In E. Tulving and W. Donaldson (Eds.), *Organization of memory* (381–403). New York: Academic Press.

Twiss, S. B. (1974). Parental responsibility for genetic health. *Hastings Center Report, 4*(1), 9–11.

Vaillant, G. E. (1977). *Adaptation to life.* Boston: Little, Brown.

Valensin, A. (1972). Satan in the Old Testament. In F. J. Sheed (Ed.), *Soundings in Satanism* (105–20). New York: Sheed & Ward.

Van Dyke, V. V. (1970). *Human rights, the United States, and world community.* New York: Oxford University Press.

Van Voorhis, P. (1985). The utility of Kohlberg's theory of moral development among adults in a situation field setting. *Genetic, Social, and General Psychology Monographs, 111,* 103–26.

Veatch, H. B. (1971). *For an ontology of morals.* Evanston: Northwestern University Press.

Vecchio, R. P. (1981). Workers' belief in internal versus external determinants of success. *Journal of Social Psychology, 114,* 199–207.

Vinacke, W. E. (1984). Healthy personality. *Genetic Psychology Monographs, 109,* 279–329.

Von Mises, S. (1957). *Theory and history.* New Haven: Yale University Press.

Wagner, W. (1984). Social comparison of opinions. *Journal of Psychology, 118,* 197–202.

Wahrman, I. (1981). The relationship of dogmatism, relgious affiliation, and moral judgment development. *Journal of Psychology, 108,* 151–54.

Walster, E., Berscheid, E., and Walster, G. W. (1970). The exploited. In J. Macaulay and L. Berkowitz (Eds.), *Altruism and helping behavior* (179–204). New York: Academic Press.

Walster, E., Walster, G. W., and Traupmann, J. (1978). Equity and premarital sex. *Journal of Personality and Social Psychology, 36,* 82–92.

Warshaw, P. R., and Davis, F. D. (1986). The accuracy of behavioral intention versus expectation for predicting behavioral goals. *Journal of Social Psychology, 126.* In press.

Warwick, D. P., and Pettigrew, T. F. (1983). Toward ethical guidelines for social science research in public policy. In D. Callahan and B. Jennings (Eds.), *Ethics, the social sciences, and policy analysis* (335–68). New York: Plenum.

Webster, M., and Driskell, J. E. (1983). Beauty as status. *American Journal of Sociology, 89,* 140–65.

Wedel, T. O. (1963). Review of J. A. T. Robinson. (q.v.). In D. L. Edwards

(Ed.), *The honest to god debate* (180–86). Philadelphia: Westminster Press.

Weischedel, W. (1976). *Skeptische Ethik*. Frankfurt: Suhrkamp Verlag.

Weiss, P. (1952). Some neglected ethical questions. In R. N. Anshen (Ed.), *Moral principles of action* (207–20). New York: Harpers.

Wertheimer, M. (1961). Some problems in the theory of ethics. In M. Henle (Ed.), *Documents of gestalt psychology* (29–41). Berkeley: University of California Press.

White, R. K. (1983). Empathizing with the rulers of the USSR. *Political Psychology, 4,* 121–37.

Wiesenthal, D. L., Austrom, D., and Silverman, I. (1983). Diffusion of responsibility in charitable donations. *Basic and Applied Social Psychology, 4,* 17–27.

Williams, K. B., and Kipling, D. (1983). Social inhibition and asking for help. *Journal of Personality and Social Psychology, 44,* 67–77.

Williams, R. M. (1968). Values. In D. L. Sills (Ed.), *International encyclopedia of the social sciences* (Vol. 16, 283–87). New York: Macmillan and Free Press.

———. (1979). Change and stability in values and value systems. In M. Rokeach (Ed.), *Understanding human values* (15–46). New York: Free Press.

———. (1982). Two kinds of ethics. *New York Times,* Feb. 18, p. A23.

Wilson, J., Williams, N., and Sugarman, B. (1967). *Introduction to moral education*. London: Penguin.

Wilson, M. (1985). Effects of perceived attractiveness and feminist orientation on helping behavior. *Journal of Social Psychology, 125,* 415–20.

Winch, P. (1972). *Ethics and action*. London: Routledge & Kegan Paul.

Windelband, W. (1894). *Geschichte und Naturwissenschaft*. Strassburg: Kaiser-Wilhelms Universität.

Wolff, W. (1950). *Value and personality*. New York: Greene & Stratton.

Woodcock, A., and Davis, M. (1978). *Catastrophe theory*. New York: Dutton.

Woods, W. (1975). *A history of the devil*. Frogmore, St. Albans: Panther Books.

Woodside, A. (1982). Conception of change and of human responsibility for change in late traditional Vietnam. In D. K. Wyatt and A. Woodside (Eds.), *Moral order and the question of change*. Yale University Southeast Asia Studies Monographs, n. 24.

Wright, D. (1971). *The psychology of moral behaviour*. Middlesex, England: Penguin.

Wright, D., and Cox, E. (1967). A study of the relationship between moral judgment and religious belief. *Journal of Social Psychology, 72,* 135–44.

Wyer, R. S., Skull, T. K., and Gordon, S. (1984). The effects of predicting a person's behavior on subsequent trait judgments. *Journal of Experimental Social Psychology, 20,* 29–46.

Yeats, W. B. (1956). Old play. In W. B. Yeats, *The collected poems* (97). New York: Macmillan.

Zelden, R. S., Savin-Williams, R. C., and Small, S. A. (1984). Dimensions of personal behavior in adolescent males. *Journal of Social Psychology, 123,* 159–68.

Zern, D. S., and Stern, G. W. (1983). The impact of obedience on intelligence and self-concept. *Genetic Psychology Monographs, 108,* 245–65.

Ziv, A., Shani, A., and Nebenhaus, S. (1975). Adolescents educated in Israel and the Soviet Union. *Journal of Cross-Cultural Psychology, 6,* 108–21.

Zuckerman, M., Mann, R. W., and Bernieri, F. J. (1982). Determinants of consensus estimates. *Journal of Personality and Social Psychology, 42,* 839–52.

Zweigenhaft, R. L., Phillips, B. K. G., Adams, K. A., Morse, C. K., and Horan, A. E. (1985). Religious preference and belief in a just world. *Genetic, Social, General Psychological Monograph, 111,* 331–48.

Index

Abelson, R. P., 120
Abortion, 44, 56, 61, 259
Abram, M. B., 269
Abramson, L., 77
Absolutism, 51, 56, 122, 234
Accuracy, 82–86, 140, 182;
   skeptical note, 86
Action: values from, 12–16,
   218–19; predispositions affect-
   ing, 38, 49–50, 117, 143;
   moral stages of, 141–42, 151.
   See also Behavior; Inaction
Adaptation, 238
Age, 60, 140, 168
Aggression, 151–53, 267
Aiken, W., 88, 235
Ajzen, I., 50
Altruism, 101, 103–05, 110–13,
   116, 266–67
Amato, P. R., 113
Amnesty International, 212
Amniocentesis, 239
Animals, rights of, 131, 262–63
Anthropology, 21–22, 58, 158,
   246
Anticipation, 3, 79–99, 118,
   120, 278
Applebaum, P. S., 167
Arendt, H., 70
Aristotle, 6–7, 12, 24, 53, 64,
   91, 102–03, 113, 116, 184,
   207, 217, 220–21, 258, 261

Aronfreed, J., 140
Arthur, J., 67
Asceticism, 114
Astrology, 190
Atiyah, P. S., 92
Attitude: nature of, 46–47, 54–
   55; skeptical note, 47; effects
   of, 55–56, 76, 120, 173–74
Auerbach, J. S., 205
Austin, V. D., 30
Austin, W., 205
Authority, 54–55, 60, 100–01,
   118, 131, 149, 158, 159, 176
Averill, A. K., 267
Awareness, 45, 132, 242–45,
   259–63, 277–78; skeptical
   note, 245. See also Salience
Ayer, A. J., 193

Bagarozzi, D. A., 218
Bankruptcy, moral, 279–80
Battin, M. P., 83
Bauman, Z., 7
Baumer, F. L., 9
Bay, C., 213
Beaman, A. L., 387
Beauty, 97–98, 208–09, 252;
   skeptical note, 209
Beauvoir, S. de, 76, 80, 134,
   191
Becker, C. L., 179
Becker, L. C., 110, 162, 189, 256

Behavior, 3, 115, 143–53, 176, 288
Behaviorism, 167, 186
Belief: nature of, 43–46; skeptical note, 46; effects of, 55–56, 87, 92, 120, 173–74, 232; desirable, 98–99
Berger, R. E., 56, 144
Berkowitz, L., 47, 104, 110
Bettelheim, B., 83
Bickman, L., 267
Biderman, A. D., 93
Bidney, D., 107
Black, M., 214
Blanshard, B., 133, 202
Blasi, A., 134, 142, 143
Blatt, M., 265
Bode, J., 136–37, 266
Bok, S., 124–25
Boldero, J., 218
Bonhoeffer, D., 184
Boyce, W. D., 79, 94, 135, 157, 267
Bradford, L. P., 246
Brandt, R. B., 68, 121–22, 176, 182, 192, 223
Braver, S., 178
Braybrooke, D., 243
Brazerman, M. H., 148
Brehm, J. W., 82, 108
Brehm, S. S., 82, 108
Brennan, J. G., 164, 180
Brewer, G. D., 83
Brewer, W. F., 171
Bronfenbrenner, U., 137, 221
Brown, A. L., 73
Brown, R. C. J., 164
Browning, S., 268
Buber, M., 109
Buddha, 223
Buldain, R. W., 96
Bullock, M., 160
Burger, J. M., 165
Burke, R. J., 231
Buss, A. H., 91, 245

Buss, A. R., 43, 51, 167
Bussey, K., 136

Callahan, D., 260
Calvin, J., 207
Campbell, D. T., 268
Camus, A., 8
Canetti, E., 126
Cannibalism, 42
Caplan, A. L., 260
Casuistry, 116
Catholicism, 9, 21, 68, 163, 183, 239
Causation, 162–63, 167–68. See also Responsibility
Cavendish, R., 147
Cecil, J. S., 268
Cervantes Saavedra, M. de, 23
Change, social: in values, 20–23, 219–20, 235, 238, 252–53; in rules, duties, 64–65; skeptical note, 65; vs. tradition, 233–34; inelasticity of, 238–40; in roles, 263–64
Chaos, theory of, 183
Character, 67, 140, 247–48
Cheating, 144
Childs, B., 49
Christianity: effects of, 44, 131, 198–99, 234, 245; tenets, 68, 163, 211–12, 252, 253–54, 271–72
Clemes, S., 137
Codes, ethical, 14, 124, 175, 189, 250–55, 268–70; skeptical note, 255
Cohen, A., 238
Cohen, D. K., 185
Collingwood, R. G., 188, 193
Collins, J., 237
Commons, tragedy of, 215–16, 225, 254
Communication, 29–31, 65–66, 112, 159–60, 246, 249, 264
Communist Manifesto, 262

Complexity, 233–38, 251, 252–53, 263; skeptical note, 238
Comprehensibility, 65–66, 249, 251; skeptical note, 66
Compromising, 122
Comstock, C., 90
Confucius, 22, 223
Conner, R. F., 268
Conroy, W. J., 265
Conscience, 55–56, 82, 100–01, 104, 129, 144, 225; skeptical note, 101
Consent, informed, 102, 268–70
Consequences, 3, 86–87, 88, 91, 118–19, 130–31; temporal, 86–87; skeptical note, 87
Consequentialism, 79
Consistency, 50–51, 57, 208, 225, 244. See also Exceptions
Contract, 129, 162
Control, locus of, 47, 75–78
Convention, 129–30
Costanzo, P., 389
Cox, E., 276
Crime, 60–61, 103, 121, 148, 216
Criminology, 45, 66, 119, 141–42, 161, 254–55
Cronbach, L. J., 187
Crosby, F., 207
Cross, W. O., 120
Crumbaugh, J. C., 229
Culture, 21–22, 198, 223, 232, 245, 280
Cushman, D., 22
Czartoryski, A., 169

Damon, W., 118
Danieli, Y., 96
Darden, D. K., 50
Darwin, C., 23
Davis, K. E., 49
Davis, M., 183
Dawson, C., 15

Deception, 268–69; of self, 123, 244. See also Lying
Declaration of Independence, 198, 262
Deconstruction, 166
Demography, 19–20, 112–13, 119, 131, 171, 177
Deontology, 137
Descartes, R., 169
Determinism, 77, 161
Deutsch, M., 206
Development, cognitive, 140–41, 276
Dewey, J., 6, 8, 64, 115, 264
Dicks, H. V., 70
Dickstein, E., 141
Diener, E., 268
Differential, semantic, 66
Disagreement, observer, 222–24; skeptical note, 222
Dissonance, 46–47, 144
Dixon, B., 260
Donnerstein, E., 267
Doob, L. W., 13, 22, 32, 39, 81, 96, 126, 144, 178, 197, 207, 212, 244, 246, 280
Dostoyevsky, F. M., 130
Douglas, M., 15, 146
Dreams, 197–99, 222–23, 233
Dresden, bombing of, 29, 96
Driskell, J. E., 55
Drive, 105–06. See also Motives
Dudai, T., 48
Duty, 3, 46, 58–78, 129

Eagleton, T., 252
Easterbrook, J. A., 88, 139, 163
Eccles, J. C., 116
Eclecticism, 280
Economics, 117, 165–66, 180–81, 189, 199, 201, 206, 220
Ecosystem, 200
Ecumenism, 183
Edel, A., 117, 170, 173
Edel, M., 117, 170, 173

Edgerton, R. B., 22
Education. *See* Socialization
Effects, future, 148–51, skeptical
  note, 151
Egocentricity, 129, 134–35, 169,
  233
Eimer, B. N., 149
Einstein, A., 23, 73, 86
Eisenberg-Berg, N., 110, 226,
  248
Eiser, J. R., 171
Ekman, P., 123
Emerson, W. A., 17
Emler, N., 97, 170, 181
Emmons, K. A., 141
Empathy, 111, 131, 158
Ends. *See* Means and ends
Envois: skepticism, 16; event
  perception, 31; predisposi-
  tions, 52; rules, duties, 71;
  anticipation, 94; imperatives,
  110; intention, 133; behavior,
  151; observers, 165; experts,
  184; dreams, 213; constraints,
  240; struggles, 259
Enzensberger, H. M., 225
Equality, 49, 112, 152
Equity, 112, 152, 205–06, 217,
  228
Erickson, E. H., 81
Ericson, R. V., 45
Errors, types of, 169
Ethics, 4n, 20, 25, 37, 183–84,
  191–92, 193, 262, 265–66.
  See also Philosophy
Ethnocentricity, 169
Ethnomethodology, 190
Euthanasia, 56, 61, 83, 90
Event: definition, 27–29; skepti-
  cal note, 29; perception, 23,
  29–31, 38, 63
Everett, W. G., 133
Evil, 13, 20, 197, 209, 212, 244,
  258, 279
Evolution, 23, 183

Exceptions, 51, 56, 64, 120,
  133–34, 225, 233, 234, 238;
  skeptical note, 126
Excuses, 164

Faith, 55, 199, 211–12, 233,
  257, 271
Fallacy, naturalistic, 131, 160,
  199–200, 214–15, 220, 228,
  233, 253, 257, 277; skeptical
  note, 200
Fallibility: of observer, 169–71,
  171–77; of social science,
  177–78, 180–81, 184–90; of
  science, 182–83; of ethics ex-
  perts, 183–84, 191–94
Fatalism, 77, 128, 161
Feasibility, 130–33; skeptical
  note, 133
Feather, N. T., 220
Feedback, 148
Fellner, C. H., 68
Fertilization, artificial, 217, 260
Fincham, F. D., 220
Finney, P. D., 162
Fishbein, M., 50
Fisher, J. D., 104
Fishkin, J. S., 56–57, 74–75,
  122–23, 130, 139
Fleetwood, R. S., 266
Fletcher, J., 117, 216, 230
Flugel, J. C., 273
Form, W., 112
Forsyth, D. R., 51, 56, 144
Foshay, N. N., 70
Fowler, H. W., 4n
Frailties, human, 224–28; skep-
  tical note, 228
Fraisse, P., 94
Frankena, W. K., 48, 87, 109,
  165, 175
Frankl, V. E., 63, 114, 115
Franklin, B., 223
Franklin, R. L., 116
Freedman, J. L., 106, 151

Freedom, 49, 58, 98, 107–09,
    217, 244; skeptical note, 109
Freud, S., 44, 73, 225–26, 239,
    242, 265
Friendly, J., 175
Fromm, Eberhard, 213
Fromm, Erich, 108
Frustration, 90, 107, 144, 145,
    148, 151, 152, 205, 279

Galileo, 23
Gandhi, M., 51, 73, 105
Garbarino, J., 137, 221
Garcia, J. D., 109, 262
Gardner, G. T., 145
Gardner, H., 48, 72
Garfinkel, H., 190
Geertz, C., 22
Geller, D. M., 268
Genesis of morality, 24–26, 251;
    skeptical note, 25
Genovese murder, 70
Gergen, K. J., 77, 187–88, 265
Gerlitz, P., 254
Gibb, G. D., 97
Gibbs, J. C., 138, 244
Giles, H., 97
Gillet, M., 200
Gilligan, C., 138, 217
Girvetz, H. K., 143
Glazer, M., 69
Goal, 41–43, 118; skeptical
    note, 43
Goethe, J. W., 23
Goffman, E., 240
Goldman, M., 110–11
Goldschmidt, W., 22, 245
Goleman, D., 244
Gorsuch, R. L., 139
Gottlieb, A., 267
Graham, D., 128, 140, 189
Green, W., 260
Greene, G., 65
Greet, K. G., 191, 252
Greif, E. B., 226

Grice, G. R., 43, 103, 162
Grotius, H., 207
Groups, 24–25, 26, 60, 83, 136,
    150, 201, 240. See also Others
Grube, J. W., 230
Guilt, 67, 151–53, 227
Guitton, J., 77
Gunnemann, J. P., 258
Guttman, J., 32

Haan, N., 166
Habermas, J., 177
Habit: morality as, 37–38, 58,
    63–64, 104, 115, 151, 234,
    247; skeptical note, 64; chal-
    lenges to, 80, 126, 220, 238–
    40, 242; conscience, 101–
    02
Handlin, M., 60
Handlin, O., 60
Handy, R. T., 248
Happiness, 24, 87, 105–07,
    113–14, 192, 201–02, 251,
    270; skeptical note, 107
Harder, D. W., 209
Hardin, G., 51, 215–16
Hardy, A., 118
Harris, E. E., 55
Hart, H. L. A., 163
Hartley, S. F., 268
Harvey, D., 204
Hastings Center, 259–61
Hatfield, E., 205
Hedonism, 86, 105–07, 113,
    192, 201–02, 251
Hegel, G. W. F., 71
Heider, F., 86, 167
Held, V., 8, 79, 258
Helm, B., 162
Heraclitus, 8
Hermeneutics, 166, 237
Heroes, 223, 224, 256
Hickman, F., 49
Higgins, A., 139, 172
Hill, C. A., 97

History, 178–80, 213; skeptical note, 181
Hitler, A., 95, 207, 224, 247
Hobbes, T., 20
Hoffman, M. L., 72
Hoffmann, S. H., 198
Hogan, R., 56, 72
Holmes, O. W., 94
Holocaust, 12, 95–96, 115, 149, 163, 250
Hope, 91–93; skeptical note, 93
Hopi Indians, 68, 223
Hudson, W. D., 214
Hume, D., 175
Hurreh, I. M., 32
Huxley, A., 226
Huxley, J., 226
Hypnosis, 166–67

Idealism, 40
Identifying, 25–27, 30, 32–33, 40, 158, 239; skeptical note, 27
Imperative: morality, 3, 116, 117, 118, 250, 258–59; conscience, 100–01, components, 101–14. See also Values
Inaction, 144–45; skeptical note, 145
Indoctrination, 247–50, 263–68; skeptical note, 250
Inelasticity, 64, 238–40; skeptical note, 240
Inevitability, 59–62; skeptical note, 62
Inferences, observer, 157–68, 185–86
Inheritance, genetic, 43, 232–33
Instinct, 53
Intelligence, 3, 47–48, 72, 140. See also Skill
Intention, 3, 115–42, 143, 160–65, 226, 278
Interrelation of predisposition, 19, 49–52, 120, 122, 226, 233, 248; skeptical note, 52

Intuition, 118, 174–75, 192, 227, 256
Irwin, M., 46

James, W., 239
Janis, I. L., 83
Jaspars, J. M., 164
Jennings, B., 178
Jensen, L. C., 79, 94, 135, 157, 267
Jesus, 23, 92, 105, 202, 211, 223, 253
Joad, C. E. M., 82
John Paul II, 223–34
Jones, E. E., 47, 97, 188
Jones, L., 70
Joyce, J., 226
Joyce, S., 226
Judgment: complete, 5, 116, 134, 137, 228–33; variables affecting, 12–16, 38–39, 43, 226, 278; habitual, 63–64; reasoned, 126–30, 234; effects of, 143, 165–66; skeptical note, 233; awareness of, 242–43, 262
Jung, C. G., 199
Jurisprudence, 85
Justice: value of, 9, 98, 102–03, 136, 147–49, 202, 204–07, 263; skeptical note, 207; nature of, 216–19, 227–28, 235
Justifiability, 109–10; skeptical note, 110
Just world, 148–49, 151–52, 205

Kagan, S., 168
Kahn, J. V., 140
Kanekar, S., 164
Kant, I., 12, 17, 23, 70–71, 173, 184, 193–94, 210, 220, 239, 241, 262
Kantola, S. J., 50
Katzev, R. D., 267
Kavka, G. S., 84

Keasey, C. B., 141
Kenrick, D. T., 178
Kiell, N., 226
Kierkegaard, S., 168
Kipling, D., 104
Klein, P. D., 9
Kleinberger, A., 184
Kluckhohn, F. R., 53
Knowledge, 43–46, 79, 84–85,
    170, 193, 232, 241, 278;
    skeptical note, 46
Knudson, K. A. M., 168
Kohlberg, L., 48, 129–30, 136,
    138, 139, 140, 168, 172, 200,
    216–17, 221, 226, 265
Köhler, W., 42, 116
Kolsawalls, M. B., 164
Körner, S., 6, 42, 46, 120, 133,
    144
Krimmel, H. T., 239
Kunda, Z., 111
Kurtines, W., 226
Kurtz, C. A., 226, 248

La Follette, H., 235
Laing, R. D., 199
Lamm, H., 217, 218
Language, 14, 62, 65–66, 157,
    170, 174, 227, 238–39, 246
Lappé, F. M., 237, 260
Lauterbach, A., 225
Lavoisier, A., 23
Law: failure of, 85, 206, 250,
    254; procedures of, 107, 158,
    166–67, 177, 205, 208, 218;
    content of, 162–64
Learning, theories of, 104, 105–
    06, 240, 265
Leary, D. E., 180
Lefcourt, H. M., 47
Leibnitz, G. W., 159
Leiter, K., 170
Lenin, V. I., 84, 235
Lerner, M. J., 149, 204
Leventhal, G. S., 205
Levine, C., 260

Levinson, D. J., 41
Lewis, C. I., 21
Lindblom, C. E., 185
Lindskold, S., 124
Linguistics, 246
Linton, R., 21
Lipscomb, T. J., 266
Literature, 252
Lockhart, D. C., 55
London, P., 173
Lorenz, K., 199
Love, 202–04, 215–16, 234,
    245, 259, 271; skeptical note,
    204
Luchins, A. S., 30
Luchins, E. H., 30
Luther, M., 21
Lying, 82, 116, 119, 123–26,
    188, 264–65

Macaulay, J., 104, 110
McCloskey, H. J., 116, 192
McCord, J., 137
McDougall, W., 53
McGlashan, C. F., 42
McGuire, W. J., 187
MacIver, R. M., 203
MacKaye, J., 106
McKillip, J., 55
Mader, J., 191
Maeroff, G. I., 249
Makai, M., 215
Malamuth, N. H., 267
Malmström, A.-K., 176
Mann, H., 226
Mann, L., 83
Mann, T., 226
Mannheim, K., 54, 170, 193,
    213, 234
Maqsud, M., 33, 138
March, J. G., 83
Marcus, G. E., 22
Marcuse, H., 177
Margenau, H., 14
Marks, E. L., 112
Marsden, P. V., 26

Marshall, H., 68, 167, 168
Marx, K., 23, 71, 199, 213, 235
Marxism, 44, 102, 159, 213, 222, 239
Maslow, A. H., 220
Masochism, 103
Mason, P., 217
Maughan, B., 136
Means and ends: relation of, 93–94, 106, 270–71; skeptical notes, 94, 256; search for, 97–99, 114, 230–31, 242, 244, 255–56
Media, mass, 174, 175, 245, 260, 267
Mehl, R., 272
Meiland, J. W., 116
Melden, A. I., 42, 70, 90, 118, 133, 188
Melsen, A. G., 79, 199, 205
Merton, R. K., 225
Metaethics, 109–10, 116
Metaphysics, 8, 52, 222
Method, nomothetic and idiographic, 178
Meynell, H., 200, 244
Middleton, R., 264
Midlarsky, E., 48, 112
Mikula, G., 204, 228
Milgram, S., 77, 90
Miller, J. G., 16, 20
Mills, J., 264
Milner, D., 226
Mischel, W., 51, 95
Mohammed, 23
Moodley-Rajab, D., 76
Moore, E., 15, 114
Morality, concept of, 4n
Moral reasoning, stages of, 128–30, 134–42, 267–68
Moran, J. D., 136
More, T., 207
Morris, C., 19
Motives: analysis of, 41–43; skeptical note, 43, 159; no-

menclature, 53–54; self vs. others, 101–05; effects of, 144, 173, 230, 231–32; observer, 158–59; unconscious, 173
Muelder, W. G., 7, 180
Multivariance, 117–19; skeptical note, 119
Mussen, P. H., 110

Naess, O., 8, 273
Nakamura, G. V., 171
Naroll, R., 270–71
Narr, W.-D., 230
Needs. See Motives
Nelson, J. B., 172
Nelson, R. R., 23
Newton, L. H., 243
Nielsen, K., 92, 214, 215
Nisbett, R. E., 47
Niven, W. D., 82
Normality, 210, 219–20
Norman, R., 21, 127
Nosow, S., 112
Nucci, L. P., 137
Nummendal, S. G., 168

Obedience, 126, 128–29, 135. See also Duty; Rules
Obligation, 67–71, 278; skeptical note, 71. See also Responsibility
O'Brien, G., 136
Observer: identification of, 9, 25–27, 38; definition of, 11–12; skeptical notes, 12, 27, 177; fallibility of, 109, 171–77; moral, 197–98; disagreements, 222–24
Olson, R. G., 21
O'Neill, O., 134
Ontology, 191
Opportunism, 120
Options, 80–84, 117, skeptical note, 82

Opton, E. M., 149
Osgood, C. E., 66
Ossowska, M., 15, 119, 192
Ostheimer, J. M., 92
Others, 28, 87–91, 96–97, 111,
    119; skeptical notes, 91, 105;
    self vs., 101–05, 149, 150,
    173, 227, 230, 231, 245–46

Page, R. A., 136–37, 266
Parables, 249
Parish, T. S., 266
Pascal, B., 255
Passmore, J., 21, 113, 249
Pateman, C., 94
Paton, H. J., 51, 158, 201
Patriotism, 203, 213
Patterson, O., 90
Peake, P. K., 51
Peplau, L. A., 257
Perception, 29–31, 38, 159, 221;
    of groups, 30–31; skeptical
    note, 31; person, 96–97
Percival, T. O., 137
Perfection, 113, 198, 209–10,
    222, 241; skeptical note, 212
Perrow, C., 26, 146, 245
Personality, 3, 19–20, 38–57,
    60, 142, 190, 247, 278
Persons, moral: definition of,
    197–99; dreams of, 201–21;
    constraints on, 222–40; strug-
    gles of, 241–74; future of,
    275–79
Pettigrew, T. F., 185
Philosophy: evaluation of, 6, 7,
    159, 176, 183–84, 191–94;
    variables in, 12, 133–34, 162,
    165, 167–68, 218–19, 272,
    273–74; values of, 15, 19, 58,
    105–06, 113–14; function of,
    127, 243, 261–62, 279; skep-
    tical note, 184; and naturalis-
    tic fallacy, 199–200, 214–15
Piaget, J., 72, 134–35, 217

Pike, J. A., 42
Placebo, 268–69
Planning, 86, 95, 132
Plato, 6, 24, 159, 169, 197, 223,
    271
Politics: morality in, 6, 7, 197,
    208, 232, 237, 243; changes
    in, 64; means and ends of,
    93–94; preferences in, 118–
    20, 187
Pollution, 58–59, 85, 146, 169–
    70, 216
Pornography, 84
Potentiality, 3. See also Skill
Powesland, P. F., 97
Pragmatism, 40
Prather, D. K., 82
Prayer, 115–16
Predictability, 91–93, 146, 148,
    207–08, 220; skeptical notes,
    93, 208
Predisposition, 40–41, 49–52,
    112, 175–76, 242–43; skepti-
    cal note, 41. See also Personal-
    ity
Prejudice, 171, 206–07
Prewitt, K., 83
Principal: definition of, 11–12;
    skeptical notes, 12, 27; identi-
    fication of, 24–27; as observ-
    er, 149, 164; moral, 197–98
Privacy, 244–45
Procrastination, 130–33, 144,
    244; skeptical note, 133
Projection, 175–76
Promises, 91–92, 208
Propaganda, 224
Protagoras, 8
Proverbs, 31–32, 88–89
Psychiatry, 27, 29, 97, 167, 180,
    199, 209, 230, 246. See also
    Freud, S.
Psychology: affecting morality,
    6, 38, 40; skepticism concern-
    ing, 9–10; values in, 16–20;

Psychology (*continued*)
  scope of, 25, 225, 246; fallibility of, 180, 187–89; traits
  in, 272–73
Psychophysics, 206
Pugh, G. E., 17–18
Punishment, 128–29, 146–47;
  skeptical note, 147
Putney, S., 264

Questions, probing, 3–7; origins
  of, 24–25; functions of, 29,
  79, 144, 184, 197, 228, 244,
  247, 278

Rachels, J., 263
Radcliffe, W., 100–01
Ramkisson, R. D., 76
Rationality, 83, 210, 220–21,
  222, 233, 239–40, 243, 244
Rationalization: predisposition,
  44, 46, 59, 83, 127, 244; ac-
  tion, 122, 128, 149, 167, 245
Rawls, J., 117, 204, 219
Reactance, 82, 107–08
Reasoning, 84–85, 126–30,
  144–45, 158–59, 210; skepti-
  cal note, 130
Regan, T., 263
Rein, M., 45
Reinforcement, 106, 158
Relativism, 122, 193
Religion: values of, 23, 68, 192,
  211, 234; functions of, 67,
  120, 257; changes in, 253–54,
  256
Remorse, 150
Renunciation, 94–95
Rescher, N., 9, 169
Responsibility: assigning of, 26,
  41, 95, 122, 127, 160–65,
  168, 210, 229; duty, rules,
  67–71; skeptical notes, 71,
  165
Rest, J. R., 136, 139, 140, 221

Revenge, 152
Rewards, 111, 128, 146–47;
  skeptical note, 147
Richardson, V., 257
Rights: human, 22, 90, 103,
  129, 144–45, 198, 253; ani-
  mal, 131, 262–63
Riordan, C. A., 152
Risk, 91, 118, 132, 145–46;
  skeptical note, 146
Ritt, L. G., 92
Robinson, J. A. T., 203
Rodman, J. L., 165
Roemer, J., 102
Rogers, R. W., 131
Rokeach, M., 17, 18–19, 31, 49,
  230, 269
Role, 118, 157–68; playing, 168
Roosevelt, F. D., 207, 262
Rorty, R., 256
Rosenthal, D., 218
Rosinksi, H., 86
Rosnow, R. L., 188
Rosser, R. A., 112
Rothman, G. R., 143
Rotter, J. B., 76
Roubiczek, P., 18, 25, 48, 80,
  173, 192, 203, 238, 256
Royce, J. R., 51
Rubin, Z., 257
Rule, J., 178
Rules, 3, 58–78, 118, 120–21,
  247
Rushton, J. P., 111
Russell, B., 182

Sabini, J., 12, 127, 170
Salience, 51, 100, 120, 144,
  204, 207, 217, 218, 242
Salkever, S. G., 233
Sampson, E. E., 186
Sands-Dudelezyk, K., 110
Sanford, N., 90
Sapir, E., 238
Schafer, S., 62

Scheibe, K. L., 33
Schneiderman, L., 22
Schotch, P. K., 243
Schwartz, S. H., 59, 79, 111,
    267
Schweitzer, A., 203
Schwinger, T., 205, 217
Science, natural: fallibility of,
    182–83, 207–08, 251–52;
    skeptical note, 183; function
    of, 243, 276–77
Science, social: skepticism about,
    7–10; values in, 16, 22, 166,
    182–83; fallibility of, 177–78,
    180–81, 184–90; skeptical
    note, 181; function of, 225–
    26, 246–47, 255–56
Searle, J. H., 214
Sears, D., 50
Secrecy, 124–25
Seligman, C., 164
Selman, R. L., 49
Sensitivity, interpersonal, 245–
    47, 257; skeptical note, 247
Sermon on the Mount, 44, 199,
    202, 253, 262
Sexual relations, 60–61, 64,
    202, 264
Shelton, M. L., 131
Sher, G., 261
Sherman, L. W., 261
Sides, W. H., 96
Sidgwick, H., 69, 184, 191
Sieber, J. E., 180
Sievers, B., 187
Sigall, H., 188
Silver, M., 12, 127, 170
Simmons, C., 110
Sin, 17, 54, 163, 191, 222,
    234
Singer, M. G., 8, 54
Singer, P., 93, 114, 208, 262,
    263
Situationism, 51, 56, 119–20,
    234, 240; skeptical note, 120

Skepticism: nature of, 8–10;
    skeptical note, 10; evaluation
    of, 275–79
Skill: nature of, 47–49; skeptical
    note, 49; learning of, 72, 82
Skinner, B. F., 114, 235
Slavery, 145, 238, 239
Smith, J. E., 39
Smith, M. B., 243
Snyder, C. R., 44, 164
Snyder, P. L., 179
Socialization: effects of age on,
    72–73, 81–82, 96, 108, 118,
    246, 247; parental, 54, 59, 62,
    94, 163–64, 245; of altruism,
    104, 110–11; stages of, 128–
    30, 134–42, 265, 278; differ-
    ences in, 32–33, 150–51,
    169
Social Science Research Council,
    73, 143
Societies, traditional, 31–32, 81,
    82, 234
Sociobiology, 17–18
Solipsism, 157, 172, 189, 280
Sommers, C. H., 137, 240
Sources, information, 159–60,
    175; skeptical note, 160
Spaccaquerche, M. E., 33
Speech, 96–97. See also Lan-
    guage
Sperry, R., 17, 228, 258
Staub, E., 49, 104, 112, 136,
    152, 218, 231, 262, 265
Steiner, G. A., 251
Steiner, I. D., 107
Stern, G. W., 72
Stevenson, C. L., 28, 128, 193
Strodtbeck, F. L., 53
Strong, C., 261
Subjectivism, 51, 56, 122
Superego. See Conscience
Surveys, public opinion, 186–
    87, 190
Swann, W. B., 97

Szanlawski, K., 90
Szasz, T. S., 27

Tallman, I., 219
Tanke, E. D., 268
Tanke, T. J., 268
Taylor, D. M., 96
Taylor, J. F. A., 63, 121, 180
Taylor, R., 244
Taylor, S., 125
Tedeschi, J. T., 152, 164
Teleology, 113, 137, 263–64
Ten Commandments, 44, 65, 199, 202, 251
Theology, 92, 234, 238, 239; fallibility, 183–84; skeptical note, 84
Thomas, K., 234
Thompson, J., 215
Tilker, H., 68
Tillich, P., 243
Tilly, C., 178
Tipton, R. M., 268
Toi, M., 111
Toleration, 229–30
Toulmin, S., 167
Training, sensitivity, 246
Traits, 192, 209, 223, 245, 256–59, 271–74. See also Predisposition
Trust, 88, 91–92
Truth, value of, 207–08; skeptical note, 208
Tsujimoto, R. N., 141
Tulving, E., 73
Tussle, eternal, 58, 207, 256–59; skeptical note, 259
Twiss, S. B., 261

Unconscious, 190, 205, 225–26, 227, 233, 239, 256
United Nations, 22, 98
Universality, 20–23, 129, 138, 165–66, 205

Utilitarianism, 192, 251
Utility, social, 106, 201–02; skeptical note, 202
Utopia, 92–93, 212–13, 235, 242, 258

Vaillant, G. E., 247
Valensin, A., 92
Values: definition of, 4, 12–13; salience of, 12–16, 240; scope of, 14–16, 31–32, 121–22, 165–66, 173, 234, 258–59; skeptical note, 16; nomenclature of, 17–20; universal, 20–23, 165–66, 181, 197–99, 276; effects of, 41–43, 45–46, 242, 265; imperative, 101–14, 115, 118, 250, 258–59; deficient, 229–30, 238–40; teaching of, 264–68, 269
Van der Pligt, J., 171
Van Dyke, V. V., 22
Van Voorhis, P., 141
Variability, 66–67, 108, 189; skeptical note, 67. See also Change, social
Veatch, H. B., 13, 109, 191
Vecchio, R. P., 78
Vinacke, W. E., 273
Virtue, 4n, 248
Von Mises, L., 77

Wagner, W., 174
Wahrman, I., 138
Walster, E., 151, 218
Walters, P. S., 124
War: nuclear, 6, 84, 182, 258, 279; requirements of, 29, 59, 61, 68, 90, 98, 121, 123, 174, 212; prevention of, 132, 279–80; just, 207
Warwick, D. P., 185
Weakness, moral, 120
Webster, M., 55
Wedel, T. O., 183

Weighting of variables, 117–19,
  128; skeptical note, 119
Weischedel, W., 8, 108, 274
Weiss, P., 191
Wertheimer, M., 117
White, R. K., 158
Wiesenthal, D. L., 111
Wildavsky, A., 146
Williams, K. B., 104
Williams, R. H., 14, 208
Williams, R. M., 18, 21, 55
Wilson, J., 273
Wilson, M., 112
Winch, P., 102, 150
Windelband, W., 178
Winter, S. G., 23

Wolff, W., 192–93, 210
Woodcock, A., 183
Woods, W., 147
Woodside, A., 161
Wright, D., 17, 104, 110, 135,
  267
Wyer, R. S., 170

Yeats, W. B., 197

Zelan, K., 83
Zeldin, R. S., 104
Zern, D. S., 72
Ziv, A., 150
Zuckerman, M., 30
Zweigenhaft, R. L., 149